A Comprehensive French Grammar

D0335660

Blackwell Reference Grammars
General Editor: Glanville Price

A Comprehensive French Grammar
Fourth Edition
L. S. R. Byrne and E. L. Churchill
Completely revised and rewritten by Glanville Price

A Comprehensive Russian Grammar
Terence Wade
Edited by Michael J. de K. Holman

A Comprehensive Welsh Grammar
David A. Thorne

In preparation:

A Comprehensive German Grammar
A Comprehensive Italian Grammar
A Comprehensive Portuguese Grammar
A Comprehensive Spanish Grammar

L. S. R. Byrne and E. L. Churchill's

A Comprehensive French Grammar

Fourth edition rewritten by

GLANVILLE PRICE

*Professor of French
in the University of Wales
at Aberystwyth*

BLACKWELL
Oxford UK & Cambridge USA

Fourth edition copyright © Glanville Price 1993

The right of Glanville Price to be identifid as author of this book has been asserted in accordance with the Copyright. Designs and Patents Act 1988.

First Published 1950
Reprinted 1952
Second edition 1956
Reprinted 1957, 1961, 1967, 1970, 1974, 1978
Reprinted and first published in paperback 1980
Reprinted 1982
Third edition 1986
Reprinted with corrections 1987
Reprinted 1988, 1989, 1990, 1991
Fourth edition 1993
Reprinted 1994 (twice), 1995

Blackwell Publishers Ltd
108 Cowley Road
Oxford OX4 1JF
UK

Blackwell Publishers Inc.
238 Main Street
Cambridge, Massachusetts 02142
USA

British Library Cataloguing in Publication Data
A CIP catalogue record for this book is available from the British Library.

Library of Congress Cataloging-in-Publication Data
Price, Glanville
    L.S.R. Bryne and E.L. Churchill's A comprehensive French grammar.
—4th ed./rewritten by Glanville Price.
        p. cm.
    Includes index.
    ISBN 0–631–18164–1 (acid-free paper). – ISBN 0–631–18165–2
(pbk.: acid-free paper)
    1. French language–Grammar–1950– I. Byrne, L. S. R.
(Lionel Stanley Rice). 1863–1948. Comprehensive French grammar.
    11. Title.
PC211. P83   1992
448.2'421–de20   92–84
                                                          CIP

Typeset in 10 on 12pt Times
by Photo·graphics, Honiton, Devon
Printed and bound in Great Britain by Hartnolls Limited, Bodmin, Cornwall

This book is printed on acid-free paper

Contents

Verbs

The Structure of the Sentence

Adverbs, Prepositions and Conjunctions

Appendix

Preface

The 'Preface' to the third edition (1986) of this grammar began by stating that 'this new edition of "Byrne and Churchill" has been not only extensively revised but in parts completely rewritten'. It was further pointed out that the sections on gender, the demonstratives, the subjunctive, and negation were almost completely new and that, elsewhere, 'there is barely a paragraph that has not been in some way modified'. In this fourth edition, the process has been carried further and many sections that, in the third edition, still remained fairly close to the original 'Byrne and Churchill' have been thoroughly revised and, in many cases, completely rewritten. However, the numbering of paragraphs has been kept as close as possible to that of the third edition.

No grammar can answer all the questions that an advanced learner is likely to ask. Such a student will also need to consult grammars written for native speakers. The most widely used of these is probably Maurice Grevisse's remarkably successful *Le Bon Usage* which, having been originally published in 1936, went through eleven editions in the author's lifetime and has since appeared, in its golden jubilee year, in a twelfth edition extensively revised by André Goosse, Paris and Louvain-la-Neuve, 1986 (paperback edition, 1991). But even this, which is between four and five times as long as this present grammar, leaves some questions unanswered.

A few of the literary examples in this edition have been taken from Grevisse, and others from the following works, which are widely available in university libraries but which relatively few private individuals are likely to own:

1 G. and R. L. Bidois, *Syntaxe du français moderne*, 2 vols, 2nd edn, Paris 1968.
2 J. Damourette and E. Pichon, *Des mots à la pensée. Essai de grammaire de la langue française*, 7 vols, Paris, 1931–50.

A good dictionary can often help to clear up detailed points of grammar. An excellent one-volume French–French dictionary is *Le Petit Robert*, new edition by Alain Rey and Josette Rey-Debove, Paris, 1990. The title of this dictionary is explained by the fact that it is abridged from Paul Robert's nine-volume *Dictionnaire alphabétique et analogique de la langue française* (known for short as *Le Robert*), new edition, Paris, 1985 (some of my literary examples are taken from this source).

The two best and most widely used dictionaries of French and English are:

1 J. E. Mansion, *Harrap's New Standard French and English Dictionary*, revised and edited by D. M. Ledésert and R. P. L. Ledésert: Volumes One and Two, *French–English*, London, 1972; Volumes Three and Four, *English–French*, London, 1980
2 The *Collins–Robert French–English English–French Dictionary*, 2nd edn, London and Glasgow, 1987.

It is anticipated that this edition of 'Byrne and Churchill', like its predecessors, will go through a number of reprints and so I should be grateful to anyone who might take the time and trouble to draw my attention to possible improvements.

I am grateful to my wife and to my colleague, Catherine Mahé, who have each read the text from the points of view of a native speaker of English and a native speaker of French respectively, each of them able to draw on her experience of teaching advanced English-speaking students of French. They have made many valuable suggestions and saved me from a number of errors but, of course, they are in no way responsible for any that remain.

G.P.

Technical Terms and Abbreviations

It is assumed that most users of this grammar will be familiar with the basic traditional terminology for the parts of speech (noun, adjective, verb, etc.) and a few other concepts such as 'clause', 'subject', 'gender', 'tense', 'active', 'passive', etc.

Among the terms (some of which, though now in general use, are not traditional) defined in particular sections of the book are the following (the list is not complete):

impersonal verb	343
indirect object	18, 21
intransitive verb	17
inversion	596
linking verb	518
mood	472
mute *h*	3
nominative (case)	15
noun phrase	13
partial interrogation	581
persons of the verb	342
quantifier	320
referent	248
simple tense	340
total interrogation	581
transitive verb	17

The following abbreviations have been used:

adj.	adjective
adv.	adverb
art.	article
compl.	complement
condit.	conditional
conjug.	conjugation
constr.	construction
def.	definite
demonst.	demonstrative
disjunct.	disjunctive
Eng.	English
fem.	feminine
Fr.	French
fut.	future
imper.	imperative
imperf.	imperfect
indef.	indefinite
indic.	indicative
infin.	infinitive
masc.	masculine
obj.	object
part.	participle

past ant.	past anterior
perf.	perfect
pers.	person
pluperf.	pluperfect
plur.	plural
poss.	possessive
pres.	present
pret.	preterite
pron.	pronoun
q. ch.	*quelque chose*
q. un.	*quelqu'un*
ref.	reference
refl.	reflexive
rel.	relative
sing.	singular
subjunct.	subjunctive
transl.	translated

Introduction

Alphabet

1 French has the same alphabet as English:

A	B	C	D	E	F	G	H
[a]	[be]	[se]	[de]	[ə]	[ɛf]	[ʒe]	[aʃ]
I	J	K	L	M	N	O	P
[i]	[ʒi]	[ka]	[ɛl]	[ɛm]	[ɛn]	[o]	[pe]
Q	R	S	T	U	V	W	X
[ky]	[ɛr]	[ɛs]	[te]	[y]	[ve]	*	[iks]
Y	Z						
*	[zɛd]						

*The letters *w* and *y* are known as *double v* and *i grec* ('Greek i'). For the values of the phonetic symbols used above to transcribe the names of the other letters, see 2. (Note that *w* is pronounced [v] in *le wagon* '(railway-)carriage' and in a few other, relatively uncommon, words but [w] in other borrowings from English, e.g. *le week-end, le whisky*, and in *wallon* 'Walloon'.

The names of all the letters are now usually considered to be masculine, e.g. *un a bref* 'a short *a*', *«Londres» s'écrit avec un s* '*Londres* is written with an *s*', *Le d de «pied» ne se prononce pas* 'The *d* in *pied* is not pronounced'.

Phonetic transcriptions

2   To indicate pronunciation, we use symbols of the International
Phonetic Alphabet, as follows:

Vowels

[i]	as in *lit*
[e]	as in *été, j'ai*
[ɛ]	as in *bête, faites*
[a]	as in *date*
[ɑ]	as in *pas, pâte*
[ɔ]	as in *botte*
[o]	as in *dos, beau*
[u]	as in *tout*
[y]	as in *tu*
[ø]	as in *feu*
[œ]	as in *peur*
[ə]	as in *je, premier*
[ɛ̃]	as in *vin, main*
[œ̃]	as in *un*
[ɔ̃]	as in *bon*
[ɑ̃]	as in *blanc, dent*

Semi-vowels

[j]	as in *yeux, pied*
[ɥ]	as in *huile*
[w]	as in *oui*

Consonants

[t]	as in *tout*
[d]	as in *dent*
[p]	as in *pomme*
[b]	as in *beau*
[k]	as in *camp, qui, kilo*
[g]	as in *goutte*
[f]	as in *fou*
[v]	as in *vie*
[s]	as in *sou, face*
[z]	as in *zéro, maison*

[ʃ]   as in **ch**apeau
[ʒ]   as in **j**e, rou**g**e
[l]   as in **l**une
[r]   as in **r**ouge
[m]   as in **m**adame
[n]   as in **n**ez
[ɲ]   as in si**gn**e
[ŋ]   as in parki**ng**
A colon, [ː], after a vowel indicates that the vowel is long, e.g.:

[myːr] *mur*, [pɑːt] *pâte*, [pœːr] *peur*, [mɔ̃ːd] *monde*.

The two varieties of 'H' in French

3   The French *h* is never pronounced. However, some words beginning with *h* (which is always followed by a vowel) function as if they began with a vowel, while others function as if they began with a consonant. These two varieties of *h* are known respectively as 'mute *h*' and 'aspirate *h*' (in French, *h muet* and *h aspiré*).

(i) Mute *h*. Words (most of them of Latin or Greek origin) beginning with mute *h* function as if it were not there, i.e. as if they began with a vowel. (Indeed, in many such words it used *not* to be there but has been introduced under the influence of Latin spelling, e.g. medieval French *erbe* 'grass', *abiter* 'to dwell', *ier* 'yesterday', which have since had an *h* added to them, i.e. *herbe, habiter, hier*, because it was realized that they came from Latin *herba, habitare, heri*.) Like other words beginning with a vowel, these words give rise to the processes of elision (see **12**) (e.g. *l'herbe, j'habite*) and liaison (see **7**,C) (e.g. *les hommes* [lez ɔm] 'the men'), they take the masculine demonstrative *cet* not *ce* (e.g. *cet homme* 'this man' – see **235**) and the feminine possessives *mon, ton, son* not *ma, ta, sa* (e.g. *mon habitude* 'my custom' – see **223**).

(ii) Aspirate *h*. On the other hand, a number of words beginning with *h* function as if they began with a consonant. (In fact, though the *h* is now silent, it *was* pronounced until perhaps the sixteenth century, and still remains in some provinces.) These are mainly words borrowed from languages other than Latin or Greek and, in particular, words borrowed in the early medieval period from the Germanic speech of the Franks, or, much more recently, from English. Such words do *not* give rise to elision (e.g. *le hêtre* 'beech-tree', *la hache* 'axe', *je hais* 'I hate', *je le hais* 'I hate him') or liaison (*les hiboux* [le ibu] 'the owls'), and they take the masculine demonstrative *ce* (e.g. *ce hachoir* 'this chopper') and the feminine possessives *ma*, *ta*, *sa* (e.g. *ma honte* 'my shame').

Capitals

4 Capitals (in French, *majuscules*) are used at the beginning of a sentence and with proper names (*Jean*, *Paris*), but elsewhere are much less widely used than in English. In particular, small letters (*minuscules*) are used:

(i) for months and days of the week, e.g. *septembre* 'September', *samedi* 'Saturday'

(ii) for adjectives corresponding to proper names, e.g. *la côte méditerranéenne* 'the Mediterranean coast', *un printemps parisien* 'a Parisian spring', *l'ère napoléonienne* 'the Napoleonic era'. This includes adjectives of nationality and also applies when they are used as nouns denoting a language, e.g.:

le gouvernement français	the French government
la langue italienne	the Italian language
Il comprend l'anglais	He understands English
Le russe est une langue difficile	Russian is a difficult language

but, when used as nouns with reference to people, they take a capital, e.g.:

C'est un Espagnol	He's a Spaniard
Les Allemands sont partis	The Germans have left

(iii) for titles, e.g. *le colonel Blanc, le docteur Dupont, le duc de Bourgogne* 'the Duke of Burgundy', *le président Coty* 'President

Coty', *le professeur Mornet* 'Professor Mornet', *la reine Élisabeth* 'Queen Elizabeth', *saint Paul.* Note too *monsieur, madame, mademoiselle Dupont*, without capitals except (a) when addressing someone, e.g. in a letter (*Mon cher Monsieur Dupont*), (b) when abbreviated to *M., Mme, Mlle.*

In other contexts, there is some fluctuation in the use of capitals, but note in particular their use with:

(i) titles applied to God or to any of the persons of the Trinity or to the Virgin Mary, the names of religious festivals, etc., and the names of sacred books, e.g.:

> *le Tout-Puissant* 'the Almighty', *le Rédempteur* 'the Redeemer', *le Saint-Esprit* 'the Holy Spirit', *Notre-Dame* 'Our Lady', *Noël* 'Christmas', *Mardi gras* 'Shrove Tuesday', *la Pentecôte* 'Whitsun', *l'Ancien Testament* 'the Old Testament', *l'Écriture sainte* 'Holy Scripture', *le Coran* 'the Koran'

(ii) the names of institutions, organizations, unique events, etc. (note that, in such cases, adjectives following the noun or nouns linked to the head noun by *de* are usually not capitalized), e.g.:

> *le Sénat* 'the Senate', *la Bourse* 'the Stock Exchange', *la Réforme* 'the Reformation', *la Révolution française* 'the French Revolution', *l'Académie française* 'the French Academy', *la Sécurité sociale* 'Social Security', *la Légion étrangère* 'the Foreign Legion', *l'Institut géographique national* 'the National Geographical Institute', *l'Église catholique* 'the Catholic Church', *la Légion d'honneur* 'the Legion of Honour', *la Cour d'appel* 'the Appeal Court', *le Conseil de sécurité* 'the Security Council' (but notice *la Comédie-Française* [a theatre] and the names of government departments, e.g. *le ministère des Finances* 'the Ministry of Finance', *le ministère des Affaires étrangères* 'the Foreign Ministry', etc.).

Punctuation

5   Most French and English punctuation marks are the same:

| . | *point* | full stop |
| , | *virgule* | comma |

;	*point-virgule*	semi-colon
:	*deux points*	colon
?	*point d'interrogation*	question mark
!	*point d'exclamation*	exclamation mark
–	*tiret*	dash
-	*trait d'union*	hyphen
. . .	*points de suspension*	dots
( )	*parenthèses*	round brackets
[ ]	*crochets*	square brackets

The principal difference between the two languages relates to the use of quotation marks. There are two aspects to this:

(i) Quotations or other items that in English would be enclosed in inverted commas are usually placed between *guillemets*, i.e. «...», in French, e.g. *Il a répondu: «C'est impossible!»* 'He answered: "It's impossible!"', *Comment dit-on «magnétophone» en allemand?* 'What's the German for "tape-recorder"?'

(ii) Dialogue may be enclosed in *guillemets* or not. If not, then the beginning of the dialogue is indicated by a dash. In either case, each change of speaker is indicated by a dash and *not* by *guillemets* which, when used, mark only the beginning and end of the complete exchange. Note, too, that there is no formal indication (i.e. neither a dash nor *guillemets*) that phrases such as *dit-il* 'he said', *répondis-je* 'I answered', do not form part of the quotation. These points are all illustrated by the following passage from Alexandre Dumas:

> *Joseph entra là-dessus.*
> *«Monsieur, me dit-il de l'air d'un homme enchanté de lui, les malles sont faites.*
> *– Entièrement?*
> *– Oui, monsieur.*
> *– Eh bien, défaites-les: je ne pars pas.»*

Thereupon Joseph came in.
'Sir,' he said with the air of a man who is feeling very pleased with himself, 'the trunks are packed'.
'Entirely?'
'Yes, sir.'
'Well, unpack them: I'm not leaving.'

Division into syllables

6 (i) The following rules apply to the *written* language:

(a) A single consonant between vowels goes with the following syllable, e.g. *au-to-mo-bi-le, ra-pi-di-té*; note that, for this purpose, the groups *ch* [ʃ], *ph* [f], *th* [t], *gn* [ɲ], which each represent one sound, count as single consonants and are never split, e.g. *ma-chi-nal, té-lé-pho-ner, ma-thé-ma-ti-que, si-gner.*

(b) Except for the groups mentioned under a and c, two consonants occurring together are divided, the first going with the preceding syllable, the second with the following, e.g. *ar-gent, por-ter, ap-par-te-ment, al-ti-tu-de, oc-cu-per.*

(c) Pairs of consonants, of which the second is *l* or *r* (except the groups *-rl-, -nl-, -nr-*) are not divided and go with the following syllable, e.g. *pa-trie, li-brai-rie, ou-vrir, pu-blic, rè-gle-ment* (but *par-ler, Sen-lis, Hen-ri).*

(d) Where three or more consonants come together, the first two usually go with the preceding syllable, except that the groups referred to in a and c above are not of course divided, e.g. *obs-ti-né, pers-pec-ti-ve, promp-ti-tu-de, sculp-teur, ron-fle-ment, ins-truc-tion, con-trai-re.*

(e) Occasionally, the rules set out in c and d are not observed, a division according to etymology being preferred, e.g. *hé-mi-sphè-re* (cf. *sphère*), *con-stant, in-stant* (both from a prefix and the root of the Latin verb *stare*, to stand).

(f) Adjacent vowels that fall into separate syllables in pronunciation are also theoretically in separate syllables in the written language, but see ii,c, below.

(ii) When words are divided at the end of a line, the division is indicated as in English by a hyphen. Note that:

(a) The division should always coincide with a division between syllables, e.g. *cha-ritable* or *chari-table*, not *char-itable.*

(b) A syllable consisting only of one or more consonants and *-e* should never be carried over on its own, so, *pu-blique, impossible,* not *publi-que, impossi-ble.*

(c) Adjacent vowels should never be divided even when

theoretically they fall into separate syllables, so *che-vrier* not *chevri-er*; this means that, since both *po-ète*, *thé-âtre* and (in accordance with b above) *poè-te*, *théâ-tre* are unacceptable, words such as these should not be divided.

7 In the spoken language, similar rules apply. In particular:
(a) A single consonant between vowels goes with the following syllable, e.g. [a-re-te] *arrêter*, [te-le-fɔ-ne] *téléphoner*, [vi-la] *villa*.
(b) Pairs of consonants are split except those ending in [l] or [r] (but the group [rl] is an exception to the exception), e.g. [par-ti] *parti*, [ar-me] *armée*, [ar-ʃi-tɛk-ty-ral] *architectural*, [al-tɛr-ne] *alterner*, [plas-tik] *plastique*, [ap-ti-tyd] *aptitude*, [py-blik] *public*, [a-pli-ke] *appliquer*, [a-gra-ve] *aggraver*, [a-bri] *abri*, [pa-tri] *patrie*, [par-le] *parler*, [ɔr-li] *Orly*.
(c) A final consonant that is normally silent is pronounced in certain circumstances before a word beginning with a vowel, and then counts as part of the following syllable, e.g. [le-za-ni-mo] *les animaux*, [œ̃-le-ʒɛ-rɛ̃-si-dɑ̃] *un léger incident*, [œ̃-na-mi] *un ami*. This running on of a final consonant is known as *liaison*.

Hyphens

8 (i) Hyphens must be used when a word is divided at the end of a line, in which case the division must be made at a syllable boundary, e.g. *télé-phone*, *par-tir* (see 6,i and ii).
(ii) Many compound words are hyphenated, e.g. *grand-mère* 'grandmother', *semi-conducteur* 'semiconductor', *sourd-muet* 'deaf and dumb', *ci-dessus* 'above (i.e. earlier in the same piece of writing)', *là-bas* 'over there'. There is, however, considerable inconsistency (compare, for example, *au-dessous*, *par-dessous* 'below', *le porte-monnaie* 'purse' and *vis-à-vis* 'opposite, facing', with *en dessous* 'below', *le portefeuille* 'wallet' and *face à face* 'face to face') and few rules can be given. (Note, however, that all adverbial expressions in *au-*, *ci-*, *là-* and *par-* have hyphens.) In case of doubt, consult a dictionary.
(iii) Names of French towns, departments, etc., consisting of more than one word are hyphenated, e.g. *Aix-en-Provence*, *Colombey-*

les-deux-Églises, Hautes-Pyrénées, Saint-Denis, Seine-et-Marne; this does not apply to an initial definite article, e.g. *Le Havre, La Ferté-sous-Jouarre, Les Andelys*.

Foreign place-names in which a noun is preceded by an adjective are hyphenated, e.g. *la Grande-Bretagne* 'Great Britain', *la Nouvelle-Écosse* 'Nova Scotia', as are *le Royaume-Uni* 'the United Kingdom', *les États-Unis* 'the United States', *les Pays-Bas*, 'the Netherlands', but most other names involving a following adjective are not, e.g. *l'Arabie saoudite* 'Saudi Arabia', *la Colombie britannique* 'British Columbia', nor are *le pays de Galles* 'Wales', *l'Irlande du Nord* 'Northern Ireland', *l'Afrique du Sud* 'South Africa', etc.

Note also the hyphen in such Christian names as *Anne-Marie, Jean-Pierre*.

(iv) For the use of hyphens with cardinal and ordinal numerals, e.g. *dix-sept* '17', *vingt-deux* '22', *trente-cinquième* '35th', see **178** and **180**. Note in particular that hyphens are not used before or after the conjunction *et* (e.g. *vingt et un* '21') or with *cent* '100', *mille* '1000', or *centième* '100th', *millième* '1000th' (e.g. *deux cent trente-sept* '237', *deux millième* '2000th').

(v) For the combination of personal pronouns with *-même*, e.g. *moi-même* 'myself', see **215**.

(vi) For *-ci*, *-là* with demonstratives, e.g. *cette maison-ci* 'this house', *celui-là* 'that one', see **237** and **238**.

(vii) A hyphen is used with personal pronouns (including *y* and *en*), *ce* and *on* following the verb; if there are two such personal pronouns they are also linked to one another by a hyphen except when the first is an elided form (i.e. *m'*, *t'* or *l'* for *me*, *te*, *le* or *la*), e.g.:

> *Regardez-la!* 'Look at her!', *Donnez-le-moi* 'Give it to me', *Allez-vous-en!* 'Go away!', *Réfléchissez-y!* 'Think about it', *Voulez-vous?* 'Will you?', *Puis-je vous aider?* 'May I help you?', *Oui, dit-il*, '"Yes", he said', *Est-ce vrai?* 'Is it true?', *Que peut-on dire?* 'What can one say?', *Donne-m'en trois* 'Give me three of them', *Va-t'en!* 'Go away!'

If one of the pronouns *il*, *elle* or *on* follows a verb ending in a vowel, a *-t-* preceded and followed by hyphens is inserted, e.g. *Où va-t-il?* 'Where is he going?', *Peut-être viendra-t-il demain* 'Perhaps he will come tomorrow', *Oui, ajoute-t-elle* '"Yes", she adds', *Chante-t-elle?* 'Does she sing?' *A-t-on le temps d'y aller?* 'Have we time to go there?'.

Accents and the cedilla

9 (i) The acute accent (*accent aigu*) (´) is used only on the letter *e*, e.g. *été* 'summer'.

(ii) The grave accent (*accent grave*) (`) is used:

(a) over an *e*, e.g. *très* 'very', *j'achète* 'I buy'

(b) over an *a* in a very few words, the most frequently occurring being *à* 'to, at' and *là* 'there', which also appears in *voilà* 'there is' and (*au*) *delà* (*de*) 'beyond'; note that there is no accent on *cela* 'that' and its reduced form *ça* (not to be confused with the adverb *çà*, as in *çà et là* 'here and there')

(c) over *u* in the one word *où* 'where'.

(iii) The circumflex accent (*accent circonflexe*) (^) is used with all vowels except *y*, e.g. *tâche* 'task', *être* 'to be', *dîner* 'to dine', *côte* 'coast', *sûr* 'sure'. (In some words, the circumflex, which serves no useful purpose, was introduced in the seventeenth century, though the French Academy did not adopt it in its dictionary until 1740, in place of an *s* that had disappeared from pronunciation several centuries before, e.g. *pâte, fête, maître, île, hôte* for earlier *paste, feste, maistre, isle, hoste*. Some of these words had passed into English where the [s] remains either in pronunciation, in *paste, feast, master, host*, or, in the word *isle*, in spelling only.) Accents over capitals are sometimes omitted, in particular with a capital *A* representing the preposition *à*.

10 The letter *c* with a cedilla (*cédille*), i.e. *ç*, occurs only before one or other of the vowels *a*, *o* or *u*, where it indicates that the pronunciation is [s] not [k], e.g. *je commençais* 'I was beginning', *nous commençâmes* 'we began', *nous plaçons* 'we place', *j'ai reçu* 'I have received', *nous reçûmes* 'we received', from the verbs *commencer*, *placer* and *recevoir* respectively.

Note that *c* is *always* pronounced [s] before *e* or *i* and so *never* takes a cedilla before either of these vowels.

Diaeresis

11   The diaeresis (*tréma*) (¨) has three principal functions:

(a) It indicates that the second of two adjacent vowels belongs to a separate syllable, e.g. *je haïs* 'I hated', pronounced [ai] (contrast *je hais* 'I hate' [ɛ]), *Saül* [sayl] (contrast *Paul* (pɔl]), *Noël* 'Christmas' [nɔɛl].

(b) In words such as *ambiguïté* 'ambiguity' it indicates that -*guï*- is pronounced [gɥi].

(c) Over the -*e* of such words as the feminine adjectives *aiguë* 'acute', *ambiguë* 'ambiguous', *contiguë* 'adjacent', it indicates that the pronunciation is [gy]. (Otherwise, -*gue* would be pronounced [g] as in *figue* [fig] 'fig'.)

It also occurs over an *e* in a few proper names, the best known being *Saint-Saëns* [sɛ̃sɑ̃ːs] and *madame de Staël* [stal].

Elision

12   Elision in French occurs when the final vowel of a word is dropped before another word beginning with a vowel (this term includes words beginning with mute *h* – see **3**). The fact that a vowel has been elided is indicated by an apostrophe. Note that, with the exception of the words *la* (see a and b below) and *si* (see f below), the only vowel that can be elided in French is *e*.

Elision occurs in the following circumstances (for exceptions, see the end of this section):

(a) The *e* of the pronouns *je*, *me*, *te*, *se*, *le*, *ce* and the *a* of *la* are elided before a verb beginning with a vowel or mute *h* and, provided the pronouns precede the verb, before the pronouns *y* and *en*, e.g. *J'ai* 'I have', *Il m'avait vu* 'He had seen me', *Je t'offre ce livre* 'I am offering you this book', *Il s'est levé* 'He stood up', *Elle l'adore* 'She adores him', *Je l'aime* 'I love her', *J'y habite* 'I live there', *Je l'y ai vue* 'I have seen her there', *Je t'en donnerai* 'I'll give you some'. (Note that the forms -*m'en* and -*t'en* can occur *after* a verb in the imperative, e.g. *Donnez-m'en* 'Give me some', *Va-t'en* 'Go away'.) These words are not elided in writing in other circumstances, e.g. *Puis-je en prendre?* 'May I take some?', *Dois-je y aller?* 'Am I to go there?', *Donnez-le à Henri* 'Give it to Henry'.

(b) The vowel of the definite articles *le* and *la* is elided before a noun or adjective beginning with a vowel or mute *h*, e.g. *le grand homme* 'the great man' but *l'homme* 'the man', *l'autre homme* 'the other man', *la petite île* 'the small island' but *l'île* 'the island'.

(c) The *e* of *de, ne, que* and *jusque* 'up to, until' is elided before a vowel or mute *h*, e.g. *Il est parti d'Amiens* 'He has set off from Amiens', *N'ouvrez pas la porte!* 'Don't open the door!', *Je crois qu'elle viendra* 'I think she'll come', *Il chante mieux qu'Henri* 'He sings better than Henry', *jusqu'alors* 'up till then', *jusqu'en 1984* 'up to 1984', *jusqu'où?* 'how far?'

(d) The *e* of the conjunctions *lorsque* 'when', *puisque* 'since', *quoique* 'although', is elided before the pronouns *il, elle, ils, elles, on,* and the indefinite articles *un* and *une*, e.g. *lorsqu'un enfant naît* 'when a child is born', *puisqu'on ne peut pas partir* 'since one cannot leave', *quoiqu'elle soit malade* 'although she is ill', but *quoique Alfred soit malade* 'although Alfred is ill', *lorsque arrivera le beau temps* 'when the fine weather arrives', etc.

(e) The *e* of *presque* 'almost' and *quelque* 'some' is elided **only** in the words *la presqu'île* 'peninsula', *quelqu'un* 'someone', and the infrequently used *quelqu'un de . . ., quelqu'une de . . .* 'one or other of . . .', e.g. *quelqu'une de mes publications* 'one or other of my publications', but *presque impossible* 'almost impossible', *presque à la fin* 'almost at the end', *avec quelque impatience* 'with some impatience'.

(f) The *i* of *si* 'if' is elided **only** before the pronouns *il, ils*, e.g. *s'il peut, s'ils peuvent* 'if he (they) can', but *si elle peut* 'if she can', *si Ibsen vivait toujours* 'if Ibsen were still living'.

Note that there is no elision before *oui* 'yes' (e.g. *Ce oui m'a surpris* 'That yes surprised me'), or before the numerals *huit* 'eight', *onze* 'eleven', and their ordinals, e.g. *le huit janvier* 'the eighth of January', *le onze de France* 'the French eleven (= team)', *la onzième fois* 'the eleventh time'. Note too the lack of elision before *un* and *une* meaning 'number one', e.g. *la porte du un* 'the door of (room) number one', *la une* 'page one, the front page (of a newspaper)'.

There is usually no elision (though it is possible) before the names of letters, e.g. *le a, le i, en forme de S* [də ɛs] 'S-shaped'. The *e* of *de* is sometimes not elided before the title of a book, periodical, etc., e.g. *un numéro spécial de «Arts et Modes»* 'a special number of *Arts et Modes*', or before a word that is being quoted, e.g. *la première syllabe de «autel»* 'the first syllable of *autel*'.

The Noun Phrase

Introduction

13 A noun phrase always includes either

(a) a **noun** (e.g. *book, truth, elephants*), which may be accompanied by a determiner (see **23**) and/or an adjective or adjectives, and/or an adjectival phrase (e.g. 'a *coffee* cup', 'une tasse *à café*') or adjectival clause (e.g. 'the man *who came to dinner*'), or

(b) a **pronoun** (e.g. *I, him, these, mine, someone, nothing, themselves, who?*), some of which may (like nouns, but much less frequently) be accompanied by adjectival expressions, or

(c) a **noun-clause**, i.e. a clause fulfilling similar functions to a noun (e.g. 'I believe *what he says*' = more or less 'I believe *his statement*', '*that he is angry* distresses me' = more or less '*his anger* (or *the fact of his anger*) distresses me').

For the functions of the noun phrase, see **14–22**.

The functions of the noun phrase

14 The functions of a noun phrase in a sentence, as far as English and French (but not necessarily other languages) are concerned, can be classified as follows (**15–22**). The noun phrase may be:

15   (i) The **subject**, e.g.:

The boy is reading a book
My friends work well
When **his brother** was killed
Where are **the books**?
These will never please him
If **she** speaks French
It is raining
Have **you** finished?

which in French would be:

Le garçon lit un livre
Mes amis travaillent bien
Quand son frère fut tué
Où sont les livres?
Ceux-ci ne lui plairont jamais
Si elle parle français
Il pleut
Avez-vous fini?

(In Latin, the subject was expressed by a form known as the *nominative* case, and the term is retained in some grammars with reference to English or French.)

16   (ii) The **complement of the subject**, after the verb 'to be' or another linking verb (see **518**), e.g.:

He is **a doctor**	*Il est médecin*
It's **me**!	*C'est moi!*
He became **a soldier**	*Il est devenu soldat*

17   (iii) The **direct object**, e.g.:

| The boy is reading **a book** | *Le garçon lit un livre* |
| Do you know **them**? | *Les connaissez-vous?* |

(In Latin, the direct object was expressed by the *accusative* case. Since both English and French have a distinct form of the personal pronouns (though not of nouns) to indicate the direct object – 'I see **him**, je **le** vois, he sees **me**, il **me** voit' – the use of the term 'accusative case' as occurs in many grammars of English or French is defensible.)

Note that verbs that have a direct object are known as **transitive** verbs while those that do **not** have a direct object are known as **intransitive** verbs.

18 (iv) The **indirect object**, e.g.:

> I am sending **my brother** a book (= 'to my brother')
> He will give **you** it (= 'to you')

or, in French:

> *J'envoie un livre* **à mon frère**
> *Il* **vous** *le donnera*

Note that, except with personal pronouns, the indirect object in French always requires the preposition *à* 'to' (or occasionally *pour* 'for') (see **21**).

(In Latin, the indirect object was expressed by the *dative* case. Since, in the case of the third person pronouns, French has distinct forms for the direct object (**le, la, les** 'him, her, them') and the indirect object (**lui**, '[to] him', '[to] her', **leur** '[to] them') (see **198**), the use of the term 'dative case' is defensible with reference to French.)

19 (v) The **genitive**, e.g.:

> **the lady's** book (= 'the book of the lady')
> **my brother's** children (= 'the children of my brother')

Note that in French, there is no genitive – the construction with *de* 'of' must be used (see **22**) – so the equivalents of the above phrases are:

> *le livre* **de la dame**
> *les enfants* **de mon frère**

(Latin also had a *genitive* case. Our reason for retaining this term is that English nouns do have a special genitive form, viz. a form ending in 'apostrophe *s*' (**boy's**) or in an apostrophe alone (**boys'**) (see **22**).)

20 (vi) The **complement of a preposition**, e.g.

with **his friends**	*avec* **ses amis**
under **the table**	*sous* **la table**
without **me**	*sans* **moi**

The indirect object

21 English in certain circumstances expresses the indirect object (i.e. the person or – occasionally – thing to whom or for whom something is given, sent, lent, shown, told, bought, etc.) merely by using the appropriate noun or pronoun without any preposition, e.g.:

(a) He gave John a present = He gave a present to John

(b) How many letters have you sent your brother = to your brother?

(c) He won't lend anyone his video-recorder = He won't lend his video-recorder to anyone

(d) You'll have to show someone your passport = You'll have to show your passport to someone

(e) He has bought his wife a car = He has bought a car for his wife.

This is not possible in French – the indirect object is always (except for personal pronouns, see 198) indicated by the preposition *à* 'to' (or, with some verbs, *pour* 'for'). So the equivalents of the above sentences are:

(a) *Il donna un cadeau à Jean*

(b) *Combien de lettres avez-vous envoyées à votre frère?*

(c) *Il ne veut prêter son magnétoscope à personne*

(d) *Il vous faudra montrer votre passeport à quelqu'un*

(e) *Il a acheté une voiture pour sa femme*

The possessive relationship

22 English often expresses a possessive relationship between two nouns by means of the 'genitive case' (see 19), i.e. by a form of the noun ending in 'apostrophe *s*' (*the boy's book* = 'the book of the boy', *the children's toys, Thomas's business*) or, in the case of some nouns (mainly plurals but also some personal names) ending in *-s*, by the apostrophe alone (*the boys' books* = 'the

books of the boys', *Euripides' plays* = 'the plays of Euripides').
French has no such construction and expresses the possessive
relationship by means of the preposition *de* 'of', e.g.:

le père de Jean	John's father = 'the father of John'
la maison de mon ami	my friend's house = 'the house of my friend'
le livre du garçon	the boy's book
les jouets des enfants	the children's toys
le sommet de la colline	the top of the hill

(For *du* = *de* + *le* and *des* = *de* + *les*, see 25,b.)
Similarly when the possessor is a pronoun:

la maison de quelqu'un que je connais
the house of someone I know

Je n'aime pas cette robe, je préfère la couleur de la mienne
I don't like this dress, I prefer the colour of mine

Moi, je préfère la couleur de celle-ci (de celles-ci)
I prefer the colour of this one (of these)

Note that English phrases in which a pronoun relating to the
object possessed is omitted must be rendered in French by the
construction *celui de . . ., ceux de*, etc. 'the one(s) of' (see section
245), e.g.:

Ce jardin est plus grand que celui de Jean
This garden is bigger than John's

nos enfants et ceux de mon frère
our children and my brother's

Determiners

23   French has a variety of forms that serve to introduce the
noun, and which, in most cases, also indicate the gender and
number of the noun. These are known as determiners. They are:

(i) the definite, indefinite and partitive articles (24–46), e.g. *le
livre* 'the book', *une belle maison* 'a beautiful house', *du pain*

'(some) bread', *les enfants* 'the children', *des enfants* '(some) children'

(ii) the so-called 'possessive adjectives' (222–230), e.g. *mon chapeau* 'my hat', *leurs crayons* 'their pencils'

(iii) the so-called 'demonstrative adjectives' (234–237), e.g. *cette maison* 'this/that house', *ces disques* 'these/those records'

(iv) the relative determiner, *lequel* (as in *laquelle somme*) (270)

(v) the interrogative determiner, *quel?* 'which?' (279)

(vi) the negative determiners, *aucun* (546) and *nul* (547)

(vii) various indefinites and quantifiers, viz. *certains* (294), *chaque* (295), *différents* and *divers* (297), *maint* (324,viii), *plusieurs* (331), *quelque(s)* (306), and *tout* (317)

(viii) the cardinal numerals (178).

Articles

Introduction

24 Whereas English (like many other languages) has only two articles, viz. the definite article *the* and the indefinite article *a*, *an*, French has three, viz. the definite, the indefinite and the partitive articles. The forms of the partitive article are identical with the construction '*de* + definite article' (see 25,b,c). In none of the articles is there a distinction between masculine and feminine in the plural. The basic forms are:

	masc. sing.	fem. sing.	plur.
Definite article	*le*	*la*	*les*
Indefinite article	*un*	*une*	*des*
Partitive article	*du*	*de la*	*des*

Notes
(a) for *l'* and *de l'*, see 25 and 3
(b) views differ as to whether (i) the indefinite article has no

plural, or (ii) the partitive article has no plural, or (iii) the plural form *des* is both an indefinite and a partitive; in practice, it makes no difference which view we adopt; purely for convenience, we shall deal with it under the heading of the partitive.

Definite article

25 The definite article is:

masc. sing.	fem. sing.	plur.
le	*la*	*les*

le livre, les livres	the book, the books
la porte, les portes	the door, the doors

Before a vowel or 'mute *h*' (see **3**), *le* and *la* become *l'*, e.g.:

l'arbre (m.), *l'homme* (m.)	the tree, the man
l'autre maison (f.), *l'heure* (f.)	the other house, the hour

Note, however, that an aspirate *h* (see **3**,ii), though not pronounced, counts as a consonant and so is preceded by the full form of the article, i.e. *le* or *la*, e.g.:

le hibou, owl	*la honte*, shame

Note too that:

(a) the preposition *à* combines with the articles *le* and *les* to give *au* and *aux* respectively, e.g.:

au père, au hasard	to the father, at random
aux professeurs, aux enfants	to the teachers, to the children

(b) the preposition *de* combines with the articles *le* and *les* to give *du* and *des* respectively, e.g.:

le prix du billet	the price of the ticket
Il vient du port	He's coming from the harbour
la fin des vacances	the end of the holidays

(c) *à* and *de* do not combine with *la* and *l'*, e.g.:

à la maison, à l'enfant	at the house, to the child
au sommet de la colline	at the top of the hill
à la fin de l'hiver	at the end of (the) winter

Position of the definite article

26 As in English, the definite article usually comes at the beginning of a noun phrase, e.g. *le virage dangereux* 'the dangerous bend', *la petite maison* 'the little house'. However, it follows *tout* 'all, the whole' (see **317**), e.g.:

tout le comité	the whole committee
toute la journée	all day (long), the whole day
tous les enfants	all the children

Article in English but not in French

27 Generally speaking, if a definite article is used in English there is likely to be one in the corresponding French construction also. There are, however, some exceptions to this. In particular:

(a) The article is regularly omitted in appositions such as the following, in which the apposition provides additional information about the head noun:

Alain-Fournier, auteur du «Grand Meaulnes»
Alain-Fournier, the author of *Le Grand Meaulnes*

Tolède, ancienne capitale de l'Espagne
Toledo, the former capital of Spain

If the article is used (*Alain-Fournier, l'auteur du «Grand Meaulnes»*; *Tolède, l'ancienne capitale de l'Espagne*), this serves to give greater prominence to the word or phrase in apposition.

(b) When read out in full, titles such as *François I*^{er}, *Élisabeth II*, *Pie XII* become *François premier*, *Élisabeth deux*, *Pie douze* (contrast 'Francis the First', 'Elizabeth the Second', 'Pius the Twelfth').

Article required in French but not in English

28   (i) French uses the definite article with various categories of nouns used in a generic sense, including:

(a) abstract nouns, e.g.:

La beauté n'est pas tout	Beauty isn't everything
Aimez-vous la musique?	Do you like music?
Elle s'intéresse à l'art moderne	She's interested in modern art

(b) names of languages, e.g.:

Il apprend l'anglais	He is learning English
Comprenez-vous le russe?	Do you understand Russian?
Le danois ressemble beaucoup au suédois	Danish is very like Swedish

But the article is not usually used with the verb *parler*, e.g. *Parlez-vous français?* 'Do you speak French?', *Il parle très bien anglais* 'He speaks English very well' (though the article also occurs, e.g. *Il parle l'allemand sans accent* 'He speaks German without an accent'), and never after *en*, e.g. *en français* 'in French', *en japonais* 'in Japanese'.

(c) nouns denoting substances, e.g.:

L'or est un métal précieux	Gold is a precious metal
J'aime mieux le vin que la bière	I prefer wine to beer

(d) plural nouns referring to a class, e.g.:

Les insectes ont six pattes	Insects have six legs
Les magnétoscopes coûtent cher	Video-recorders are expensive

Note, however, that in literary French the article is sometimes omitted in enumerations such as *Vieillards, hommes, femmes, enfants, tous voulaient me voir* (Montesquieu) 'Old people, men, women, children, they all wanted to see me', or when two nouns linked by *et* complement one another, e.g. *Patrons et ouvriers sont d'accord* 'Bosses and workers are in agreement'.

(ii) The article is used with words meaning 'last' or 'next' in expressions of time, e.g.:

| *le mois (l'an) dernier*⎫
le mois (l'an) passé ⎭ | last month (year) |
| *la semaine prochaine* | next week |

and with the names of religious festivals, fasts, etc., such as *la Saint-Michel* 'Michaelmas (Day)', *la Saint-Jean* 'St John's Day, Midsummer Day', *la Toussaint* 'All Saints' Day' (in these examples the article is *la* because the full form is *la fête de saint-Michel*, etc.), *la Pentecôte* 'Whitsun', *le Carême* 'Lent', *la Pâque* 'Passover', *le Ramadan* 'Ramadan', etc. Note, however, that *Pâques* 'Easter' has no article (see also **72**) and that the article is optional with *Noël* 'Christmas' (*à Noël, à la Noël* 'at Christmas').

(iii) Most titles followed by a proper name require the article, e.g.: *le président Kennedy* 'President Kennedy', *la reine Élisabeth* 'Queen Elizabeth', *le pape Léon XIII* 'Pope Leo XIII', *le capitaine Dreyfus* 'Captain Dreyfus', *le général de Gaulle* 'General de Gaulle', *le docteur Martin* 'Dr Martin', *le professeur Fouché* 'Professor Fouché', *la mère Thérèse* 'Mother Teresa'. This does not apply to the titles *saint(e)* (e.g. *saint Paul, sainte Geneviève*), *Maître* (used with reference to certain members of the legal profession, e.g. *Maître Dupont* – note the capital *M*-), or the English title *lord* (no capital, e.g. *lord Salisbury*).

(iv) The definite article is sometimes used with an exclamatory value, similar to that of *quel* 'what (a)' (see **36, 279**), e.g. *Oh! la belle fleur!* 'Oh! what a beautiful flower!'

(v) The definite article is sometimes used when hailing or addressing people, as in La Fontaine's *Passez votre chemin, la fille* 'Continue on your way, girl', or in the Communist anthem, *L'Internationale* (E. Pottier):

> *Debout! les damnés de la terre!*
> *Debout! les forçats de la faim!*

the equivalent of which in the English translation is 'Arise, ye starvelings from your slumbers! Arise, ye criminals of want!'

29 (i) French uses the definite article where English uses the indefinite article:

(a) To express measures of quantity in relation to price, e.g. *cent francs le mètre* 'a hundred francs a metre', *six francs le kilo/la douzaine* 'six francs a kilo/dozen'.

(b) After the verb *avoir* with nouns referring to parts of the body or mental faculties and followed by an adjective, e.g. *Il a le nez pointu* 'He has a pointed nose', *Il avait les lèvres gonflées* 'He had swollen lips (His lips were swollen)', *Elle a la mémoire fidèle* 'She has a retentive memory'. But the indefinite article may also be used with reference to permanent or lasting features, e.g. *Il a un nez pointu et des yeux bleus* 'He has a pointed nose and blue eyes', and must be used if the adjective precedes the noun, e.g. *Il a un grand nez* 'He has a big nose', *Elle avait une très jolie voix et une excellente mémoire* 'She had a very pretty voice and an excellent memory'.

(ii) In contexts in which articles of clothing or other items normally carried on one's person are mentioned as part of the circumstances accompanying the action, the definite article is frequently used in French where English uses either 'with' and a possessive determiner, e.g.:

Il est entré dans la cuisine le chapeau sur la tête et la pipe à la bouche
He came into the kitchen with his hat on his head and his pipe in his mouth

or no determiner at all, e.g.:

Il courait le long de la rue la serviette à la main
He was running along the street briefcase in hand

For the use of the definite article in French where English uses the possessive determiner with reference to parts of the body, see **228–229**.

30   The article is repeated with each of a series of nouns regarded as separate entities, e.g.:

J'ai mis le beurre et le fromage dans le frigo
I've put the butter and cheese in the fridge

Les Belges, les Hollandais et les Allemands s'y opposent
The Belgians, Dutch and Germans are opposed to it

but not when they are regarded as forming a single entity, e.g. *les ministres et secrétaires d'état* 'the ministers and junior ministers'.

Geographical names

31 The definite article is used with most names of continents, countries, regions and rivers, e.g.:

(a) (masculine) *le Brésil* 'Brazil', *le Portugal, l'Anjou, le Périgord, le Transvaal, le Valais, le Yorkshire, le Danube, le Nil* 'Nile', *le Rhône*

(b) (feminine) *l'Afrique* 'Africa', *l'Europe, l'Égypte, la France, la Grande-Bretagne* 'Great Britain', *l'Andalousie* 'Andalusia', *la Bavière* 'Bavaria', *la Bohême* 'Bohemia', *la Moldavie* 'Moldavia', *la Normandie* 'Normandy', *la Sibérie* 'Siberia', *la Toscane* 'Tuscany', *la Seine, la Tamise* 'Thames'

But it is not used:

(a) after the preposition *en* – see **656**,ii,1

(b) with *Israël* (which was originally a personal name, that of the patriarch Jacob)

(c) with the names of the following islands (see **33**) that are also countries: *Chypre* 'Cyprus', *Cuba, Malte* 'Malta' (all feminine).

32 There is some fluctuation in the use of the definite article with names of countries and regions after the preposition *de* 'of, from', but in general the following indications apply:

(a) with masculine singular names, the article is used, e.g.:

Il revient du Portugal	He's coming back from Portugal
la reine du Danemark	the Queen of Denmark
l'histoire du Japon	the history of Japan
l'ambassade du Brésil	the Brazilian Embassy
les vins du Languedoc	Languedoc wines

(b) with feminine singular names, the article is not used when *de* means 'from' e.g.:

Il revient de Grande-Bretagne	He's coming back from Britain
Il arrive d'Espagne	He's arriving from Spain

and after certain nouns such as *roi* 'king', *reine* 'queen', *ambassade* 'embassy', *histoire* 'history', *vin* 'wine', e.g.:

le roi d'Angleterre	the King of England
l'histoire de France	the history of France
les vins d'Italie	Italian wines
l'ambassade de Suède	the Swedish Embassy

But, on the other hand, note for example *l'histoire littéraire de la France* 'the literary history of France', *la géographie de la France* 'the geography of France', *le président de l'Italie* 'the President of Italy', *le nord de la France* 'the north of France', *la politique agricole de la Grande-Bretagne* 'Britain's agricultural policy'. The distinction seems to be that expressions like *le roi de* . . ., *les vins de* . . ., etc., in most cases go back to a period when the article was not normally used with names of countries ('France' was just *France*, not *la France*), while those that involve the use of the article are usually of more recent coinage.

(c) with plural names, masculine or feminine, the article is used (as it is in English), e.g.:

l'ambassade des États-Unis	the United States Embassy
l'histoire des Pays-Bas	the history of the Netherlands
Il arrive des Philippines	He's arriving from the Philippines

33   As a rule the definite article is not used with the names of towns and islands, e.g. *Londres* 'London', *New-York*, *Paris*, *Aurigny* 'Alderney', *Bornéo*, *Corfou* 'Corfu', *Guernesey* 'Guernsey', *Java*, *Jersey*, *Madagascar*, *Madère* 'Madeira', *Majorque* 'Majorca', *Sercq* 'Sark', *Taïwan*.
    The principal exceptions to this rule are:

(a) a considerable number of towns in France, e.g. *Les Andelys*, *La Baule*, *Le Creusot*, *Le Havre*, *L'Isle-Adam*, *Le Mans*, *Le Puy*, *La Rochelle*

(b) a few foreign towns, e.g. *Le Caire* 'Cairo', *La Havane* 'Havana', *La Haye* 'the Hague', *La Mecque* 'Mecca', *La Nouvelle-Orléans* 'New Orleans'

(c) certain islands, some of which are also countries, e.g. *la Barbade* 'Barbados', *la Grande-Bretagne* 'Great Britain', *la Grenade* 'Grenada', *l'Irlande* 'Ireland', *l'Islande* 'Iceland', *la Jamaïque* 'Jamaica', *la Nouvelle-Zélande* 'New Zealand', *la Trinité* 'Trinidad', and some of which are not, e.g.: *la Corse* 'Corsica', *la Crète, la Guadaloupe, la Martinique, la Réunion, la Sardaigne* 'Sardinia', *la Sicile* 'Sicily'.

34 There is a certain amount of inconsistency in the use of *de* + definite article on the one hand and of *de* alone on the other, e.g.:

le vent du nord, le vent du sud	the north wind, the south wind
l'armée de l'air	the Air Force
le mal de la route, le mal de l'air	carsickness, airsickness
l'office du tourisme	tourist office (in some towns)

but, on the other hand:

le vent d'est, le vent d'ouest	the east wind, the west wind
l'armée de terre, l'armée de mer	the Army, the Navy
le mal de mer	seasickness
l'office de tourisme	tourist office (in other towns)

In general, however, if the prepositional phrase functions more or less as an adjectival phrase, *de* alone is likely to be used, e.g. *un vaisseau de guerre* 'a warship' (cf. *un vaisseau marchand* 'a merchant ship') but *le ministère de la Guerre* (= 'the War Office').

For similar inconsistencies in relation to place-names, see **32**.

Indefinite article

35 The forms of the indefinite article in the singular are:

masc.	fem.
un	*une*

Its use corresponds broadly to that of the English indefinite article, 'a, an'; see **36** to **39** for exceptions.

On the form *des* as the plural of the indefinite article, see **24**, note b, and **40**.

36 The indefinite article is not used in French:

(i) In apposition, e.g. *Son père, boucher de son état, est mort en 1950* 'His father, a butcher by trade, died in 1950'

(ii) After *être* 'to be', *devenir* 'to become', *paraître* 'to appear', *sembler* 'to seem', and verbs such as *faire* 'to make', *nommer* 'to appoint', *élire* 'to elect', *croire* 'to believe' } when the noun that follows denotes nationality, profession, rank, family status or some other long-term situation in life,

e.g. *Le père était avocat. Son fils est devenu général pendant la guerre. Plus tard, il a été élu sénateur, et finalement de Gaulle l'a nommé ministre* 'The father was a barrister. His son became a general during the war. Later, he was elected a senator, and finally de Gaulle appointed him a minister'

Elle est Française	She is a Frenchwoman
Je vous croyais citoyen américain	I thought you were an American citizen
Il est grand-père	He is a grandfather

But the article is inserted if the noun is qualified, e.g. *Son père était un avocat distingué* 'His father was a distinguished barrister'.

(iii) After *quel* (m.), *quelle* (f.) 'what a . . .!', e.g. *Quel homme intelligent!* 'What an intelligent man!', *Quelle famille!* 'What a family!'.

(iv) When the direct object of a verb in the negative is introduced by *pas de* (or, but much less usually, *point de*) (see **568**), e.g.:

Je n'ai pas de crayon	I haven't got a pencil
Il n'a pas acheté de voiture	He didn't buy a car

(v) When the subject of the verb is preceded by *jamais* 'never', e.g. *Jamais enfant n'a été plus charmant* 'Never was a child more charming'.

(vi) In a number of miscellaneous expressions where the English equivalent has an indefinite article, e.g.:

nombre de	a number of
C'est chose facile	That's an easy thing (easily done)
C'est mauvais signe	That's a bad sign
porter plainte contre	to lodge a complaint against
à grande/faible allure	at a great/slow speed
en lieu sûr	in a safe place

37 French uses *par* where English uses the indefinite article in a distributive sense in such contexts as the following:

trois fois par semaine	three times a week
gagner dix mille francs par mois	to earn ten thousand francs a month
dix francs par personne	ten francs a head (per person)

Le son . . . se propage à une vitesse de 340 mètres par seconde
(*Petit Larousse*)
Sound travels at 340 metres a second

Note, however, the constructions *une fois tous les trois mois* 'once every three months', *rouler à cent kilomètres à l'heure* 'to travel at a hundred kilometres an hour'.

38 French makes considerable use of adverbial expressions of the type preposition + noun, e.g. *par hasard* 'by chance', *en hâte* 'speedily', *avec soin* 'with care, carefully', *avec patience* 'with patience, patiently', *sans difficulté* 'without difficulty', *sans enthousiasme* 'without enthusiasm, unenthusiastically'. In appropriate contexts, the noun may be modified by the adjective *grand*, e.g. *en grande hâte, avec grand soin, sans grande difficulté.* Nouns introduced by *sans* are also sometimes modified by other adjectives, e.g. *sans raison valable* 'without good reason', *sans difficulté excessive* 'without inordinate difficulty'. Otherwise, if the noun is modified by an adjective, the indefinite article is introduced, e.g. *par un hasard malheureux* 'by an unfortunate chance', *avec un soin particulier* 'with special care', *avec une patience admirable* 'with admirable patience'.

39 The indefinite article is repeated with each of two nouns linked by *et* 'and' or *ou* 'or', e.g.:

Il a cassé une tasse et une soucoupe
He broke a cup and saucer

Je sais qu'il a un fils ou une fille
I know he has a son or daughter

Likewise with a series of three or more nouns:

Vous trouverez sur la table un stylo, un crayon et une règle
You'll find a pen, pencil and ruler on the table

Partitive article

40   The forms of the partitive article are:

masc. sing.	fem. sing.	plural
du, de l'	*de la, de l'*	*des*

The form *de l'* is used instead of *du* or *de la* before a vowel or a mute *h* (cf. **25**, notes b and c), e.g. *du pain* 'bread', *de la viande* 'meat', but *de l'or* (m.) 'gold', *de l'eau* (f.) 'water'.

The form *des* can also be considered as the plural of the indefinite article (see **24**, note b).

41   English has no partitive article and no plural of the indefinite article, and nouns taking either of these forms in French often stand alone in English, e.g.:

Il boit de la bière	He's drinking beer
Elle a des cousins au Canada	She has cousins in Canada

Not infrequently, however, English uses 'some' or 'any' where French has a partitive article, e.g.:

Il y a du pain sur la table	There's (some) bread on the table
Il a acheté des biscuits	He bought (some) biscuits
Voulez-vous du vin?	Do you want (some/any) wine?
S'il y a de l'eau chaude, je vais prendre un bain	If there's any hot water, I'll have a bath

42   The distinction between these and the definite article (which can also be used when English has no article, see **28**) is that the definite article indicates that the noun is being used in a general sense whereas the partitive article refers to only a part of the whole (and, likewise, the plural indefinite article indicates 'some' as opposed to 'all' members of a class), e.g.:

J'aime le café	I like coffee (in general)
J'aimerais du café	I'd like (some) coffee
Je bois du café	I'm drinking coffee
Les moutons ont quatre pattes	Sheep have four legs

Il y a des moutons dans le champ	There are (some) sheep in the field

43 After (*ne . . .*) *pas* or *point* 'not', *guère* 'scarcely, hardly', *jamais* 'never', *plus* 'no longer, no more', the partitive article is normally replaced by *de* alone (see **568** – but see also **569–570**), e.g.:

Je ne veux pas de fromage	I don't want (any) cheese
Je n'ai pas acheté de pain	I haven't bought any bread
Ils n'ont guère d'argent	They have hardly any money
Vous ne buvez jamais de bière?	Don't you ever drink beer?
Nous ne mangeons plus d'œufs	We don't eat eggs any more

Note that this does not apply to *ne . . . que* 'only' which is not negative but restrictive in sense, e.g.:

Il n'achète que du vin	He only buys wine
Nous n'avons que des cerises	We only have cherries

44 The plural partitive (or indefinite) article *des* is replaced by *de* when an adjective precedes the noun, e.g.:

Il nous a dit d'affreux mensonges
He told us (some) dreadful lies

Vous avez de belles fleurs dans votre jardin
You have (some) beautiful flowers in your garden

This does not apply when adjective and noun are virtually combined, expressing one idea, e.g. *des jeunes gens* 'youths, young men', *des petits pains* 'rolls', *des petits pois* 'peas'. The rule is often ignored elsewhere, especially in speech, e.g. *des vieilles chansons* 'old songs', *des petits yeux* 'small eyes'. A similar rule used to apply in the singular (*de bon vin* 'good wine', *de belle musique* 'beautiful music'), but nowadays it has virtually ceased to apply, in writing as well as in speech, e.g. *du bon vin, de la belle musique.*

45 The partitive article is not used after *de*, in the following circumstances in particular:

(a) after expressions of quantity such as:

assez, enough
autant, as much, as many
beaucoup, much, many, a lot of
combien? how much? how many?
moins, less
peu, little, few
un peu, a little
plus, more
tant, as much, so much, as many, so many
trop, too much, too many

e.g. *assez de pain* 'enough bread', *J'ai autant de problèmes que vous* 'I have as many problems as you (have)', *beaucoup de difficulté* 'much (a lot of) difficulty', *beaucoup de gens* 'many (a lot of) people', *combien de fois?* 'how many times?', *peu de difficulté* 'little difficulty', *un peu de difficulté* 'a little (= some) difficulty', *trop de temps* 'too much time'.

Similarly after nouns expressing quantity, e.g.:

une bouteille de vin	a bottle of wine
un kilo de viande	a kilo of meat
l'absence de témoins	the absence of witnesses
son manque d'intelligence	his lack of intelligence
un certain nombre de personnes	a certain number of people
une tranche de jambon	a slice of ham

(b) when *de* means 'with' or 'by' after one of the verbs listed in **526** (which see for further examples), e.g.:

Nous étions entourés d'ennemis
We were surrounded by enemies

Il me comble d'amitié	He overwhelms me with friendship
couronné de succès	crowned with success
couvert de boue	covered with mud
rempli de sable	filled with sand

(c) after certain adjectives, e.g.:

Le verre est plein d'eau
The glass is full of water

La place était vide de passants
The square was empty of passers-by

dépourvu d'intelligence
devoid of intelligence

But if *de* is followed by a definite article, then it combines with it in the normal way (see **25**,b), e.g.:

La boîte est pleine du sable que j'ai rapporté de la plage
The box is full of the sand that I brought back from the beach

Beaucoup des timbres qu'il a achetés sont sans valeur
Many of the stamps he bought are worthless

In these examples, *pleine du sable* = *pleine de* 'full of' + *le sable* 'the sand' (so not 'full of sand'), and *beaucoup des timbres* = *beaucoup de* 'many of' + *les timbres* 'the stamps' (so not 'many stamps').

46 The partitive article can, however, be used after prepositions other than *de*, e.g.:

Il m'a écrit sur du papier à en-tête
He wrote to me on headed paper

On le fait avec de la farine
You make it with flour

Il l'a pris pour de l'or
He thought it was gold (*lit.* He took it for gold)

Il réfléchit à des problèmes graves
He is thinking about some serious problems

Nous allons passer par des chemins dangereux
We are going to travel by dangerous roads

Note, however, the existence of numerous expressions of the type preposition + noun, including:

(a) *à* indicating either purpose, e.g. *une cuiller à café* 'a coffee spoon', *un verre à vin* 'a wineglass', or a characteristic feature, e.g. *un verre à pied* 'a stemmed glass', *une bête à fourrure* 'an animal with fur', *une chemise à rayures vertes* 'a shirt with green stripes'

(b) *avec* with an abstract noun forming an adverbial expression, e.g. *avec difficulté* 'with difficulty', *avec patience* 'with patience, patiently' (but *avec du sucre* 'with sugar', etc.)

(c) *en*, especially with abstract nouns, e.g. *être en colère* 'to be angry', *en guerre* 'at war', *en réparation* 'under repair', *en théorie* 'in theory', or to indicate the substance that something is made of, e.g. *une cuiller en bois* 'a wooden spoon', *une jupe en laine* 'a woollen skirt', *une statue en bronze* 'a bronze statue'

(d) *sans*, e.g. *sans arrêt* 'ceaselessly', *sans difficulté* 'without difficulty', *sans délai* 'without delay', *une robe sans manches* 'a sleeveless dress', *sans sucre* 'without sugar'

(e) a number of fixed expressions involving other prepositions, e.g. *par pitié* 'through pity', *sous verre* 'under glass', *fait sur commande* 'made to order'.

Gender

Introduction

47 Although the two grammatical genders of French are referred to by the terms 'masculine' and 'feminine', in the case of most (though not all) words these terms are utterly meaningless and, were it not for the fact that they are so well established, we might do better to abandon them altogether and use some such terms as 'class A' and 'class B'. It is impossible to give simple – or, indeed, complicated – rules that will enable learners to determine the gender of each and every noun they come across. However, it is possible to draw up certain categories of words that are likely to be of one gender rather than the other. In particular:

(1) Words standing for male or female human beings are likely to be masculine or feminine respectively – but not necessarily so (see **48**). (For animals, see **49**.)

(2) Words falling into certain other categories depending on their meaning are likely to be of one gender rather than the other even though, in this case, sex is not a relevant factor (see **50–52**).

(3) Words with certain endings are likely to be of one gender rather than the other (see **53–55**); in most cases, not only sex (as in 1 above) but meaning in general (as in 2 above) is irrelevant.

(4) Special rules apply to compound nouns (see **57–63**).

Gender according to meaning

Gender and sex

48 (i) **Humans**

(a) Generally speaking, nouns referring to male humans are masculine and nouns referring to female humans are feminine, e.g.:

masc.	fem.
un avocat, barrister	*la cantatrice*, (opera) singer
le boucher, butcher	*la couturière*, seamstress
un étudiant, (male) student	*une étudiante*, (female) student
le musicien, musician	*une ouvreuse*, usherette
le père, father	*la princesse*, princess
le prêtre, priest	*la reine*, queen
le romancier, novelist	*la tante*, aunt
le voyageur, traveller	*la veuve*, widow

(b) Some nouns, however, are masculine even when they refer to females, in particular:

un architecte
un auteur, author(ess)
le brise-fer ⎫
le brise-tout ⎬ destructive child
le contralto ⎭
le docteur, doctor
un écrivain, writer
le médecin, doctor
le ministre, (government) minister
le peintre, painter
le professeur, teacher, professor
le sculpteur, sculptor, sculptress
le témoin, witness

Many of these may be preceded by *femme* when it is wished to specify that the individual concerned is a woman, e.g. *une femme auteur, une femme médecin, une femme sculpteur. La doctoresse* also exists as the feminine of *docteur. Soprano* is usually masculine but occasionally feminine.

Un ange 'angel', even when referring to a woman or a girl (or a heavenly being in female form), is always masculine.

(c) Some nouns are always feminine, even when they refer to males, e.g.:

la brute
la connaissance, acquaintance
la dupe
la personne, person
la recrue, recruit
la sentinelle, sentry
la vedette, (film-)star, etc.
la victime, victim

(d) Some nouns take either gender, depending on the sex of the person concerned, e.g.:

un or *une aide*, assistant
le or *la camarade*, friend
le or *la collègue*, colleague
le or *la concierge*, caretaker
un or *une élève*, pupil
un or *une enfant*, child
un or *une hypocrite*
le or *la locataire*, tenant
le or *la propriétaire*, owner
le or *la secrétaire*, secretary

and all words ending in -*iste* referring to humans:

le or *la socialiste*   *le* or *la touriste*

49   (ii) Animals
The relation between gender and sex is far less close in the case of animals than it is in the case of humans. Note the following categories:

(a) Many nouns referring to animals have only a masculine form, used for both males and females, e.g.:

le blaireau, badger
le chacal, jackal
un écureuil, squirrel
un éléphant

le gorille, gorilla
le hérisson, hedgehog
un hippopotame, hippopotamus
le jaguar
le léopard
le rat
le renne, reindeer
le rhinocéros

If it is necessary to specify that the animal is female, one can say *un léopard femelle* 'leopardess', *un éléphant femelle*, etc.
Many nouns referring to the young of animals are of this type, e.g.:

l'éléphanteau, elephant calf   *un ourson*, bear-cub
le levraut, leveret   *le poulain*, foal
le lionceau, lion-cub   *le renardeau*, fox-cub
le louveteau, wolf-cub   *le veau*, calf

(b) Many nouns that are normally used in the masculine as generic terms, i.e. with reference both to males and females, do however have a feminine equivalent for use when one wishes to specify that a particular animal is female. In some cases, the two words are related, e.g.:

un agneau, une agnelle, lamb
un âne, une ânesse, donkey
le chameau, la chamelle, camel
le chien, la chienne, dog, bitch
le lapin, la lapine, rabbit, doe
le lion, la lionne, lion(ess)
le loup, la louve, wolf
un ours, une ourse, bear
le renard, la renarde, fox, vixen
le tigre, la tigresse, tiger, tigress

In other cases, quite different words are used, e.g.:

le cerf, la biche, stag (*or* deer), doe
le lièvre, la hase, hare, doe
le singe, la guenon, monkey

(c) With reference to some animals, there is a generic word (which in every case is masculine) referring to individuals of either sex, but also special words for specifying male and female respectively:

le chat, cat	*le matou*, tomcat	*la chatte*, female cat
le cheval, horse	*un étalon*, stallion	*la jument*, mare
le mouton, sheep	*le bélier*, ram	*la brebis*, ewe
le porc, le cochon, pig	*le verrat*, boar	*la truie*, sow

Note that, corresponding to *le taureau* 'bull', *la vache* 'cow', there is no generic term in the singular, though the collective noun *le bétail*, and the plural *les bestiaux*, both meaning 'cattle', exist.

(d) For certain animals, the generic (and only) word is feminine, e.g.:

la baleine, whale	*la loutre*, otter
la belette, weasel	*la panthère*, panther
la girafe, giraffe	*la souris*, mouse
la grenouille, frog	*la taupe*, mole
une hyène, hyena	*la tortue*, tortoise

Note that *la chèvre* 'goat' is used as a generic but that there is also a specifically 'male' word, *le bouc* 'he-goat'.

La bête 'animal' is always feminine, even with reference to male animals.

Gender according to meaning – other categories

50   (i) **Masculine**
Most nouns falling into the following categories are masculine:

(a) Names of trees and shrubs

(b) Names of common fruits and vegetables not ending in -*e* (no exceptions)

(c) Names of metals and minerals

(d) Names of languages (no exceptions)

(e) Names of colours

(f) Names of weights and measures of the metric system, cardinal numbers, fractions, letters of the alphabet

(g) Names of days of the week, months, seasons, points of the compass.

Examples:

(a) Names of trees and shrubs, e.g.:

le chêne, oak	*le platane*, plane-tree
un érable, maple	*le pommier*, apple-tree
le hêtre, beech	*le sapin*, fir
le laurier, laurel	*le chèvrefeuille*, honeysuckle

The principal exceptions are:

une aubépine, hawthorn	*la ronce*, bramble
la bruyère, heather	*la vigne*, vine

(b) Names of common fruits and vegetables *not* ending in -*e* (for those ending in -*e*, see 51), e.g.:

un abricot, apricot	*un artichaut*, artichoke
le brugnon, nectarine	*le céleri*, celery
le citron, lemon	*le chou*, cabbage
le melon	*le haricot*, bean

(c) Most names of metals and minerals (including precious stones), e.g.:

le cuivre, copper	*le sel*, salt
le fer, iron	*le silicium*, silicon
le plomb, lead	*le souffre*, sulphur
l'anthracite	*le diamant*, diamond
le carbone, carbon	*le rubis*, ruby
le charbon, coal	*le saphir*, sapphire

Exceptions:

la chaux, chalk	*une émeraude*, emerald
la pierre, stone	*la perle*, pearl
la roche, rock	

and some technical names of minerals in -*ite* (e.g. *la malachite*, see 56).

(d) Names of languages are all masculine, e.g.:

le français, French	*le russe*, Russian
le grec, Greek	*le swahili*

(e) Most names of colours, e.g.:

le bleu, blue	*le jaune*, yellow	*le rouge*, red

Exceptions: *l'écarlate* 'scarlet' and *l'ocre* 'ochre' are feminine.

(f) Names of weights and measures of the metric system, cardinal numbers, most fractions, and the letters of the alphabet, e.g.:

le gramme	*un tiers*, one third
le kilogramme	*un quart*, a quarter
le litre	*un dixième*, a tenth
le mètre	*un e*
un sept, a seven	*un m*

Exception: *la moitié*, 'half'. Note that numerals in *-aine* indicating approximate quantities are feminine, e.g. *une dizaine* 'about ten', *une trentaine* 'about thirty', *une centaine* 'about a hundred'.

(g) The names of days of the week, months, seasons, and points of the compass, e.g.:

lundi dernier, last Monday
janvier prochain, next January
au printemps, in spring
en plein été, in the middle of summer
le nord, north
le sud, south
l'est, east
l'ouest, west

51   (ii) **Feminine**
The names of most common fruits and vegetables ending in *-e* (for others, see **50,i,b**) are feminine, e.g.:

la banane, banana	*la betterave*, beetroot
la fraise, strawberry	*la carotte*, carrot
la pomme, apple	*la fève*, broad bean

Exceptions: *le pamplemousse* 'grapefruit', *le concombre* 'cucumber'.

The gender of place-names

52   (a) There are no clear rules for determining the gender of names of towns. In many cases there is a good deal of hesitation and fluctuation but there is a marked tendency to treat them as masculine, e.g. *Paris est plus grand que Lyon* 'Paris is bigger than

Lyons', *Venise est beau* 'Venice is beautiful', *le grand Londres* 'Greater London', *Grenoble est devenu un centre industriel* 'Grenoble has become an industrial centre', *le musée du vieux Marseille* 'the Museum of Old Marseilles'. However, names in *-e* and *-es* and occasionally others can also be treated as feminine, e.g. *Londres fut sévèrement bombardée en 1940* 'London was heavily bombed in 1940', *Bruxelles fut libérée en 1944* 'Brussels was liberated in 1944', *Nice fut fondée en 350 av. J.-C.* 'Nice was founded in 350 BC', *Marseille contemporaine* 'present-day Marseilles'.

(b) As a general rule, names of countries, of French provinces and regions, and of French rivers, are feminine if they end in *-e*, masculine if they do not:

Countries, e.g.:

le Canada	*la Chine*, China
le Danemark, Denmark	*la Finlande*, Finland
le Japon, Japan	*la Norvège*, Norway
le Maroc, Morocco	*la Roumanie*, Romania
le Nigeria	*la Suisse*, Switzerland
le Portugal	*la Syrie*, Syria

Exceptions: *le Cambodge* 'Cambodia', *le Mexique* 'Mexico', *le Mozambique*, *le Zaïre*, and, with the *-e* pronounced, *le Zimbabwe*.

French provinces and regions, e.g.:

le Languedoc	*l'Aquitaine*
le Limousin	*la Bourgogne*, Burgundy
le Poitou	*la Champagne*
le Roussillon	*la Provence*

Exceptions: *le Maine*, *la Franche-Comté*

French rivers:

le Doubs	*la Durance*
le Lot	*la Loire*
le Rhin, Rhine	*la Maine*
le Tarn	*la Seine*

Exceptions: *le Rhône*, *la Lys*. Note that the rule does not apply to foreign rivers, many of which are masculine even though they end in *-e*, e.g. *le Danube*, *le Gange* 'Ganges', *le Tage* 'Tagus', *le Tibre* 'Tiber', *le Tigre* 'Tigris'.

(c) The gender of the names of French *départements* is as follows:

Names based on river-names take the gender of the corresponding river or, where there are two, of the first, e.g. *le Doubs*, *le Haut-Rhin*, *la Somme*, *la Loire-Atlantique*, *le Loir-et-Cher*, *le Lot-et-Garonne*, *la Meurthe-et-Moselle*.

Plural names (based on the names of mountains or other geographical features) happen in most cases to be feminine, e.g. *les Alpes-Maritimes*, *les Ardennes*, *les Bouches-du-Rhône*, *les Côtes-du-Nord*, *les Deux-Sèvres*, *les Landes*, *les Pyrénées-Orientales*, *les Vosges*, *les Yvelines*. One, *les Hauts-de-Seine*, is masculine. In practice, however, the need to indicate gender with these names rarely arises.

Others are masculine if the name (or, in the case of compounds, the first element) does **not** end in *-e*, feminine if it does:

le Calvados	*la Corse-du-Sud*
le Cantal	*la Haute-Corse*
le Jura	*la Haute-Savoie*
le Morbihan	*la Lozère*
le Nord	*la Manche*
le Puy-de-Dôme	
le Val-de-Marne	
le Val-d'Oise	

Exception: *le Vaucluse*.

Gender shown by ending

53 We shall discuss successively endings that always or usually indicate that the noun is (i) masculine or (ii) feminine, and (iii) a few problematic endings.

54 (i) **Masculine endings**
-age
A few monosyllables:

le gage, pledge, guarantee
le mage, Magus (*les rois Mages*, the Three Wise Men)
le page, page-boy
le sage, wise man
le stage, short course, training period

and several hundred polysyllables (many of them corresponding to English words in *-ing*), e.g.:

l'atterrissage, landing (of a plane)
le barrage, dam
le bavardage, chatter(ing)
le chômage, unemployment
le cirage, waxing, polishing
le courage
l'étage, floor, storey
le fromage, cheese
le garage
le gaspillage, waste, wasting
le mariage, marriage, wedding
le message
le nettoyage, cleaning
l'orage, (thunder)storm
le paysage, scenery
le potage, soup
le pourcentage, percentage
le village
le visage, face
le voyage, journey

Exceptions: five monosyllables:

la cage
la nage, swimming (in certain expressions only)
la page
la plage, beach
la rage, fury, rabies

and four polysyllables (three of them names of plants):

l'image	*la solidage*, golden rod
la passerage, pepperwort	*la saxifrage*, saxifrage

-ai, -oi
Most nouns in *-ai*, *-oi* are masculine, e.g.:

le balai, broom	*le beffroi*, belfry
le délai, time limit	*l'emploi*, use, job
l'essai, attempt	*l'envoi*, sending
le geai, jay	*le roi*, king

le quai, quay, platform   *le tournoi*, tournament

Exceptions: *la foi* 'faith', *la loi* 'law', *la paroi* '(inside) wall'.

-ail, -eil (including **-ueil**), **-euil**
All masculine, e.g.:

l'ail, garlic
le chandail, sweater
le corail, coral
le détail
l'émail, enamel
l'épouvantail, scarecrow
l'éventail, fan
le portail, portal
le travail, work
le vitrail, stained-glass window
l'appareil, apparatus
le conseil, piece of advice
l'orteil, toe
le réveil, waking up
le soleil, sun
le sommeil, sleep
l'accueil, welcome
le cercueil, coffin
l'écueil, reef
l'orgueil, pride
le recueil, collection (of poems, etc.)
le deuil, mourning
l'écureuil, squirrel
le seuil, threshold

-at
All masculine, e.g.:

le championnat, championship   *l'état*, state
le chocolat, chocolate   *le forçat*, convict
le climat, climate   *le nougat*
le combat, fight   *le résultat*, result
le consulat, consulate   *le secrétariat*
le contrat, contract   *le sénat*, senate
le débat, debate   *le syndicat*, trade-union

-c, -d, etc.

All words ending in -c or -d, and the relatively few words ending in -b, -g, -k, -p, -q or -z, are masculine, whether or not the consonant is pronounced, e.g.:

(a) **-c**:

l'aqueduc, aqueduct	*le jonc*, reed
le bec, beak	*le lac*, lake
l'estomac, stomach	*le sac*, bag
le franc	*le porc*, pig

(b) **-d**:

le bord, edge
l'étendard, flag, standard
le fond, bottom
le gland, acorn
le pied, foot
le regard, glance, look
le retard, delay
le standard, (telephone) switchboard

(c) others:

le club	*le steak*
le plomb, lead	*le coup*, blow
l'étang, pond	*le loup*, wolf
le hareng, herring	*le coq*, cock
le poing, fist	*le gaz*, gas
le bifteck, steak	*le nez*, nose
le snack, snack-bar	*le riz*, rice

-é

Nearly all words ending in -é except those in -té, tié (see below, 55) are masculine, e.g.:

le blé, wheat	*le délégué*, delegate
le café, café, coffee	*le fossé*, ditch
le carré, square	*le gué*, ford
le clergé, clergy	*le marché*, market
le cuirassé, battleship	*le pavé*, paving-stone
le dé, dice, thimble	*le péché*, sin
le défilé, procession	*le pré*, meadow
le degré, degree, step	*le thé*, tea

Exceptions: *l'acné* 'acne', *la clé* 'key', *la psyché* 'psyche'.

-eau

Four monosyllables:

> *le beau*, that which is beautiful
> *le sceau*, seal
> *le seau*, bucket
> *le veau*, calf, veal

and some two hundred polysyllables, e.g.:

l'anneau, ring	*le gâteau*, cake
le bateau, boat	*le marteau*, hammer
le bouleau, birch-tree	*le morceau*, piece
le cadeau, present	*le niveau*, level
le cerveau, brain	*le râteau*, rake
le chapeau, hat	*le réseau*, network
le château, castle	*le rideau*, curtain
le couteau, knife	*le tableau*, picture
le drapeau, flag	*le tombeau*, tomb

Exceptions: Only two: *l'eau* 'water', *la peau* 'skin'.

-ède, -ège, -ème

> *l'intermède*, interlude
> *le quadrupède*, quadruped
> *le remède*, remedy
> *le collège*, type of secondary school
> *le cortège*, procession
> *le liège*, cork
> *le manège*, merry-go-round
> *le piège*, trap
> *le sacrilège*
> *le siège*, seat, siege
> *le sortilège*, magic spell
> *le chrysanthème*, chrysanthemum
> *le diadème*, diadem
> *l'emblème*, emblem
> *le poème*, poem
> *le problème*, problem
> *le système*, system
> *le thème*, theme, etc.

and the names of fractions, *un dixième* 'a tenth', *un vingtième* 'a twentieth', *un centième* 'a hundredth', etc.

Exceptions: The only common exception is *la crème* 'cream' (but note the use of *un crème*, short for *un café crème* 'coffee with cream or milk'). A few rare or technical terms include *la pinède* 'pine-forest', *l'allège* 'lighter (boat)', *la drège* 'drag-net', *la trirème* 'trireme'.

-er (for **-ier** see below):

(a) (*-r* pronounced). Nearly all masculine, e.g.:

> *le cancer*
> *l'enfer*, hell
> *le fer*, iron
> *l'hiver*, winter
> *le laser*
> *le leader*
> *le reporter*
> *le revolver*
> *le starter*, choke (of a car)
> *le speaker*, (radio, TV) announcer

Only two exceptions: *la cuiller* 'spoon', *la mer* 'sea'.

(b) (*-r* not pronounced). All masculine, e.g.:

> *le boucher*, butcher   *le foyer*, hearth
> *le boulanger*, baker   *le laisser-passer*, pass, permit
> *le clocher*, church tower   *le loyer*, rent
> *le déjeuner*, lunch   *l'oranger*, orange-tree
> *le dîner*, dinner   *le plancher*, floor

-ès

All masculine, e.g.:

(a) (Final *-s* pronounced)

> *l'aloès*, aloe   *le palmarès*, list of winners
> *le cacatoès*, cockatoo   *le xérès*, sherry

(b) (Final *-s* not pronounced)

> *l'abscès*, abscess   *le grès*, sandstone
> *l'accès*, access   *le procès*, trial
> *le congrès*, congress   *le progrès*, progress
> *le cyprès*, cypress   *le succès*, success

-et

Some three hundred words, all masculine, e.g.:

le ballet	*le perroquet*, parrot
le banquet	*le poulet*, chicken
le béret	*le projet*, project
le billet, ticket	*le regret*
le bonnet	*le robinet*, tap
le buffet	*le roitelet*, wren
le carnet, notebook	*le secret*
le filet, net	*le sommet*, summit
le fouet, whip	*le sujet*, subject
le jouet, toy	*le ticket*

-i (pronounced [i], i.e. excluding **-ai, -oi**)

Most nouns in *-i* are masculine, e.g.:

l'abri, shelter	*le merci*, thanks
l'appui, support	*le pari*, bet
le colibri, humming bird	*le parti*, (political) party
le cri, shout	*le pli*, fold
le défi, challenge	*le raccourci*, short cut
l'ennui, boredom	*le ski*, ski, skiing
l'épi, ear (of corn)	*le souci*, care, worry

and the days of the week, *le lundi*, *le mardi*, etc.

Exceptions: *la fourmi* 'ant', *la merci* 'mercy'.

Note that *un après-midi* and *une après-midi* 'afternoon' are both used.

-ier

A couple of hundred words, many of them referring to (a) male humans, or (b) trees, and all masculine:

(a) Male humans, e.g.:

le banquier, banker	*l'héritier*, heir
le chevalier, knight	*l'hôtelier*, hotel-keeper
le conférencier, lecturer	*l'officier*, officer
l'épicier, grocer	*le romancier*, novelist
le guerrier, warrior	*le sorcier*, sorcerer

(b) Trees, e.g.:

le dattier, date-palm	*le figuier*, fig-tree

le laurier, laurel	*le peuplier*, poplar
le marronnier, chestnut tree	*le poirier*, pear-tree
le noisetier, hazel-tree	*le pommier*, apple-tree
le palmier, palm-tree	*le rosier*, rose-bush

(c) Others, e.g.:

l'acier, steel	*le guêpier*, wasps' nest
le cahier, note-book	*le métier*, job, profession
le casier, pigeonhole	*le palier*, landing
le cendrier, ashtray	*le panier*, basket
le chantier, building site	*le papier*, paper
le clavier, keyboard	*le pétrolier*, (oil) tanker
le collier, necklace	*le quartier*, district (of a
le dossier, file, dossier	town)
le gosier, throat	*le saladier*, salad-bowl
le grenier, attic	*le sentier*, path
	le tablier, apron

-ing
A few words borrowed from English (or, in the case of *schilling*, from German), are all masculine, e.g.:

le brushing, blow-dry
le building, office-block, etc.
le camping, camp-site
le jogging, jogging, track-suit
le meeting, rally, (political) meeting
le parking, car-park
le schilling, (Austrian) schilling
le shopping

-isme
Some four hundred words, all masculine, e.g.:

le catéchisme	*le rhumatisme*, rheumatism
le christianisme, Christianity	*le romantisme*, Romanticism
le cubisme	*le socialisme*
l'idiotisme, idiom	*le tourisme*
le prisme, prism	*l'urbanisme*, town-planning

-ment
With one exception, the scores of words in *-ment* are all masculine, e.g.:

l'abonnement, subscription	*le gouvernement*, government
l'avertissement, warning	*le logement*, lodging
le bâtiment, building	*le moment*
le ciment, cement	*le monument*
le commencement, beginning	*le mouvement*, movement
le désarmement, disarmament	*le recensement*, census

Exception: *la jument* 'mare'.

-oir
Over a hundred words, all masculine, e.g.:

le couloir, corridor	*le mouchoir*, handkerchief
le désespoir, despair	*le rasoir*, razor
le dortoir, dormitory	*le soir*, evening
l'espoir, hope	*le tiroir*, drawer
le miroir, mirror	*le trottoir*, pavement

-ou
All masculine, e.g.:

le bijou, jewel	*le genou*, knee
le caillou, pebble	*le hibou*, owl
le chou, cabbage	*le pou*, louse
le clou, nail	*le trou*, hole
le cou, neck	*le verrou*, bolt
le coucou, cuckoo	*le voyou*, lout

55 (ii) Feminine endings
-ace
Words in *-ace* are nearly all feminine, e.g.:

l'audace, daring	*la race*, breed, race
la glace, ice, mirror	*la surface*
la menace, threat	*la trace*
la place, (public) square	

Un espace 'space' is an exception (but note that with reference to a typographical space the word is feminine, *une espace*).

-ade
Some two hundred words (many of them uncommon), the great majority of them feminine, e.g.:

l'ambassade, embassy	*la cascade*
la bourgade, large village	*la façade*

l'œillade, wink	*la saccade*, jerk
l'orangeade	*la salade*, salad
la promenade, walk	*la tornade*, tornado

Exceptions:

le or *la camarade*, friend
le or *la garde-malade*, home nurse
le or *la malade*, sick person
le or *la nomade*, nomad
le grade, rank
le jade
le stade, stadium

-aie
All nouns in *-aie* are feminine:
(a) Collective nouns for trees, etc.:

la châtaigneraie, chestnut grove
l'oliveraie, olive grove
la palmeraie, palm grove
la peupleraie, poplar grove
la ronceraie, bramble patch
la roseraie, rose garden

(b) Others, e.g.:

la baie, bay, berry	*la plaie*, wound
la haie, hedge	*la raie*, furrow, stripe
la monnaie, currency, change	*la taie*, pillow-case

-aine, -eine, -oine
Most nouns with these endings are feminine, e.g.:

l'aubaine, windfall	*la semaine*, week
la fontaine, fountain	*la baleine*, whale
la gaine, sheath	*la peine*, trouble, difficulty
la graine, grain	*la reine*, queen
la haine, hatred	*la veine*, vein
la laine, wool	*l'avoine*, oats
la migraine	*la macédoine (de légumes)*,
la plaine, plain	mixed vegetables
la porcelaine	*la pivoine*, peony

Also *la douzaine* 'dozen', *la quinzaine* 'about fifteen, a fortnight', *la vingtaine* 'score', *la centaine* 'about a hundred', and similar forms derived from other numerals.

Exceptions:

le capitaine, captain	*le chanoine*, canon
le domaine, domain	*le moine*, monk
l'antimoine, antimony	*le patrimoine*, heritage

-aison

All feminine, e.g.:

la comparaison, comparison	*la maison*, house
la conjugaison, conjugation	*la raison*, reason
la crevaison, puncture	*la saison*, season
la liaison	*la terminaison*, ending (of a
la livraison, delivery	word)

-ance, -anse, -ence, -ense

With only two exceptions, these words are feminine, e.g.:

l'ambulance	*la panse*, paunch
la confiance, confidence	*la transe*, trance
la correspondance,	*l'agence*, agency
correspondence	*la conscience*
la croyance, belief	*la différence*
la distance	*l'essence*, petrol
l'espérance, hope	*l'influence*
la lance	*la patience*
la naissance, birth	*la présence*
la puissance, power	*la violence*
la souffrance, suffering	*la défense*, defence
l'anse, handle (of cup, etc.)	*la dépense*, expenditure
la danse, dance	

Exceptions: *le silence, le suspense.*

-èche, -èque, -èse, -ève

The great majority of these are feminine, e.g.:

la brèche, breach	*la pastèque*, water-melon
la crèche, crib, creche	*la genèse*, genesis
la flèche, arrow	*l'hypothèse*, hypothesis
la mèche, wick	*la synthèse*, synthesis
la bibliothèque, library	*la thèse*, thesis
la discothèque, disco, record	*la fève*, broad bean
library	

la grève, strike	*la sève*, sap

Exceptions: *le chèque* 'cheque', *le* or *la métèque* (derogatory term for a foreigner), *le diocèse, un* or *une élève* 'pupil'.

-ée

Most nouns in *-ée* (but with a substantial number of exceptions, mostly technical or otherwise uncommon words) are feminine, e.g.:

l'araignée, spider	*la fusée*, rocket
la buée, condensation, steam	*la journée*, day
la cactée, cactus	*la marée*, tide
la cuillerée, spoonful	*la mosquée*, mosque
la dictée, dictation	*la pensée*, thought
la durée, duration	*la poignée*, fistful, handful
l'épée, sword	*la rosée*, dew
l'épopée, epic	*la traversée*, crossing
la fée, fairy	*la vallée*, valley

Exceptions include:

un or *une athée*, atheist	*le mausolée*, mausoleum
l'apogée, peak, climax, apogee	*le musée*, museum
le camée, cameo	*le pygmée*, pygmy
le colisée, coliseum	*le scarabée*, scarab (beetle)
le lycée, (French) secondary school	*le trophée*, trophy

-euse

All feminine:

(a) Female humans, e.g.:

la blanchisseuse, laundress	*l'ouvreuse*, usherette
la maquilleuse, make-up girl	*la religieuse*, nun
la menteuse, liar	*la vendeuse*, saleswoman

(b) Mechanical objects, e.g.:

l'agrafeuse, stapler	*la tondeuse (de gazon)*, lawnmower
la cireuse, floor polisher	
la mitrailleuse, machine-gun	*la tricoteuse*, knitting-machine
la moissonneuse, harvester	*la tronçonneuse*, chain-saw
la perceuse, drill	

(c) Others, e.g.:

la berceuse, lullaby	*la vareuse*, kind of tunic
la nébuleuse, nebula	*la veilleuse*, night-light

-ie (including **-uie**, but excluding **-aie** and **-oie**)
Several hundred words (including about four hundred in *-erie*),
of which all except a handful are feminine, e.g.:

la biologie, biology	*la géographie*, geography
la boucherie, butcher's shop	*la jalousie*, jealousy
la bougie, candle	*la librairie*, bookshop
la chimie, chemistry	*la magie*, magic
la colonie, colony	*la maladie*, illness
la compagnie, company	*la partie*, part
la copie, copy	*la pharmacie*, pharmacy
la démocratie, democracy	*la pie*, magpie
la folie, madness	*la plaisanterie*, joke
la galerie, gallery	*la pluie*, rain
la prairie, meadow	*la symphonie*, symphony
la scie, saw	*la tragédie*, tragedy
la série, series	*la truie*, sow
la suie, soot	*la vie*, life

Exceptions:

l'amphibie, amphibian	*l'incendie*, fire
le coolie, coolie	*le Messie*, Messiah
le génie, genius; engineering corps	*le parapluie*, umbrella
	le sosie, double, look-alike

-ière
Well over a hundred words, nearly all feminine, e.g.:

la bannière, banner	*la lumière*, light
la barrière, barrier	*la manière*, manner, way
la bière, beer	*la matière*, matter
la cafetière, coffee-pot	*la paupière*, eye-lid
la chaumière, cottage	*la poussière*, dust
la croisière, cruise	*la prière*, prayer
la fermière, farmer's wife	*la rivière*, river
la frontière, frontier	*la thière*, tea-pot

Exceptions: *le cimetière* 'cemetery', *le derrière* 'backside, rear'.

-ine

Over a hundred words, nearly all feminine, e.g.:

la colline, hill
la cuisine, kitchen
la farine, flour
la guillotine
la machine
la marine, navy
la médecine
la narine, nostril
la pénicilline
la piscine, swimming-pool
la platine, tape-deck, etc.

la poitrine, chest
la racine, root
la routine
la ruine, ruin
la saccharine
la sardine
la scarlatine, scarlet fever
la turbine
la vitrine, shop window,
  showcase

Only two exceptions: *le magazine, le platine* 'platinum'.

-ise

About fifty words, nearly all of them feminine, e.g.:

la bêtise, folly
la brise, breeze
la cerise, cherry
la chemise, shirt
la crise, crisis

une église, church
la franchise, frankness
la marchandise, goods
la surprise
la valise, suitcase

Exceptions: *le cytise* 'laburnum', *le pare-brise* 'windscreen'.

-sion, -tion

With one exception, the many nouns in *-sion, -tion* are all feminine, e.g.:

la confusion
la décision
l'émission, broadcast
l'occasion, opportunity
la possession
la pression, pressure
la provision
la télévision
la tension
la vision, eyesight

l'action
la civilisation
la condition
la destination
la fiction
la nation
la position
la question
la situation
la traduction, translation

Exception: *le bastion*.

-lle, -sse, -tte, -ffe, -nne, -ppe

Many hundreds of words ending in a double consonant + *-e* are feminine. This does not apply to words in *-mme* and *-rre* (see 56 below), but, otherwise, there are relatively few exceptions, all of which, apart from a few highly technical or very rare words, are listed below.

(a) **-lle** (pronounced [l]), e.g.:

la balle, ball	*la poubelle*, dustbin
la malle, trunk	*la selle*, saddle
la salle, room, hall	*la semelle*, sole (of shoe)
la chapelle, chapel	*la vaisselle*, dishes, crockery
la dentelle, lace	*la voyelle*, vowel
l'échelle, ladder	*la ville*, town
la ficelle, string	*la bulle*, bubble

Note that even *la sentinelle* 'sentry', referring to a male human, is feminine.

Exceptions:

l'intervalle, interval	*le violoncelle*, cello
le libelle, lampoon	*le bacille*, bacillus
le polichinelle, Punch, buffoon	*le mille*, thousand
le or *la rebelle*, rebel	*le vaudeville*
le vermicelle, vermicelli	*le tulle*

(b) **-ille** (pronounced [j] – see 2), e.g.:

la bataille, battle	*l'aiguille*, needle
la ferraille, scrap iron	*l'anguille*, eel
la muraille, (high) wall	*la bille*, marble
la paille, straw	*la cheville*, ankle
la taille, waist, size	*la famille*, family
la volaille, poultry	*la faucille*, sickle
la bouteille, bottle	*la fille*, daughter
l'oreille, ear	*la pupille*, pupil (of eye)
la veille, eve, day before	*la grenouille*, frog
la feuille, leaf	*la patrouille*, patrol

Exceptions:

le chèvrefeuille, honeysuckle	*le gorille*, gorilla
le portefeuille, wallet	*le* or *la pupille*, ward

(c) -sse

All nouns in *-esse* are feminine; many of them denote either female beings, e.g.:

la déesse, goddess	*la princesse*, princess
la maîtresse, mistress	*la tigresse*, tigress

or qualities, e.g.:

la faiblesse, weakness	*la tendresse*, tenderness
la jeunesse, youth	*la tristesse*, sadness
la paresse, laziness	*la vieillesse*, old age
la politesse, politeness	*la vitesse*, speed

Other feminine nouns in *-sse* include:

la chasse, hunting	*la forteresse*, fortress
la classe, class	*la messe*, (religious) mass
la potasse, potassium	*la presse*, press
la tasse, cup	*la cuisse*, thigh
la terrasse, terrace	*la saucisse*, sausage
la baisse, lowering	*la brosse*, brush
la caisse, cash-desk	*la fosse*, pit
la graisse, grease, fat	*l'angoisse*, anxiety
la hausse, rise (in prices, etc.)	*la paroisse*, parish
la caresse, caress	*la mousse*, moss, mousse

Exceptions:

le or *la gosse*, kid
le or *la Russe*, Russian
le carrosse, (horse-drawn) coach
le colosse, colossus, giant
le molosse (rare), huge dog
le mousse, cabin-boy
le narcisse, narcissus
le pamplemousse, grapefruit
le petit-suisse, kind of cream cheese
le Suisse, Swiss

(d) -tte

A large group of nouns in *-ette*, the vast majority of them feminine, e.g.:

l'allumette, match	*la camionnette*, van

la chaussette, sock	*l'omelette*
la cigarette	*la recette*, recipe
la côtelette, chop, cutlet	*la serviette*, towel, brief-case
la dette, debt	*la silhouette*
la fourchette, fork	*la trompette*, trumpet

Exceptions: *le squelette* 'skeleton', *le trompette* 'trumpeter'.

Note that *la vedette* '(film-)star', etc., is feminine even when it refers to a man.

Other nouns in *-tte*, **all** feminine, include:

la datte, date (fruit)	*la botte*, boot, bunch
la patte, paw	*la carotte*, carrot
la grotte, cave, grotto	*la hutte*, hut
la goutte, drop	*la lutte*, struggle

(e) **-ffe, -nne, -ppe**
Most of these words are feminine, e.g.:

l'étoffe, cloth, material
la gaffe, blunder
la greffe, graft, transplant
la griffe, claw
la touffe, tuft
la truffe, truffle
l'antenne, aerial
la colonne, column
la couronne, crown
la panne, (mechanical) breakdown
la personne, person
la tonne, ton, tonne
l'enveloppe, envelope
la grappe, bunch (of grapes)
la grippe, flu
la nappe, tablecloth
la trappe, trap-door

Exception: *le renne* 'reindeer'.

-té, -tié
Several hundred nouns in *-té* and **all** nouns in *-tié* (there are only four) are feminine, e.g.:

la bonté, goodness	*la cécité*, blindness

la cité, city	*la quantité*, quantity
la cruauté, cruelty	*la santé*, health
la difficulté, difficulty	*la vérité*, truth
la fierté, pride	*l'amitié*, friendship
la lâcheté, cowardice	*l'inimitié*, enmity
la majorité, majority	*la moitié*, half
la qualité, quality	*la pitié*, pity

Exceptions:

l'aparté, (theatrical) aside
l'arrêté, order, decree
le comité, committee
le comté, county
le côté, side
le décolleté, low neckline
le doigté, fingering, tact
l'été, summer
le pâté, pie, pâté; block of houses; etc.
le traité, treaty, treatise

-tude
All feminine, e.g.:

l'attitude	*l'inquiétude*, anxiety
la certitude, certainty	*la multitude*
l'étude, study	*la servitude*
l'habitude, habit	*la solitude*

-ure
Over three hundred words, nearly all of them feminine, e.g.:

la ceinture, belt	*la lecture*, reading
la confiture, jam	*la nature*
la couverture, blanket	*la nourriture*, food
la créature	*la peinture*, painting, paint
la dictature, dictatorship	*la reliure*, binding (of a book)
la doublure, lining	*la serrure*, lock
la fermeture, closing	*la signature*
la figure, face	*la température*
la fourrure, fur	*la torture*
une injure, insult	*la voiture*, car, carriage

Exceptions:

(i) Chemical substances, e.g.:

le bromure, bromide	*l'hydrocarbure*, hydrocarbon
le carbure, carbide	*le mercure*, mercury
le chlorure, chloride	*le phosphure*, phosphide
le fluorure, fluoride	*le sulfure*, sulfide

(ii) Others:

l'augure, soothsayer	*le* or *la manucure*, manicurist
le murmure, murmur	*le* or *la pédicure*, chiropodist
le parjure, perjury	

56   (iii) Problematic endings

-a

Those who know Latin, Italian or Spanish, in which languages nouns in *-a* are usually feminine, may well think the same is true of French. This is not so – many, though by no means at all, French nouns in *-a* are masculine.

(a) Masculine nouns in *-a* include:

l'agenda, diary	*le sofa*
l'opéra	*le tapioca*
le panda	*le tibia*
le panorama	*le visa*
le rutabaga, swede	

and a number of names of flowers, e.g. *le bégonia*, *le dahlia*, *le gardénia*, *le pétunia*.

(b) Feminine nouns in *-a* include:

la malaria	*la toundra*, tundra
la marina	*la vendetta*
la paranoïa	*la véranda*
la razzia, raid, foray	*la villa*
la tombola, lottery	*la vodka*

and a number of names of dances, including *la mazurka*, *la polka*, *la rumba*, *la samba*.

-ène

(a) Masculine nouns in -*ène* are mainly technical terms of chemistry, e.g.:

l'acétylène	*l'hydrogène*

le kérosène	*le molybdène*, molybdenum
le méthylène	*l'oxygène*

but also include:

un or *une aborigène*	*le troène*, privet
le phénomène, phenomenon	

(b) Feminine nouns in -*ène* include:

l'arène, arena	*l'hygiène*
l'ébène, ebony	*la patène*, paten
la gangrène, gangrene	*la scène*, scene, stage
l'hyène, hyena	*la sirène*, siren; mermaid

-ère (excluding **-ière**, see 55)
Nouns in -*ère* referring to humans are male or female according to the sex of the individual concerned. Apart from that, no very helpful rules can be given for determining the gender of nouns in -*ère*.

(a) Masculine nouns include:

Referring to males:

le confrère, colleague, confrere
le frère, brother
le père, father
le trouvère, trouvère (medieval bard)

Others:

le caractère, character	*l'hémisphère*
le conifère, conifer	*le ministère*, ministry
le cratère, crater	*le monastère*, monastery
le critère, criterion	*le mystère*, mystery
le débarcadère, landing stage	*le réverbère*, street lamp
le gruyère, Gruyère cheese	*l'ulcère*, ulcer
l'hélicoptère, helicopter	

(b) Feminine nouns include:

Referring to females:

la bergère, shepherdess	*l'étrangère*, foreigner
la boulangère, baker's wife	*la ménagère*, housewife

Others:

l'artère, artery
l'atmosphère
la bruyère, heather
la colère, anger
la cuillère, spoon
l'ère, era

la misère, dire poverty
la panthère, panther
la sphère
la stratosphère
la vipère, viper

-ète

(a) Masculine nouns include:

   le diabète, diabetes

le prophète, prophet

(b) Feminine nouns include:

l'arbalète, crossbow
la cacahuète, peanut
la comète, comet

la diète, diet (assembly)
l'épithète, epithet
la planète, planet

(c) Nouns that can be of either gender, in accordance with the sex of the individual referred to, include:

   un or *une ascète*, ascetic
   un or *une athlète*
   un or *une esthète*, aesthete
   un or *une interprète*, interpreter

-eur

Words in *-eur* fall into four groups:

(a) Nouns referring to male humans are masculine, e.g.:

le cambrioleur, burglar
le facteur, postman
le lecteur, reader
le menteur, liar

le pêcheur, fisherman
le sculpteur, sculptor
le voleur, thief
le voyageur, traveller

Note that *le professeur* 'teacher, professor', is masculine, even with reference to a woman.

(b) Nouns referring to physical (in many cases mechanical) objects are masculine, e.g.:

l'accélérateur, accelerator
l'aspirateur, vacuum-cleaner
le carburateur, carburettor
le condenseur, condenser
le croiseur, cruiser

le moteur, engine
l'ordinateur, computer
le démarreur, starter (of car)
l'échangeur, interchange (on motorway)

le radiateur, radiator	*le tracteur*, tractor
le récepteur, receiver	*le vapeur*, steamship
le téléviseur, TV set	

(c) Abstract nouns, referring to qualities, feelings, colours, etc., are in most cases feminine, e.g.:

la blancheur, whiteness	*l'humeur*, mood
la couleur, colour	*la largeur*, width
la douceur, sweetness, softness	*la pâleur*, paleness
la douleur, pain, grief	*la peur*, fear
la faveur, favour	*la profondeur*, depth
la fraîcheur, coolness	*la rougeur*, redness
la fureur, fury	*la stupeur*, daze
la grandeur, size	*la terreur*, terror
la hauteur, height	*la valeur*, value

Exceptions:

le bonheur, happiness	*le labeur*, toil
le déshonneur, dishonour	*le malheur*, misfortune
l'honneur, honour	

(d) Miscellaneous, e.g.:

masc.	fem.
le chœur, choir	*la fleur*, flower
le cœur, heart	*la liqueur*
le dénominateur, denominator	*la lueur*, glow
l'équateur, equator	*la sueur*, sweat
l'extérieur, outside	*la vapeur*, steam
le secteur, sector	

-ite

(a) Words referring to humans are masculine or feminine according to the sex of the person referred to, e.g.:

le Jésuite, Jesuit
la Carmélite, Carmelite nun
un or *une antisémite*
un or *une Israélite*
le or *la Maronite*, Maronite (Christian)
le or *la Moscovite*, Muscovite
le or *la Sunnite*, Sunni Muslim

(b) Names of salts of acids are masculine:

l'arsénite	*le nitrite*
l'hypochlorite	*le phosphite*
l'hyposulfite	*le sulfite*

(c) Some names of minerals in fairly common use are masculine:

l'anthracite	*le graphite*
le granite (also *le granit*)	*le lignite*

but more technical names of minerals in *-ite* are feminine, e.g.:

la bauxite	*la magnésite*
la calcite	*la marcassite*
la ferrite	*la mélanite*
la lazalite	*la néphrite*
la malachite	*la wolframite*

(d) Medical terms in *-ite* (corresponding to English *-itis*) referring to various types of inflammation are feminine, e.g.:

l'appendicite	*la gastrite*
l'amygdalite, tonsilitis	*la laryngite*
l'arthrite	*la méningite*
la bronchite	*la phlébite*
la conjonctivite	*la poliomyélite*

(e) Other masculine nouns include:

le mérite, merit	*le satellite*
le parasite	*le termite*
le plébiscite	

(f) Other feminine nouns include:

la dynamite	*l'orbite*, orbit, eye-socket
la faillite, bankruptcy	*la réussite*, success
la guérite, sentry-box	*la stalactite*
la marguerite, ox-eye daisy	*la stalagmite*
la marmite, cooking-pot	*la site*
la mite, clothes moth	*la visite*

-mme, -rre

Note that there are more masculine than feminine words in *-mme* and *-rre*, e.g.:

(a) Masculine

le dilemme, dilemma   *le somme*, nap
l'homme, man

Also masculine are *le gramme* 'gram', other metric units of measurement in -*gramme* (*le centigramme*, *le kilogramme*, etc.), and *le cryptogramme*, *le diagramme*, *le monogramme*, *le parallélogramme*, *le programme*, and *le télégramme* (for two feminine words in -*gramme*, see below).

le beurre, butter
le cimeterre, scimitar
le leurre, snare, delusion
le lierre, ivy
le paratonnerre, lightning conductor
le parterre, flowerbed, stalls (theatre)
le tintamarre, din, racket
le tonnerre, thunder
le verre, glass

(b) Feminine

une anagramme, anagram   *la pomme*, apple
une épigramme, epigram   *la somme*, sum, amount
la femme, woman   *la barre*, bar
la flamme, flame   *la guerre*, war
la gamme, scale, gamut   *la pierre*, stone
la gemme, gem   *la serre*, greenhouse
la gomme, rubber (eraser)   *la terre*, earth

-o

A majority of the small group of words in -*o* are masculine, but there are some important exceptions.

(a) Masculine words include:

le bistro(t), pub, café   *le piano*
le cargo, cargo-boat   *le porto*, port (drink)
le casino   *le radio*, radio operator,
le duo, duet   radiogram
le credo, creed   *le studio*, studio, flatlet
l'écho   *le verso*, back (of page)
le kilo, kilo(gram)   *le zéro*
le numéro, number, numeral

(b) Feminine nouns include:

une auto, car
la dactylo, typist, typing
la dynamo
la photo

la polio
la radio, radio, X-ray photo

-oire

(a) Masculine nouns include:

l'auditoire, audience
l'ivoire, ivory
l'observatoire, observatory
le pourboire, tip
le promontoire, headland

le laboratoire, laboratory
le mémoire, memoir
le réfectoire, refectory
le répertoire
le territoire, territory

(b) Feminine nouns include:

l'armoire, cupboard
la balançoire, swing
la baignoire, bath-tub
la bouilloire, kettle
la foire, fair
la gloire, glory

l'histoire, history, story
la mâchoire, jaw
la nageoire, fin
la mémoire, memory
la poire, pear
la victoire, victory

-te (other than **-ète, -ite** and **-tte**, see above)

(a) Nouns referring to humans are masculine or feminine according to the sex of the individual concerned, e.g.:

un or *une adulte*
un or *une artiste*
un or *une astronaute*
le or *la démocrate*
le or *la dentiste*
le or *la diplomate*
un or *une enthousiaste*, enthusiast
un or *une hôte*, guest
le or *la linguiste*
le or *la patriote*

Note *le comte* 'count, earl' (feminine *la comtesse*), *le despote, un hôte* 'host, landlord' (feminine *une hôtesse*), *le pilote, le pirate*.

(b) Names of chemicals and minerals in *-ate, -lte, -ste* are masculine, e.g.:

le carbonate	*le sulfate*, sulphate
le chlorate	*l'asphalte*
le nitrate	*le basalte*
le phosphate	*l'asbeste*, asbestos
le silicate	*le schiste*, schist

(c) Most other nouns in -*te* (but with some important exceptions) are feminine, e.g.:

l'arête, fish-bone	*la boîte*, box
la bête, animal	*la carte*, map, card
la chute, fall	*la perte*, loss
la côte, coast	*la peste*, plague
la crainte, fear	*la piste*, track, runway
la cravate, tie	*la plainte*, complaint, groan
la crête, crest	*la porte*, door
la croûte, crust	*la poste*, postal service
la date	*la récolte*, crop
la découverte, discovery	*la route*, road
la dispute	*la sieste*, siesta
l'émeute, riot	*la sonate*, sonata
la faute, mistake	*la sorte*, sort
la fente, crack	*la tarte*, tart
la flûte, flute	*la tempête*, storm
la honte, shame	*la tente*, tent
la minute	*la tomate*, tomato
la note, note, bill	*la vente*, sale
la pâte, dough	*la veste*, jacket
la pente, slope	*la voûte*, vault

Exceptions include:

l'acte, act	*le faîte*, top, summit
l'antidote	*l'insecte*, insect
l'arbuste, small shrub	*le jute*
le buste, bust	*le parachute*
le compte, count, account	*le poste*, job, etc.
le conte, tale	*le reste*, remainder, rest
le contexte, context	*le texte*, text
le contraste, contrast	*le tumulte*, tumult
le doute, doubt	*le vote*

The gender of compound nouns

57 In what follows, only nouns formed of two or more words joined by hyphens are counted as compound nouns. Nouns that were originally compounds but are now written as one word without hyphens (e.g. *le chèvrefeuille*, honeysuckle) are treated as simple nouns and so are covered by the rules given above.

Compound nouns can be divided, for our present purposes, into six classes:

58 (i) **Nouns composed of a noun and a preceding or following adjective**
The gender of the compound is normally that of the simple noun, e.g.:

le bas-relief, low relief, bas
   relief
le cerf-volant, kite, stag-
   beetle

le bas-côté, aisle
le coffre-fort, safe

la basse-cour, farmyard
la belle-fille, daughter-in-law

Exceptions:

le Peau-Rouge, Redskin
le terre-neuve, Newfoundland dog (short for *le chien de Terre-Neuve*)

and some birds' names, including *le rouge-gorge* 'robin', *le rouge-queue* 'redstart'.

59 (ii) **Nouns having the construction noun + noun**
The gender is that of the principal noun, which is normally the first noun, e.g.:

le bateau-école, training-ship (i.e. a ship, *bateau*, serving as a school)
le camion-citerne, tanker (-lorry)
le chou-fleur, cauliflower (i.e. a 'flowering' cabbage)
un homme-grenouille, frogman
le mot-clé, keyword
un oiseau-mouche, humming-bird

le timbre-poste, (postage-) stamp
le wagon-lit, sleeping-car
une année-lumière, light-year
la porte-fenêtre, french window (i.e. a door, *porte*, serving
also as a window)
la voiture-restaurant, dining-car (i.e. a coach, *voiture*, serving
as a restaurant)

60 (iii) **Nouns having the construction noun + preposition +
noun**
The gender is usually that of the first noun, e.g.:

masc.

un arc-en-ciel, rainbow
le chef-d'œuvre, masterpiece
le mont-de-piété, pawnshop
le pot-de-vin, bribe

fem.

la bourse-à-pasteur, shepherd's purse
la langue-de-chat, type of biscuit
la main-d'œuvre, work-force
la tête-de-loup, ceiling brush

Exceptions: *le face-à-main* 'lorgnette', *le tête-à-queue* 'spin, slew
round (in horse-riding)', *le tête-à-tête*.

61 (iv) **Nouns having the construction adverb or prefix + noun**
The gender is that of the simple noun, e.g.:

masc.

l'arrière-plan, background
l'ex-roi, ex-king
le demi-tarif, half-fare
le mini-budget
le non-paiement, non-payment
le vice-président

fem.

l'arrière-pensée, mental reservation
l'ex-femme, ex-wife
la demi-bouteille, half-bottle
la mini-jupe, mini-skirt

la non-agression
la vice-présidence, vice-presidency

62 (v) Nouns having the construction preposition + noun
These are usually masculine, e.g.:

l'après-guerre, post-war period (even though *la guerre*, war, is feminine)
l'en-tête, heading (e.g. headed writing-paper)
le sans-gêne, lack of consideration for others
le sous-main, desk blotter

Exceptions: words referring to a female person, e.g.:

une sans-abri, homeless woman
une sans-cœur, heartless woman

Many apparent exceptions are accounted for by the fact that the first element is not a preposition but an adverb (so they are, in fact, type iv nouns), e.g. *l'avant-scène* 'proscenium, apron-stage' is feminine because the word is to be analysed not as something that is in front of the stage (*scène*), but as that part of the stage, *scène*, which is in front, *avant*, and so it takes the feminine gender of *scène*; *la contre-attaque* 'counter-attack' is not something that is against (*contre*) an attack, but an attack that goes counter to a previous one; *la sous-alimentation* 'malnutrition, under-feeding' is obviously not something that is beneath (*sous*) nutrition (*alimentation*), but nutrition that is of an inferior level.
Likewise:

une avant-garde, vanguard
la sous-commission, sub-committee
la sous-location, sub-letting
la sous-préfecture, sub-prefecture

63 (vi) Words having the construction verb + noun
These are nearly all masculine, e.g.:

le casse-noisettes, nutcracker
le coupe-papier, paper-knife
le cure-dent, toothpick
un essuie-main, hand-towel
le fume-cigarette, cigarette-holder
le gratte-ciel, skyscraper

l'ouvre-boîte, tin-opener
le pare-brise, windscreen
le porte-avions, aircraft carrier
le porte-monnaie, purse
le taille-crayon, pencil sharpener
le tire-bouchon, corkscrew

Exceptions: *le or la garde-barrière* 'level-crossing keeper', *le or la garde-malade* 'home nurse', according to the sex of the individual, *la garde-robe* 'wardrobe'.

A few uncommon names of fruit and flowers in *passe-* or *perce-* are feminine, e.g. *la passe-crassane* (variety of winter pear), *la passe-pierre* or *perce-pierre* 'samphire', *la passe-rose* 'hollyhock', *la perce-feuille* 'hare's ear', *la perce-muraille* 'wall pellitory' (but *le perce-neige* 'snowdrop').

Note that *le brise-fer*, *le casse-tout* 'a child who breaks everything', are masculine even with reference to girls.

Words that are identical in form but different in gender

64 As we have seen (in particular in 48,i,d), words such as *élève* 'pupil', *secrétaire* 'secretary', and many others can be of either gender depending on the sex of the person concerned. Quite apart from these, French has a number of pairs or sets of words whose members are identical in spelling and pronunciation but different in gender and meaning. They include:

	masc.	fem.
aide	male assistant	help; female assistant
aigle	eagle	female eagle; eagle standard
cartouche	scroll	cartridge
crêpe	crepe	pancake
critique	critic	criticism, review

	masc.	fem.
enseigne	sub-lieutenant, ensign (officer)	(shop-)sign, ensign (flag)
faune	faun	fauna
faux	forgery	scythe
finale	finale	last letter or syllable of a word
foudre	tun	thunderbolt, lightning
garde	keeper, guardsman	guard (duty), guardianship
greffe	record office (of law court, etc.)	graft(ing), (heart) transplant, etc.
guide	(male) guide; guidebook, etc.	(female) guide; *les guides* 'reins'
laque	lacquer ware	shellac, lacquer, hairspray
livre	book	pound
manche	handle (e.g. of a broom)	sleeve; *la Manche* 'English Channel'
manœuvre	labourer	manoeuvre
martyre	martyrdom (a male martyr is *un martyr*)	female martyr
matricule	reference number	membership list
mauve	mauve	mallow (plant)
mémoire	memorandum	memory
merci	thank-you (e.g. *un grand merci*)	mercy
mode	method, way; (grammatical) mood	fashion
mort	dead man	death
mousse	cabin-boy	moss, froth, lather, mousse, etc.

	masc.	fem.
page	page(-boy)	page (of book)
palme	handsbreadth	palm leaf, (symbolic) palm
parallèle	resemblance; line of latitude	parallel line
pendule	pendulum	clock
période	climax	period
physique	physique, that which is physical	physics
pique	spades (cards)	pike (weapon); cutting remark
platine	platinum	deck, turntable (of record-player)
pneumatique	tyre (now abbreviated to *pneu*)	pneumatics
poêle	stove; pall	frying-pan
poste	position, job; (police) station, etc.; (radio, TV) set; (telephone) extension; etc.	post (= postal service)
radio	radiogram; wireless (radio) operator	radio; X-ray (photograph)
rose	pink (colour)	rose
sixième	sixth (fraction); sixth floor, etc.	lowest form in a *lycée*
solde	balance (of account); sale	(soldier's) pay
somme	sleep, nap	sum, amount
souris	(archaic, poetical) smile	mouse
tonique	tonic (medical)	keynote, tonic (in music)
tour	turn, walk, lathe, trick, etc.	tower

	masc.	fem.
trompette	trumpeter	trumpet
vague	vagueness	wave
vapeur	steamship	steam, vapour
vase	vase	silt
voile	veil	sail

Some anomalies of gender

65 *Amour* 'love' is normally masculine, but in the plural, in the sense of 'love affairs', it is sometimes (but not necessarily) feminine.

66 *Chose* 'thing' is feminine (*une bonne chose* 'a good thing'), but *quelque chose* 'something' is masculine; *un petit quelque chose* 'a little something', *quelque chose s'est produit qui m'a beaucoup étonné* 'something happened which surprised me very much' in which the masculine agreement of *produit* (see **461**) shows that *quelque chose* is masculine. (Note too the construction *quelque chose d'intéressant* 'something interesting' – see **667**.)

67 *Délice* 'delight' is masculine in the singular but feminine in the plural.

68 *Gens* 'people' was originally the plural of the feminine noun *la gent* 'people, race' which survives only as a (usually humorous or ironic) archaism, e.g. *la gent ailée* 'the wingèd race (i.e. birds)'. This is reflected in the fact that, if an adjective that precedes the noun has a distinct feminine form (e.g. *bonne* 'good', *meilleure* 'best', *vieille* 'old', as distinct from masculine *bon*, *meilleur*, *vieux*), then the feminine form is used, e.g. *les vieilles gens* 'old people'. In such circumstances, if the noun is introduced by *tout* 'all' or *quel* 'what! which?', these also take the feminine form, e.g. *toutes les vieilles gens* 'all old people', *quelles bonnes gens!* 'what good people!' Note:

(a) that this **does not** apply when the adjective immediately preceding the noun does not have a distinct feminine form (e.g. *honnête* 'honest', *brave* 'fine'), so we have for example *tous les honnêtes gens* 'all honest people', *quels braves gens!* 'what fine people!', *ces bons et honnêtes gens* 'these good, honest people'.

(b) that adjectives in other positions are always masculine, e.g. *les gens heureux* 'happy people'; this applies even when the noun is preceded by an adjective taking the feminine form, e.g. *Les vieilles gens peuvent être ennuyeux* 'Old people can be boring'.

69 *Œuvre* 'work' is usually feminine (*une œuvre littéraire* 'a literary work', *une œuvre de longue haleine* 'a long-term piece of work') and is always feminine in the plural (*de bonnes œuvres* 'good works', *les dernières œuvres de Balzac* 'Balzac's last works'). It may, however, be masculine when referring to the complete work of a writer, composer or other artist (*l'œuvre entier* or *l'œuvre entière de Balzac* 'the complete works of Balzac').

70 *Orge* 'barley' is feminine (*cette orge est mûre* 'this barley is ripe') except in the terms *orge mondé* 'husked barley' and *orge perlé* 'pearl barley'.

71 *Orgue* 'organ' is masculine (*un orgue électrique* 'an electric organ', *deux orgues excellents* 'two excellent organs'), but note the use of a feminine plural (e.g. *les grandes orgues* 'the great organ') with reference to a singular instrument, especially a church organ.

72 *Pâque(s)*. The Jewish festival of Passover is feminine, *la Pâque* (*célébrer la Pâque* 'to celebrate Passover').

The Christian festival of Easter, *Pâques* (no article), is feminine plural in a few expressions such as *bonnes Pâques!* or *joyeuses Pâques!* 'Happy Easter', *souhaiter de bonnes* (or *joyeuses*) *Pâques à quelqu'un* 'to wish someone a happy Easter', *faire de bonnes Pâques* 'to take communion at Easter' (also *Pâques fleuries* 'Palm Sunday'), but elsewhere is usually treated as masculine singular, e.g. *quand Pâques sera arrivé* 'when Easter arrives', *à Pâques prochain* 'next Easter'.

73 *Personne*. The noun *personne* 'person' is feminine, e.g. *Une certaine personne est venue* 'A certain person came', but the negative pronoun *personne* 'nobody' (see **551**) is masculine, e.g. *Personne n'est venu* 'Nobody came'.

Gender of other parts of speech used as nouns

74 (i) Apart from the exceptions noted in ii–iv below, other parts of speech used as nouns are masculine, e.g.:

(a) (adjectives) *le beau* 'the beautiful' (as in *le culte du beau* 'the cult of the beautiful, of beauty'), *distinguer le vrai d'avec le faux* (Descartes) 'to distinguish the true from the false, what is true from what is false, truth from falsehood', *tenter l'impossible* 'to attempt the impossible', *le blanc* 'white (as a colour), the white (of an egg, of the eye)', *un liquide* 'a liquid'

(b) (verbs) *le va-et-vient* 'to-ing and fro-ing', *le rendez-vous* 'appointment', *le sourire* 'smile', *le voyant* '(luminous) signal, indicator', *le reçu* 'receipt'

(c) (adverbs and prepositions) *le mieux* 'best' (as in *faire de son mieux* 'to do one's best'), *le devant* 'front', *le pour et le contre* 'the pros and cons'

(ii) Nouns derived from the feminine forms of past participles are of course feminine, e.g. *l'arrivée* 'arrival', *la portée* 'reach', *la vue* 'sight'

(iii) Nouns derived from adjectives and referring to people take the gender corresponding to the sex of the individual concerned, e.g. *un* or *une aveugle* 'a blind person', *un* or *une malade* 'a patient, sick person', *un blanc, une blanche* 'a white man or woman'

(iv) Adjectival nouns originating in expressions of the type noun + adjective (see **176**) take the gender of the noun that is understood, e.g.:

(a) (masculine) *le rouge* 'red wine' (for *le vin rouge*), *le complet* 'suit; breakfast' (for *le costume complet* or *le petit déjeuner complet*), *le garni* 'furnished accommodation' (for *l'appartement garni*)

(b) (feminine) *la capitale* 'capital (city)' (for *la ville capitale*), *la majuscule* 'capital (letter)' (for *la lettre majuscule*), *la liquide* 'liquid (consonant)' (for *la consonne liquide*).

The feminine of nouns and adjectives

Introduction

75 The question of what words are used for corresponding male and female beings (e.g. *le père* 'father', *la mère* 'mother'; *le roi* 'king', *la reine* 'queen'; *le taureau* 'bull', *la vache* 'cow'; *le jars* 'gander', *l'oie* 'goose') is a matter of lexicon not of grammar and so will not be dealt with here (but see **48** and **49** above). The student should refer to a dictionary.

76 However, in certain cases corresponding masculine and feminine nouns were originally adjectives. In other cases, the feminine is derived from the masculine by change of suffix. These types can be considered as being on the fringes of grammar and so will be dealt with here.

Spoken French

77 In this section we shall deal only with adjectives.

There is no constant relationship between the masculine and feminine forms of adjectives in the spoken language. The main types of relationship are the following (for the phonetic symbols, see **2**):

78 The feminine is identical with the masculine, e.g.:

[ʃɛːr] *cher–chère*, dear	[naval] *naval–navale*
[dirɛkt] *direct–directe*	[ruːʒ] *rouge,* red
[fɛrm] *ferme*, firm	[vrɛ] *vrai–vraie*, true

79 The feminine is formed from the masculine by the addition of a consonant, e.g.:

[blɑ̃] *blanc* – [blɑ̃ːʃ] *blanche*, white
[fo] *faux* – [foːs] *fausse*, false
[ʒɑ̃ti] *gentil* – [ʒɑ̃tij] *gentille*, nice
[grɑ̃] *grand* – [grɑ̃ːd] *grande*, big
[o] *haut* – [oːt] *haute*, high
[œrø] *heureux* – [œrøːz] *heureuse*, happy
[lɔ̃] *long* – [lɔ̃ːg] *longue*
[su] *soûl* – [sul] *soûle*, drunk
[vɛːr] *vert* – [vɛrt] *verte*, green

80 The feminine is formed from the masculine by changing the final consonant, e.g.:

[sɛk] *sec* – [sɛʃ] *sèche*, dry
[vif] *vif* – [viːv] *vive*, living, etc.

81   The feminine is formed from the masculine by changing the
vowel and adding a consonant, e.g.:

[bo] *beau* – [bɛl] *belle*, beautiful
[fu] *fou* – [fɔl] *folle*, mad
[leʒe] *léger* – [leʒɛːr] *légère*, light, slight
[so] *sot* – [sɔt] *sotte*, foolish
[vjø] *vieux* – [vjɛj] *vieille*, old
[bɔ̃] *bon* – [bɔn] *bonne*, good
[brœ̃] *brun* – [bryn] *brune*, brown
[fɛ̃] *fin* – [fin] *fine*, fine, delicate
[peizɑ̃] *paysan* – [peizan] *paysanne*, peasant
[sɛ̃] *sain* – [sɛn] *saine*, healthy

Written French

82   The vast majority of adjectives form their feminine by
adding -*e* to the masculine, e.g.:

masc.	fem.
bleu, blue	*bleue*
clair, clear	*claire*
différent, different	*différente*
grand, big	*grande*
gris, grey	*grise*
musulman, Muslim	*musulmane*
royal, royal	*royale*
vrai, true	*vraie*

Nouns falling into this category include many deriving from adjectives of nationality, e.g.:

un Américain, American	*une Américaine*
un Espagnol, Spaniard	*une Espagnole*
le Français, Frenchman	*la Française*

83   If the masculine already ends in -*e* the masculine and the
feminine are the same, e.g.:

faible, weak	*faible*
rouge, red	*rouge*
le Russe, Russian	*la Russe*

84   In adjectives and nouns with the following endings, some further change, besides the addition of *-e*, takes place in the feminine:

-c becomes

(1) *-che* in

blanc, white	*blanche*
franc, frank, candid	*franche*
sec, dry	*sèche*

(2) *-que* in

ammoniac	*ammoniaque*
caduc, deciduous, etc.	*caduque*
franc, Frankish	*franque*
le Franc, Frank	*Franque*
public, public	*publique*
turc, Turkish	*turque*
le Turc, Turk	*la Turque*

(3) *-cque* in

grec, le Grec, Greek	*grecque, la Grecque*

-f becomes *-ve*, e.g.:

bref, brief	*brève*
neuf, new	*neuve*
(*le*) *veuf*, widowed, widower	(*la*) *veuve*, widowed, widow
vif, lively	*vive*

-g becomes *-gue* in

long, long	*longue*
oblong, oblong	*oblongue*

85   Adjectives and nouns in *-l* are regular except that:

-el becomes *-elle*, e.g.:

cruel, cruel	*cruelle*
mortel, mortal, deadly	*mortelle*

-eil becomes *-eille*, e.g.:

pareil, like	*pareille*
vermeil, vermilion	*vermeille*

Note too

gentil, nice	*gentille*
nul, no, none	*nulle*

86   Five adjectives have an alternative masculine form in *-l* when they occur before a noun beginning with a vowel or mute *h*, and it is from this second form that the feminine is derived:

beau, bel, beautiful	*belle*
fou, fol, mad	*folle*
mou, mol, soft	*molle*
nouveau, nouvel, new	*nouvelle*
vieux, vieil, old	*vieille*

The use of the second masculine forms is illustrated in such contexts as *un bel arbre* 'a beautiful tree' (cf. *un beau jour* 'a beautiful day'), *un fol espoir* 'an insane hope' (cf. *il est fou* 'he's mad'), *un mol oreiller* 'a soft pillow' (cf. *cet oreiller est mou* 'this pillow is soft'), *un nouvel élève* 'a new pupil' (cf. *un nouveau professeur* 'a new teacher'), *un vieil ami* 'an old friend' (cf. *un vieux film* 'an old film').

The following nouns in *-eau* form their feminine in the same way as *beau* and *nouveau*:

le chameau, camel	*la chamelle*
(le) jumeau, twin	*(la) jumelle)*
le Tourangeau, native of Tours or of Touraine	*la Tourangelle*

87   Words in *-n* are regular except that:
-en becomes *-enne*, e.g.:

ancien, former	*ancienne*
européen, European	*européenne*
italien, Italian	*italienne*

-on becomes *-onne*, e.g.:

le baron	*la baronne*, baroness

bon, good	*bonne*
breton, Breton	*bretonne*
le lion	*la lionne*, lioness

and *-an* becomes *-anne* in:

(le) paysan, peasant	*(la) paysanne*
rouan, roan	*rouanne*

(but *afghan*, *musulman* 'Muslim', *persan* 'Persian', *le sultan*, etc., are regular – *afghane*, *la sultane*, etc.)

Notice also:

bénin, kindly, benign	*bénigne*
malin, cunning, malign	*maligne*

88 Words in *-r*, other than those in *-er* (see below) and *-eur* (see **89**) are regular, e.g.:

dur, hard	*dure*
noir, black	*noire*

The ending *-er* becomes *-ère*, e.g.:

le boulanger, baker	*la boulangère*, female baker, baker's wife
cher, dear	*chère*
un écolier, schoolboy	*une écolière*, schoolgirl
(un) étranger, foreign(er)	*(une) étrangère*
premier, first	*première*

89 Words in *-eur* are of various kinds:

(a) Comparatives, including all adjectives in *-érieur* (which derive from Latin comparatives), are regular:

majeur, major	*majeure*
mineur, minor	*mineure*
(le) meilleur, better, best	*(la) meilleure*
supérieur, superior	*supérieure*
ultérieur, later	*ultérieure*

(also *antérieur*, *extérieur*, *inférieur*, *intérieur*, *postérieur*).

(b) A number of adjectives and nouns in *-eur* form their feminine in *-euse*, e.g.:

le chanteur, singer	*la chanteuse*
le danseur, dancer	*la danseuse*
(le) flatteur, flattering, flatterer	*(la) flatteuse*
(le) menteur, lying, liar	*(la) menteuse*
pleureur, weepy	*pleureuse*
trompeur, deceitful, deceptive	*trompeuse*
(le) voleur, thieving, thief	*(la) voleuse*
le vendeur, shop assistant	*la vendeuse*

Note that these all have the same stem as that of the corresponding verb (*danseur* like *danser*, *menteur* like *mentir*, etc.).

(c) Three forms in *-eur* that correspond to verbs have, however, a feminine in *-eresse*:

(un) enchanteur, enchanting, enchanter	*(une) enchanteresse*
(le) pécheur, sinful, sinner	*(la) pécheresse*
(le) vengeur, avenging, avenger	*(la) vengeresse*

Two legal terms also fall into this category:

| *le défendeur*, defendant | *la défenderesse* |
| *le demandeur*, plaintiff | *la demanderesse* |

(Note that 'defender' is *le défenseur*, which has no feminine, and that *le demandeur* in the more general sense of 'someone who asks' has the feminine *la demandeuse*.)

Five others that also share a stem with a corresponding verb form their feminine in *-trice* (cf. d below):

(un) émetteur, transmitting (station etc.), transmitter	*émettrice*
un exécuteur, executor	*une exécutrice*
un inspecteur, inspector	*une inspectrice*
un inventeur, inventor	*une inventrice*
(le) persécuteur, persecuting, persecutor	*(la) persécutrice*

(d) A large number of nouns and a few adjectives in *-teur* whose stem is *not* also that of a corresponding verb (e.g. *protecteur* 'protective, protector' but *protéger* 'to protect', *collaborateur* but *collaborer*) form their feminine in *-trice*, e.g.:

(un) accusateur, accusing, accuser	*(une) accusatrice*
un acteur, actor	*une actrice*, actress
(le) consolateur, comforting, comforter	*(la) consolatrice*
(le) destructeur, destructive, destroyer	*(la) destructrice*
un instituteur, schoolmaster	*une institutrice*, schoolmistress
le lecteur, reader	*la lectrice*
le traducteur, translator	*la traductrice*

(e) Note the following: *l'ambassadeur* 'ambassador', *l'empereur* 'emperor', have the feminine forms *l'ambassadrice* 'ambassador's wife' (a woman ambassador is either *l'ambassadeur* or *l'ambassadrice*), *l'impératrice* 'empress'. *Le docteur* (but only in the sense of a medical doctor) sometimes has the feminine *la doctoresse*, but *la femme docteur* or just *le docteur* (cf. *ma femme est docteur* 'my wife is a doctor') are more usual.

(f) Some nouns in *-eur* have no feminine, including *l'amateur*, *l'auteur* 'author', *le défenseur* 'defender', *l'imprimeur* 'printer', *l'orateur* 'speaker, orator', *le possesseur* 'owner', *le professeur* 'teacher, professor', *le sculpteur* 'sculptor', *le vainqueur* 'winner, victor'.

90 Forms in *-s* are regular (e.g. *gris, grise* 'grey'), except for:

bas, low	*basse*
épais, thick	*épaisse*
exprès, formal, express	*expresse*
gras, fat	*grasse*
gros, big	*grosse*
las, weary	*lasse*
frais, fresh, cool	*fraîche*
tiers, third	*tierce*

91 Forms in *-t* are regular (e.g. *plat, plate* 'flat', *idiot, idiote*), except that:

(a) The feminine of *le chat* 'cat' is *la chatte*

(b) Nine adjectives in *-et* make their feminine in *-ète*, viz.:

complet, complete	*complète*
incomplet, incomplete	*incomplète*

concret, concrete	*concrète*
désuet, antiquated, obsolete	*désuète*
discret, discreet	*discrète*
indiscret, indiscreet	*indiscrète*
inquiet, uneasy	*inquiète*
replet, stout, podgy	*replète*
secret, secret	*secrète*

The rest make their feminine in *-ette*, e.g. *muet* 'dumb', *muette*; *net* 'clean', *nette*.

(c) A few adjectives in *-ot* make their feminine in *-otte*, in particular:

boulot, tubby	*boulotte*
maigriot, skinny	*maigriotte*
pâlot, palish	*pâlotte*
sot, foolish	*sotte*
vieillot, antiquated, quaint	*vieillotte*

92 Forms in *-u* are regular except that *-gu* becomes *-guë*, e.g.:

aigu, sharp	*aiguë*
ambigu, ambiguous	*ambiguë*
exigu, exiguous, scanty	*exiguë*

(otherwise the *-ue* would not be pronounced – e.g. *aigue*, with no *ë*, would be pronounced [ɛg] not [egy].)

93 In most cases, *-x* becomes *-se*, e.g.:

heureux, happy	*heureuse*
jaloux, jealous	*jalouse*

But note:

doux, sweet, soft	*douce*
faux, false	*fausse*
roux, reddish-brown	*rousse*
vieux, old	*vieille*

94 The following are irregular:

andalou, Andalusian	*andalouse*
favori, favourite	*favorite*

Also *coi*, feminine *coite*, now used only in the expressions *se tenir coi(te)* 'to remain silent', *en rester coi(te)* 'to be rendered speechless'.

Note that though both *hébreu* and *hébraïque* 'Hebrew' exist in the masculine (e.g. *le peuple hébreu* 'the Hebrew people', *l'alphabet hébraïque* 'the Hebrew alphabet'), only *hébraïque* occurs in the feminine (e.g. *l'Université hébraïque de Jérusalem* 'the Hebrew University of Jerusalem').

95 A certain number of adjectives (in addition to those having *-e* in the masculine, see **83**) have no special feminine form (and no special plural form, see **125** and **126**). They are:

(i) some words that were originally nouns but are now used as adjectives of colour, e.g. *une chaussure marron* 'a brown shoe', *une robe lilas* 'a lilac dress', *une jupe saumon* 'a salmon-pink skirt'; also *chamois* 'fawn, buff', *indigo*

(ii) a very few other adjectives, mainly of foreign origin, e.g.:

une femme chic	a smartly dressed woman
une toile kaki	a khaki cloth
une pendule rococo	a rococo clock
une langue standard	a standard language
une livre sterling	a pound sterling

96 The following adjectives occur only in one or other gender and, in the case of those asterisked, only in the contexts quoted:

masc. only

un nez aquilin*, a hooked nose
benêt, simple-minded
un vent coulis*, a draught
un piano discord, an out-of-tune piano
un esprit dispos, an alert mind
le feu grégeois*, Greek fire
pantois, flabbergasted
un hareng saur*, a smoked herring

fem. only

bouche bée*, open-mouthed
une année bissextile*, a leap-year
une porte cochère*, a carriage entrance
de l'ignorance crasse, crass ignorance

la pierre philosophale*, the philosopher's stone
une œuvre pie*, a pious or charitable work

The plural of nouns

Spoken French

97 In spoken French, most nouns are invariable in the plural –
that is, there is no *audible* distinction between singular and plural,
e.g.:

le lit, bed, plur. *les lits*, both pronounced [li]
la ville, town, plur. *les villes*, both pronounced [vil]

The principal exceptions are:

(i) Most nouns ending in *-al* (see **105**), e.g. *le cheval* [ʃəval]
'horse', plural *les chevaux* [ʃəvo]

(ii) Some nouns in *-ail* (see **106**), e.g. *le travail* [travaj] 'work',
plural *les travaux* [travo]

(iii) *l'aïeul* [ajœl] 'grandfather', plural *les aïeux* [ajø] 'ancestors';
le ciel [sjɛl], 'sky', plural *les cieux* [sjø]; *l'œil* [œj] 'eye', plural *les
yeux* [jø] (see **108**)

(iv) *monsieur* [məsjø], *madame* [madam], *mademoiselle*
[madmwazɛl], plurals *messieurs* [mesjø], *mesdames* [medam], *mesdemoiselles* [medmwazɛl]; *un bonhomme* [bɔnɔm] 'chap, bloke',
plural *des bonshommes* [bɔ̃zɔm]; *un gentilhomme* [ʒɑ̃tijɔm]
'gentleman, squire', etc., plural *des gentilshommes* [ʒɑ̃tizɔm] (see
109)

(v) *l'os* [ɔs] 'bone', plural *les os* [o], *le bœuf* [bœf] 'ox', and *l'œuf*
[œf] 'egg', plurals *les bœufs* [bø], *les œufs* [ø].

98 In fact, the main indication as to whether a noun is singular
or plural is provided not by the form of the noun itself but by its
determiner (article, demonstrative, possessive, etc., see **23**), e.g.:

le chat [lə ʃa], the cat   *les chats* [le ʃa], the cats
la femme [la fam], the   *les femmes* [le fam], the
  woman   women

l'enfant [lɑ̃fɑ̃], the child	*les enfants* [lez ɑ̃fɑ̃], the children
un pied [œ̃ pje], a foot	*des pieds* [de pje], feet
une boîte [yn bwat], a box	*des boîtes* [de bwat], boxes
mon fils [mɔ̃ fis], my son	*mes fils* [me fis], my sons
sa main [sa mɛ̃], his/her hand	*ses mains* [se mɛ̃], his/her hands
votre jardin [vɔtrə ʒardɛ̃], your garden	*vos jardins* [vo ʒardɛ̃], your gardens
ce livre [sə liːvr], this book	*ces livres* [se liːvr], these books
cette pomme [sɛt pɔm], this apple	*ces pommes* [se pɔm], these apples

But sometimes the system breaks down – there is, for example, no audible distinction between *leur chapeau* 'their hat' and its plural *leurs chapeaux*, both pronounced [lœr ʃapo], or between *quelle porte?* 'which door?' and *quelles portes?* 'which doors?', both pronounced [kɛl pɔrt].

99 Sometimes the distinction between singular and plural is made clear in pronunciation by the presence of a liaison [z] in the plural, e.g. *leur enfant* [lœr ɑ̃fɑ̃] 'their child', *quel arbre?* [kɛl arbr] 'which tree?', plural *leurs enfants* [lœrz ɑ̃fɑ̃], *quels arbres?* [kɛlz arbr]. (Liaison can of course also occur even when the determiner itself indicates whether the noun is singular or plural, e.g. *mon cher ami* [mɔ̃ ʃɛr ami] 'my dear friend', plural *mes chers amis* [me ʃɛrz ami].)

100 Occasionally, when all else fails, the form of the verb may be the only way in which one can tell whether the subject of the sentence is singular or plural, e.g. *Leur frère va* [va] *partir demain* 'Their brother is going to leave tomorrow', plural *Leurs frères vont* [vɔ̃] *partir demain* 'Their brothers are going to leave tomorrow'. But sometimes all possible devices fail. There is, for example, no way at all of distinguishing in pronunciation between *Quel livre voulez-vous acheter?* 'What book do you want to buy?' and the plural *Quels livres voulez-vous acheter?* 'What books do you want to buy?' If it is essential to make the distinction, then the sentence must be phrased differently, e.g.:

Quel est le livre ⎱ *que vous voulez acheter?*
Quels sont les livres ⎰

Written French

101   In the written language, the plural is regularly formed by adding *-s* to the singular, e.g.:

le livre, book	*les livres*
la femme, woman	*les femmes*

102   Nouns that end in *-s*, *-x* or *-z* in the singular remain unchanged, e.g.:

le mois, month	*les mois*
la voix, voice	*les voix*
le nez, nose	*les nez*

103   Nouns ending in *-au*, *-eau* or *-eu* form their plural in *-x*, e.g.:

le noyau, stone (of fruit), nucleus	*les noyaux*
le tuyau, tube, pipe	*les tuyaux*
le chapeau, hat	*les chapeaux*
le seau, bucket	*les seaux*
le jeu, game	*les jeux*
le neveu, nephew	*les neveux*
le vœu, wish, vow	*les vœux*

Exceptions: *le landau* 'pram, landau', *les landaus*; *le bleu* 'blue, bruise', *l'émeu* 'emu', *le pneu* 'tyre', *les bleus* (which also means 'overalls'), *les émeus, les pneus*.

104   Seven nouns in *-ou* also form their plural in *-x*:

le bijou, jewel	*le hibou*, owl
le caillou, pebble	*le joujou*, toy
le chou, cabbage	*le pou*, louse
le genou, knee	

– plurals *les bijoux*, *les cailloux*, *les choux*, etc.

Other nouns in *-ou* add *-s*, e.g. *le clou* 'nail', *le voyou*, 'lout, yobbo', *les clous, les voyous*.

105 Most nouns ending in *-al* form their plural in *-aux*, e.g.:

le cheval, horse	*les chevaux*
le général, general	*les généraux*
le journal, newspaper	*les journaux*

Exceptions: *un aval* 'backing, guarantee', *le bal* 'dance', *le cal* 'callus', *le carnaval* 'carnival', *le chacal* 'jackal', *le choral* 'chorale', *le festival* 'festival', *le narval* 'narwhal', *le récital* 'recital', *le régal* 'treat', form their plural in *-s*, e.g. *les avals*, *les bals*, *les chacals*, *les récitals*, etc. *Le val* 'dale' has the plural *vals*, but note the expression *par monts et par vaux* 'over hill and dale'. *L'idéal* 'ideal' has both *idéals* (the more usual form) and *idéaux*.

106 About ten nouns ending in *-ail* form their plural in *-aux*. Of these, the only ones in even moderately frequent use are:

le bail, lease	*les baux*
le corail, coral	*les coraux*
l'émail, enamel	*les émaux*
le soupirail, basement window	*les soupiraux*
le travail, work	*les travaux*
le vantail, leaf of door	*les vantaux*
le vitrail, stained-glass window	*les vitraux*

107 Nouns in *-ail* forming their plural in *-ails* include:

le chandail, (thick) sweater	*les chandails*
le détail, detail	*les détails*
l'épouvantail, scarecrow	*les épouvantails*
l'éventail, fan	*les éventails*
le gouvernail, helm	*les gouvernails*
le portail, portal	*les portails*
le rail, rail	*les rails*

L'ail 'garlic' has both *les ails* and *les aulx*, the latter being somewhat archaic. *Le bétail* 'cattle, livestock' is a collective word and has no plural.

108 The following words have two plurals which differ in sense:

aïeul, grandfather *aïeuls*, grandfathers *aïeux*, ancestors

ciel, sky	*ciels*, skies in paintings, canopies of beds, climates	*cieux*, skies, heavens
œil, eye	*œils*, in compound nouns with *de*; e.g. *œils-de-bœuf*, round or oval windows, *œils-de-perdrix*, corns (on the feet)	*yeux*, eyes

Of these, the only ones in everyday use are *cieux* and *yeux*.

Compound nouns

109   As in the section on gender (57–63), only nouns formed of two or more words joined by hyphens are here counted as compound nouns.

Nouns that were originally compounds but are now fused, i.e. written as one word without hyphens, present little difficulty as far as their plural goes – they are treated like any other noun, e.g.:

une entrecôte, (rib) steak	*des entrecôtes*
le passeport, passport	*les passeports*
le pourboire, tip	*les pourboires*

Note, however, the following exceptions (for their pronunciation, see 97,iv):

(le) monsieur, gentleman, Mr	*(les) messieurs*
madame, mademoiselle, Mrs, Miss	*mesdames, mesdemoiselles*
le bonhomme, chap, bloke	*les bonshommes*
le gentilhomme, gentleman, squire, etc.	*les gentilshommes*

Locutions like *la pomme de terre* 'potato', in which the various elements are neither fused nor joined by hyphens, present even less difficulty: the first noun, and the first noun only, is made plural, *les pommes de terre*, cf.:

le coup d'œil, glance	*les coups d'œil*
l'hôtel de ville, town hall	*les hôtels de ville*
le ver à soie, silk-worm	*les vers à soie*
le verre à vin, wine-glass	*les verres à vin*

110 Compound nouns are constantly coming and going, in the sense that new ones are being created and others, that still figure in many grammars, have largely or entirely gone out of use. What is more, in many cases opinions differ as to the recommended plural. In these circumstances, the following indications do not aim to be exhaustive but only to cover most cases that the student is likely to come across. They must be supplemented by reference to a good dictionary.

The following classes are the same as those adopted with reference to gender (sections **58–63**).

111 (i) **Nouns composed of a noun and a preceding or following adjective**
Both elements become plural:

la basse-cour, farmyard	*les basses-cours*
la belle-mère, mother-in-law	*les belles-mères*
le grand-père, grandfather	*les grands-pères*
le haut-relief, high relief	*les hauts-reliefs*
le rouge-gorge, robin	*les rouges-gorges*
le cerf-volant, kite, stag-beetle	*les cerfs-volants*
le coffre-fort, safe	*les coffres-forts*

Note the following:

(a) Feminine nouns in *grand-* (which represents an early form of the feminine adjective – it is **not** a shortened form of *grande*): generally speaking, *grand* remains invariable – *la grand-mère* 'grandmother', *la grand-route* 'main road', plural *les grand-mères*, *les grand-routes* – but *grands-mères*, *grands-routes*, etc. are also acceptable.

(b) In *le haut-parleur* 'loudspeaker', *le nouveau-né* 'newly born child', *le sauf-conduit* 'safe conduct', the first element is not an adjective but an adverb (*haut* = 'aloud', *nouveau* = 'newly', *sauf* = 'safely') and so does not change: *les haut-parleurs*, *les nouveau-nés*, *les sauf-conduits*. (But, inconsistently, *le premier-né* 'firstborn', *le dernier-né* 'lastborn', *le nouveau-marié* 'newly-wed', and *le nouveau-venu* 'newcomer' have the plurals *les premiers-nés, les derniers-nés, les nouveaux-mariés, les nouveaux-venus.*)

112   (ii) Nouns composed of noun + noun
In most cases, both nouns become plural, e.g.:

le bateau-phare, light-ship	*les bateaux-phares*
le camion-citerne, tanker (lorry)	*les camions-citernes*
le chef-lieu, county town	*les chefs-lieux*
l'homme-grenouille, frogman	*les hommes-grenouilles*
l'oiseau-mouche, humming-bird	*les oiseaux-mouches*
le wagon-lit, sleeper	*les wagons-lits*

Exceptions include:

l'année-lumière, light-year	*les années-lumière*
le soutien-gorge, bra	*les soutiens-gorge*
le timbre-poste (for *timbre de poste*), postage-stamp	*les timbres-poste*

113   (iii) Nouns having the construction noun + preposition + noun
In most cases the first noun (only) becomes plural, e.g.:

l'arc-en-ciel, rainbow	*les arcs-en-ciel*
le chef-d'œuvre, masterpiece	*les chefs-d'œuvre*
le face-à-main, lorgnette	*les faces-à-main*
la langue-de-chat (type of biscuit)	*les langues-de-chat*

Some nouns, however, remain invariable, e.g.:

le pied-à-terre	*les pied-à-terre*
le pot-au-feu, stew	*les pot-au-feu*
le tête-à-tête	*les tête-à-tête*

114   (iv) Nouns having the construction adverb or prefix + noun
The second element, i.e. the noun, becomes plural, e.g.:

l'arrière-pensée, mental reservation	*les arrière-pensées*
l'avant-projet, pilot study	*les avant-projets*
la demi-heure, half-hour	*les demi-heures*

l'ex-roi, ex-king	*les ex-rois*
le haut-parleur, loudspeaker	*les haut-parleurs*
la mini-jupe, mini-skirt	*les mini-jupes*
le sous-titre, subtitle	*les sous-titres*
le vice-président	*les vice-présidents*

115   (v) Nouns having the construction preposition + noun

Here, there is considerable fluctuation. Some, including *le*, *la sans-cœur* 'heartless person', *le sous-main* 'desk blotter', are invariable, *les sans-cœur*, *les sous-main*. *L'à-côté* 'side issue', *l'en-tête* 'heading', usually have the plurals *les à-côtés*, *les en-têtes*, while *l'après-midi* 'afternoon' has either *les après-midi* or *les après-midis*.

116   (vi) Words having the construction verb + noun

To say that chaos reigns would be an unfair comment on the rules for the formation of the plural of nouns of this type. But that there are numerous uncertainties and inconsistencies is indisputable. We shall, however, try and give as much reliable guidance as possible, based on two general principles, and advise readers, in cases not covered here, to consult a good dictionary (while warning them that, if they consult *two* dictionaries, they may well find two different answers).

The first general principle is that the first element, being a verb, never varies. The apparent exception found in the case of a few compounds in *garde-*, all of them referring to people, is accounted for by the fact that *garde-*, though originally it *was* a verb, is here treated as a noun – e.g. *le garde-chasse* 'game-keeper', *les gardes-chasse* (*chasse* remains invariable – cf. c below), *le/la garde-malade* 'home-nurse', *les gardes-malade(s)* (*malade* may or may not take the plural *-s*, cf. a and b below).

The second principle, by no means always observed in practice as we shall see, is that the second element takes an *-s* when, and only when, it stands for a noun that can itself be plural in the particular sense in question. On this basis, the nouns in question fall into three groups:

(a) Those that have an *-s* even in the singular, e.g. *le compte-tours* 'rev counter', i.e. an instrument serving to count revolutions, *compter les tours* (in the plural), or *le brise-lames* 'breakwater', a construction serving to break the force of the waves, *briser les* *lames.* Such words are, of course, invariable in the plural – *les compte-tours*, *les brise-lames.* Other examples are:

le chauffe-plats, dish-warmer
le coupe-tomates, tomato-slicer
le gobe-mouches, flycatcher (bird)
le pare-balles, bullet-shield
le pare-chocs, bumper (of a car)
le porte-avions, aircraft carrier
le porte-cigarettes, cigarette-case
le porte-clefs, key-ring
le presse-papiers, paper-weight
le protège-dents, gum-shield

(b) Those that add a plural marker to the noun; the justification for this is presumably that, to take an obvious example, *un tire-bouchon* 'a corkscrew', can only be used for drawing one cork at a time, whereas several corkscrews can draw several corks, hence the plural *des tire-bouchons.* Cf.:

un accroche-cœur, kiss-curl	*des accroche-cœurs*
le bouche-trou, stop-gap, stand-in	*les bouche-trous*
le couvre-lit, bedspread	*les couvre-lits*
le cure-pipe, pipecleaner	*les cure-pipes*
un ouvre-boîte, tin-opener	*des ouvre-boîtes*
le pèse-lettre, letter-scales	*les pèse-lettres*
le perce-oreille, earwig	*les perce-oreilles*
le vide-pomme, apple-corer	*les vide-pommes*

At least one category b noun, *le cure-dent* 'tooth-pick', which can be defined as something one uses *pour se curer les dents* (in the plural), and one which hesitates between categories a and b, viz. *le porte-cartes* or *le porte-carte* 'card-holder, map-case', i.e. something for containing cards or maps (in the plural), might have been expected to fall clearly into category a. Others that hesitate, e.g. *le coupe-cigare* or *le coupe-cigares* 'cigar cutter', *le taille-crayon* or *le taille-crayons* 'pencil sharpener', are very similar to *ouvre-boîte*, *vide-pomme*, and so ought to fall clearly into category b.

The inconsistencies in fact relate mainly to those nouns that do, or ought to but do not, fall into this category. They are well illustrated by the absurdity of the fact that *le coupe-tomates* 'tomato-slicer' falls into category a, *le vide-pomme* 'apple-corer' into category b, and *le presse-citron* 'lemon-squeezer' into category c.

(c) Where the sense of the second element clearly remains singular (i.e. where we have to do with mass-nouns), the compound as a whole is invariable in the plural – e.g. several ice-breakers break ice (in the singular), so *le brise-glace*, *les brise-glace*, several waterheaters heat water (in the singular), so *le chauffe-eau*, *les chauffe-eau*. Cf.:

un abat-jour, lamp-shade	*des abat-jour*
un aide-mémoire, memorandum	*des aide-mémoire*
le coupe-feu, fire-break	*les coupe-feu*
le garde-boue, mudguard	*les garde-boue*
le garde-manger, larder, pantry	*les garde-manger*
le gratte-ciel, skyscraper	*les gratte-ciel*
le pare-brise, windscreen	*les pare-brise*
le porte-bonheur, lucky charm	*les porte-bonheur*
le porte-monnaie, purse	*les porte-monnaie*
le rabat-joie, killjoy, spoilsport	*les rabat-joie*

Unfortunately, and inexplicably, a few nouns whose second element is not a mass-noun, i.e. it *could* have taken the plural marker, follow the same pattern as category c instead of falling, as might have been expected, into b, e.g.: *le fume-cigarette* 'cigarette-holder', *les fume-cigarette*, *le porte-plume* 'pen-holder', *les porte-plume*, *le presse-citron* 'lemon-squeezer', *les presse-citron*. Others fluctuate between the two forms, e.g. *un attrape-nigaud* 'con(fidence) trick', *des attrape-nigaud* or *attrape-nigauds*, *le porte-couteau* 'knife-rest', *les porte-couteau* or *porte-couteaux*. Likewise *les essuie-main(s)* 'hand-towels', *les essuie-glace(s)* 'windscreen-wipers', *les grippe-sou(s)* 'skinflints', *les porte-drapeau(x)* 'standard-bearers', *les porte-savon(s)* 'soap-dishes'.

Miscellaneous

117   The letters of the alphabet, phrases used as nouns, numerals, and various other parts of speech such as adverbs or prepositions when used as nouns, do not vary in the plural, e.g.:

'Cannes' s'écrit avec deux n
'Cannes' is spelt with two *n*'s

mettre les points sur les i
to dot the *i*'s

Ce ne sont que des on-dit
It's only hearsay

des meurt-de-faim
paupers

des va-et-vient
comings and goings

les oui et les non
the ayes (yeses) and the noes

des laissez-passer
passes, permits

écrire deux quatre
to write two fours

les ci-devant
pre-Revolutionary aristocrats

118   (i) Generally speaking, words of foreign origin, even when they keep their original form, are treated as French words and form their plural in -*s*, e.g. (from Latin) *les albums, les ultimatums, les référendums, les sanatoriums, les tumulus*; (from English) *les best-sellers, les meetings, les snack-bars, les week-ends*; (from Italian) *les adagios, les concertos, les solos, les pizzas*; (from Spanish) *les matadors*.

(ii) Latin phrases used as nouns (cf. 117) and a few Latin words (many though not all of them to do with the Church) are invariable, e.g. *des ex-voto, des Te Deum, des confiteor* 'general confessions', *des credo* 'creeds', *des post-scriptum* 'postscripts'. *Le maximum* and *le minimum* have the Latin plurals *les maxima, minima*, in addition to the more usual *les maximums, minimums*.

(iii) English words in *-man* (including such false anglicisms as *le rugbyman* 'rugby player') normally form their plural in *-men*, e.g. *les gentlemen*, *les rugbymen*, but *le barman* has both *les barmen* and *les barmans*, and (obsolete) *le wattman* 'tram-driver' has only *les wattmans*.

English words in *-y* have either *-ies* or *-ys* (depending perhaps on how well the writer knows English), e.g. *les dandies* or *dandys*, *les ladies* or *ladys*, *les whiskies* or *whiskys*.

Le match, *le sandwich* have *les matches* or *matchs*, *les sandwichs* or *sandwiches*, but *le flash* has only *les flashes*.

(iv) Among words of Italian origin, *le dilettante* and *le*, *la soprano* have *les dilettanti*, *les soprani* beside the more usual *les dilettantes*, *les sopranos*.

119 Personal names
Considerable uncertainty remains as to when personal names take a plural. The following indications cover most cases that occur with any frequency:

(i) Names of dynasties and certain eminent families, etc., usually take a plural form, e.g. *les Ptolémées*, *les Césars*, *les Bourbons*, *les Tudors* (but note *les Romanov*, *les Habsbourg*).

(ii) Otherwise, a name referring to a number of people of the same name is usually invariable, e.g. *les deux Corneille* (i.e. Pierre and Thomas Corneille), *le 'Journal' des Goncourt* (i.e. of the Goncourt brothers), *les Dupont* (i.e. the members of the Dupont family), *les Borgia* (the Borgias).

(iii) Personal names taken as representing a *type* of person are usually plural, e.g. *Combien de Mozarts naissent chaque jour en des îles sauvages!* (J. Rostand) (i.e. potential Mozarts), *il n'y a pas beaucoup de Pasteurs* (i.e. people like Pasteur); but some writers leave such names invariable, e.g. *les Boileau de l'avenir* (A. Hermant), *il y a peut-être eu des Shakespeare dans la lune* (Duhamel).

(iv) Names referring to makes of car, aeroplane, etc., are usually invariable, e.g. *des Ford et des Chevrolet, plusieurs Boeing, deux Leica* (cameras).

(v) Usage varies considerably in respect of personal names denoting the works (e.g. editions of literary texts, paintings) of the individual concerned. These sometimes take a plural form and are sometimes invariable, *des Rembrandts* or *des Rembrandt*

'Rembrandts' (i.e. paintings by Rembrandt), *trois Picassos* or *Picasso*, *il possède plusieurs Racines* or *Racine* (i.e. editions of Racine).

The conclusion seems to be that, except in cases such as those included under (i) above, it is never wrong to leave a personal name invariable even if, in some circumstances, it is more usual to add an *-s* in the plural.

120   Though this is not strictly a grammatical point, it is worth pointing out that some words in the plural have a different meaning or an additional meaning to that which they have in the singular. In particular:

l'affaire, matter	*les affaires*, affairs, business
le ciseau, chisel	*les ciseaux*, chisels, scissors
le gage, pledge	*les gages*, pledges, wages
la lettre, letter	*les lettres*, letters, arts (subjects), literature
la lunette, telescope, etc.	*les lunettes*, telescopes, etc., spectacles
l'ouïe, (sense of) hearing	*les ouïes*, gills
la vacance, vacancy (i.e. time during which a post is vacant)	*les vacances*, vacation, holiday(s)

121   Finally, note that some words are singular in French but correspond to a plural in English, in particular various words denoting items consisting of two symmetrical parts such as *une lorgnette* 'opera-glasses', *un soufflet* '(a pair of) bellows', and a number of words for items of leg-wear that may or may not be preceded by 'a pair of' in English, e.g. *un caleçon* '(a pair of) (men's) (under) pants', *un collant* 'tights', *une culotte* '(women's) pants', *un maillot (de bain)* 'swimming trunks', *un pantalon* 'trousers', *un short* 'shorts', *un slip* 'panties'.

Note too a number of words in *-ique* (many of them referring to academic disciplines), such as *la gymnastique* 'gymnastics', *la linguistique* 'linguistics', *la phonétique* 'phonetics', *la physique* 'physics', *la politique* 'politics'.

The plural of adjectives

122   Adjectives form their plural in much the same ways as nouns. Note in particular:

(a) that, apart from the exceptions dealt with below (123–126), masculine adjectives form their plural in -*s*, e.g.:

le grand chien, the big dog   *les grands chiens*
un livre difficile, a difficult   *des livres difficiles*
   book

(b) that all feminine adjectives apart from a few that are invariable for gender or number (see **126**) form their plural by adding -*s* to the singular, e.g.:

la grande maison, the big   *les grandes maisons*
   house
une fleur blanche, a white   *des fleurs blanches*
   flower

123   Adjectives in -*eau*, like nouns in -*eau* (see **103**), form their plural in -*x*, viz. *beau* 'fine, beautiful', *nouveau* 'new', *tourangeau* (the adjective corresponding to *Tours* and *Touraine*), plural *beaux*, *nouveaux*, *tourangeaux*.

Hébreu 'Hebrew' has the plural *hébreux*, but *bleu* 'blue' has *bleus*.

124   Most adjectives in -*al*, like nouns in -*al* (see **105**), form their plural in -*aux*, e.g. *égal* 'equal', plural *égaux*, *social*, plural *sociaux*, *normal*, plural *normaux*, *spécial*, plural *spéciaux*. But *banal*, *bancal* 'rickety, wobbly' (of a piece of furniture), *fatal*, *final*, *natal* and *naval* take -*s*, e.g. *des incidents banals*, *des enfants bancals*, *des chantiers navals* 'naval dockyards', *fatals*, *finals*, *natals*. *Idéal* usually has *idéaux*, though *idéals* also occurs. Much uncertainty surrounds the plural of some adjectives in -*al*, e.g. *estival* '(to do with) summer', *frugal*, *glacial*, *pascal* '(to do with) Easter', and in consequence there is a tendancy to avoid using them in the masculine plural.

125   Masculine adjectives (like nouns, see **102**) ending in -*s* or -*x* (there are no adjectives ending in -*z*) do not change in the plural, e.g. *un gros livre* 'a big book', *trois gros livres* 'three big books', *il est heureux* 'he is happy', *ils sont heureux* 'they are happy'.

126 Adjectives that are invariable for gender (see 95) are also invariable for number, i.e. they have no special plural form:

(i) Words that were originally nouns but are now used as adjectives of colour: *des gants marron* 'brown gloves', *des rubans cerise* 'cherry-coloured ribbons', *des rideaux orange* 'orange curtains', *crème* 'cream', *olive* 'olive(-green)', *paille* 'straw-coloured', *puce*, etc. But note that the adjectives *écarlate* 'scarlet', *mauve*, *pourpre* 'crimson', *rose* 'pink', that were also originally nouns, are now treated as ordinary adjectives and so agree in number, e.g. *des rubans écarlates et mauves* 'scarlet and mauve ribbons', *des nuages roses* 'pink clouds'.

(ii) Miscellaneous, e.g. *des vêtements chic* 'smart clothes', *des uniformes kaki* 'khaki uniforms', *des églises rococo* 'rococo churches', *cinq livres sterling* 'five pounds sterling'.

Agreement of adjectives

127 (i) Adjectives are used either attributively (e.g. *une belle maison* 'a beautiful house', *des livres intéressants* 'interesting books') or predicatively (e.g. *Ce livre est intéressant* 'This book is interesting', *elle paraît heureuse* 'she seems (to be) happy', *je les croyais intelligents* 'I thought them (I thought they were) intelligent').

(ii) Whether used attributively or predicatively, adjectives take the gender and number of (i.e. they 'agree with') the noun or pronoun they qualify, e.g.:

masc. sing.	*un livre intéressant* 'an interesting book'
fem. sing.	*cette leçon intéressante* 'this interesting lesson'
masc. plur.	*ils sont intéressants* 'they are interesting'
fem. plur.	*je trouve ses idées intéressantes* 'I find his ideas interesting'

(iii) When an adjective qualifies two or more nouns or pronouns, each of which is in the singular, the adjective is put in the plural, e.g. *le gouvernement et le parlement italiens* 'the Italian government and parliament', *la marine et l'aviation françaises* 'the French navy and airforce'.

If the nouns or pronouns are of different genders, the adjective takes the masculine plural form, e.g. *Lui et sa femme sont très intelligents* 'He and his wife are very intelligent'. However, though it is not impossible to find constructions such as *un père et une mère excellents* 'a fine father and mother', in which a feminine noun is followed immediately by a masculine adjective, they are much better avoided except in contexts in which the masculine and feminine forms sound the same, e.g. *un dictionnaire et une grammaire espagnols* 'a Spanish dictionary and grammar'. The problem can usually be avoided by putting the feminine noun first, e.g. *une grammaire et un dictionnaire allemands* 'a German grammar and dictionary', *la politesse et le charme français* 'French politeness and charm'. (Some such constructions might well be theoretically ambiguous, e.g. the last example *could* mean 'politeness and French charm', but in practice it will usually be clear from the context that the adjective refers to both nouns.)

(iv) Two or more adjectives, each in the singular, can modify the same plural noun when each refers to one instance of the plurality expressed by the noun, e.g. *les dix-neuvième et vingtième siècles* 'the nineteenth and twentieth centuries', *les religions chrétienne, musulmane et juive* 'the Christian, Muslim and Jewish religions', *les gouvernements espagnol et italien* 'the Spanish and Italian governments'.

(v) Past participles used adjectivally agree in the same way as other adjectives, e.g. *une occasion perdue* 'a missed opportunity', *une école et une église détruites pendant la guerre* 'a school and a church destroyed during the war'.

128 Where the adjective refers to two nouns linked by *ou* 'or', the adjective is usually plural if the idea is 'either [of the nouns mentioned] – it does not much matter which', e.g. *Je cherche un livre ou un journal allemands* 'I'm looking for a German book or [a German] newspaper', *Il mange chaque jour une pomme ou une poire mûres* 'He eats a ripe apple or pear every day'.

129 Note that an adjective qualifying two nouns is singular when the nouns are joined by *ainsi que, aussi bien que, autant que, comme, de même que* ('as, as well as, as much as, in the same way as, like', etc.), *plus que* ('more than'), and the like; e.g. *Sa* *main, ainsi que (aussi bien que, pas moins que) son pied, a été échaudée* 'His hand, as well as his foot, was scalded'.

The reason is that the basic structure of the sentence is *sa main a été échaudée* (note that the verb is singular) and the sentence as a whole could be translated as 'his hand was scalded, and so was his foot'. This is therefore not in fact an exception to the general rule. (See also **393**.)

130 In certain contexts, the agreement of the adjective is illogical and inconsistent. In particular:

(i) Logically, we would expect an adjective used with the expression *avoir l'air* to agree with *air*, i.e. one would expect to find not only *Il a l'air heureux* 'He looks happy' (literally 'He has a happy air'), but also *Elle a l'air heureux*. In practice, however, *avoir l'air* is often treated as the equivalent of *sembler, paraître*, etc., and the adjective usually (though not always) agrees with the subject, e.g. *Elle a l'air heureuse* 'She looks happy', *Ils ont l'air tristes* 'They look sad', etc.

(ii) *On* 'one' (see **302**) is normally masculine singular (in conformity with its origin – it comes from the Latin *homo* 'man'). However, there is a growing tendency in familiar speech to use it as the equivalent of any personal pronoun, i.e. to mean 'I, we, you, he, she or they' (especially 'we'). In such cases, adjectives relating to it agree according to the sense, i.e. they may be feminine and/or plural (even though the verb is always singular), e.g. *On est malades?* 'Are you [plural] ill?', *On a été contentes de les voir* 'We [feminine] were glad to see them'.

(iii) For the agreement of adjectives with *gens* 'people' (e.g. *Certaines* [feminine] *gens ne sont jamais heureux* [masculine] 'Some people are never happy'), see **68**.

131 For the agreement or otherwise of *demi* 'half', see **188**.

132 Note that *nu-* 'bare' before a noun referring to a part of the body is treated as an invariable prefix, e.g.:

travailler nu-tête	to work bareheaded
marcher nu-pieds	to walk barefoot
nu-jambes	barelegged

In other circumstances it agrees in the normal way, *travailler (la) tête nue* 'to work bareheaded', *un enfant aux jambes nues* 'a barelegged child', *boxer à main nue* 'to box with bare hands', *ils étaient nus* 'they were naked'.

133 *Possible*, after a superlative and a plural noun, is invariable:

les plus grands malheurs possible
the greatest possible misfortunes

les robes les plus élégantes possible
the smartest dresses possible

J'ai fait le moins d'erreurs possible
I made the fewest possible mistakes (= as few mistakes as possible)

The reason is that *possible* is taken as agreeing with an unexpressed impersonal pronoun subject *il* (e.g. the first example above is the equivalent of something like *les plus grands malheurs qu'il est possible d'imaginer* 'the greatest misfortunes that it is possible to imagine').

Elsewhere, it agrees quite normally with its noun, e.g. *tous les malheurs possibles* 'all possible misfortunes'.

134 When placed before a noun, certain past participles and in particular *attendu*, *compris* (especially in the expression *y compris* 'including', *non compris* 'not including'), *excepté*, *passé*, and *vu* are treated as prepositions and so remain invariable; some of them can also follow the noun, in which case they agree with it in gender and number:

vu les conditions
considering the conditions

tous mes parents, y compris ma tante (or *ma tante (y) comprise*)
all my relations including my aunt

Personne n'est venu, excepté sa mère (or *sa mère exceptée*)
Nobody came except his mother

Passé dix heures, je ne travaille plus
After ten o'clock, I don't work any more

Passé ces maisons, on est en pleine campagne
Beyond these houses you are right out in the country

The expression *étant donné* 'given, in view of', is also usually invariable when it precedes, but may agree, e.g. *étant donné* or *étant données les difficultés* 'given the difficulties'.

The expressions *ci-joint*, *ci-inclus* 'enclosed (herewith)', agree when they follow the noun immediately (*la lettre ci-jointe* 'the enclosed letter'), but elsewhere may either agree or (more usually) remain invariable, e.g.:

> *Vous trouverez ci-joint* (or *ci-jointe*) *une copie de ma lettre du 10 juin*
> You will find enclosed a copy of my letter of 10 June
>
> *Je me permets de vous envoyer ci-joint(es) les lettres dont je vous ai parlé*
> I take the liberty of enclosing the letters I told you about
>
> *Ci-joint(s) les documents que vous avez demandés*
> Herewith the documents you asked for

135   Note the following special cases:

Plein 'full' is invariable when it precedes both the noun and its article in such expressions as *avoir de l'argent plein les poches* 'to have plenty of money' (literally 'to have one's pockets full of money'), *J'ai de l'encre plein les mains* 'I've got ink all over my hands', *en avoir plein la bouche de (quelque chose)* 'to be always on about (something)' (literally 'to have one's mouth full of it').

The little-used adjective *feu* 'late, deceased' (which virtually never occurs in the plural) agrees with a feminine noun when preceded by a determiner (which can only be either the definite article or a possessive); it may, however, come before the determiner, in which case it is invariable, e.g.:

la feue reine	the late queen
feu la reine	
ma feue mère	my late mother
feu ma mère	

Note that *feu* is now obsolescent and indeed, in everyday usage, obsolete – use some such expression as *ma pauvre mère* 'my late mother', *le regretté Charles Dupont* 'the late Charles Dupont'.

136   Compound adjectives

(i) The rule for compound adjectives formed from two simple adjectives, e.g. *aigre-doux* 'bitter-sweet', is that both parts agree, e.g.:

une jeune fille sourde-muette	a deaf and dumb girl
les partis sociaux-démocrates	the Social Democrat parties
des chansons aigres-douces	bitter-sweet songs

(ii) *Tout-puissant* 'almighty, all-powerful, omnipotent', agrees as follows:

masc.	fem.
sing. *tout-puissant*	*toute-puissante*
plur. *tout-puissants*	*toutes-puissantes*

(iii) *Soi-disant* 'so-called' does not agree, e.g. *ces soi-disant professeurs* 'these so-called teachers', *une soi-disant preuve* 'a so-called proof'. (The reason is that it is treated as though it were still a present participle, 'calling oneself' – cf. the non-agreement of the participle in *Voyant cela, elle est partie* 'seeing that, she left'.)

(iv) Note that in compounds such as *haut-placé* 'highly placed', *court-vêtu* 'short-skirted', *nouveau-né* 'newborn' (in all of which the second element is a past participle), the first element is an adverb, not an adjective, and so does not agree, e.g.:

une femme court-vêtue	a short-skirted woman
des gens haut-placés	highly placed people
des fillettes nouveau-nées	newborn baby girls

There are, however, some inconsistencies:

(a) *mort-né* 'stillborn (i.e. born dead)', whose first element is not an adverb, behaves like *nouveau-né*, e.g. *une idée mort-née* 'a stillborn idea', *des enfants mort-nés* 'stillborn children'

(b) On the agreement of *frais*, *grand* and *large* when they are used adverbially in contexts comparable to the above, see **610,i**.

137 Adjectives of colour that are themselves modified by another adjective (or a noun used as an adjective) do not agree in either gender or number, e.g. *une robe vert foncé* 'a dark-green dress', *une écharpe bleu vif* 'a bright-blue scarf', *la mer gris perle* 'the pearl-grey sea', *des chaussures vert pomme* 'apple-green shoes', *des yeux bleu clair* 'pale blue eyes', *des cheveux brun foncé* 'dark brown hair', *des uniformes bleu marine* 'navy-blue uniforms', *gris ardoise* 'slate grey', *jaune citron* 'lemon yellow', *rouge sang* 'blood-red', etc.

138   For adjectives that are invariable for gender and number (*une robe marron, des vêtements chic*, etc.), see **95** and **126**.

The position of adjectives

139   Adjectives in French tend to follow the noun (e.g. *un livre difficile* 'a difficult book'). However, some adjectives must and others may precede the noun (e.g. *un petit garçon* 'a little boy'), and there is indeed an increasing tendency on the part of journalists and others to put in front of the noun adjectives that would more usually be found after it (e.g. *une importante décision* for *une décision importante* 'an important decision') (see **148**). A safe principle to follow is that the adjective should be placed after the noun unless there is some reason for doing otherwise. The main rules and tendencies relating to contexts in which the adjective must or may come before the noun are set out in sections **140–151**.

140   The following adjectives usually precede the noun:

beau, beautiful, fine	*mauvais*, bad
bon, good	*meilleur*, better, best
bref, brief	*moindre*, less, least
grand, big, great	*petit*, little, small
gros, big	*sot*, foolish
haut, high	*vaste*, immense
jeune, young	*vieux*, old
joli, pretty	*vilain*, ugly, nasty

This remains true even when these adjectives are preceded by one or other of the short adverbs *assez* 'rather, quite', *aussi* 'as', *bien* 'very', *fort* 'very', *moins* 'less', *plus* 'more', *si* 'so', *très* 'very', e.g. *un assez bon rapport* 'quite a good report', *une plus jolie robe* 'a prettier dress', *un très grand plaisir* 'a very great pleasure'.

Note, however: (i) *d'un ton bref* 'curtly', *une voyelle brève* 'a short vowel'; (ii) *la marée haute* 'high tide', *à voix haute* (or *à haute voix*) 'aloud'; (iii) *un sourire mauvais* 'a nasty smile' (and also with various other nouns – consult a good dictionary).

If modified by a longer adverb or adverbial phrase these

adjectives normally follow the noun, e.g. *une femme exceptionnellement jolie* 'an exceptionally pretty woman', *un homme encore jeune* 'a man still young', *des différences tout à fait petites* 'quite slight differences'.

141   *Court* 'short' and *long* 'long' tend to precede the noun (e.g. *un court intervalle* 'a short interval', *une courte lettre* 'a short letter', *un long voyage* 'a long journey', *une longue liste* 'a long list') except when (as frequently happens) there is a contrast or an implied contrast, i.e. 'short as opposed to long' or vice versa, e.g. *une robe courte*, *une robe longue* 'a short/long dress', *des cheveux courts/longs* 'short/long hair', *une voyelle courte/longue* 'a short/long vowel'.

142   *Dernier* 'last' (see also **183**) and *prochain* 'next' meaning 'last or next as from now' follow words designating specific moments or periods of time such as *semaine* 'week', *mois* 'month', *an, année* 'year', *siècle* 'century', names of the days of the week or of the seasons, and (in the case of *dernier* only) *nuit* 'night', e.g. *la semaine dernière* 'last week', *le mois prochain* 'next month', *l'an dernier/prochain*, *l'année dernière/prochaine* 'last/next year', *le siècle dernier* 'last century', *lundi prochain* 'next Monday', *l'été dernier* 'last summer', *la nuit dernière* 'last night'. Otherwise they precede the noun, e.g. *la dernière/prochaine fois* 'last time, next time', *la dernière semaine des vacances* 'the last week of the holidays', *la prochaine réunion* 'the next meeting', *le dernier mardi de juin* 'the last Tuesday in June', *le prochain village* 'the next village'.

143   *Nouveau* 'new' follows the noun when it means 'newly created' or 'having just appeared for the first time', e.g. *du vin nouveau* 'new wine', *des pommes (de terre) nouvelles* 'new potatoes', *un mot nouveau* 'a new (i.e. newly coined) word', *une mode nouvelle* 'a new fashion'; otherwise – and most frequently – it precedes the noun, e.g. *le nouveau gouvernement* 'the new government', *j'ai acheté une nouvelle voiture* 'I've bought a new (i.e. different) car'.

144   *Faux* 'false' usually precedes the noun, e.g. *un faux problème* 'a false problem', *une fausse alerte* 'a false alarm', *une fausse fenêtre* 'a false window', *un faux prophète* 'a false prophet', *de faux papiers* 'false papers', but follows it in certain expressions such as *des diamants faux* 'false diamonds', *des perles fausses* 'false pearls', *un raisonnement faux* 'false reasoning', *des idées fausses* 'false ideas'.

145 *Seul* before the noun means 'single, sole, (one and) only', e.g. *c'est mon seul ami* 'he is my only friend', *la seule langue qu'il comprenne* 'the only language he understands'. After the noun it means 'alone, on one's own', e.g. *une femme seule* 'a woman on her own'. Note too the use of the adjective *seul* in contexts where English uses 'only' as an adverb, e.g. *Seuls les parents peuvent comprendre* 'Only parents can understand', *Seule compte la décision de l'arbitre* 'Only the referee's decision (the referee's decision alone) counts'.

146 Some other adjectives have one meaning when they precede the noun and a different one when they follow the noun. In some cases the two meanings are very clearly distinguishable. In other cases, the distinction is less sharp but there is a tendency for the adjective to have a literal meaning or to be used objectively when it follows the noun and to have a more figurative meaning or to be used more subjectively when it precedes the noun. It is not possible to give a full list of all such adjectives, nor is a grammar the place to attempt to cover the full range of meanings of each adjective that *is* listed – a dictionary should be consulted. The following list includes only the more common of the adjectives in question and some of their more usual meanings (others whose usage should be looked up in a dictionary include *chic, digne, fameux, franc, maudit, plaisant, sacré, véritable*):

	Meaning before the noun	Meaning after the noun
ancien	former, ex-	old, ancient
brave	nice, good, decent	brave
certain	certain, some	sure, certain
cher	dear, beloved	dear, expensive
différent	(plural) various	(sing. and plural) different
divers	(plural) various, several	(sing. and plural) differing
méchant	poor, second-rate, nasty	malicious
même (see **300**)	same	very, actual
pauvre	poor (pitiable, of poor quality)	poor, needy
propre	own	clean, suitable
sale	nasty	dirty
simple	mere	simple, single
triste	wretched, sad	sad, sorrowful
vrai	real, genuine	true

Examples:

un ancien cinéma	*la ville ancienne*
a former cinema	the old city
au bout d'un certain temps	*une preuve certaine*
after a certain time	definite proof
certains Français	*des indications certaines*
certain French people	sure indications
différentes personnes	*des avis différents*
various people	different opinions
un méchant petit livre	*des propos méchants*
a wretched little book	malicious remarks
les mêmes paroles	*ses paroles mêmes*
the same words	his very (actual) words
pauvre jeune homme!	*un jeune homme pauvre*
poor young man!	a penniless young man
ma propre maison	*une maison propre*
my own house	a clean house
	le mot propre
	the right word
un sale tour	*des mains sales*
a dirty trick	dirty hands
une simple formalité	*une explication simple*
a mere formality	a simple explanation
	un aller simple
	a single ticket

147 A preceding adjective refers only to the noun that immediately follows; where there is, in English, an implication that an adjective refers to more than one following noun, it must be repeated in French, e.g.:

un beau printemps et un bel été
a fine spring and summer

les mêmes mots et les mêmes expressions
the same words and expressions

(On following adjectives qualifying more than one noun, see **127**, iii.)

148   The following normally go after the noun:

(a) Adjectives denoting nationality or derived from proper names, or relating to political, philosophical, religious, artistic movements, etc., e.g.:

la langue française
the French language

une actrice américaine
an American actress

les provinces danubiennes
the Danubian provinces

la politique gaulliste
Gaullist policy (i.e. that of General de Gaulle)

un personnage cornélien
one of Corneille's characters

les théories marxistes
Marxist theories

la religion chrétienne
the Christian religion

la peinture surréaliste
surrealist painting

(b) Adjectives denoting colour, shape or physical qualities (other than those, many of which relate to size, listed in **140**), e.g.:

une robe blanche	a white dress
une fenêtre ronde	a round window
un toit plat	a flat roof
une rue étroite	a narrow street
un oreiller mou	a soft pillow
une voix aiguë	a shrill voice
de l'or pur	pure gold
un goût amer	a bitter taste

Some of these, however, may occur in front of the noun, particularly when they are used figuratively, e.g. *le noir désespoir* 'black despair', *une étroite obligation* 'a strict obligation', *une molle résistance* 'feeble resistance', *la pure vérité* 'the plain truth'. But they by no means invariably precede the noun even when used figuratively (e.g. *l'humour noir* 'sick humour', *une amitié étroite* 'a close friendship').

(c) Present and past participles used as adjectives, e.g.:

un livre amusant	an amusing book

| *du verre cassé* | broken glass |
| *la semaine passée* | last week |

Note, however, that *prétendu* 'so-called, alleged' and the invariable adjective *soi-disant* 'so-called' (see **136**, iii) precede the noun, e.g. *mon prétendu ami* 'my so-called friend', *la prétendue injustice* 'the alleged injustice', *la soi-disant actrice* 'the so-called actress'.

149 In general, polysyllabic adjectives tend to follow rather than precede the noun. However, there seems to be an increasing tendency for such adjectives to be placed before the noun when they express a value judgement or, even more so, a subjective or emotional reaction. Such adjectives include *adorable, affreux* 'dreadful', *délicieux* 'delightful', *effrayant* 'frightful', *effroyable* 'appalling', *énorme* 'enormous', *épouvantable* 'terrible', *excellent, extraordinaire* 'extraordinary', *important, inoubliable* 'unforgettable', *magnifique* 'magnificent', *superbe, terrible*, and many others, e.g. *un adorable petit village* 'a delightful little village', *une épouvantable catastrophe* 'a terrible catastrophe', *un magnifique coucher de soleil* 'a magnificent sunset'.

150 It is perfectly possible for a noun to take adjectives both before and after it, as in *une belle robe bleue* 'a beautiful blue dress', *un jeune homme habile* 'a capable young man'.

151 A noun may be preceded and/or followed by two or more adjectives; except in the type of construction dealt with in **152** below, two adjectives preceding or following the noun are linked by *et* 'and' (or by *ou* 'or' if two following adjectives are presented as alternatives), e.g.:

une belle et vieille cathédrale
a beautiful old cathedral

un étudiant intelligent et travailleur
an intelligent, hard-working student

des journaux anglais ou français
English or French newspapers

Where more than two adjectives are associated in a similar way with the same noun, the last two are linked by *et* or *ou*, e.g. *des étudiants intelligents, travailleurs et agréables* 'intelligent, hard-working, pleasant students'.

152 In the examples given in 151, each adjective modifies the noun so to speak independently and equally. Sometimes, however, one adjective modifies not just the noun but the group adjective + noun or noun + adjective, in which case there is no linking *et*, e.g. in *un gentil petit garçon* 'a nice little boy' the adjective *gentil* modifies the whole phrase *petit garçon*, and in *la poésie française contemporaine* 'contemporary French poetry' (in which the reference is not to poetry which happens to be both French and contemporary but to French poetry of the present time) *contemporaine* modifies the whole of the phrase *la poésie française*.

153 (i) When an adverb precedes the verb and governs a predicative adjective, English places the adjective immediately after the adverb it is linked to by grammar and sense, while French keeps the adjective in the usual position for predicative adjectives, viz. after the verb. This affects adjectives used with:

(a) the adverbs of comparison *plus* 'more' and *moins* 'less', e.g.:

> *Plus le problème devenait complexe, moins il paraissait inquiet*
> The more complex the problem got, the less worried he seemed

(b) with adverbs meaning 'how', viz. *combien*, *comme* and *que*, e.g.:

> *Je comprends combien vous devez être inquiet*
> I understand how worried you must be

> *Comme il est facile de se tromper!*
> How easy it is to be wrong!

> *Qu'il est bête!*
> How stupid he is!

(ii) French uses a parallel construction with *tant*, *tellement* 'so' where English tends to put the group 'so' + adjective after the verb, e.g.:

> *On aurait cru l'été, tant le soleil était beau* (Loti)
> You would have thought it was summer, the sun was so beautiful

(This could also be translated 'so beautiful was the sun' or, more idiomatically, 'The sun was so beautiful that you would have thought it was summer'.)

Il n'y arrivera jamais, tellement il est nerveux
He'll never manage to do it, he's so nervous (He's so nervous he'll never manage)

154   In English, adjectives precede the adverb 'enough' but in French they follow the adverbs *assez* 'enough', *suffisamment* 'enough, sufficiently', e.g.:

Elle n'est pas assez intelligente pour comprendre
She isn't intelligent enough to understand

Il est suffisamment grand pour voyager seul
He's old enough to travel on his own

The comparison of adjectives and adverbs

155   As adjectives and adverbs have the same degrees of comparison and as the constructions involved are the same in each case we shall discuss them together.

156   There are four degrees of comparison, but one, the comparative of equality or inequality, sometimes known as the equative, has no special forms in either English or French (see **157**). They are:

(i)   the absolute – e.g. (in English) *good, hard, difficult, easily*
(ii)   the equative – e.g. *(not) as good as, (not) as easily as*
(iii)   the comparative, which can be subdivided into:
        (a) the comparative of superiority, e.g. *better, harder, more difficult, more easily*
        (b) the comparative of inferiority, e.g. *less good, less easily*
(iv)   the superlative – e.g. *the best, the hardest, the most difficult, (the) most easily*.

The comparative of equality or inequality (the equative)

157   In affirmative sentences the comparative of equality (English 'as . . . as . . .') is expressed by *aussi . . . que . . .*, e.g.:

Il est aussi grand que vous
He is as big as you (are)

Elle est aussi intelligente que belle
She is as intelligent as she is beautiful

Il comprend aussi facilement que vous
He understands as easily as you (do)

Ils sont aussi charmants que vous le dites
They are as charming as you say

In negative sentences, *aussi* is usually replaced by *si*, e.g.:

Il n'est pas si grand que vous
He is not as big as you (are)

Ils ne sont pas si charmants que vous le dites
They are not as charming as you say

though *aussi* is possible (*Il n'est pas aussi grand que vous*).
   On constructions of the type *Il est aussi grand que vous* 'He is as big as you (are)', *Vous travaillez aussi énergiquement que nous* 'You work as energetically as we (do)', i.e. where English has the option of using after a comparative a verb that repeats or stands for that of the previous clause, see **173**.

158   As in English, the second half of the comparison may be omitted, e.g.:

Je n'ai jamais vu un si (or *aussi*) *beau spectacle*
I never saw so fine a sight

The comparative and superlative of superiority or inferiority

159   The comparative of superiority or of inferiority is formed (apart from the cases noted in **161**) by means of the adverbs *plus* 'more' or *moins* 'less', e.g.:

absolute	comparative of superiority	comparative of inferiority
intelligent intelligent	*plus intelligent* more intelligent	*moins intelligent* less intelligent
facilement easily	*plus facilement* more easily	*moins facilement* less easily
souvent often	*plus souvent* more often	*moins souvent* less often

The adjective agrees in the normal way, e.g. *Elle est plus grande que moi* 'She is taller than me', *dans des circonstances moins heureuses* 'in less happy circumstances'.

160   (i) The superlative of adjectives of superiority or of inferiority is formed (apart from the cases noted in 161) by placing the definite article, in the appropriate gender and number, before the comparative, e.g.:

absolute	superlative of superiority	superlative of inferiority
intelligent intelligent	*le plus intelligent* the most intelligent	*le moins intelligent* the least intelligent

Adjectives that normally precede the noun (see 140) also do so in the superlative, e.g.:

le plus jeune garçon	the youngest boy
la moins belle vue	the least beautiful view
les plus grandes difficultés	the greatest difficulties

With adjectives that follow the noun, the superlative is constructed as follows:

l'homme le plus intelligent	the most intelligent man
la femme la plus intelligente	the most intelligent woman
les hommes les moins intelligents	the least intelligent men
les femmes les moins intelligentes	the least intelligent women

Note that, with either a preceding or a following adjective, a possessive determiner (see 223) may be substituted for the definite article according to the following models:

(a) with a preceding adjective:

mon plus grand plaisir	my greatest pleasure
sa moins belle sœur	his least beautiful sister
nos plus vieux amis	our oldest friends

(b) with a following adjective:

son livre le plus célèbre	his most famous book
ma cousine la moins intelligente	my least intelligent cousin
nos montagnes les plus élevées	our highest mountains

(ii) The superlative of adverbs is formed by placing *le* before the comparative, e.g.:

le plus agréablement	the most pleasantly
le moins souvent	the least often

Note that, since adverbs cannot agree (like adjectives) with nouns or pronouns, these forms are invariable, i.e. the article is always *le*, e.g.:

C'est elle qui travaille le plus intelligemment
She is the one who works the most intelligently

(For the superlative adverb modifying an adjective, see **170**.)

161 The comparative and superlative of the adjectives *bon* 'good', *mauvais* 'bad', *petit* 'small' and of the corresponding adverbs have the following irregular forms (but see also **163** and **164**):

absolute	comparative	superlative
bon, good	*meilleur*, better	*le meilleur*, best
mauvais, bad	*pire*, worse	*le pire*, worst
petit, small	*moindre*, less(er)	*le moindre*, least
bien, well	*mieux*, better	*le mieux*, best
mal, badly	*pis*, worse	*le pis*, worst
peu, little	*moins*, less	*le moins*, least

The adjectives agree in gender and number with their noun as follows:

masc. sing.	fem. sing.	masc. plur.	fem. plur.
(le) meilleur	*(la) meilleure*	*(les) meilleurs*	*(les) meilleures*
(le) pire	*(la) pire*	*(les) pires*	
(le) moindre	*(la) moindre*	*(les) moindres*	

The adverbs are of course invariable.

Note that some, but not all, of these forms are subject to certain restrictions and that, for some of them, 'regular' comparatives and superlatives such as *(le) plus mauvais* occur – see **163–164**.

162   The comparative and superlative of *bon* and *bien* are always *(le meilleur)* and *(le) mieux* respectively, e.g.:

Ce pain est meilleur que l'autre
This bread is better than the other

Leurs meilleurs amis
Their best friends

Il chante mieux que vous
He sings better than you (do)

C'est le matin que je travaille le mieux
It's in the morning that I work (the) best

The rule applies even to expressions such as *bon marché* 'cheap' (*meilleur marché* 'cheaper', *le meilleur marché* 'cheapest') and *de bonne heure* 'early' (*de meilleure heure* 'earlier' – though a more usual rendering for 'earlier' is *plus tôt*).

163   The comparative and superlative of *mauvais* are either *(le) pire* or *(le) plus mauvais*. The two are often interchangeable, but in so far as there is any distinction it is (a) that *(le) pire* occurs more widely in literary than in spoken usage, and (b) that *(le) pire* in any case tends to be restricted to contexts in which it refers to abstract nouns, e.g.:

Votre attitude est pire que la sienne
Your attitude is worse than his

le pire danger
the worst danger

but:

Ce vin est plus mauvais que l'autre
This wine is worse than the other

le plus mauvais restaurant de la ville
the worst restaurant in town

(Note however that French often says *moins bon* 'less good' where English says 'worse', e.g. *Cette route est moins bonne que l'autre* 'This road is worse than (*or* not as good as) the other'.)

The adverb *(le) pis* 'worse, worst' is even less used than *pire* and, for practical purposes, it can be assumed that the normal comparative and superlative of *mal* 'badly' are *plus mal* and *le plus mal. Pis* can never be used as an alternative to *plus mal* in, for example, a context such as *Il chante plus mal que vous* 'He sings worse than you'. Apart from the one expression *tant pis (pour vous, pour lui,* etc.) 'so much the worse (for you, for him, etc.)', it is rarely heard in conversational usage and even in literary usage it is confined to a few expressions like *aller de mal en pis* 'to go from bad to worse', *qui pis est* 'what is worse', *rien de pis* 'nothing worse', *le pis* 'the worst thing', *mettre les choses au pis* 'to put things at their worst, to assume the worst', and even in some of these it can be replaced by *pire*, e.g. *ce qui est pire* 'what is worse', *rien de pire, le pire, mettre les choses au pire.* (Note too the use of *moins bien* 'less well' as a frequent alternative to *plus mal.*)

164   As the comparative and superlative of *petit*, the form *(le) plus petit* must always be used when reference is to physical size, e.g.:

Il est plus petit que je ne croyais
He is smaller than I thought

le plus petit verre
the smallest glass

The form *moindre* occasionally occurs as the equivalent of 'less', e.g. *des choses de moindre importance* 'things of less importance', but is more common as a superlative, particularly as the equivalent of English 'least, slightest', e.g.:

son moindre défaut	his slightest failing
les moindres détails	the smallest details
sans la moindre difficulté	without the slightest difficulty
Je n'ai pas la moindre idée	I haven't the slightest idea
la loi du moindre effort	the law of least effort

On the other hand, the comparative and superlative of the adverb *peu* are invariably *moins* and *le moins* 'less, (the) least', e.g.:

moins difficile
less difficult

J'ai moins de temps que vous
I have less time than you

C'est lui que j'aime le moins
He is the one I like (the) least

Note that where English uses 'the least' with a noun, meaning 'the least amount of', French uses *le moins de* (with the optional addition, as in English, of the adjective *possible*), e.g.:

C'est comme ça qu'on le fait avec le moins de difficulté
That's the way to do it with the least difficulty

Do not confuse this with constructions involving a negative or *sans* 'without', e.g.:

De cette façon vous n'aurez pas la moindre difficulté	In this way you will not have the slightest difficulty
De cette façon vous le ferez sans la moindre difficulté	In this way you will do it without the slightest difficulty

in which the meaning is not 'the least amount of difficulty' but 'the smallest difficulty'.

165 The adverb *beaucoup* 'much, many, a lot' has as its comparative and superlative *plus* and *le plus*, e.g.:

J'ai plus de temps que vous
I have more time than you (have)

C'est le soir que je travaille le plus
It's in the evening that I work most

166 'Than' (except when followed by a numeral, see **167**) is translated by *que*. In an affirmative sentence *ne* is often put before the following verb (see **563**), e.g.:

Il est plus fort que son frère
He is stronger than his brother

Il travaille mieux que je (ne) croyais
He works better than I thought

167   Except in the type of sentence referred to in **168** below, 'than' followed by a numeral (including fractions) is translated by *de* instead of *que*, e.g.:

> *J'en ai plus de trente*
> I have more than thirty of them

> *Cela coûte plus de dix mille francs*
> That costs more than ten thousand francs

> *Il en a mangé plus de la moitié*
> He has eaten more than half of it

> *Il a vécu moins de dix ans*
> He lived less than ten years

168   In the type of sentence discussed in **167**, 'more than' means 'in excess of' and 'less than' means 'a quantity less than'. There is, however, a totally different construction in which 'than' is followed by a numeral and in which it is translated not by *de* but, as in most other contexts, by *que*, e.g.:

> *Un seul œuf d'autruche pèse plus que vingt œufs de poule*
> A single ostrich egg weighs more than twenty hen's eggs

The reason is that this does not, of course, mean 'more than twenty' in the sense of 'at least twenty-one'. What is being compared is the weight of an ostrich egg, and the weight of hen's eggs; *vingt œufs de poule* is in fact the subject of a clause whose verb is understood but which could have been expressed, in either French or English:

> *Un seul œuf d'autruche pèse plus que vingt œufs de poule ne pèsent*
> A single ostrich egg weighs more than twenty hen's eggs weigh

The sentence in question is therefore an exact parallel with a sentence such as the following which does not involve a numeral:

> *Cet œuf pèse plus que celui-là*
> This egg weighs more than that one

169   When a comparative or superlative relates to two or more adjectives or adverbs, *(le) plus* or *(le) moins* is repeated with each, even if the corresponding adverb is not repeated in English, e.g.:

Il est plus intelligent et plus travailleur que son frère
He is more intelligent and hard-working than his brother

Elle parle moins couramment et moins correctement que vous
She speaks less fluently and correctly than you

le problème le plus compliqué et le plus difficile
the most complicated and difficult problem

170   (i) When *le plus* 'the most', *le moins* 'the least', *le mieux* 'the best' followed by an adjective or a participle have the value of 'to the highest (lowest, best) extent', i.e. when the comparison is not between different persons or things but between different conditions relating to the same person(s) or thing(s), the article is invariable (i.e. always *le*), e.g.:

C'est en été qu'elle est le plus heureuse
She is happiest in summer (It is in summer that she is happiest)

(i.e. in summer 'she' is happier than the same 'she' in other conditions)

C'est quand ils sont fatigués qu'ils sont le moins tolérants
It's when they are tired that they are (at their) least tolerant

C'est ici qu'elles seront le mieux placées pour voir
This is where they'll be best placed (i.e. in the best position) to see

(ii) When other adverbs in the superlative (i.e. adverbs themselves qualified by *le plus* or *le moins*) qualify an adjective or participle, either construction is sometimes possible, with a slight (almost negligible) difference in meaning, e.g. *les soldats les plus gravement blessés* 'the most seriously wounded soldiers' interpreted as a parallel construction to *les soldats les plus malades* (i.e. the construction is *les plus + gravement blessés*), or *les soldats le plus gravement blessés*, interpreted as 'the soldiers who are wounded to the most serious extent' (i.e. *le plus gravement + blessés*). However, it seems that in practice, and regardless of logic, the former construction, with a definite article agreeing with the noun, is the usual one.

171   Note the following uses of *de* in comparative or superlative constructions:

(i) to express the 'measure of difference' (i.e. the extent to which the items compared differ), e.g.:

Il est plus grand que vous de trois centimètres
He is three centimetres taller than you

Ce dictionnaire est de beaucoup le plus cher
This dictionary is by far the most expensive

(this is not restricted to comparative and superlative constructions – cf. *dépasser quelqu'un d'une tête* 'to be a head taller than someone', *gagner de trois longeurs* 'to win by three lengths')

(ii) as the equivalent of English 'in' in such contexts as:

l'élève le plus paresseux de la classe
the laziest boy in the class

le meilleur restaurant de Paris
the best restaurant in Paris

172   *Le plus* and *le moins* are always superlatives in French, never comparatives. Consequently, *plus* and *moins* alone, with no article, are used in such contexts as the following where English uses the definite article 'the' with a comparative:

Plus il gagne, moins il est content
The more he earns, the less contented he is

Plus tôt vous arriverez, plus tôt vous pourrez partir
The earlier you arrive the earlier you'll be able to get away

In literary usage, the second term of the comparison is sometimes introduced by *et*, e.g.:

Plus je vieillis, et moins je pleure (Sully Prudhomme)
The older I grow, the less I weep

173   After a comparative of equality (see the end of section **157**), superiority or inferiority, French normally does not use a second verb that merely repeats or stands for (like 'did' in the third example below) the verb of the previous clause, e.g.:

Il est aussi grand que moi
He is as tall as I (am)

J'ai plus de temps que vous
I have more time than you (have)

Il a chanté mieux que son frère
He sang better than his brother (did)

Absolute superlative

174   (i) There is an important distinction to be made between
the type of superlative adjective discussed in **160** (i.e. the type
l'enfant le plus intelligent 'the most intelligent child') and a not
dissimilar construction in which English uses not the definite
article 'the' but the indefinite article (e.g. 'a most intelligent
child') or, in the plural, no article (e.g. 'those are most dangeous
ideas'). The former, which characterizes a noun in relation to
others of the same kind, is known as the 'relative superlative'.
The latter, which expresses the idea that the person or thing
denoted by the noun is characterized by a high degree of the
quality denoted by the adjective, is known as the 'absolute
superlative'.
   The absolute superlative in French is constructed as follows:

un enfant des plus exaspérants
a most exasperating child

une situation des plus difficiles
a most difficult situation

Ces idées-là sont des plus dangereuses
Those ideas are most dangerous

The use of a plural adjective even when the noun is in the singular
will be understood if it is appreciated that *un enfant des plus
exaspérants*, for example, means something like 'a child from
among the most exasperating ones of his kind'.
   Alternatively (and very frequently), an intensifying adverb may
be used, e.g. *un enfant tout à fait exaspérant, Ces idées-là sont
extrêmement dangereuses*.
   Ambiguity may arise in English from the fact that 'most' can
express either a relative or an absolute superlative. For example,
the sentence 'The situation is most difficult in Paris' may mean
either

(a) 'It is in Paris that the situation is (the) most difficult', i.e. we have a relative superlative, *C'est à Paris que la situation est le plus difficile* (see 170), or

(b) 'The situation in Paris is extremely difficult', i.e. we have an absolute superlative, *La situation à Paris est des plus difficiles.*

In such contexts, care must be taken to select the appropriate French equivalent.

(ii) Unlike English 'most', *plus* is not used in French to express the absolute superlative with adverbs; various other equivalents exist, however, e.g.:

> *Il conduit avec beaucoup de prudence*
> He drives most carefully

> *Elle s'exprime d'une manière extrêmement intelligente*
> She expresses herself most intelligently

Adjectives used as nouns

175 (i) Many adjectives of colour and some others are used as nouns with a variety of meanings for which a dictionary must be consulted, e.g.:

le beau	the beautiful, that which is beautiful
le blanc	the white (of an egg, of the eye)
un bleu	a bruise
le noir	darkness

176 (ii) Some adjectival nouns originate in expressions of the type noun + adjective; as a result of ellipsis of the noun, the adjective has taken on the function of a noun carrying the meaning of the whole expression, e.g.:

du bleu	for *du fromage bleu*, 'blue cheese'
un (petit) noir	for *un café noir*, 'a black coffee'
du rouge	for *du vin rouge*, 'red wine'
un complet	for *un costume complet*, 'a suit'
la capitale	for *la ville capitale*, 'capital (city)'
la majuscule	for *la lettre majuscule*, 'capital (letter)'

177 (iii) Adjectives can be used as nouns with reference to humans more freely in French than in English. Note in particular that, whereas in English a nominalized adjective with reference to humans is normally plural (e.g. 'the poor' = 'poor people', 'the blind' = 'blind people'), the fact that French has distinct masculine singular, feminine singular, and plural articles and other determiners (see **23**) means that one can have, e.g., *un pauvre* 'a poor man', *une pauvre* 'a poor woman', *des pauvres* 'poor people', *le muet* 'the dumb man', *la muette* 'the dumb woman', *cet aveugle* 'this blind man', *cette aveugle* 'this blind woman', *les aveugles* 'blind people', and, in cases where there are distinct forms for the masculine and feminine adjectives, a distinction in the plural between, for example, *les sourds* 'the deaf men' or 'the deaf (in general)' and *les sourdes* 'the deaf women'.

Numerals

178 Cardinal numbers express numerical quantity, i.e. 'one, two, three, etc.', while ordinal numbers express numerical sequence, i.e. 'first, second, third, etc.'.

The French cardinals and ordinals are:

	Cardinal		Ordinal
0	*zéro*		
1	*un* (m.), *une* (f.)	1st	*premier* (m.), *première* (f.)
2	*deux*	2nd	*deuxième, second* (m.), *seconde* (f.)
3	*trois*	3rd	*troisième*
4	*quatre*	4th	*quatrième*
5	*cinq*	5th	*cinquième*
6	*six*	6th	*sixième*
7	*sept*	7th	*septième*
8	*huit*	8th	*huitième*
9	*neuf*	9th	*neuvième*
10	*dix*	10th	*dixième*
11	*onze*	11th	*onzième*
12	*douze*	12th	*douzième*
13	*treize*	13th	*treizième*
14	*quatorze*	14th	*quatorzième*
15	*quinze*	15th	*quinzième*
16	*seize*	16th	*seizième*

17	*dix-sept*	17th	*dix-septième*
18	*dix-huit*	18th	*dix-huitième*
19	*dix-neuf*	19th	*dix-neuvième*
20	*vingt*	20th	*vingtième*
21	*vingt et un* (or *une*)	21st	*vingt et unième* (not *premier*)
22 etc.	*vingt-deux*, etc.	22nd etc.	*vingt-deuxième*, etc.
30	*trente*	30th	*trentième*
31	*trente et un* (or *une*)	31st	*trente et unième* (not *premier*)
32 etc.	*trente-deux*, etc.	32nd etc.	*trente-deuxième*, etc.
40	*quarante*	40th	*quarantième*
41	*quarante et un* (or *une*)	41st	*quarante et unième* (not *premier*)
42 etc.	*quarante-deux*, etc.	42nd etc.	*quarante-deuxième*, etc.
50	*cinquante*	50th	*cinquantième*
51	*cinquante et un* (or *une*)	51st	*cinquante et unième* (not *premier*)
52 etc.	*cinquante-deux*, etc.	52nd etc.	*cinquante-deuxième*, etc.
60	*soixante*	60th	*soixantième*
61	*soixante et un* (or *une*)	61st	*soixante et unième* (not *premier*)
62 etc.	*soixante-deux*, etc.	62nd etc.	*soixante-deuxième*, etc.
70	*soixante-dix*	70th	*soixante-dixième*
71	*soixante et onze*	71st	*soixante et onzième*
72 etc.	*soixante-douze*, etc.	72nd etc.	*soixante-douzième*, etc.
80	*quatre-vingts*	80th	*quatre-vingtième*
81	*quatre-vingt-un* (or *une*)	81st	*quatre-vingt-unième* (not *premier*)
82 etc.	*quatre-vingt-deux*, etc.	82nd etc.	*quatre-vingt-deuxième*, etc.
90	*quatre-vingt-dix*	90th	*quatre-vingt-dixième*
91	*quatre-vingt-onze*	91st	*quatre-vingt-onzième*
92 etc.	*quatre-vingt-douze*, etc.	92nd etc.	*quatre-vingt-douzième*, etc.
100	*cent*	100th	*centième*
101	*cent un* (or *une*)	101st	*cent unième* (not *premier*)
102 etc.	*cent deux*, etc.	102nd etc.	*cent deuxième*, etc.
200 etc.	*deux cents*, etc.	200th etc.	*deux centième*, etc.
257	*deux cent cinquante-sept*	257th	*deux cent cinquante-septième*

1000	*mille*	1000th	*millième*
1001	*mille un* (or *une*)	1001st	*mille unième* (not *premier*)
1500	*mille cinq cents* or *quinze cents*	1500th	*mille cinq centième* or *quinze centième*
10 000	*dix mille*, etc.	10,000th	*dix millième*, etc.
etc.		etc.	

179 Notes on pronunciation (for phonetic symbols, see 2):

(a) *Cinq* is pronounced [sɛ̃ːk] when final (e.g. *j'en ai cinq* 'I have five of them') and [sɛ̃k] in liaison (e.g. *cinq enfants* 'five children') but [sɛ̃] before a consonant (see note c) (e.g. *cinq jours* 'five days', though there is an increasing tendency in conversational speech to pronounce [sɛ̃k] even there).

(b) *Six* and *dix* are pronounced [sis] and [dis] when final (e.g. *j'en ai six* 'I have six of them'), [siz] and [diz] in liaison (e.g. *dix ans* 'ten years'), and [si] and [di] before a consonant (see note c), (e.g. *six francs* 'six francs', *dix jours* 'ten days').

(c) 'Before a consonant' in notes a and b relates only to contexts in which the numeral directly governs a following noun (as in *cinq jours*) or adjective (as in *dix beaux livres* 'ten beautiful books'); in contexts such as *dix pour cent* 'ten per cent' this does not apply and the numerals are pronounced [sɛ̃k, sis, dis].

(d) *Neuf* is pronounced [nœf] except in the two phrases *neuf ans* [nœvɑ̃] 'nine years' and *neuf heures* [nœvœːr] 'nine o'clock', so *neuf jours* [nœf ʒuːr] 'nine days', *neuf arbres* [nœf arbr] 'nine trees', etc.

(e) *Vingt* on its own is pronounced [vɛ̃] but it is pronounced [vɛ̃t] not only in liaison (i.e. *vingt et un* [vɛ̃t e œ̃]) but also before a consonant in the numbers '22' to '29' (e.g. *vingt-quatre* [vɛ̃tkatr]); but note that the *-t* of *quatre-vingt(s)* is never pronounced, not even in *quatre-vingt-un*.

(f) In Belgium and Switzerland, '70' and '90' are *septante* (pronounced [sɛptɑ̃t] – contrast *sept* [sɛt] and *septième* [sɛtjɛm]) and *nonante* respectively, and hence *septante et un* '71', *nonante-trois* '93', etc. However, '80' is usually *quatre-vingts* though *huit-ante* does exist in some parts of Switzerland (but not in Belgium).

180 Remarks:

(a) Hyphens are used in compound numbers except before or after *et*, *cent* (or *centième*), *mille* (or *millième*), e.g.:

vingt-deux, twenty-two   *vingt et un*, twenty-one

(b) *Et* is used in *vingt et un* '21' and likewise in '31', '41', '51' and '61' and also in *soixante et onze* '71' (and in '121', '231', '371', etc.), but not in other numerals ending in '1', *quatre-vingt-un* '81', *quatre-vingt-onze* '91', *cent un* '101', *deux cent un* '201', etc.

(c) *Quatre-vingts* '80' loses its *-s* before another numeral, e.g. *quatre-vingt-trois* '83'.

(d) *Cent* '100' takes a plural *-s* in round hundreds, e.g. *deux cents* '200', but not before another numeral, e.g. *deux cent trois* '203', while *mille* '1000' never takes an *-s*, e.g. *deux mille* 'two thousand'.

(e) *Un* is not used with *cent* '100' or *mille* '1000', e.g. *Il vécut cent ans* 'He lived for a hundred years', *Il possède mille hectares de vignes* 'He owns a thousand hectares of vines'.

(f) The normal form for '1100' is *onze cents* 'eleven hundred' (*mille cent* is virtually unused); from '1200' to '1900' (and particularly from '1200' to '1600'), the forms *douze cents* 'twelve hundred', etc., are preferred to *mille deux cents*, etc. The same is true of dates of the Christian era, but note in addition that in this case, if the form in 'one thousand' is used, then the spelling is *mil*, e.g. *en l'an mil huit cent* (no *-s* – see **182**) 'in the year 1800' (but 'the year one thousand' is *l'an mille*).

(g) When 'a thousand and one' means a large indefinite number ('umpteen'), it is *mille et un(e)*, e.g. *J'ai mille et une choses à faire* 'I have a thousand and one things to do'; note, too, as an exception, *Les Mille et une nuits* 'The Thousand and One Nights (i.e. The Arabian Nights)'.

(h) For the translation of 'than' before a numeral, see **167**.

(i) Apart from a few fixed expressions, such as (*apprendre quelque chose) de seconde main* '(to learn something) at second hand', *en second lieu* 'secondly', *second* and *deuxième* are interchangeable; the 'rule' that *second* is preferred with reference to the second of two (only) and *deuxième* when there are more than two can safely be ignored. Note that *second* is pronounced [səgɔ̃].

181 Note that *de* is used after *un millier* '(about) a thousand', *un million* 'a million' and multiples thereof and *un milliard* 'a thousand million' (or a 'billion' in American and now increasingly in British usage – the older sense of 'a billion' in British usage is 'a million million', which is also now the official definition of *un billion* in French though it used to be the equivalent of *un milliard*), e.g.:

des milliers de francs
thousands of francs

cinquante millions de Français
fifty million Frenchmen

deux milliards de francs
two thousand million francs

182 Cardinal numbers (not ordinals as in English) are used:

(a) in dates, e.g.:

le trois janvier	the third of January
le vingt et un juin	the twenty-first of June

(b) with names of monarchs, popes, etc., e.g.:

Louis XV (= 'quinze')	Louis XV (= 'the Fifteenth')
Élisabeth II (= 'deux')	Elizabeth II (= 'the Second')
le pape Jean XXIII	Pope John XXIII
(= 'vingt-trois')	(= 'the Twenty-third')

In both such contexts, however, the ordinal *premier* is used, e.g.:

le premier mai	the first of May
François premier	Francis the First

The ordinal is invariably used with reference to the *arrondissements* (districts) of Paris, e.g. *habiter dans le seizième (arrondissement)* 'to live in the sixteenth *arrondissement'*, and usually with reference to floors, e.g. *habiter au troisième (étage)* 'to live on the third floor'. It may also be used, as in English, with reference to chapters, etc., e.g. *au dixième chapitre* 'in the tenth chapter'. However, as in English the cardinal is normally used in contexts such as the following:

la page vingt-cinq	page twenty-five
le chapitre dix	chapter ten
habiter au (numéro) trente	to live in (house) number thirty
Je suis au vingt-quatre	I'm in (room) number twenty-four

Note that in such contexts, i.e. when they serve as the equivalent of ordinals, *quatre-vingt* '80' and *cent* '100' (in the plural) do not take a final *-s* (contrast **178**, and **180** c and d), e.g.:

à la page quatre-vingt	on page eighty
habiter au numéro trois cent	to live in number three hundred
l'an sept cent	the year seven hundred

(For 'every other, every third', etc., see 317,ii,b.)

183 Conversely to what happens in English, cardinals precede *premier* 'first' and *dernier* 'last', e.g.:

les dix premières pages	the first ten pages
les trois derniers mois	the last three months

184 For 'both', 'all three', etc., see 317,ii,f.

185 The following ten nouns ending in *-aine* express an approximate number:

une huitaine, about eight
une dizaine, about ten
une douzaine, a dozen
une quinzaine, about fifteen
une vingtaine, a score, about twenty
une trentaine, about thirty
une quarantaine, about forty
une cinquantaine, about fifty
une soixantaine, about sixty
une centaine, about a hundred

e.g. *J'ai écrit une vingtaine de lettres*
I've written about twenty letters

Une huitaine is used particularly in the expression *une huitaine de jours* (i.e. 'a week') and *une quinzaine* whether or not followed by *de jours* frequently means 'a fortnight'. As in English, *une douzaine* 'a dozen' can mean 'precisely twelve' in such expressions as *une douzaine d'œufs* 'a dozen eggs'. The terms *trentaine, quarantaine, cinquantaine* and *soixantaine* can refer to age in such expressions as *atteindre la quarantaine* 'to reach the age of forty', *Elle a dépassé la cinquantaine* 'She is over fifty'.

Note that similar forms based on other numerals either do not exist or are no longer in use (apart from *une neuvaine* which is used only in the sense of 'novena').

186 French has no adverbs to express numerical frequency (corresponding to English 'once, twice, thrice'). The word *fois* 'time' is used, e.g. *une fois* 'once', *deux fois* 'twice', *trente-six fois* 'thirty-six times'. Note the construction *dix fois sur vingt* 'ten times out of twenty'.

187 The multiplicatives *double* 'double, twofold', *triple* 'triple, treble, threefold', *quadruple* 'quadruple, fourfold', *centuple* 'hundredfold' are used both as adjectives (in which case they often precede the noun), e.g. *une consonne double* 'a double consonant', *un triple menton* 'a treble chin', and (preceded by the definite article) as nouns, e.g. *le double de ce que j'ai payé* 'double what I paid', *le quadruple de la récolte de l'an dernier* 'four times (as much as) last year's harvest'.

Apart from the forms quoted above, only the following exist, and some of these are not much used: *quintuple* 'fivefold', *sextuple* 'sixfold', *septuple* 'sevenfold', *octuple* 'eightfold', *nonuple* (very rarely used) 'ninefold', *décuple* 'tenfold'.

Fractions

188 A 'half' is either *(un) demi* or *la moitié*, but the two are by no means interchangeable (and see also **189**). We can distinguish three types of function, viz. (i) as nouns, (ii) as adjectives, (iii) as adverbs:

(i) Apart from a few contexts in which it is a nominalized adjective (see ii,c, below), *un demi* exists as a noun only as a mathematical term, e.g. *Deux demis font un entier* 'Two halves make a whole'. Otherwise, *la moitié* must be used (and note that, when it is the subject of the verb, the verb may be either singular or plural, depending on the sense – the same is also true of other fractions), e.g.:

Il n'a écrit que la moitié de son roman
He has only written half his novel

couper une orange en deux moitiés
to cut an orange into two halves

La moitié de la ville a été inondée
Half the town was flooded

La moitié de mes amis habitent à Paris
Half my friends live in Paris

la première (seconde) moitié
the first (second) half

(ii) *Demi* occurs in the following circumstances:

(a) before a noun in the sense of 'half (a) ...'; it is then invariable and is linked to the noun by a hyphen, e.g. *un demi-pain* 'half a loaf', *un demi-frère* 'a half-brother', *une demi-heure* 'half an hour', *une demi-bouteille* 'half a bottle', *des demi-mesures* 'half-measures';

(b) after the noun and preceded by *et*, meaning '... and a half'; it is then written as a separate word and takes an *-e* if the noun is feminine, e.g. *un kilo et demi* 'a kilo and a half, one and a half kilos', *une heure et demie* 'an hour and a half, one and a half hours, half past one', *trois heures et demie* 'three and a half hours, half past three';

(c) with an implied noun (as in a above), in contrast to a noun expressing a whole object, e.g. *Vous voulez un pain? Non, un demi* 'Do you want a loaf? No, a half (half a loaf)'; note (in contrast to *une demi-bouteille*, etc., see a above) that *demi* takes *-e* in agreement with a feminine noun when the noun itself is omitted, e.g. *Nous allons commander une bouteille de vin? – Une demie suffira* 'Shall we order a bottle of wine?' 'A half (bottle) will be enough'. Note too the following instances in which the noun has been completely dropped and the adjective has therefore become fully nominalized (see **176**):

> *un demi* 'glass of beer' (originally *un demi-litre*, but now contains less)
>
> *un demi* 'half-back' (in football – for *un demi-arrière*)

(iii) As adverbs, *à demi* and *à moitié* are in most cases interchangeable (but see below), in particular:

(a) before an adjective or participle, e.g.:

> *à demi plein/vide, à moitié plein/vide*
> half full/empty
>
> *à demi ouvert/pourri, à moitié ouvert/pourri*
> half open/rotten

(b) after a verb, e.g.:

> *ouvrir la porte à demi/à moitié*
> to half-open the door
>
> *Vous avez fait le travail à demi/à moitié*
> You have (only) half done the work
>
> *remplir un verre à demi/à moitié*
> to half-fill a glass

Note, however, the use of *à moitié* (but not of *à demi*) in a small number of expressions with nouns, in particular *à moitié prix* '(at) half-price' and *à moitié chemin* 'half-way' (but *à mi-chemin*, see below, is more usual). *Moitié* (without *à*) also occurs in various other expressions such as *moitié moitié* 'half-and-half, fifty-fifty', *(diviser quelque chose) par moitié* '(to divide something) in half, in two', *être pour moitié dans quelque chose* 'to be half responsible for something' (for other such expressions, consult a good dictionary).

189   The old noun *mi* 'a half' is still used adverbially in such constructions as *mi pleurant et mi souriant* 'half weeping and half smiling', *mi-fil et mi-coton* 'half linen and half cotton', in the expression *mi-clos* 'half-shut', and in a number of expressions with *à mi* including the following (for others, consult a dictionary):

> *à mi-chemin*, half-way
> *à mi-distance*, half-way, midway
> *à mi-hauteur*, half-way up
> *à mi-pente*, half-way up or down the slope
> *(travailler) à mi-temps*, (to work) half-time
> *à mi-voix*, in an undertone

190   'A third' and 'a quarter' are *un tiers* and *un quart* respectively, e.g.:

un tiers des votants	one third of those voting
un quart d'heure	a quarter of an hour

> *La bouteille est aux trois quarts vide*
> The bottle is three-quarters empty

Other fractions have (as in English) the same form as the ordinals, e.g. *un cinquième* 'a fifth', *sept huitièmes* 'seven eighths', *un centième* 'a hundredth', etc.

191   When a fraction refers to part of a specific whole (i.e. to one introduced by the definite article or by a demonstrative or possessive determiner), French uses the definite article where English uses the indefinite article or (especially in the plural) no article, e.g.:

> *Il a perdu le quart de ses biens*
> He lost a quarter of his possessions
>
> *la moitié de la classe*
> half (of) the class
>
> *les sept huitièmes de la population*
> seven eighths of the population

192   The decimal system as used in France is based not on the point but on the comma, and the figures coming after the comma are often expressed as if they were whole numbers, e.g. 2.35 'two point three five' becomes 2,35 *deux virgule trente-cinq.*

Pronouns and pronominal determiners

Personal pronouns

Introduction

193   Personal pronouns in French are either 'conjunctive' or 'disjunctive'.

Conjunctive pronouns (see 198–213) are used only in direct association with a verb. They include (a) subject pronouns, e.g. *Je vois* 'I see', (b) direct and indirect object pronouns, e.g. *(Pierre) la connaît* '(Peter) knows her', *(Marie) leur écrit* '(Mary) writes to them', and (c) the adverbial pronouns *y* (see 200) and *en* (see 201).

Disjunctive pronouns (see 215–220) usually stand independently of the verb, e.g. *Moi (je sais)* or *(Je sais) moi* 'I know', *avec eux* 'with them', though they are directly associated with the verb in imperative constructions such as *Pardonnez-moi* 'Forgive me' (see 207).

194   *Je* 'I' and *nous* 'we' are known as the first person singular and the first person plural respectively; *tu* 'you' and *vous* 'you'

(see **196**) are the second person singular and the second person plural respectively; *il* 'he, it' and *elle* 'she, it' are the third persons singular, masculine and feminine, and *ils* and *elles* 'they' are the third persons plural, masculine and feminine.

195 *Je* can be either masculine or feminine, depending on the sex of the speaker, e.g. *Je suis heureux* (masc.), *Je suis heureuse* (fem.) 'I am happy'. Likewise, *nous* can be either masculine or feminine, e.g. *Nous sommes heureux/heureuses*, 'We are happy' (when *nous* includes persons of both sexes, the masculine agreement is used).

Similarly with the direct object forms, e.g. *Il me croit intelligent(e)* 'He considers me (*masc., fem.*) intelligent', *Il nous croit intelligent(e)s* 'He considers us (*masc., fem.*) intelligent'.

196 *Tu* refers to one person only and is normally used only when addressing a friend, a relative, a child, God, or an animal; used in other contexts it can (and can be intended to be) offensive. Note that, whereas the corresponding English form *thou* has long since gone out of use (except in some dialects and sometimes in poetic or religious style), the use of *tu* is on the increase, particularly among young people. It may take either masculine or feminine agreement, depending on the sex of the person addressed, e.g. *Tu es heureux* (masc.)/*heureuse* (fem.) 'You are happy'; likewise with the direct object pronoun *te*, e.g. *Il te croit intelligent(e)* 'He considers you (*masc., fem.*) intelligent'.

Those to whom one does not say *tu* are addressed as *vous*, which is therefore both singular and plural depending on whether one is addressing one person or more than one; whether it is singular or plural makes no difference to the verb, but adjectives and participles vary both for gender and for number, e.g. *Vous êtes fou* (masculine singular)/*folle* (feminine singular)/*fous* (masculine plural)/*folles* (feminine plural) 'You're crazy'. Likewise with the direct object pronoun, e.g. *Il vous croit fou* (masc. sing.)/*folle* (fem. sing.)/*fous* (masc. plur.)/*folles* (fem. plur.) 'He thinks you crazy'. (As with *nous*, when *vous* includes persons of both sexes, the masculine agreement is used.)

197 Masculine nouns, whether relating to humans, animals, abstractions or inanimate objects, are referred to as *il* and feminine nouns as *elle*; *il* and *elle* therefore both mean 'it' as well as 'he' and 'she' respectively, e.g. *Où est ma cuiller? Elle est sur la* *table* 'Where is my spoon? It's on the table'. When 'they' refers to persons of both sexes or to nouns of both genders, *ils* is used.

Conjunctive personal pronouns

198   (i) The forms of the conjunctive personal pronouns are as follows:

subject	direct object	indirect object
je, I	*me*, me	*me*, to me
tu, you	*te*, you	*te*, to you
il, he, it	*le*, him, it	*lui*, to him ⎫ sometimes
elle, she, it	*la*, her, it	*lui*, to her ⎬ 'to it', see **200**,iii
nous, we	*nous*, us	*nous*, to us
vous, you	*vous*, you	*vous*, to you
ils, they (masc.)	*les*, them	*leur*, to them
elles, they (fem.)	*les*, them	*leur*, to them

(For the terms 'direct object' and 'indirect object', see **17**, **18** and **21**.)

Je, *me*, *te*, *le* and *la* become *j'*, *m'*, *t'* and *l'* before a verb beginning with a vowel or mute *h* and before *y* or *en*, e.g. *J'arrive* 'I arrive', *J'y habite* 'I live there', *M'aimes-tu?* 'Do you love me?', *Il t'en envoie* 'He's sending you some', *Il l'achète* 'He buys it'.

(ii) The indirect object pronouns are used:

(a) with such verbs as *dire* 'to say', *donner* 'to give', and other verbs of comparable meaning, e.g. *avouer* 'to admit', *confier* 'to entrust', *envoyer* 'to send', *léguer* 'to bequeath', *offrir* 'to offer', *parler* 'to speak', *recommander* 'to recommend', *rendre* 'to give back', *transmettre* 'to convey':

Il me dit que c'est vrai	He tells me it's true
Donnez-lui cette lettre	Give him this letter
Il va nous l'envoyer	He is going to send it to us
Je vous recommande ce restaurant	I recommend this restaurant to you

(b) with a number of other verbs, among the most common being *appartenir* 'to belong', *écrire* 'to write', *falloir* 'to be necessary', *paraître* 'to seem', *pardonner* 'to forgive', *plaire* 'to please', *sembler* 'to seem', e.g.:

Ce livre ne m'appartient pas	This book does not belong to me
Cela me paraît difficile	That seems difficult to me
Il lui faut un bureau	He needs an office
Je leur pardonne tout	I forgive them everything
Cette robe vous plaît?	Do you like this dress?

For verbs taking *à* + the disjunctive pronoun (e.g. *Je pense à vous* 'I am thinking of you'), see **220**.

(iii) With reference to things, the indirect object is often expressed by *y* rather than by *lui* or *leur* – see **200**.

199   As a reflexive pronoun (for reflexive verbs see **379–381**), *se* replaces all the third person pronouns, singular and plural (i.e. *le, la, les, lui, leur*), e.g.:

elle se lave	she washes (herself)
ils s'écrivent	they write to one another

In the first and second persons, the forms *me, te, nous* and *vous* also function as reflexive pronouns, e.g.:

je me lave	I wash (myself)
tu te laves	you wash (yourself)
nous nous écrivons	we write to each other
vous vous fatiguez	you are tiring yourselves

For the reciprocal use of reflexive pronouns see **292**.
For the full conjugation of a reflexive verb see **381**.
For the use of *soi* see **219**.

200   (i) The adverbial conjunctive pronoun *y* corresponds to the preposition *à* + noun, when the noun refers to an animal, a thing, a place or an abstract idea (or any of these in the plural), e.g. *Je réponds à la lettre* 'I reply to the letter' and *J'y réponds* 'I reply to it', *Il travaille à Paris* 'He works in Paris' and *Il y travaille* 'He works there'. (On *y* with reference to people, see ii below.)

(a) It frequently has the meaning 'there', e.g.:

Connaissez-vous Dijon? – Oui, j'y suis né et j'y vais souvent
Do you know Dijon? – Yes, I was born there and I often go there

However, it can be so used only to refer back to a place mentioned or implied in what has gone before. It does *not* have a demonstrative value, i.e. it does not, so to speak, 'point' to the place indicated by 'there' (or, to put it differently, it does not express the idea of 'there' as opposed to 'here'); in such circumstances, *là* is used, e.g. *Ton parapluie est là* 'Your umbrella is *there*'.

(b) With many verbs, *y* has the meaning 'to it, to them', e.g.:

Il s'y accrochait
He was hanging on to it (*or* them)

Je suis flatté de cet honneur, d'autant plus que je n'y avais jamais aspiré
I am flattered by this honour, the more so since I had never aspired to it

Ses observations ne me dérangent pas: je n'y fais pas attention
His remarks don't bother me: I pay no attention to them

In such instances as the following, the French verb takes *à* where the corresponding English verb either has a direct object (e.g. *renoncer à quelque chose* 'to give something up', *succéder à* 'to succeed, follow') or takes a preposition other than 'to' (e.g. *viser à* 'to aim at', *penser à, songer à, réfléchir à* 'to think about'):

Vous ne fumez plus? – Non, j'y ai renoncé
Don't you smoke any more? – No, I've given it up

la IIIe République et tous les régimes qui y ont succédé
the Third Republic and all the regimes that succeeded it

Il y réfléchit
He is thinking about it (considering it)

Note that, with reference to people, these verbs take *à* and the disjunctive pronouns, *lui, elle, eux, elles*, not the conjunctive indirect object pronouns, *lui* and *leur*, e.g. *Elle a renoncé à lui* 'She has given him up', *Je pensais à eux* 'I was thinking of them'.

(c) *Y* is sometimes the equivalent of *sur* and a noun, e.g. *écrire sur une feuille de papier* 'to write on a sheet of paper' and *Il y écrit une lettre d'amour* 'He's writing a love-letter on it', *Je compte sur sa discrétion* 'I am counting on his discretion' and *Vous pouvez y compter* 'You can count on it'.

(d) *Y* sometimes corresponds to *à* + a verb, as in *obliger quelqu'un à faire quelque chose*, hence:

Ne partez pas. Rien ne vous y oblige
Don't go. Nothing obliges you to (do so)

(ii) *Y* sometimes refers to people, particularly in substandard French, e.g. *J'y pense souvent* 'I often think of him (her, them)', for *Je pense souvent à lui* (*à elle, à eux, à elles*). This construction occasionally occurs in literary French, especially in that of a somewhat archaic kind, but it should not be imitated.

(iii) *Lui* and *leur* are sometimes used instead of *y* with reference to animals, things or abstract ideas, particularly:

(a) when it is necessary to make it clear that the meaning is 'to it' or 'to them' and not 'there', e.g.:

Les dames de la ville lui donnaient leur clientèle (Theuriet)
The ladies of the town gave it [= a shop] their custom

or (b) when the noun is to some extent personified, e.g.:

Je suis heureux de $\begin{Bmatrix} ma\ maladie \\ mes\ malheurs \end{Bmatrix}$*, puisque je* $\begin{Bmatrix} lui \\ leur \end{Bmatrix}$

dois votre amitié

I am glad of $\begin{Bmatrix} \text{my illness} \\ \text{my misfortunes} \end{Bmatrix}$ since I owe to $\begin{Bmatrix} \text{it} \\ \text{them} \end{Bmatrix}$

your friendship

201 (i) The conjunctive pronoun *en* (not to be confused with the preposition *en* which is a totally different word, see **654–658**) corresponds to the preposition *de* + a noun, especially with reference to animals, things, places and abstract ideas, e.g. *Nous parlons souvent de votre visite* 'We often talk about your visit' and *Nous en parlons souvent* 'We often talk about it', *Il est arrivé hier de Paris* 'He arrived yesterday from Paris' and *Il en est arrivé hier* 'He arrived from there yesterday'. (On *en* with reference to people, see ii below.)

(ii) In partitive constructions, it serves as a pronominal equivalent of *de* + a noun, with the value of 'some of it (*or* of them)', or 'any of it (*or* of them)'; and note that, though 'of it, of them' is frequently omitted in English, *en* must be inserted in French, e.g.:

Avez-vous du pain? – Oui, j'en ai acheté
Have you any bread? – Yes, I've bought some

Voulez-vous de la bière? – Oui, s'il y en a
Do you want some beer? – Yes, if there is any

Si vous voulez des billets, je peux vous en donner
If you want tickets, I can give you some

Il n'y en a pas
There isn't (*or* aren't) any

Il a plus d'argent qu'il n'en veut
He has more money than he wants

This construction frequently occurs with numerals and expressions of quantity, e.g.:

Combien de timbres pouvez-vous me prêter? – Je vais vous en prêter dix
How many stamps can you lend me? – I'll lend you ten

Voulez-vous du fromage? – J'en prends cent grammes
Do you want (any) cheese? – I'll take a hundred grammes

Note that, in this construction, *en* is used (and *must* be used) with reference to people just as with reference to animals, things, etc. (cf. i above and iv below), e.g.:

Combien d'enfants avez-vous? – J'en ai quatre
How many children have you? – I have four

(iii) In contexts such as the following, where in English one often (but not always) has the option of using either 'of it, of them' or the possessive determiner 'its, theirs', *en* is used in French, e.g.:

Je n'en aime pas la forme
I don't like the shape of it (*or* its shape)

Regarde ces fleurs! La couleur en est si jolie
Look at those flowers! The colour of them (their colour) is so pretty

(iv) Except in partitive constructions (see ii above), *de lui, d'elle, d'eux* and *d'elles* rather than *en* are normally used with reference to people, e.g.:

Il rêve d'elle chaque nuit
He dreams of her every night

J'ai reçu de lui une très longue lettre
I have had a very long letter from him

However, *en* is used much more widely than *y* (see **200**,ii) with reference to people, not only in colloquial French (e.g. *Il en rêve chaque nuit* 'He dreams of her every night') but also in the literary language, e.g.:

Il s'efforçait de lier conversation avec lui, comptant bien en tirer quelques paroles substantielles (A. France)
He tried to engage him in conversation, fully expecting to extract from him a few words of substance

Je le vois rarement, mais j'en reçois de très longues lettres
I rarely see him, but I get very long letters from him

On n'a d'ouverture sur un être que si on en est aimé (Chardonne)
One can have no real understanding of another person unless one is loved by him (*or* by her)

202   Conjunctive pronouns are used in French in such contexts as the following, where their equivalents may be merely implied in English:

Qui vous l'a dit?
Who told you?

Quand allez-vous à Paris? – J'y vais demain
When are you going to Paris? – I'm going (there) tomorrow

(For examples with *en*, see **201**,ii.)

The position of conjunctive personal pronouns

Subject

203   The subject pronoun normally comes before the verb; however, it follows the verb

(i) in certain types of questions (see **583–584, 589–592**)

(ii) in certain non-interrogative constructions (see **476–478, 596, 599–600**).

As a rule the subject pronoun is best repeated with each verb; but, provided both verbs are in the same tense, it may be omitted with *et, mais* and *ou* (see examples in **210**), and generally is with *ni* 'nor' (see **571**).

No subject is expressed with verbs in the imperative (see **514**).

Pronouns other than subject pronouns

204   Except with the affirmative imperative (see **207**), the pronouns stand immediately before the verb of which they are the object, e.g.:

Je t'aime	I love you
La connaissez-vous?	Do you know her?
Mon frère leur écrit souvent	My brother often writes to them
J'en prends six	I'll take six of them
Nous n'y allons pas	We are not going there
Ne les perdez pas	Don't lose them
Nous voulons les vendre	We want to sell them

(In the last of the above examples, 'them' is the object of 'sell' not of 'wish' and so, in accordance with the rule, comes immediately before the infinitive *vendre* 'to sell'.)

In the case of compound tenses (see **448–456**) the pronouns come before the auxiliary and are *never* placed immediately before the past participle, e.g.:

Je vous ai écrit	I have written to you
Ne les avez-vous pas trouvés?	Haven't you found them?
Mon père y est allé	My father has gone there

205   In a negative sentence, the *ne* stands immediately before the object pronouns, e.g. *Je ne les aime pas* 'I don't like them'.

206   When there is more than one object pronoun, they stand in the following order:

1 *me, te, se, nous, vous*
2 *le, la, les*
3 *lui, leur*
4 *y*
5 *en*

Examples:

Il me les donne	He gives me them (them to me)

Je le lui ai donné	I gave it to him (to her)
Les y avez-vous vus?	Did you see them there?
Vous en a-t-il offert?	Did he offer you any?
Ne me l'envoyez pas	Don't send it to me
Ne les lui donnez pas	Don't give them to him

Note:

(a) that is not possible for more than one member of any one of groups 1 to 3 above to occur with the same verb (see **208**)

(b) that, though it is possible for up to three of the above pronouns to occur together provided they are from different groups (e.g. *Je m'y en achète* 'I buy some for myself there'), in practice this very rarely happens.

207 With the affirmative imperative (see **514**):

(a) all pronouns follow the verb

(b) *moi* and *toi* are used instead of *me* and *te* except with *en* and *y* (see below)

(c) direct object precedes indirect object

(d) *y* and *en* come last

(e) except for elided forms (*m'*, *t'*, *l'*), pronouns are linked to the verb and to one another by hyphens.

Examples:

Croyez-moi	Believe me
Prends-en	Take some (of it, of them)
Donnez-le-moi	Give it to me
Menez-nous-y	Take us there
Offrez-lui-en	Offer him some
Donnez-m'en	Give me some
Menez-l'y	Take him (*or* her) there
Va-t'en	Go away!

Note, however, that the theoretically possible forms *m'y* and *t'y* are avoided in practice after an imperative, as are, in the literary language and in careful speech, the alternatives *y-moi* and *y-toi* that occur in colloquial speech (e.g. *Menez-y-moi* 'Take me there'). The solution is to use a different construction, e.g. *Voulez-vous m'y mener?* 'Will you take me there?' or *Pourriez-vous m'y mener?* 'Could you take me there?'.

208   It is not possible to combine:

(i) any two of *me, te, se, nous, vous* (see **206**, note a), or

(ii) any of *me, te, se, nous, vous* as direct object with *lui* or *leur* as indirect object.

In circumstances that might seem to require one of these impossible constructions, the direct object pronoun follows the ordinary rule but the indirect object is expressed by *à* 'to' and a disjunctive pronoun (see **215–220**), e.g.:

> *Il vous présentera à moi*
> He will introduce you to me

> *Voulez-vous me présenter à elles?*
> Will you introduce me to them?

> *Ils se sont rendus à moi*
> They surrendered to me

> *Nous ne nous rendrons pas à eux*
> We shall not surrender to them

> *Présentez-moi à lui*
> Introduce me to him (to her)

209   When an infinitive is governed by a modal verb (e.g. *devoir, pouvoir, vouloir*) or some other verb such as *aller, compter, oser, préférer* (see **529**), any conjunctive pronouns precede the infinitive, e.g.:

Je veux lui écrire	I want to write to him
Il doit y aller demain	He is to go there tomorrow
Vous allez le regretter	You are going to regret it
Il ose me contredire	He dares to contradict me
Je compte vous les envoyer demain	I expect to send them to you tomorrow

(In a somewhat archaic style, which should not be imitated, the pronoun sometimes precedes the modal verb, e.g. *Ils la peuvent apercevoir* (H. Bordeaux) 'They can see her'.)

For the constructions used when *faire, laisser, envoyer*, verbs of the senses, and certain other verbs, are followed by an infinitive, see **430–438**.

210   In English, the same pronoun may serve as the direct or indirect object of more than one verb, e.g. 'He loves and understands her'. In such circumstances, conjunctive pronouns in French are repeated with each verb, e.g.:

Il l'aime et la comprend   He loves and understands her

(In compound tenses, in which the pronoun always precedes the auxiliary verb, see **204**, the pronoun cannot be repeated if the auxiliary is not repeated, e.g. *Il l'a toujours aimée et respectée* 'He has always loved and respected her'.)

211 French makes much greater use than English of conjunctive pronouns referring either back or forward to nouns occurring in the same clause.

(i) This is normal (i.e. the conjunctive pronoun should be used) when attention is drawn to any element in the sentence by bringing it forward from its more usual position after the verb, e.g.:

Ce poème je le connais par cœur
I know this poem by heart

A mon cousin je ne lui écris jamais
I never write to my cousin

A Paris j'y vais souvent
I often go to Paris

De ces romans-là j'en ai plusieurs
I have several of those novels

(In examples such as these last three, the introductory preposition is sometimes omitted.)

(ii) In spoken French, anticipation of a direct or indirect object or of a prepositional phrase (introduced by *à* or *de*) by a conjunctive pronoun is very frequent, e.g.:

Je la connais ta soeur
I know your sister

Je lui écris souvent à mon frère
I often write to my brother

Il n'y va jamais à Paris
He never goes to Paris

J'en ai plusieurs de ces romans-là
I have several of those novels

See also **602**, 'Dislocation and fronting'.

212 *Le* frequently refers not to a specific noun but to a concept. This may be:

(i) a quality or status expressed by an adjective, participle or noun (but see also **213**), e.g.:

En sont-ils contents? – Je suis sûr qu'ils le sont
Are they pleased with it? – I am sure they are

Ce livre qui vient d'être publié n'aurait pas dû l'être
This book which has just been published ought not to have been

Est-elle étudiante? – Elle le sera l'année prochaine
Is she a student? – She will be next year

Cet édifice était autrefois une église mais il ne l'est plus
This building used to be a church but it is not (one) any more

(ii) the idea expressed in a previous clause, e.g.:

Est-ce qu'il arrive aujourd'hui? – Je l'espère
Is he arrive today – I hope so

Si vous comptez réserver des places, je vous conseille de le faire sans tarder
If you want to book seats, I advise you to do so without delay

Je viendrai dès qu'on me le permettra
I shall come as soon as I am allowed to

Son explication n'est pas très lucide, je l'avoue
His explanation is not very clear, I admit

Note that after *comme* and after comparatives the use of *le* is optional, e.g.:

Je suis essoufflé, comme vous (le) voyez
I am out of breath, as you see

Il est plus intelligent que je ne (le) croyais
He is more intelligent than I thought

213 The literary language sometimes uses the pronouns *le, la, les*, with the verb *être* (or occasionally with other verbs such as *rester* 'to remain') to refer back to a noun used with the definite article or another 'definite' determiner (such as a demonstrative, interrogative or possessive). The pronoun agrees with this noun in gender and number, e.g. *Tu devrais être ma femme, n'est-ce pas fatal que tu la sois un jour?* (Zola) 'You ought to be my wife, is it not inevitable that one day you will be?' (*la* agrees with *ma femme*). This, however, is an exclusively literary construction. In speech, one would be likely either to use the invariable *le* (see 212,i), e.g.:

Elle n'est pas sa femme et elle ne le sera jamais
She is not his wife and never will be

or to use some other construction, such as repeating the noun, e.g.:

Vous êtes son fils? – Oui, je suis son fils
Are you his son – Yes, I am

214 Note, on the other hand, that in contexts such as the following where English uses an anticipatory 'it' with reference to a following clause or infinitive serving as the direct object of the preceding verb, there is no equivalent pronoun in French:

J'estime essentiel que tu lui écrives
I consider it essential that you write to him

J'ai entendu dire qu'il va démissionner
I have heard it said that he is going to resign

Je crois préférable de ne pas y aller
I think it best not to go there

Il a jugé bon de partir tout de suite
He thought it advisable to leave at once

Il s'est mis dans la tête d'aller à Paris
He got it into his head to go to Paris

This is particularly common after a verb of thinking + an adjective, as in some of the above examples.

Disjunctive personal pronouns

215 The disjunctive pronouns are:

moi, I, me	*lui*, he, him
toi, you	*elle*, she, her

nous, we, us	*eux*, they, them (masc.)
vous, you	*elles*, they, them (fem.)

They can be combined with *-même(s)* as follows:

moi-même, myself	*nous-mêmes*, ourselves
toi-même, yourself	*vous-même*, yourself
	vous-mêmes, yourselves
lui-même, himself	*eux-mêmes*, themselves (masc.)
elle-même, herself	*elles-mêmes*, themselves (fem.)

as in *Je le ferai moi-même* 'I'll do it myself'.

In addition to these there is the reflexive disjunctive pronoun *soi* (see **219**).

The disjunctive pronouns can be used either as a subject of a verb (e.g. *Mon frère et moi partons demain* 'My brother and I are leaving tomorrow'), or as the object (e.g. *Je la connais, elle* 'I know *her*'), or after prepositions (e.g. *avec eux* 'with them') (see succeeding paragraphs).

216 The disjunctive pronouns (other than *soi*, see **219**) are used in the following circumstances:

(i) whenever the personal pronoun is to be emphasized (see also **602**, 'Dislocation') or is contrasted with another pronoun or noun; in such circumstances, the disjunctive pronouns are used *in addition to* the conjunctive pronouns (this applies even when the two forms are the same, i.e. to *nous* and *vous*) (but see also **217**), e.g.:

Toi, tu ne peux pas venir or *Tu ne peux pas venir, toi*
You can't come

Mon frère part demain mais moi je reste ici
My brother is leaving tomorrow but *I*'m staying here

Vous, vous ne pouvez pas comprendre
You can't understand

Il ose m'accuser, moi!
He dares to accuse *me*!

Lui, je l'aime beaucoup
I like *him* very much

If the conjunctive pronoun expresses an indirect object, the disjunctive is preceded by *à*, e.g.:

Il te l'a donné à toi
He gave it to *you*

Je leur obéirai à eux mais pas à mon oncle
I will obey them but not my uncle

Note too the use of disjunctive *nous, vous* + *autres* as emphatic forms, particularly when there is an expressed implied distinction between 'us' or 'you' on the one hand and some other group (or other people in general) on the other, e.g.:

Nous autres Français, nous mangeons beaucoup de pain
We French eat a lot of bread

Vous n'êtes jamais contents, vous autres fermiers
You farmers are never content

Nous n'aimons pas ça, nous autres
We do not like that

(ii) when there are two or more coordinate subjects (i.e. the type 'X and Y' or 'X, Y and Z'), e.g.:

Mon frère et moi nous partons demain
My brother and I are leaving tomorrow

Lui et moi nous savons que ce n'est pas vrai
He and I know it isn't true

Je croyais que ton frère et toi vous n'arriveriez jamais
I thought your brother and you would never arrive

Son père et lui ne s'entendent pas très bien
His father and he don't get on very well together

In this construction, the conjunctive pronouns *nous* and *vous* are usually inserted (as in the first three examples above), particularly in speech, though *Mon frère et moi partons demain*, etc., are also possible, especially in writing. This insertion of the conjunctive pronoun is less usual, especially in writing, with the third person pronouns *ils* and *elles* (cf. the fourth example above where no conjunctive pronoun is used).

When the word-order is inverted (i.e. the subject follows the verb) in questions or after one of the adverbs or adverbial expressions that cause inversion (see **600**), the conjunctive pronoun *must* be used, e.g.:

Ton frère et toi comptez-vous partir demain?
Do you and your brother expect to leave tomorrow

Sans doute Anne et lui en seront-ils contents
Anne and he will doubtless be pleased

(iii) as the complement of *c'est, c'était,* etc., e.g. *C'est moi* 'It's me' (see also **255** and **258**)

(iv) after prepositions, e.g. *pour moi* 'for me', *sans lui* 'without him', *avec vous* 'with you'

(v) after *ne … que* 'only', e.g.:

Je ne connais que lui
I only know him (i.e. him only)

Je ne le dis qu'à toi
I'm only telling you (you only)

(vi) as the subject or object of an unexpressed verb:

(a) subject (note that in the corresponding English utterances a verb, which may be just the verb 'to do' standing in for another verb, often *is* expressed), e.g.:

Qui a dit ça? – Moi
Who said that? – I did (*or* Me)

Qui le fera? – Lui
Who will do it? – He will

Je suis plus grand que toi
I am taller than you (are)

Jean va peut-être rester, mais moi non (or *moi pas*)
John may be staying, but I'm not

(b) object, e.g.:

Qui a-t-il vu? – Toi
Whom did he see? – You

(vii) as the subject of an infinitive in exclamations (see **429**), e.g.:

Lui, nous trahir!   *He* betray us!

217 The third person disjunctive pronouns are sometimes used as the direct subjects of a verb (i.e. in the absence of the corresponding conjunctive pronoun), e.g.:

Les autres l'ignoraient, mais lui le savait
The others were unaware of it, but *he* knew

Nous, nous étions trop loin, mais eux l'ont vu
We were too far away, but *they* saw it

This is not possible in the case of the other disjunctive pronouns, with which the corresponding conjunctive pronoun must be inserted as grammatical subject (see examples in 216,i, above).

218 The functions of the reflexive disjunctive pronoun *soi* are much more restricted than those of the corresponding conjunctive pronoun *se*. Except in the circumstances referred to below (see 219), the third person disjunctives, *lui, elle, eux, elles*, are used instead. So, whereas, corresponding to *Je me lave* 'I wash (myself)', *Tu t'habilles* 'You dress (yourself), you get dressed', we have *Je ne suis pas fier de moi* 'I am not proud of myself', *Tu ne penses qu'à toi(-même)* 'You only think of yourself', *Vous l'avez acheté pour vous(-même)* 'You bought it for yourself', the forms that correspond to *Il/Elle se lave* 'He/she washes (himself/herself)', *Ils/Elles s'habillent* 'They get dressed' are, for example, *Il n'est pas fier de lui* 'He is not proud of himself', *Elle ne pense qu'à elle(-même)* 'She only thinks of herself', *Ils/Elles l'ont acheté pour eux-mêmes/elles-mêmes* 'They bought it for themselves'.

If there is any possibility of ambiguity, i.e. if it might otherwise not be clear whether the pronoun is being used reflexively (with reference to the subject) or not (i.e. with reference to someone else), the form with *-même(s)* should be used.

219 (i) In normal usage, *soi* and *soi-même* are used only:

(a) with reference to an indefinite pronoun such as *chacun* 'each (one)', *personne* 'no one', *on* 'one', *quiconque* 'whoever', or to a noun introduced by one of the indefinite determiners *chaque* 'each' or *aucun* 'no', e.g.:

On le ferait pour soi(-même)	One would do it for oneself
Chacun pour soi	Every man for himself

or (b) when no antecedent is expressed, e.g.:

Il faut tout faire soi-même	One has to do everything oneself
aimer son prochain comme soi-même	to love one's neighbour as oneself

> *Pourquoi toujours penser à*   Why always think of oneself?
> *soi-même?*

and likewise in a number of noun phrases such as *respect de soi* 'self-respect', *contentement de soi* 'self-satisfaction', *confiance en soi* 'self-confidence'.

(ii) *Lui*, etc., are usually used, however, when *chacun, chaque* refer to 'each (of a specific set)', e.g.:

> *Après la réunion, chacun (chaque membre du comité) rentra chez lui*
> After the meeting, everyone (each member of the committee) went home

(iii) Some modern authors affect the faintly archaic use of *soi* with reference to a definite subject, e.g. *Elle pense toujours à soi* 'She is always thinking of herself', but this usage should not be imitated.

220 'To me, to him, etc.' are frequently expressed by the conjunctive pronouns *me, lui*, etc., e.g. *Je lui écris* 'I write to him' (see **198**). However, with certain verbs, *à* and the disjunctive pronoun are used instead. This construction is found in particular:

(a) with *être* 'to belong', e.g. *Ce livre est à moi* 'This book belongs to me (This book is mine)' (but note that *appartenir* 'to belong' takes a conjunctive pronoun, *Ce livre m'appartient*)

(b) with verbs of motion, e.g. *Il courut à moi* 'He ran to me', *Il viendra à nous* 'He will come to us' – but *L'idée me vient que …* 'The idea comes to me that …', etc., when no physical motion is implied.

(c) with *penser, songer* 'to think' and *rêver* 'to dream', e.g. *Je pensais à toi* 'I was thinking of you'

(d) with a few miscellaneous verbs including *en appeler* 'to appeal', *recourir* 'to have recourse', *renoncer* 'to give up', e.g. *J'en appelle à vous* 'I appeal to you (i.e. to your judgement)', *Elle recourt toujours à lui* 'She always turns to him (i.e. for help)', *J'ai renoncé à elle* 'I have given her up'; note too such expressions as *Il aura affaire à moi* 'He will have me to deal with', *Prends garde à toi!* 'Watch out!'

Adverb replacing preposition + pronoun

221 In English, an adverb of place is often used instead of a preposition + 'it' (or, less frequently, 'them', with reference to things), e.g. 'Here's the table but there's nothing underneath (*or* under(neath) it)'. A similar possibility exists in French and it should be noted that in some contexts French uses the adverb where the prepositional construction is more likely in English.

The following adverbs are particularly common in this construction (the forms in *là* have a slightly stronger demonstrative value than those without and can sometimes, but not always, be translated 'in there, under there, on there'):

dedans, là-dedans	inside, in it
dessous, là-dessous	underneath, under it
dessus, là-dessus	on top, on it

Examples:

Il n'y a personne là-dedans
There is no one in there

J'ai ouvert la boîte mais il n'y avait rien dedans
I opened the box but there was nothing inside (in it)

Voici l'enveloppe: son adresse est dessus
Here's the envelope: his address is on it

In spoken French, *avec* 'with' (and, to a lesser extent, *pour* 'for' and *sans* 'without') are similarly used, e.g. *Il a emprunté mon parapluie et il est parti avec* 'He borrowed my umbrella and went off with it'.

Possessive determiners and pronouns

Introduction

222 French, like English, has two sets of possessives, each having different functions, viz.:

(i) possessive determiners (see **23**) (more frequently but less satisfactorily known as 'possessive adjectives'), corresponding to English *my*, *your*, etc. (see **223–226**)

(ii) possessive pronouns, corresponding to English *mine*, *yours*, etc. (see 231–233).

Possessive determiners

223 The possessive determiners in French are:

masc. sing.	fem. sing.	masc. and fem. plur.	
mon	*ma*	*mes*	my
ton	*ta*	*tes*	your
son	*sa*	*ses*	his, her, its
notre	*notre*	*nos*	our
votre	*votre*	*vos*	your
leur	*leur*	*leurs*	their

These forms function in a similar way to the definite article, agreeing in gender and number with the noun they introduce (e.g. *mon livre* 'my book', *ma maison* 'my house', *mes crayons* 'my pencils') and preceding not only the noun but any accompanying adjectives (e.g. *ma nouvelle voiture* 'my new car'). The only member of a noun phrase that can normally precede the possessive (but see also *feu*, **135**) is the predeterminer *tout* 'all, whole' (see **317**), e.g. *toute ma vie* 'my whole life', *tous vos amis* 'all your friends'.

Before a noun or adjective beginning with a vowel or mute *h*, *mon*, *ton*, *son*, are used in the feminine instead of *ma*, *ta*, *sa*, e.g. *mon idée* 'my idea', *son habileté* 'his skill'.

The distinction between *ton*, etc., and *votre*, etc., corresponds to that between *tu* and *vous* (see **196**).

224 Like the definite article (see **30**) the possessive determiner is repeated with each of a series of nouns referring to different entities, e.g. *mon frère et ma sœur* 'my brother and sister', but not with nouns referring to the same item or individual, e.g. *mon collègue et ami Jean Dubois* 'my colleague and friend Jean Dubois', *leur appartement ou studio à Paris* 'their flat or flatlet in Paris'.

In a few fixed expressions, a single determiner refers to two or more nouns, e.g. (with any possessive determiner) *mes allées et venues* 'my comings and goings', *vos nom, prénom(s) et qualité* 'your full name and occupation', *à ses risques et périls* 'at his own risk'.

225   The possessive determiners cannot be stressed. When any degree of emphasis is required, the appropriate disjunctive pronoun preceded by *à* is used, in addition to the determiner, e.g. *mon frère à moi* '*my* brother', *leur maison à eux (à elles)* '*their* house'.

The same procedure may be used to distinguish between 'his' and 'her' where the determiner alone could be unclear or ambiguous, e.g.:

Sa mère à lui est plus jeune que sa mère à elle
His mother is younger than her mother

Il conduisait sa voiture à elle
He was driving her car

226   The first person singular possessives *mon*, etc., are used in certain circumstances when addressing someone; in particular:

(i) as a sign of familiarity or affection; e.g. a parent speaking to his or her son or daughter may well use the forms *mon fils* and *ma fille* (where English would probably just use their names), or, speaking to one's children in general, *mes enfants* (which could also be used by a teacher addressing a class); likewise *mon amour* 'darling', etc.

(ii) as a sign of respect or deference, e.g. *mon père* 'father' (i.e. when one of his children is speaking), or 'Father' (i.e. with reference to a Catholic priest), *mon oncle* 'uncle', *ma tante* 'aunt', etc., and, in the army, when addressing those of higher rank (i.e. where 'Sir!' would be used in English), e.g. a captain and a colonel would be addressed as *mon capitaine* and *mon colonel* respectively by their inferiors, but as *capitaine* and *colonel* by their superiors and by civilians. This practice is at the origin of the forms *monsieur* (originally = 'my lord'), *madame, mademoiselle* (whose plurals are still formed in *mes*, viz. *messieurs, mesdames, mesdemoiselles*) and the ecclesiastical title *monseigneur*, plur. *messeigneurs*.

227   Just as 'of it, of them' may sometimes be substituted in English for 'its' or 'their' (with reference to things), so, in French, the conjunctive pronoun *en* 'of it, of them' (see **201**) may be substituted for the possessive determiners in the following circumstances (but the possessive is also fully acceptable and, in speech at least, more usual):

(a) with reference to the subject of *être* or another 'linking verb' (e.g. *devenir, paraître*, see **518**), e.g.:

> *Vous devriez visiter le château. Les jardins en sont superbes*
> You ought to visit the château. Its gardens (the gardens of it) are superb

> *Cette robe est jolie mais les manches en paraissent trop courtes*
> That dress is pretty but its sleeves seem too short

(b) with a direct object, e.g.:

> *J'ai reçu sa lettre mais je n'en comprends pas le premier paragraphe*
> I have had his letter but I don't understand the first paragraph of it (its first paragraph)

> *Le proviseur du lycée en connaît tous les élèves*
> The headmaster of the school knows all its pupils

> *Il achetait des livres afin d'en dévorer le contenu plutôt que d'en admirer la reliure*
> He bought books in order to master their contents rather than to admire their bindings

(but not when the possessive refers back to the subject of the same clause, e.g. *en* could not be substituted for the possessive determiner in *Le château domine ses jardins* 'The castle towers above its gardens').

228 With reference to parts of the body, French commonly uses the definite article where English uses the possessive determiner. Two different constructions have to be noted:

(i) When the reference is to something the subject does *with* a part of his or her body, the definite article alone is used, e.g.:

> *J'ai ouvert les yeux*
> I opened my eyes

> *Elle hausse les épaules*
> She shrugs her shoulders

> *Ils étendirent les bras*
> They stretched out their arms

and likewise with *fermer la bouche (les yeux)* 'to close one's mouth (eyes)', *lever le doigt* ' to put one's hand up', *secouer la tête* 'to shake one's head', etc. Cf. too expressions such as *avoir mal aux dents, … à la gorge, … à la tête, … aux reins* 'to have toothache, a sore throat, a headache, backache', etc. However, when the part of the body is in any way qualified, the possessive is used, e.g. *Elle ouvrit ses grands yeux bleus* 'She opened her big blue eyes'.

(ii) When the reference is to something one does *to* a part of one's body, the reflexive pronoun (functioning as an indirect object) is used, as in *Elle se lave les cheveux* 'She washes her hair (*lit.* She washes the hair to herself)'; cf.:

Vous vous êtes cassé le bras	You have broken your arm
Je me suis coupé le doigt	I have cut my finger
Elle s'est tordu le bras	She wrenched her arm

A similar construction, using the indirect object pronoun referring to the person affected, occurs when the action is something one does to a part of someone else's body, e.g.:

Il m'a tordu le bras	He twisted my arm
Elle lui lave les cheveux	She washes his hair
Il lui a craché à la figure	He spat in his face

229 With some verbs two different constructions are possible, e.g.:

$$Elle\ s'est \begin{Bmatrix} bless\acute{e}e \\ br\hat{u}l\acute{e}e \end{Bmatrix} au\ genou$$

$$She\ has \begin{Bmatrix} hurt \\ burnt \end{Bmatrix} her\ knee$$

(*lit.* 'she has hurt/burnt herself in the knee' – *se* is a direct object and so the past participle agrees with it, see **461**), or alternatively:

$$Elle\ s'est \begin{Bmatrix} bless\acute{e} \\ br\hat{u}l\acute{e} \end{Bmatrix} le\ genou$$

(*lit.* 'She has hurt/burnt the knee to herself' – *se* is an indirect object and so the past participle does not agree.)

230 For the use of the definite article in expressions of the type *le chapeau sur la tête* 'with his hat on his head', see **29**,ii.

Possessive pronouns

231 The French possessive pronouns are

masc. sing.	fem. sing.	masc. plur.	fem. plur.	
le mien	*la mienne*	*les miens*	*les miennes*	mine
le tien	*la tienne*	*les tiens*	*les tiennes*	yours
le sien	*la sienne*	*les siens*	*les siennes*	his, hers
le nôtre	*la nôtre*	*les nôtres*	*les nôtres*	ours
le vôtre	*la vôtre*	*les vôtres*	*les vôtres*	yours
le leur	*la leur*	*les leurs*	*les leurs*	theirs

232 (i) The possessive pronouns take the gender and number of the noun they stand for, e.g.:

tes enfants et les miens
your children and mine

Notre maison est en face de la leur
Our house is opposite theirs

(ii) After the verb *être*, 'mine, yours', etc. are usually rendered by *à moi, à vous,* etc. (i.e. 'it belongs to me' rather than 'it is mine'), e.g.:

Ces livres-ci sont à moi
These books are mine

Laquelle de ces clefs est à vous?
Which of these keys is yours?

However, when a contrast is being drawn not so much between two possessors (as in, for example, *Ces livres-ci sont à lui, les autres sont à nous* 'These books are his, the others are ours') as between two sets of things possessed, *le mien*, etc., are used, e.g.:

Ces livres-ci sont les vôtres; les miens sont en bas
These books are yours; mine are downstairs

233 The forms listed in **231** also occur very occasionally without the definite article as adjectives, in particular:

(i) in such expressions as *faire sien* 'to adopt as one's own', *regarder comme sien* 'to consider as one's own', e.g. *Je fais mienne votre réponse* 'I adopt your answer as my own', *Il regardait comme siens tous les revenus de sa femme* 'He considered all his wife's income as his own';

(ii) in the archaic construction, that one still sometimes comes across, *un* or *ce* + demonstrative + noun, e.g. *un mien ami* 'a friend of mine', *ce mien ami* 'this friend of mine'; the normal equivalents of these are *un ami à moi* (or, with a slightly different meaning, *un de mes amis* 'one of my friends') and *cet ami à moi.*

Demonstrative determiners and pronouns

Introduction

234 Unlike English, which uses *this* and *that*, *these* and *those*, both as determiners (see **23**) and as pronouns, French (as in the case of the possessives, see **222, 223, 231**) has two sets of demonstratives, each having different functions, viz.:

(i) demonstrative determiners (more usually but less satisfactorily known as demonstrative adjectives) (see **235–237**)

(ii) demonstrative pronouns (see **238**).

Demonstrative determiners

235 The demonstrative determiners in French, meaning both 'this/these' and 'that/those' (see **237**) are:

masc. sing.	fem. sing.	plur.
ce, cet	*cette*	*ces*

In the masculine singular, *ce* is used except before a vowel or mute *h* when *cet* is used, e.g. *ce livre* 'this/that book', *cet arbre* 'this/that tree', *ce soldat* 'this soldier', *cet ancien soldat* 'this former soldier', *cet homme* 'this man'.

Note that, as in the case of the other principal determiners, viz. the articles *les* and *des* (**24**) and the possessives, *mes*, *nos*, etc. (**223**), there is no distinction of gender in the plural.

236 The demonstrative determiners agree in gender and number with the noun they introduce, e.g. *cette maison* 'this house', *ces idées* 'those ideas'.

Like other determiners (cf. the definite article, **30**, and the possessive, **224**), the demonstrative is repeated with each of two or more nouns referring to separate entities, e.g. *ce pain, ce jambon et cette bière* 'this bread, ham and beer', *ces femmes et ces enfants* 'these women and children'.

Also like the definite article and the possessive determiner, the demonstrative determiner may be preceded by the predeterminer *tout* 'all (of), whole' (see **317**,ii,b), e.g. *tous ces enfants* 'all these/those children', *toute cette foule* 'this whole crowd'.

237 The French determiners mean both 'this/these' and 'that/those'. It is possible to make a distinction comparable to the English one by adding after the noun either *-ci* (an archaic form of *ici* 'here') for 'this/these' or *-là* (= 'there') for 'that/those', e.g. *ces jours-ci* 'these days', *ce jour-là* 'that day', but this is usually not necessary. Indeed, it is frequently not only unnecessary but incorrect to add *-ci* or *-là* to the noun. They should be used *only* in the following circumstances:

(i) to express emphasis

(ii) to mark a contrast between 'this' and 'that', or 'these' and 'those'

(iii) when an object is, literally, pointed out.

Examples:

Je déteste cette couleur-là
I hate that colour

Prenez ce livre-ci plutôt que l'autre
Take this book rather than the other (one)

C'est bien ce train-ci pour Paris, n'est-ce pas?
It is *this* train for Paris, isn't it?

Qui est ce monsieur-là?
Who is that gentleman (there)?

Note that, in familiar speech, the forms in *-là* are frequently used instead of the forms in *-ci* when the context makes it clear what particular item is being referred to, e.g.:

Ce train-là va à Paris?   Does this train go to Paris?

If necessary, *là-bas* 'over there' can be used to make it clear that the meaning is 'that' not 'this', e.g. *ce train là-bas* 'that train (over there)'.

Demonstrative pronouns

238   Whereas, in the case of the demonstrative determiners, French often does not distinguish between 'this/these' and 'that/those' (see **237**), in the case of the demonstrative pronouns strictly so called (see **245–246** for other pronouns that are sometimes also considered to be demonstratives) the distinction is compulsory and is expressed, as in the case of the determiners (see **237**), by adding *-ci* or *-là* to the pronoun itself. The forms of the demonstrative pronouns are:

	masc. sing.	fem. sing.	masc. plur.	fem. plur.
this, these	*celui-ci*	*celle-ci*	*ceux-ci*	*celles-ci*
that, those	*celui-là*	*celle-là*	*ceux-là*	*celles-là*

Note that, in the singular, English frequently uses 'this one, that one' instead of 'this, that'; in French, *celui-ci*, *celle-là*, etc., are all that is required – do not attempt to translate the English 'one'. The gender of the pronoun is determined by that of the noun it refers to – 'this one' with reference to a book (*le livre*), for example, is *celui-ci* but with reference to a bottle (*la bouteille*) the feminine, *celle-ci*, is required. *Celui-ci*, etc., also mean 'the latter' (i.e. the one just mentioned, so, in that sense, the nearer, 'this one'), while *celui-là*, etc., mean 'the former'. Examples:

J'ai acheté deux journaux. Celui-ci est pour vous et celui-là est pour votre père
I have bought two newspapers. This one is for you and that one is for your father

A qui sont ces disques? – Ceux-ci sont à moi mais ceux-là sont à mon frère
Whose are these records? – These are mine but those are my brother's

Laquelle de ces chemises préférez-vous? – Je préfère de beaucoup celle-ci
Which of these shirts do you prefer? – I much prefer this one

*Marlborough et Eugène étaient presque comme deux frères;
celui-ci avait plus d'audace, celui-là l'esprit plus froid et
calculateur*
Marlborough and Eugene were almost like two brothers;
the latter was more impetuous, the former more coldly
calculating

Celui-là, etc., are frequently used in familiar speech instead of
celui-ci, etc., when the meaning is clear from the context (cf.
237), e.g.:

Quelle robe as-tu choisie? – Je prends celle-là
Which dress have you chosen? – I'll take this one

The neuter demonstrative pronouns

239 French has three so-called 'neuter' demonstrative pronouns,
viz. *ce*, *ceci* and *cela* (note that the *-a* of *cela* does not have an
accent).

240 *Ce.* Although *ce* is very widely used (i) when followed by
a relative clause and meaning 'what, that which' (see **274**), and
(ii) as the subject of *être* and meaning 'it' (see **248–261**), it has
almost entirely gone out of use as a real demonstrative. It survives
as such only in a few phrases (all of them characteristic of literary
rather than of spoken usage) such as:

sur ce
thereupon, whereupon
pour ce, pour ce faire
to this end, for this purpose
ce disant
saying this, so saying, with these words
ce faisant
doing this, doing which

and *et ce* 'and that' (in the sense of 'for the reason that', or 'and
I did so', etc.) as in, for example, *J'ai promis de l'aider, et ce
pour le convaincre de mon amitié* 'I promised to help him, and
that (*or* and I did so) in order to convince him of my friendship'.

241 Whereas *celui-ci, celui-là*, etc. refer to specific nouns and
can usually be translated as 'this one, that one' (see **238**), *ceci*

and *cela* (or its reduced form *ça*, see **242**,i) do not. These so-called 'neuter' pronouns refer:

(i) to the general content of a statement, in which case *ceci* generally refers forward to something that still has to be stated, whereas *cela* refers back to something already stated, e.g.:

> *Écoutez ceci*
> Listen to this (i.e. to what I have to say)

> *Cela n'est pas vrai*
> That is not true

> *Si vous croyez cela, vous êtes fou*
> If you believe that, you're crazy

> *On dit qu'il est parti mais cela me paraît bizarre*
> They say he's left but that seems odd to me

Note, however, that *ceci* refers back in the expression *ceci dit* 'that said', as in *Ceci dit, parlons d'autre chose* 'That said, let us talk about something else'.

Note too the construction *ceci/cela* + *de* + adjective + a noun-clause, e.g.:

> *Le problème a ceci (cela) d'intéressant que personne ne sait ce qu'elle fera demain*
> The problem is interesting in this respect that (*or* What is interesting about the problem is that) no one knows what she will do tomorrow

(ii) to some unspecified object, i.e. meaning 'this, that' not 'this one, that one' (which must be *celui-ci*, etc), e.g.:

Je prends ceci	I'll take this
Ceci est son chef d'œuvre	This is his masterpiece
Jetez cela!	Throw that away!

242 Note:

(i) that frequently in speech and sometimes, in an informal style, in writing, *cela* is reduced to *ça*, e.g. *Ça suffit!* 'That's enough!',

(ii) that *ceci* is characteristic particularly of literary usage and is not very much used in conversational French in which it tends to be replaced by *cela* (*ça*).

243 *Cela (ça)* is widely used as a strengthening particle in what would otherwise be one-word questions, e.g.:

Je l'ai vu ce matin. – Où cela?
I saw him this morning. – Where?

Quelqu'un me l'a dit. – Qui ça?
Someone told me. – Who (did)?

and likewise *Comment ça?* 'How?', *Pourquoi ça?* 'Why (so)?',
Quand ça? 'When?' (but it is **not** used with *quoi?* 'what?').

244 With the verb *être* and a following noun phrase, the two
parts of which *cela* originally consisted are still frequently separated, with *ce* serving as the subject of the verb and *là* coming
between the verb and the noun phrase (without a hyphen); the
meaning, however, is still 'that' (with sometimes a slight degree
of emphasis), e.g.:

C'est là le problème
That's (just) the problem

C'était là ce qu'il voulait dire
That was what he meant

Est-ce là la maison dont vous parlez?
Is that the house you are talking about?

Note that this construction can also occur with a plural verb (cf.
255), e.g.:

Ce sont là les messieurs qui sont arrivés hier
Those are the gentlemen who arrived yesterday

(but the form *sont-ce* should be avoided.)

The simple demonstrative pronouns

245 The simple demonstrative pronouns, i.e. *celui, celle, ceux,
celles* without -*ci* or -*là*, can no longer be used as demonstratives
in the strict sense of the word, i.e. meaning 'this one, that one,
these', etc. They are used as the equivalent of English 'the one(s)'
(or, in the literary language, 'that, those') when standing for some
previously expressed noun and followed by a defining clause or
phrase. The pronoun agrees in gender and number with the noun
it stands for, e.g. 'these letters and the ones I wrote yesterday' is
ces lettres et celles que j'ai écrites hier (*celles* because it stands for
lettres which is feminine plural).

The defining element may be:

(i) a prepositional phrase introduced by *de*, corresponding to an English phrase of the type 'that of my brother' (or, more frequently, 'my brother's' with no expressed pronoun), e.g.:

sa décision et celle du président
his decision and that of the President

Son jardin est plus grand que celui de Jean
Her garden is bigger than John's

J'aime mieux les romans de Balzac que ceux de Zola
I prefer the novels of Balzac to those of Zola

Nous mangeons ces pommes-ci ou celles de mon frère?
Shall we eat these apples or my brother's?

(ii) a relative clause (see also **246**), e.g.:

Votre maison est plus grande que celle que je viens d'acheter
Your house is bigger than the one I have just bought

ces messieurs et ceux qui arrivent demain
these gentlemen and those (the ones) who are arriving tomorrow

Ce parc n'est pas celui dont je vous ai parlé
This park isn't the one I told you about

Quelle dame cherchez-vous? Celle à qui j'ai parlé hier
Which lady are you looking for? The one I spoke to yesterday

(iii) a phrase introduced by a preposition other than *de* or by a past participle, e.g.:

ces livres-ci et ceux sur la table
these books and the ones on the table

les nouvelles mesures et celles adoptées l'an dernier
the new measures and those adopted last year

However, such constructions are often considered stylistically inelegant and, for that reason, it is as well to avoid them, at least in writing. This can be done by means of a relative clause (e.g. *ceux qui sont sur la table, celles qui furent adoptées*). It is even more advisable to avoid the use of other defining elements even though these occur (but only rarely) in the French of good writers, e.g. *Elle le dégoûta . . . des tomates, même de celles comestibles* (Proust) 'She put him off tomatoes, even edible ones'.

246   *Celui qui* (*que,* etc.) and *ceux qui* (*que,* etc.) can also be used in a general sense, i.e. 'he who(m) . . .', e.g.:

> *Heureux celui qui craint le Seigneur!*
> Blessed is he who fears the Lord!

> *Ceux qui voyagent beaucoup ont de la chance*
> Those who travel a lot are lucky

> *ceux que les dieux aiment*
> those whom the gods love

247   In a similar construction to the use of *celui qui,* etc., in a general sense (**245**), the 'neuter' pronoun *ce,* which now rarely serves as a strict demonstrative (see **240**), frequently occurs as the antecedent of a relative clause with the meaning 'what, that which', e.g. *ce que je veux* 'what I want' (for fuller details see **274**).

c'est and il est

248   It is a curious fact that such a basic problem as how to translate the expression 'it is' into French is the source of considerable uncertainty and difficulty. No French grammar deals with it entirely adequately. Fortunately, for at least part of the problem, namely the use of *c'est* or *il est* + adjective, we have an illuminating study in Professor Samuel N. Rosenberg's book, *Modern French Ce* (Paris and The Hague: Mouton, 1970), to which section **250** below in particular owes a lot.

The basic problem, i.e. that of distinguishing between *c'est* and *il est* as equivalents of 'it is', is complicated by two others. One is the fact that *il (est)* in French may be the equivalent either of the English impersonal 'it is', as in 'It is easy to understand him', or of 'he is', or of 'it is' with reference to a specific object, as in 'If you want my dictionary, it is on the desk'. The other is the fact that in some contexts French uses *c'est* where English uses 'he is' or 'she is' (see **251**).

We cannot hope in a few pages to deal with all facets of the problem but what follows will cover the majority of cases in which it arises.

In what follows, 'complement' refers to what comes after the verb 'to be' and 'referent' to whatever the pronoun (*ce, il, elle,* etc.) stands for; for example, in *Jean ne vient pas, il est malade* 'John isn't coming, he's ill' and *C'est beau, la neige* 'Snow is beautiful', *malade* and *beau* respectively are the complements and *Jean* and *la neige* the referents.

Finally note that (as in, for example, *C'est beau, la neige,* above), an adjectival complement after *c'est* always agrees with *ce*, i.e. it is masculine, even if the referent is a feminine noun or a plural noun (e.g. *C'est important, les traditions* 'Traditions are important').

249   As the subject is a complicated one and a number of different rules and sub-rules are involved, it may help to simplify matters if we give a summary of the contents of sections **250–261**:

I.   *C'est* or personal *il est, elle est,* etc.?

250   (i) The complement is an adjective:

(a) The referent is a person

(b) The referent is a thing

(c) The referent is an unspecified object, a neuter pronoun, an adverbial expression of place, or a phrase including a numeral

251   (ii) The complement is a noun or pronoun:

(a) *C'est*

(b) *Il est, elle est,* etc.

(c) The difference between a and b

(d) Some exceptions

252   (iii) The complement is neither an adjective nor a noun or pronoun:

(a) The referent is a person or thing

(b) The referent is *ceci* or *cela*, a noun phrase introduced by *ce qui*, etc., or the name of a place

II.   *C'est* or impersonal *il est*?

253   (i) The complement is an adjective

254   (ii) With reference to the time of day

255   (iii) The complement is a noun or pronoun

256   (iv) The complement is an indirect object, adverb, adverbial phrase, prepositional phrase, or verb phrase

257 *Ce doit être, ce peut être*, etc.

III. *C'est* or *est?*

258 *C'est* is compulsory

259 *C'est* is preferred to *est*

260 Free choice between *c'est* and *est*

261 *C'est* + *que de* + infinitive

I. C'est *or personal* il est, elle est, *etc.?*

250 (i) **The complement is an adjective**
(a) The referent is a person:
Use *il est, elle est*, etc., e.g.:

1 *Je connais sa fille. Elle est très jolie*
   I know his daughter. She is very pretty

2 *Si mon frère arrive, il sera content de vous voir*
   If my brother arrives, he will be pleased to see you

3 *Jean ne vient pas. Il est malade*
   John isn't coming. He's ill

(b) The referent is a thing – either *c'est* or *il est, elle est*, etc., is possible, but with a difference in meaning. Generally speaking, if *il est, elle est*, etc., are used, then the adjective relates strictly to the referent, whereas, if *c'est* is used, the adjective has a somewhat wider application, referring for example, as the following examples will show, to the context of the referent as well as to the referent itself, or to the referent in a general rather than in a specific sense, or to what is implied by the referent:

4 *Est-ce que cette robe vous plaît – Oui, elle est très jolie*
5 *Est-ce que cette robe vous plaît? – Oui, c'est très joli*

Both of these could be translated 'Do you like this dress? – Yes, it is very pretty', but whereas, in 4, *elle est très jolie* refers only to the dress itself, there is an implication in 5, *c'est très joli*, that the general effect is pretty (the meaning borders on something like 'It looks very pretty on you').

6 *Regardez cette table! Elle est affreuse!*
7 *Regardez cette table! C'est affreux!*

Both 6 and 7 mean 'Look at that table! It's awful!', but 6 refers rather to the table itself as a piece of furniture and 7 to the table and whatever is on it, the way it is laid or decorated, etc.

  8 *Voulez-vous du cognac? Il est très bon*
    Would you like some cognac? It's very good

  9 *Voulez-vous du cognac? C'est très bon pour la digestion*
    Would you like some cognac? It's very good for the digestion

In 8, the reference is to the quality of the particular cognac that is being offered; in 9, to a quality attributed to cognac in general.

  10 *Elle est belle, la neige!*
     The snow is beautiful!

  11 *C'est beau, la neige!*
     Snow is beautiful!

In 10, the speaker is commenting on the snow that is on the ground, or falling, as he speaks and that he can see; in 11, to snow in general (and note the use of the English definite article 'the' in 10 but not in 11).

  12 *Je comprends votre idée. Elle est très simple*
     I understand your idea. It is very simple

  13 *J'ai une idée. C'est très simple*
     I have an idea. It is very simple

12 means specifically that the idea itself is simple; 13 has rather the meaning of 'what I have in mind is simple'.

  14 *J'aime ce livre. Il est très beau*
     I like this book. It's very handsome

  15 *Je n'aime pas ce livre. C'est trop triste*
     I don't like this book. It's too sad

Whereas 14 refers to the physical appearance of the book, 15 refers to its contents.

  16 *C'est important, les traditions*
     Traditions are important

refers by implication to all that traditions represent.

(c) The referent is an unspecified object (as in sentence 17 below), or a 'neuter' pronoun such as *cela (ça), ce (qui, que, dont),* or *le,* or a clause introduced by *comme,* or an adverbial expression of place or the name of a locality (in which case the explanation of the use of *ce* is similar to that given for sentence 15 above), or a phrase including a numeral (including *un*) (and this list is not necessarily complete), e.g.:

17 *Attention! C'est lourd!*   Careful! It's heavy!

In 17, the speaker and his hearer(s) know of course what it is that is heavy (e.g. a rock, a box, a piece of furniture) but the speaker has not specifically mentioned it, hence the use of *ce.*

18 *Ne buvez pas ça! C'est trop fort*
   Don't drink that! It's too strong

19 *C'est vrai, ça!*
   That's true

20 *C'est inquiétant ce que vous dites*
   What you say is worrying

21 *Elle le croit mais ce n'est pas vrai*
   She believes it but it isn't true

22 *C'est incroyable comme on oublie*
   It's unbelievable how one forgets

23 *C'est charmant ici*
   It's delightful here

24 *C'est beau, la Provence*
   Provence is beautiful

In 24, the reference is to all that is conjured up by the name of Provence.

25 *C'est long, une heure!*
   It's a long time, an hour!

26 *Vingt francs, c'est très cher*
   Twenty francs is very expensive

In 26, note that English uses a singular not a plural verb after 'twenty francs' – a further indication that the adjective refers not so much to the nominal referent as to what is implied by it.

251 (ii) The complement is a noun or pronoun
(a) The general rule is that one uses *c'est* when the complement

is introduced by a determiner (article, possessive or demonstrative) or when it is a pronoun such as *un, celui, quelqu'un*, e.g.:

> *C'est un médecin*
> He is a doctor

> *C'est l'ami dont je vous parlais*
> He is the friend I was telling you about

> *Je connais cette étudiante; c'est ma cousine*
> I know that student; she's my cousin

> *Qui est ce monsieur? – C'est celui qui vous a écrit*
> Who is that gentleman? – He's the man who wrote to you

> *C'était quelqu'un d'important*
> He was someone important

(b) With nouns indicating a long-term state in life, such as nationality, profession or family status, it is possible to use *il est, elle est*, etc., with no article before the complement, e.g.:

Il est médecin	He is a doctor
Elle est étudiante	She is a student
Elle est Américaine	She is an American
Il est grand-père	He is a grandfather

(c) The distinction between types a and b above is basically that in type b (*Il est médecin*) the noun has a primarily adjectival function, it serves only to characterize the person, e.g.:

> *Puis-je présenter mon mari? Il est médecin*
> May I introduce my husband? He is a doctor

whereas, once any other idea is introduced, type a (*C'est un médecin*) is likely to be used, e.g.:

> *Mon mari n'aime pas qu'on fume. C'est un médecin*
> My husband doesn't like people to smoke. He's a doctor

> *Elle fait beaucoup de gestes lorsqu'elle parle. Après tout, c'est une Italienne*
> She makes a lot of gestures when she speaks. After all, she's an Italian

Consequently, type a must be used whenever the noun is qualified, e.g.:

C'est un excellent médecin
He is an excellent doctor

C'est un étudiant qui travaille bien
He is a student who works well

(d) In spite of a and b above, the construction *il est, elle est* + complement introduced by a determiner sometimes occurs, e.g. when the subject pronoun is strengthened by a disjunctive pronoun, e.g.:

Elle, elle était une petite veuve de trente-trois ans (Courteline)
She was a little thirty-three-year-old widow

or when the uniqueness of the complement is stressed, e.g.:

Elle est la reine   She *is* the Queen
Après tout, il est mon père   After all, he *is* my father

But such nuances are delicate and difficult to define and, in general, it is advisable to follow the rules set out in a and b above.

252 (iii) **The complement is neither an adjective nor a noun or pronoun**
(a) The referent is a person or a thing expressed by a noun or pronoun – use *il est, elle est,* etc., e.g.:

Où est votre frère? – Il est en France
Where is your brother? – He is in France

Où est mon dictionnaire? – Il est sur la table
Where is my dictionary? – It is on the table

A qui est cette voiture? – Elle est à moi
Whose is this car? – It's mine

Si vous cherchez le chat, il est dans le jardin
If you are looking for the cat, he (it) is in the garden

Je ne comprends pas cettre lettre. Elle est en allemand
I don't understand this letter. It's in German

(b) The referent is *ceci* or *cela (ça)*, or a noun phrase introduced by *ce qui*, etc., or the name of a place, or the idea contained in a preceding clause – use *c'est*, e.g.:

Ça, c'est à voir
That remains to be seen

Je ne comprends pas ce qu'il a écrit. C'est en allemand
I don't understand what he has written. It's in German

Où est Neuchâtel? C'est en Suisse
Where is Neuchâtel? It is in Switzerland

J'aime jouer aux échecs. C'est très intéressant
I like playing chess. It's very interesting

II. C'est *or impersonal* il est*?*

253 (i) **The complement is an adjective** (see also end of this section)
When the referent has already been expressed, i.e. when the adjective refers *back* to it, *c'est* must be used, but when the referent follows, i.e. when the adjective refers *forward* to it, *il est* is used (but see below), e.g.:

1 *Pourquoi est-il parti? – Je ne sais pas; c'est difficile à comprendre*
   Why has he left? – I don't know; it's difficult to understand

2 *Il est difficile de comprendre pourquoi il est parti*
   It is difficult to understand why he has left

3 *C'est lui qui l'a cassé – Oui, c'est évident*
   It is he who broke it. – Yes, it's obvious

4 *Il est évident que c'est lui qui l'a cassé*
   It is obvious that it was he who broke it

In 1 and 3, the adjectives *difficile* and *évident* refer *back* to what is difficult to understand (viz. his departure) or obvious (the fact that he broke the window) and so *c'est* is used, but in 2 and 4 the adjectives refer *forward* to the same events and so *il est* is used.

However, in speech *c'est* is widely used instead of *il est* with reference forward (e.g. *C'est difficile de comprendre pourquoi il est parti*) and this is usual even in literary usage when the adjective expresses a subjective reaction or carries any kind of emphasis, e.g. *C'est curieux qu'il ne soit pas venu* 'It is strange that he has not come'.

Other adjectives with which both constructions occur include *agréable* 'pleasant', *certain, essentiel* 'essential', *étonnant* 'surprising', *facile* 'easy', *impossible, juste* 'fair', *nécessaire* 'necessary', *possible, probable, rare, regrettable, surprenant* 'surprising', *triste* 'sad', *vrai* 'true', etc.

Though these constructions occur mainly with adjectival complements, they also apply when the complement is an infinitive governed by the preposition *à*, e.g.:

> *Est-il sain et sauf? C'est à espérer*
> Is he safe and sound? It is to be hoped so
>
> *Il est à espérer qu'il est sain et sauf*
> It is to be hoped that he is safe and sound

254   (ii) **With reference to the time of day**, *il est* is used, e.g.:

Quelle heure est-il?	What time is it?
Il est trois heures et demie	It is half past three

255   (iii) **The complement is a noun or pronoun**, which may or may not be qualified by a relative clause – *c'est* must be used, e.g.:

> 1 *Qui est-ce? – C'est moi*
>   Who is it? – It's me
>
> 2 *C'est lui qui l'a fait*
>   (It's) he (who) did it
>
> 3 *C'est vous que je cherche*
>   It's you I'm looking for
>
> 4 *C'est Jean qui travaille le mieux*
>   (It's) John (who) works best
>
> 5 *Avez-vous trouvé votre livre? – Oui, c'est celui-ci*
>   Have you found your book? – Yes, it's this one

If the complement is a plural noun or pronoun, then, in the literary language, *ce sont* is used, e.g.:

> 6 *Ce sont mes frères qui le feront*
>   (It is) my brothers (who) will do it
>
> 7 *Ce sont eux qui le feront*
>   (It is) they (who) will do it

In speech, however, *c'est* is normally used, e.g. *C'est mes frères qui le feront*, and, even in the literary language, *c'est* is always used with *nous* and *vous* even with reference to more than one person, e.g. *(C'est) nous (qui) le ferons* '(It is) we (who) will do it'. (Note that the verb of the relative clause agrees in person with the complement of the preceding clause, as in the example just given or as in *C'est moi qui l'ai dit* 'It is I who said so'.)

This construction must be used when, in English, the subject is emphasized with the value 'it is . . . who', as in '*John* is coming' (= 'It is John who is coming') and sentences 2, 4, 6 and 7 above. Likewise with the direct object, except that in English the word-order is different and the form of the personal pronoun may change, e.g.:

8 *C'est Paul qu'elle aime*
  It is Paul she loves, *or* She loves *Paul*

9 *C'est lui que je cherchais*
  It is he I was looking for, *or* I was looking for *him*

Note that *c'est* generally remains in the present tense even though the tense of the relative clause may be different, as in sentences 2, 6 and 9 above. The present tense would still be used in French even if one were translating 'It was he who did it', 'It will be my brothers who will do it', and 'It was he I was looking for'. However, sentences like *C'était lui qui chantait* 'It was he who was singing', *Ce sera Jean qui le fera* 'It will be John who will do it', are not impossible.

256 (iv) **The complement is an indirect object, an adverb or adverbial phrase, a prepositional phrase, or a verb phrase** (either a subordinate clause or a phrase based on an infinitive other than one governed by *à* – see **253**, end – or on a present participle) – *c'est . . . que . . .* must be used, e.g.:

1 *C'est à Pierre que je l'ai donné*
  It was Peter I gave it to, *or* I gave it to *Peter*

2 *C'est là qu'il habite*
  It's there (that) he lives, *or* He lives *there*

3 *C'est à Paris que nous l'avons rencontré*
  It was in Paris (that) we met him, *or* We met him in
  Paris

4 *C'est aujourd'hui qu'il va venir*
  It is today that he is coming, *or* He is coming *today*

5 *Ce n'est pas assez (que) de vous excuser: il faut vous expliquer*
It is not enough to apologize: you must explain yourself

6 *C'est avec le plus grand plaisir que je vous accompagnerai*
It is with the greatest of pleasure that I will go with you

7 *C'est parce qu'il est bête qu'il a fait ça*
It is because he is a fool that he did that

8 *C'est pour vous protéger que je l'ai dit*
It was to protect you that I said it, *or* I said it to protect you

9 *C'est après vous avoir vu que votre frère est parti*
It was after seeing you that your brother left

10 *C'est en travaillant dur que vous y arriverez*
It's by working hard that you'll get there

As in the construction discussed in **255**, *c'est . . . que . . .* serves to emphasize the complement (see all the above examples) and the tense of *c'est* generally remains unchanged (see sentences 1, 3, 7, 8, 9 and 10).

The following idioms are exceptions to what has been said above:

Il en est ainsi
It is so, that is how things are

il en est de même pour . . .
the same is true of . . .

257 (i) In all the examples given in **248–256**, the verb is *être*. Note, however, that *ce* can still be used when the modal verbs *devoir* and *pouvoir* (and occasionally *aller* and, in the conditional tense only, *savoir*) are followed by *être*, e.g.:

Ce doit être un gros problème
It must be a big problem

Ce ne peut être que lui
It can only be he

Ce pourrait être vrai
It could be true

Ç'allait être difficile
It was going to be difficult

Ce ne saurait être que lui
It could only be he

(Note the cedilla on ç' before the *a-* of *allait*; the same is true before the *a-* of *avoir* in compound tenses of *être*, e.g. *ç'avait été* 'it had been'.)

(ii) Note that *c'est* can be combined with other tenses in a following clause introduced by *qui* or *que*, e.g.:

Si vous faites ça, tout ce qui arrivera $\left\{ \begin{array}{c} c'est \\ or \\ ce\ sera \end{array} \right\}$ *que vous*

offenserez tout le monde

If you do that, all that will happen $\left\{ \begin{array}{c} \text{is } or \\ \text{will be} \end{array} \right\}$ that you will

offend everybody

C'est moi (or *C'était moi*) *qu'elle attendait*
It is me (*or* It was me) she was waiting for

C'est (or *Ce fut*) *Zola qui prit la défense de Dreyfus*
It was Zola who defended Dreyfus

But if *c'est* is not used, then the tense of the two verbs must be the same; in particular, avoid the trap that foreigners often fall into of beginning with *C'était* . . . and then continuing with a preterite or a perfect in the following clause.

III. C'est *or* est?

258 Note that *c'est* rather than *est* alone must be used

(i) when the complement is a personal pronoun, e.g.:

Mon meilleur ami c'est vous   My best friend is you

(ii) when the referent is singular and the complement plural (in which case *ce sont* would be preferred in literary usage, see **255**), e.g.:

Ce que je crains, c'est (or *ce sont*) *mes prétendus amis*
What I fear is (the reaction of) my so-called friends

(iii) when both referent and complement are positive infinitives, e.g.:

Voir c'est croire   Seeing is believing

Tout comprendre c'est tout pardonner
To understand all is to forgive all

(but, if the second infinitive is negative, either *c'est* or *est* may be used, e.g. *Consentir (ce) n'est pas approuver* 'To consent is not to approve').

259 *C'est*, though not absolutely compulsory, is generally used:

(i) when the referent is a clause introduced by *celui*, etc., or *ce* and a relative pronoun, or by a nominalized adjective conveying the same sense as a clause with *ce qui* (e.g. *l'essentiel* = *ce qui est essentiel*); this is particularly true whenever a superlative is involved, in which case *c'est* rather than *est* should always be used, e.g.:

> *Celui qui travaille le mieux, c'est Paul*
> The one who works best is Paul (it's Paul who works best)

> *Ce qui m'agace* ⎫
> *Ce que je déteste* ⎬ *le plus, c'est la paresse*
> What infuriates me ⎫
>   What I hate   ⎬ most is idleness

and, without a superlative:

> *Celui qui travaille bien c'est Paul*
> The one who works well is Paul

> *Ce qui m'agace, c'est* (or *est*) *sa paresse*
> What infuriates me is his idleness

However, when the complement is an element (usually an adjective) that could not function as the subject, *est* not *c'est* is used, e.g.:

> *Ce qu'il propose est tout à fait raisonnable*
> What he suggests is perfectly reasonable

(it would be impossible to turn this round and make *tout à fait raisonnable* the subject – contrast *Ce qui m'agace, c'est sa paresse* 'What infuriates me is his idleness' and *Sa paresse est ce qui m'agace* 'His idleness is what infuriates me').

(ii) when the complement is an infinitive or a clause introduced by *que*, e.g.:

> *Le problème (c')est de le persuader que tout ira bien*
> The problem is to persuade him that all will be well

> *La difficulté (c')est qu'il ne comprend rien*
> The difficulty is that he understands nothing

260 In various circumstances, there is virtually a free choice between *c'est* and *est*, e.g.:

Se moquer de lui (c')est très facile
To make fun of him is very easy

This is particularly so when the two halves of the sentence are virtually interchangeable, e.g.:

Son grand défaut (c')est la paresse
His great defect is laziness

La paresse (c')est son grand défaut
Laziness is his great defect

In such cases, the insertion of *ce* gives slightly more emphasis.

But when such a sentence is negative, it is more usual not to insert *ce*, e.g.:

Son grand défaut n'est pas la paresse, mais l'obstination
His great defect is not laziness, but obstinacy

261 In the construction *c'est* + complement + infinitive, when the infinitive is the 'logical subject' of the verb (as in 'It would be a mistake to leave' which is the equivalent of 'To leave would be a mistake'), the infinitive is introduced by *de* or *que de*, e.g.:

C'est une erreur (que) de répondre à cette lettre
It is a mistake to reply to that letter

Ce serait manquer de tact (que) de partir maintenant
It would be tactless (lacking in tact) to leave now

C'est agaçant (que) d'être mécompris
It is infuriating to be misunderstood

Relative pronouns

262 English has, on the one hand, the invariable relative pronoun 'that', and, on the other, the following which vary according to their function in the sentence *and* according to whether they refer on the one hand to people or, on the other, to things (including animals):

	referring to people	referring to things
Subject	*who*	*which*
Direct object	*whom*	*which*
Genitive (see 19)	*whose, of whom*	*of which, whose*
After prepositions	*whom*	*which*

In French, the distinction between people and things is found only after prepositions and, sometimes, in the genitive; after prepositions there is yet another form used with reference to various 'neuter' pronouns. The distinctions between the various forms are discussed in some detail below (263–275), but in summary form they are:

	referring to people	referring to things	referring to neuter pronouns
Subject	*qui*	*qui*	*qui*
Direct object	*que*	*que*	*que*
Genitive	*dont*	*dont*	*dont*
	duquel, etc. *de qui*	*duquel,* etc.	
After prepositions	*qui* *lequel,* etc.	*lequel,* etc.	*quoi*

Note in particular

(i) that *que* can never be used after a preposition (see **263, 270, 271**)

(ii) that *dont* always comes first in its clause (see **268**).

263　After prepositions, the forms are:

	referring to people
after *de*	(see **268–269**)
after *à*	*à qui*
after other prepositions	*avec qui, par qui,* etc.

	referring to things			
	masc. sing.	fem. sing.	masc. plur.	fem. plur.
after *de*	*duquel*	*de laquelle*	*desquels*	*desquelles*
after *à*	*auquel*	*à laquelle*	*auxquels*	*auxquelles*
after other prepositions	*lequel*	*laquelle*	*lesquels*	*lesquelles*

Note that *lequel*, etc. may also be used as alternatives to *qui* with reference to people (e.g. *auxquels* = *à qui*, masc. plur., *sans laquelle* = *sans qui*, fem. sing.) but *qui* is the more usual (except after *parmi*, see **270**).

264 With three important exceptions, the use of the relatives in French is much the same as in English. The exceptions are:

(i) the direct object pronoun, which is often omitted in English, must always be inserted in French (**265**)

(ii) clauses of the type 'the man I gave it to, the table you left it on' always take in French the form 'the man to whom I gave it, the table on which you left it' (**266**)

(iii) there is no French form corresponding exactly in function to the English 'whose'; forms meaning 'of whom' or 'of which' must be used (**267–268**).

265 In English, the direct object relative pronoun is very frequently omitted; this is not possible in French – the pronoun *que* must *never* be omitted, e.g.:

Connaissez-vous la jeune fille que Paul a épousée?
Do you know the girl (that) Paul married?

Voici les livres que j'ai achetés
Here are the books I bought

266 In English one can omit not only the direct object relative pronoun (see **265**) but also a relative pronoun serving as the complement of a preposition, in which case the preposition is moved to the end of the clause, e.g. 'the children for whom he bought these presents' becomes 'the children he bought these presents for'. In French, the full form 'for whom he bought . . .', must be used, e.g.:

Où est l'homme à qui j'ai donné les billets?
Where is the man I gave the tickets to?

Je connais les enfants pour qui il achète ces cadeaux
I know the children he is buying those presents for

Quelle est la table sur laquelle vous avez laissé mes livres?
Which is the table you left my books on?

267 As French has no word whose functions correspond closely to those of English 'whose', the choice of the correct equivalent can present some problems. We shall divide the relevant sentences into two types (**268** and **269**).

268 **Clauses introduced by 'whose' + noun (subject or direct object)**

(i) In these clauses, *dont* is the relative to use and the word-order is always **subject** + **verb** + **direct object**, i.e. the normal French word-order. The English practice of placing the direct object immediately after the relative 'whose' as in the second of the following examples must **not** be followed in French.

Examples:

> *Voici mon ami dont le fils vous a écrit*
> Here is my friend whose son wrote to you
>
> *Voici mon ami dont vous avez rencontré le fils*
> Here is my friend whose son you met

Note that *dont* always precedes the noun, even when the English equivalent is 'of whom' or 'of which' following the noun, e.g.:

> *Cette histoire, dont l'origine est inconnue, a eu de graves conséquences*
> This story, the origin of which is unknown, had serious consequences

Likewise with an indefinite pronoun or a numeral, e.g. *les enfants, dont plusieurs (trois) étaient malades* 'the children, several (three) of whom were ill'.

(ii) Note too the following construction (*dont . . . que*) which combines a relative clause and a noun-clause (see **13**) in a way that provides an equivalent to a very different construction in English:

> *un oncle, dont on dit qu'il serait actuellement détenu au Mexique (Le Monde)*
> an uncle who they claim is at the moment under arrest in Mexico (*literally* about whom they claim that . . .)
>
> *Elle étouffait sous un poids énorme dont elle découvrait soudain qu'elle le traînait depuis vingt ans* (Camus)
> She was weighed down by an immense burden that she suddenly discovered she had been carrying around for twenty years (about which she discovered that . . .)
>
> *un luxe dont j'imagine aujourd'hui qu'il devait être affreux* (Mauriac)
> a luxury that I imagine today must have been dreadful

This is a literary construction. In speech, or in a simpler literary style, it is more usual to treat the verb or expression of saying, thinking, etc., as a parenthesis, e.g.:

Il a écrit une pièce qui, je crois, vous surprendra (rather than
. . . *dont je crois qu'elle vous surprendra*)
He has written a play that I think will surprise you

C'est un livre que vous allez vouloir acheter, j'en suis convaincu (rather than . . . *dont je suis convaincu que vous allez vouloir l'acheter*)
It is a book that I am sure you will want to buy

Sometimes, however, this seems barely possible, e.g.:

une force dont on se demande si elle existe (*L'Express*)
a force that one wonders if it exists

une fièvre pernicieuse, dont on ne pouvait encore dire si elle était contagieuse (Camus)
a pernicious fever of which it was not yet possible to say whether it was contagious

269 Preposition + 'whose' + noun
When the noun determined by 'whose' is governed by a preposition (or prepositional phrase), *dont* cannot be used; *de qui* or *duquel*, etc., must be used instead, e.g.:

les amis avec le fils de qui je voyageais
the friends with whose son I was travelling

la tour du haut de laquelle on voit la mer
the tower from whose top (from the top of which) one can see the sea

Lequel

270 (i) The appropriate form of *lequel*, not *qui*, is used after prepositions when the antecedent is an animal, a thing or an abstract idea, e.g. *la feuille sur laquelle j'écris* 'the sheet of paper I am writing on', *les chiens avec lesquels il jouait* 'the dogs he was playing with'.

(ii) With reference to people, either *qui* or *lequel*, etc., may be used after prepositions, e.g. *les amis pour qui* (or *pour lesquels*) *j'ai acheté ces cadeaux* 'the friends for whom I bought these presents'; *qui* is the commoner of the two except after *parmi* 'among' when *lesquel(le)s* is used, e.g. *les Belges parmi lesquels nous travaillions* 'the Belgians among whom we were working'.

(iii) *Lequel* rather than *qui* should be used if any ambiguity would otherwise occur, e.g.:

Le fils de ma cousine, lequel vient d'arriver, est gravement malade
My cousin's son who has just arrived is seriously ill

(*qui vient d'arriver* could well be interpreted as meaning that it is the cousin who has just arrived).

271 *Lequel* is usually a pronoun, but it is sometimes used as a determiner, e.g.:

Voici cent francs, laquelle somme vous est due depuis long-temps
Here are a hundred francs, which sum has long been due to you

272 When two successive relative clauses have the same ante-cedent, they are linked by *et* even though 'and' is not necessary (but can be used) in English if the meaning is clear, e.g.:

Cet étudiant qui a été absent et dont l'ami vous a téléphoné vient vous voir aujourd'hui
That student who has been absent whose friend rang you is coming to see you today

273 *Quoi* is used as a relative pronoun after a preposition

(i) when the antecedent is one or other of the 'neuter' pronouns *ce* (see **274**) or *rien* 'nothing', e.g.:

Ce avec quoi j'écris, c'est une plume d'oie
What I am writing with is a goose quill

Il n'a rien de quoi se plaindre
He has nothing to complain of

(ii) when the antecedent is not a noun or pronoun but the content of a previous clause, e.g.:

Il va bientôt démissioner, après quoi tout sera changé
He is going to resign soon, after which everything will be different

Il a toujours été compréhensif, sans quoi je n'aurais pas pu continuer
He has always been understanding, without which I could not have gone on

(iii) when there is no antecedent expressed, e.g.:

Voilà en quoi je suis sûr d'avoir raison
That is a matter in which I know I am right

and particularly with *avoir* and a few other verbs + *de quoi* + infinitive, meaning 'to have (etc.) the means, the wherewithal, enough, etc., to do something', e.g.:

Il a de quoi vivre
He has enough to live on

Pourriez-vous me donner de quoi écrire?
Could you give me something to write with?

Il n'y a pas de quoi être fier
There is nothing to be proud of

Note that some writers sometimes use *quoi* instead of *lequel* when the antecedent is a noun (singular or plural) referring to a thing, e.g.:

Cette case, vers quoi convergeaient les regards de presque tous les joueurs . . . (Malraux)
This square (i.e. in a board-game) on which the gaze of nearly all the players converged . . .

Les manuscrits anciens par quoi nous connaissons la Grèce . . . (Gide)
The ancient manuscripts from which we know Greece

This usage should not be imitated.

274 When English 'what' is the equivalent of 'that which, that of which', etc., that is how it must be expressed in French. The forms are:

Subject	*ce qui*
Direct object	*ce que*
'that of which'	*ce dont*
With other prepositions	*ce à quoi, ce avec quoi*, etc.

Examples:

Ce qui m'intéresse, c'est la peinture moderne
What interests me is modern painting

Ce que vous craignez est absurde
What you fear is absurd

Ce dont ils parlent m'intéresse beaucoup
What they are talking about interests me a lot

Ce à quoi je pense ne vous regarde pas
What I am thinking about does not concern you

This construction is sometimes used in French in contexts such as the following where English uses 'what' as a determiner meaning 'that amount of . . . which':

Il ramassa ce qu'il lui restait de forces
He summoned up what strength he had left

Avec ce que j'ai d'argent je vais me débrouiller
With what money I have I shall manage

275 Note the following archaic constructions that survive *only* in the circumstances stated and must not be used otherwise:

(i) *Qui* with the value of *celui qui* in a general sense, 'he who', remains in a number of proverbs and sayings, e.g.:

Qui dort dîne
A sleep is as good as a meal (*lit.* Who sleeps dines)

Qui vivra verra
Time will tell (*lit.* Who lives will see)

Qui va lentement va sûrement
Slowly but surely

Qui s'excuse, s'accuse
To excuse oneself is to accuse oneself

(ii) *Qui* as the equivalent of *ce qui* 'what, that which' (see **274**) survives only in the three expressions:

qui mieux est	what is better
qui pis est	what is worse
qui plus est	what is more

and after *voici* and *voilà*, e.g.:

Voilà qui est intéressant
That is (something) interesting

Voici qui distingue profondément le pessimisme de Tourguen-
iev et celui de Flaubert (P. Bourget)
This is what profoundly distinguishes Turgenev's pessimism
and that of Flaubert

(iii) An even more archaic construction than those discussed in i
and ii above is the use of *que* with the value of *ce qui* or *ce que*
in the following fixed expressions:

Faites ce que bon vous semblera
Do as you think fit (*lit.* what seems good to you)

Advienne que pourra
Come what may

Coûte que coûte
At all costs (*lit.* Let it cost what it may cost)

Vaille que vaille
For what it is worth

276   *Où* 'where' is frequently used as the equivalent of a preposition like *à* 'to, at', *dans* 'in' or *sur* 'on' + *lequel*, with reference
either to place, e.g.:

l'endroit où je l'ai laissé   the place where (in which) I left it

or to time (and note that in examples such as the following, in
which 'when' may be omitted, *où* is essential in French):

le jour où il est parti   the day (when, on which) he left

Où may be preceded by a preposition, in particular *de* 'from,
out of' and *par* 'by, through' (or occasionally by others such as
jusque 'up to, as far as', *vers* 'towards'), e.g.:

la maison d'où il sortait	the house he was coming out of
la ville par où vous êtes passé	the town you came through

277   With reference to time, *où* or *que*, not *quand* (see below),
must be used in relative clauses (e.g. in phrases of the type 'the
day when . . .', 'one day when . . .', 'at the time when . . .'). No
absolute distinction can be made between *où* and *que* but the
following comments will cover most cases:

(i) if the noun is preceded by an indefinite article, use *que*, e.g.:

> *un jour qu'il pleuvait*
> one day when it was raining

(ii) when nouns like *jour* 'day', *moment, instant, temps* 'time', *époque* 'time', are preceded by a definite article, *où* is preferred, particularly with *le jour où* 'the day when' and *au moment où* 'at the time when'; with other nouns, it is usually possible to use either *où* or *que*, but note that *où* is by far the more usual in speech. Examples:

> *le jour où vous êtes arrivé*
> the day (when) you arrived

> *au moment où je partais*
> at the moment I was leaving

> *les jours où il* (or *qu'il*) *pleuvait*
> the days (when) it rained

> *du* (or *au*) *temps où* (or *que*) *nous étions étudiants*
> at the time (when) we were students

> *dès le moment où* (or *que*) *je l'ai vu*
> from the moment I saw him

(Note that *du moment que* means 'since' in the sense of 'seeing that', e.g.:

> *Du moment que vous n'y allez pas, moi je n'y vais pas non*
> *plus*
> Since you are not going, I am not going either.)

When the clause introduced by 'when' is not a relative (and the conjunction therefore cannot be omitted in English as in the examples above), the appropriate French conjunction is *quand* or *lorsque*, e.g.:

> *A cette époque-là, quand elle était étudiante, elle était souvent*
> *malade*
> At that time, when she was a student, she was often ill

Interrogative determiners and pronouns

Introduction

278 The interrogative determiners (often termed interrogative adjectives) in English are 'what?' and 'which?' used before a noun, e.g. 'what day, which book?'.

The interrogative pronouns are 'who(m)?, what? which?'.

The situation in French, as we shall see, is considerably more complicated.

Interrogative determiners

279 French has no distinction comparable to the English distinction between 'which?' and 'what?' as determiners. The forms are:

	sing.	plur.
masc.	*quel*	*quels*
fem.	*quelle*	*quelles*

These are used both in direct questions, e.g.:

Quel garçon a répondu?
Which boy replied?

Quelle réponse allez-vous donner?
What reply are you going to give?

and in indirect questions, e.g.:

Il veut savoir quelle réponse vous allez donner
He wants to know what rely you are going to give

Quel can also have an exclamatory value, i.e. 'What (a) . . . !', e.g.:

Quelle réponse!	What an answer!
Quelle merveilleuse idée!	What a marvellous idea!
Quel temps superbe!	What superb weather!
Quelles jolies fleurs!	What pretty flowers!

For *quel* as an interrogative pronoun, see **280**.

Interrogative pronouns

280 All the forms of the interrogative determiner *quel* (see **279**) are also used as interrogative pronouns meaning 'which?' or 'what?', in both direct and indirect questions, but only as the subject of the verb *être* (or one of the modal verbs *devoir* and *pouvoir* followed by *être*), e.g.:

> *Quel est le chemin le plus court?*
> Which is the shortest way?
>
> *Quelles sont vos impressions?*
> What are your impressions?
>
> *Quelle peut être son idée?*
> What can his idea be?
>
> *Dites-moi quelles sont vos impressions*
> Tell me what your impressions are

Note that in sentences of this type, which could be rephrased in such a way as to treat 'which' or 'what' as a determiner (e.g. 'Which way is the shortest?', 'What idea can he have?'), *quel* (and not *que*, *qu'est-ce qui*, *quoi* etc. – see **283**) must be used.

281 'Who?' and 'whom?' (both as direct object and as the complement of a preposition) are both rendered by *qui?*, while 'whose?' is *de qui?* except in the construction 'Whose is X?', meaning 'To whom does X belong?', which is *A qui est X?*

Examples:

Direct questions

Subject	*Qui a dit ça?* Who said that?
Direct object	*Qui avez-vous vu?* Who(m) did you see?
'whose?' (with *de*)	*De qui a-t-il épousé la fille?* Whose daughter did he marry?
'whose?' (with *à*)	*A qui est cette valise?* Whose is this suitcase?
After other prepositions	*Avec qui voyage-t-il?* Who(m) is he travelling with?

Pour qui achetez-vous ce livre?
For whom are you buying that
book?

Indirect questions

Subject

*Je ne sais pas qui a cassé la
fenêtre*
I do not know who has broken the
window

Direct object

Dites-moi qui vous avez vu
Tell me who(m) you saw

After prepositions

Je ne sais pas à qui est cette valise
I don't know whose this suitcase
is

Dites-moi avec qui il voyage
Tell me who(m) he is travelling
with

Note that French uses *qui* where English uses 'which (one)'
with reference to specific individuals, e.g.:

*De votre père ou de votre mère qui serait le plus compréhen-
sif?*
Which would be the more sympathetic, your father or your
mother?

Qui de vous ou de moi partira le premier?
Which of us, you or I, will leave first?

Qui des deux?
Which of the two?

Je me demande qui d'entre elles arrivera la première
I wonder which of them will arrive first

282   The following exist, *in direct questions only*, as alternatives
to the forms given for 'who(m)' in **281** (there are no comparable
alternatives for 'whose'):

Subject	*qui est-ce qui*
Direct object	*qui est-ce que*
After preposition	*avec qui est-ce que*, etc.

These are specific instances of the general question form in *est-ce que* that is discussed in **585** and **589**. Some of the questions given as examples in **281** could also have been expressed as follows:

> *Qui est-ce qui a dit ça?*
> Who said that?
>
> *Qui est-ce que vous avez vu?*
> Who(m) did you see?
>
> *Avec qui est-ce qu'il voyage?*
> Who(m) is he travelling with?

283   In direct questions, the forms for 'what?' are:

Subject	*qu'est-ce qui*
Direct object	*que* or *qu'est-ce que*
After any preposition	*quoi*

Examples:

Subject	*Qu'est-ce qui fait ce bruit?*
	What is making that noise?
Direct object	*Qu'est-ce que vous faites?*
	Que faites-vous?
	What are you doing?
After prepositions	*De quoi parlez-vous?*
	What are you talking about?
	A quoi pensez-vous?
	What are you thinking about?
	Avec quoi écrit-il?
	What is he writing with?

Note the construction used in the last three examples, which, in English, begin with 'what' and end with a preposition. In French, a construction corresponding to the alternative but less usual English construction, 'About what are you talking?', etc., must be used.

Que and *qu'est-ce que* also serve as the complement of *être* and *devenir*, e.g.:

> *Que sera-t-il?*
> What will he be?

Qu'est-ce que c'était?
What was it?

Qu'est-ce qu'il est devenu ensuite?
What did he become next?

Que deviendrai-je?
What will become of me? (*lit.* What shall I become?)

Qu'est-il devenu?
What has become of him? (*lit.* What has he become?)

Qu'est-ce que . . .? and (particularly in speech) *Qu'est-ce que c'est que . . .?* are used without a following verb in contexts such as the following to mean 'What is . . .?' or 'What are . . .?':

Qu'est-ce que la vérité?
What is truth?

Qu'est-ce que c'est qu'une alêne?
What is an awl?

Qu'est-ce que c'est que ces petits trous?
What are these little holes?

The latter form often has an exclamatory value, e.g.:

Qu'est-ce que c'est que ce chapeau-là!
What on earth is that hat you're wearing!

284 *Quoi* occurs as the direct object of a verb in the following circumstances:

(i) for emphasis, when asking for confirmation of what has been said, e.g.:

J'ai perdu le magnétoscope. – Tu as perdu quoi?
I've lost the video-recorder. – You've lost what?

Il va devenir prêtre. – Il va devenir quoi?
He's going to become a priest. – He's going to become what?

(In conversational usage, this has become a normal, unemphatic, way of asking a question, so *Tu as perdu quoi? = Qu'as-tu perdu?* or *Qu'est-ce que tu as perdu?* 'What have you lost?')

(ii) with the infinitive of certain common verbs such as *dire*, *faire*, *répondre*, particularly to express hesitation or uncertainty, e.g.:

Quoi dire?   What can one say?

(Note that 'what?' as the object of an infinitive is usually *que*, e.g. *Que dire?*)

(iii) in the expression *pour quoi faire* 'for what purpose, etc.', e.g.:

Je vais à Londres demain. – Pour quoi faire?
I'm going to London tomorrow. – What for?

285 *Quoi* is used without a verb:

(i) with *de* and an adjective, e.g.:

Quoi de neuf? Quoi de nouveau?
What news?

Quoi de plus simple?
What could be easier?

(ii) on its own or with an adverb, particularly as an exclamation or other expression of surprise, e.g.:

Quoi! Il est déjà parti?!
What! He's gone already?!

J'ai fait quelque chose de stupide. – Quoi donc?
I've done something stupid. – What?

Quoi encore!
What next!

Il est fou ou quoi?
Is he crazy or what?

Quoi? (but *Comment?* is a more polite form)
What (did you say)?

286 Two different constructions are possible with the verbs *arriver* and *se passer* 'to happen', viz.:

(i) 'What?' may be treated as the subject, so:

Qu'est-ce qui arrive?
Qu'est-ce qui se passe? } What is happening?

(ii) the verbs may be treated as impersonal, with impersonal *il* as subject (as in *Il est arrivé un accident* 'There has been an accident'), in which case 'What?' is treated as the complement, viz.:

Qu'arrive-t-il?
Que se passe-t-il? } What is happening?

287 At this point it may help if we summarize the forms **most generally used** for 'who(m)?' and 'what?', i.e. excluding forms for 'whose?' (see **281**) and various restricted uses of *quoi* (see **284** and **285**); we use *avec* to represent any preposition:

(i) 'Who? Whom?'

	short forms	long forms
Subject	*qui*	*qui est-ce qui*
Direct object	*qui*	*qui est-ce que*
After prepositions	*avec qui*	*avec qui est-ce que*

(ii) 'What?'

	short forms	long forms
Subject	—	*qu'est-ce qui*
Direct object	*que*	*qu'est-ce que*
After prepositions	*avec quoi*	*avec quoi est-ce que*

Note:

(a) that there is no short form for 'what?' as subject

(b) that the long forms for 'who(m)' all begin with *qui* and those for 'what?' with *que*

(c) that the long forms for the subject end in the subject relative pronoun *qui* and that those for the direct object end in the direct object relative pronoun *que*.

288 The forms for 'what' in indirect questions are:

Subject	*ce qui*
Direct object	*ce que*
After prepositions	*quoi (à quoi, de quoi, avec quoi*, etc.)*

Examples:

Subject	*Dites-moi ce qui vous inquiète*
	Tell me what is worrying you

Direct object	*Je me demande ce qu'il va faire*
	I wonder what he is going to do

After prepositions

Dites-moi de quoi vous parliez
Tell me what you were talking about

On ne sait jamais à quoi il pense
One never knows what he is
thinking about

*Savez-vous avec quoi il a ouvert la
boîte?*
Do you know what he opened the
box with?

Ce que is also the complement of the verbs *être* and *devenir* (cf. the use of *que* with these verbs in direct questions, **283**), e.g.:

Je me demande ce qu'elle est maintenant
I wonder what she is now

Savez-vous ce qu'il est devenu?
Do you know what he became (*or* what became of him)?

289   As the object of an infinitive in indirect questions, 'what' is not *ce que* but *que* or sometimes (especially in speech) *quoi* (cf. the use of *quoi* in direct questions, **284**,ii), e.g.:

Si j'avais su que (or *quoi*) *répondre*
If I had known what to reply

Il ne sait plus que (or *quoi*) *dire*
He no longer knows what to say

Note that *je ne sais*, etc. (i.e. without *pas* – see **561**,b), being characteristic of literary usage, takes *que*, whereas the more colloquial form *je ne sais pas* tends to take *quoi*, e.g.:

Je ne sais que faire/dire ⎱ I don't know what to do/to say
Je ne sais pas quoi faire/dire ⎰

290   The forms for 'which?' as a pronoun (and note that, as pronouns, there *is* a distinction between 'what?' and 'which?' – contrast **279**), both in direct and in indirect questions, are:

	masc. sing.	fem. sing.	masc. plur.	fem. plur.
Subject ⎱	*lequel*	*laquelle*	*lesquels*	*lesquelles*
Direct object ⎰				
With *de*	*duquel*	*de laquelle*	*desquels*	*desquelles*
With *à*	*auquel*	*à laquelle*	*auxquels*	*auxquelles*

Note that, though these forms are made up of the definite article and *quel*, etc., the two parts cannot be separated, even when combined with *à* or *de* (as in *auxquels*, *duquel*, etc.).

Examples:

Laquelle de ces maisons préférez-vous?
Which of these houses do you prefer?

Je viens de rencontrer ton cousin. – Lequel?
I have just met your cousin. – Which one?

Je ne sais plus dans laquelle de ces boîtes je l'ai caché
I can't remember in which of these boxes I hid it

Savez-vous auquel de ses frères il a écrit?
Do you know which of his brothers he has written to?

Note that in English 'which?' can be either singular or plural and so, unless accompanied by 'one' or 'ones', could sometimes be ambiguous. There is no such ambiguity in French, e.g.:

Lequel de ces livres avez-vous lu?
Which (*singular*) of these books have you read?

Lesquels de ces livres avez-vous lus?
Which (*plural*) of these books have you read?

Indefinite adjectives, adverbs, determiners and pronouns

291 The various so-called 'indefinites' are grouped together here primarily for convenience. As will be seen below, they function in many different ways. Consequently, many of them could have been, and in some cases are, discussed under other headings (see cross-references). In particular, quantifiers and negatives are discussed separately (see **320–337** and **542–558** respectively).

292 *Autre(s)*

(i) *Autre* 'other', plural *autres*, is used both as an adjective and as a pronoun:

(a) As an adjective, it is normally preceded by a determiner, e.g. *l'autre jour* 'the other day', *une autre difficulté* 'another difficulty', *cet autre problème* 'this other problem', *nos autres amis* 'our other friends', *toute autre solution* 'any other solution'.

Relics of an earlier state of affairs when a determiner was not essential are found in *autre chose* 'something else, anything else', *autre part* 'elsewhere', and in the proverb *autres temps autres mœurs* 'other times other manners (*or* customs) (i.e. times change and manners with them)'.

(b) As a pronoun, *autre* is usually preceded by a determiner or a quantifier, e.g.:

J'ai perdu ma clef; en avez-vous une autre?
I have lost my key; have you another?

Les autres arrivent demain
The others are arriving tomorrow

J'en ai beaucoup d'autres
I have plenty of others

Note that 'others' (meaning 'some others') is *d'autres*, e.g.:

Certains sont déjà arrivés; d'autres arriveront demain
Some have already arrived; others will arrive tomorrow

This is in accordance with the rule that *de* replaces *des* when a plural noun is preceded by an adjective, e.g. *de jolies fleurs* 'pretty flowers' (see **44**), *d'autres* being here the equivalent of *d'autres personnes* (cf. *d'autres préoccupations* 'other anxieties'); this applies even after *bien* meaning 'many' (see **325**), e.g. *Bien d'autres seront d'accord* 'Many others will agree'.

Relics of *autre* without a preceding determiner or quantifier exist in such fixed expressions as *de temps à autre* 'from time to time' and *entre autres* 'among others, *inter alia*'.

(ii) The expressions *l'un(e) l'autre* (with reference to two individuals only) and *les un(e)s les autres* (when more than two individuals are involved) correspond to 'each other, one another'. The gender and number of each component are determined by the nouns they stand for, and both parts must be of the same number, i.e. both singular or plural, e.g.:

(a) *Ils se regardent l'un l'autre avec hostilité*
(b) *Ils se regardent les uns les autres avec hostilité*
They look at one another in a hostile manner

(the difference is that in (a) there is only one individual on each side whereas in (b) there are several); similarly in the feminine,

Elles se regardent l'une l'autre and *Elles se regardent les unes les autres*.

Note that the reflexive pronoun (see **199**) on its own is often fully adequate to convey the meaning 'one another' provided there is no ambiguity, e.g. *Ils se détestent* 'They hate one another' (provided it is quite clear that the meaning is not 'They hate themselves').

When the meaning is 'to one another' the construction is:

Elles se racontent des histoires l'une à l'autre
Elles se racontent des histoires les unes aux autres
They tell one another stories

– here too the reflexive pronoun alone would be sufficient (*Elles se racontent des histoires*) provided no ambiguity would arise.

When the meaning is 'of, about one another' the construction is:

Ils disaient toujours du mal l'un de l'autre
Ils disaient toujours du mal les uns des autres
They always spoke ill of one another

– note that, in this case, a reflexive pronoun cannot be used and the expression *l'un(e) de l'autre* (or its plural equivalent) is therefore essential.

Other prepositions may also be introduced into the expression, e.g. *Ils sont faits l'un pour l'autre* 'They are made for one another', *l'un après l'autre* or *les uns après les autres* 'one after another'.

(iii) Note the construction *les uns . . . les autres* 'some . . . others' which, though superficially similar to that discussed in ii above, is in reality quite different, e.g.:

Les uns sont arrivés hier, les autres arriveront demain
Some arrived yesterday, the others (the rest) will arrive tomorrow

The difference between *les autres* and *d'autres* (see i above), both meaning 'others', is that *les autres* means '(all) (the) others' whereas *d'autres* means '(some) others'.

(iv) Another superficially similar construction is found in *l'un(e) et l'autre* 'either, both', *l'un(e) ou l'autre* 'either', *ni l'un(e) ni l'autre* 'neither', with or without a following noun, e.g.:

Je les connais l'un(e) et l'autre
I know them both (both of them)

l'un ou l'autre parti
either party

Quelle robe as-tu achetée? – Ni l'une ni l'autre
Which dress did you buy? – Neither

Je n'accepte ni l'une ni l'autre solution
I do not accept either solution

When these are the subject of the verb, the verb may in most circumstances be either singular (which implies that each entity is considered separately from the other) or plural (which implies that the two entities are being considered together, as a group). The plural is more usual, especially with *l'un et l'autre*, e.g.:

L'une et (or *ou*) *l'autre solution sont acceptables* (or *est acceptable*)
Either solution is acceptable (*or* Both solutions are acceptable)

Ni l'un ni l'autre ne viendront (or *ne viendra*)
Neither will come [but they could both have come]

but the singular should be used when the two alternatives are mutually exclusive, e.g.:

L'un ou l'autre viendra
One or other of them will come [but not both]

Ni l'un ni l'autre ne remportera le premier prix
Neither of them will win first prize [and only one of them could have done so]

(v) For *nous autres*, *vous autres*, see **216**,i.

293   *Autrui* 'others, other people'
Although *autrui* can be used as the subject or the direct object of a verb, this is uncommon and it is most frequently found as the complement of a preposition, e.g.:

Ne fais pas à autrui ce que tu ne voudrais pas qu'on te fasse
Do not do to others what you would not wish one to do to you

chercher le bien d'autrui
to seek the happiness of others

Autrui is found in literary usage only – elsewhere, use *les autres*.

'Someone else' can occasionally be translated by *autrui* when it is used in a general sense, e.g. *agir au nom d'autrui* 'to act on someone else's behalf', but note that, whenever the reference is to a specific person, *autrui* cannot be used – use *quelqu'un d'autre*, e.g.:

Je le fais pour quelqu'un d'autre
I'm doing it for somebody else

294 *Certains* 'some (people)'
Certains is a plural pronoun meaning 'some people, certain people', e.g.:

Certains disent que . . .
Some people say that . . .

Certains de ces mots sont incompréhensibles
Some of these words are incomprehensible

Certains d'entre vous vont pouvoir partir demain
Some of you are going to be able to leave tomorrow

As an adjective preceding the noun (see **146**), *un certain*, *une certaine*, plural *certains*, *certaines* (with no article), mean 'a certain (one), certain (ones)', or, in the plural, 'some', e.g.:

Un certain écrivain français a dit que . . .
A certain French writer has said that . . .

Certains jours, je ne me sens vraiment pas bien
Some days I don't feel at all well

295 *Chaque, chacun* 'each'
Chaque is a determiner, e.g. *chaque* jour 'each day', *chaque enfant* 'each child'.
Chacun, feminine *chacune*, is a pronoun, e.g.:

Chacun fera ce qu'il veut
Each (one) will do as he pleases

J'ai acheté un cadeau pour chacune de mes sœurs
I have bought a present for each of my sisters

Problems may arise when it comes to deciding which possessive determiner to use with reference to *chaque* or *chacun*. The following indications cover the vast majority of cases:

(a) When *chaque* + a noun or *chacun(e)* is the subject of the verb, the possessive is *son*, etc., e.g.:

Chaque membre du groupe a son billet et ses papiers
Each member of the group has his or her ticket and documents

This applies even when *chacun* is followed by *de nous, de vous, d'eux, d'elles*, or by *d'entre nous*, etc., or by *de* and a plural noun or pronoun (e.g. *chacun de mes amis, chacun de ceux-ci*), e.g.:

Chacun de nous a son billet
Each of us has his or her ticket

(b) When *chaque* + a noun or *chacun* is not itself the subject of the verb but refers to either *nous* or *vous* which is in fact the grammatical subject, the possessive is *notre* or *votre*, etc., e.g.:

Nous avons chacun notre billet
We each have our ticket

Vous pouvez exprimer chacun vos idées
You may each of you express your own ideas

and likewise with the imperative:

Montrez-moi chacun votre passeport
Each of you show me your passport

(c) When the subject is *ils* or *elles* or a plural noun (or, occasionally, pronoun, e.g. *ceux-ci* 'these'), the possessive may be either *son*, etc., or *leur(s)*, e.g.:

Ils ont chacun leur (or *son*) *billet*
They each have their ticket (*or* Each of them has his/her ticket)

For *chacun* with a reflexive pronoun, see 219. See also *tout*, 317.

296   *De quoi* 'the wherewithal', etc.'

For the use of *de quoi* with an infinitive, meaning 'the wherewithal, the means, etc.' to do something, see 273,iii.

297   *Différents, divers* 'various'

In the plural only, and when placed before the noun (see 146) and with no article, the adjectives *différents* and *divers* (which in this construction are more or less interchangeable) mean 'various', etc., e.g.:

en différents endroits
in various places

pour différentes raisons
for a variety of reasons

divers amis
various friends

en diverses occasions
on several occasions

Différentes (or *Diverses*) *personnes m'en ont parlé*
A number of people have spoken to me about it

298   *D'aucuns* 'some (people)'

D'aucuns, which now occurs mainly in the literary language, is an invariable pronoun (and only a pronoun) serving as an equivalent of *certains* (see **294**) or *quelques-uns* (see **306**), e.g.:

D'aucuns estiment que cela est faux
Some consider that that is untrue

299   *Je ne sais qui, quel, quand*, etc.

There is a whole series of indefinites formed with *je ne sais* and a determiner (*quel*), pronoun (*qui, quoi*), or adverb (*combien, comment, où, pourquoi, quand*) and all expressing uncertainty as to the person, object, time, place, etc., involved, e.g.:

Ils distribuaient je ne sais quel tract politique
They were distributing some political tract or other

Il a demandé à je ne sais qui ce qu'il fallait faire
He asked somebody or other what had to be done

Mon départ a été remis à je ne sais quand
My departure has been postponed till Heaven knows when

Il y a eu je ne sais combien de tués
There were I don't know how many people killed

Also *je ne sais quoi* (see **289**), *je ne sais comment, je ne sais où, je ne sais pourquoi*. Parallel constructions with *on* or another personal pronoun instead of *je* and with *Dieu sait* also occur, but much less frequently than those formed with *je ne sais*, e.g.:

Il a réussi on ne sait comment à s'évader
Somehow he managed to escape

Il est allé s'enterrer Dieu sait où
He has gone and hidden himself away somewhere

300 *Même*

Même can be either an adjective (see i and ii below) or an adverb (see iii, iv and v below):

(i) As an adjective preceding the noun and itself preceded by a determiner, *même* means 'same'; the most frequent determiner is the definite article but others, in particular the indefinite article and the demonstrative, also occur – *un(e) même* is usually best translated by 'one and the same'; note that 'as' in 'the same as' is rendered by *que*.

Examples:

Ils habitent la même ville
They live in the same town

Je ne lis pas les mêmes journaux que vous
I do not read the same newspapers as you

Ce même individu est revenu un quart d'heure plus tard
That same individual came back a quarter of an hour later

Un même mot peut avoir plusieurs sens différents
One and the same word can have several different meanings

Note the expression *en même temps* 'at the same time' (e.g. *ils sont arrivés en même temps* 'they arrived at the same time', *en même temps que moi* 'at the same time as me'), and the possibility of omitting the definite article with a small number of nouns after *de*, e.g. *de même couleur* 'of the same colour', *de même espèce* 'of the same kind', *de même nationalité* 'of the same nationality', *de même origine* 'of the same origin', *de même taille* 'of the same size', *de même type* 'of the same type', but also *de la même couleur*, etc., and always *du même âge* 'of the same age'.

(ii) When it follows the noun, the adjective *même* means 'itself' (cf. the pronouns *moi-même* 'myself', etc., see **215**) or 'very, actual', e.g.:

le jour même du mariage
the very day of the wedding

Je vous cite ses paroles mêmes
I am quoting his very words

Vous êtes la générosité même
You are generosity itself

and likewise with the pronouns *celui-là*, etc. (see **238**) and with *cela*, e.g.:

Ceux-là mêmes qui me contredisent demandent mon avis
The very people who contradict me ask my opinion

Cela même est important
That (in) itself is important

(iii) As a preceding adverb, *même* means 'even', e.g.:

même maintenant
even now

même à Londres
even in London

Même moi je ne le sais pas
Even I don't know

Même mes cousins sont venus
Even my cousins came

As the lack of a plural *-s* shows, adverbial *même* is (like all adverbs) invariable.

Note that, with comparatives, 'even' must be translated by *encore* and not by *même*, e.g.:

Elle est encore plus intelligente que son père
She is even more intelligent than her father

(iv) As a following adverb, *même* has an intensifying value (similar to that of adjectival *même* following a noun or pronoun – see ii above), e.g.:

Il arrive aujourd'hui même
He is arriving *today* (this very day)

Je l'ai rencontrée ici même
It was *here* I met her (I met her in this very place)

(v) Adverbial *même* occurs in a number of idiomatic expressions:

(a) *à même*

As a prepositional phrase, *à même* means 'level with, flush with, right up against', etc., e.g. *à même la peau* 'next to one's skin', *coucher à même le sol* 'to lie on the bare ground', *boire à même la bouteille* 'to drink straight out of the bottle' (for other examples, consult a good dictionary).

Être à même de + infinitive means 'to be able to (to be in a position to) do something', e.g. *Je suis à même de vous aider* 'I am in a position to help you'; likewise, with *être* understood, *Je vous crois à même de me comprendre* (Simenon) 'I think you capable of understanding me', and the expression *mettre quelqu'un à même de faire quelque chose* 'to enable someone (put someone in a position to be able) to do something'.

(b) *de même (que)*
This occurs in a variety of contexts, with the meaning 'likewise, like, in the same way (as)', etc., e.g.:

> *Il en est* (or *va*) *de même pour vous*
> It's the same for you (The same applies to you)

> *De même que vous, j'ai répondu tout de suite*
> Like you, I replied immediately

For further examples, consult a good dictionary. Note that *tout de même* means 'nevertheless'.

(c) The compound conjunction *quand même* is used with the conditional (or the past conditional) to mean 'even if', e.g. *Quand même il m'inviterait, je refuserais d'y aller* 'Even if he invited me, I should refuse to go' (and likewise *quand même il m'aurait invité* 'even if he had invited me'). However, the most widespread use of *quand même* is to mean 'all the same, nevertheless', e.g.:

> *Il ne m'a pas invité mais j'y vais quand même*
> He hasn't invited me but I'm going all the same

(This results from a reduction of clauses introduced by the conjunction *quand même*, e.g. *Je le ferais quand même [il s'y opposerait]* 'I would do it even if [he opposed it]', i.e. 'I would do it nevertheless'.)

301   *N'importe qui*, etc.

Another set of indefinites (cf. **299**) is introduced by *n'importe* which means 'it doesn't matter (which, etc.)' and so gives the members of this set the value of 'any (one, etc.) at all', as in *n'importe qui* 'anyone (at all) (*lit.* it doesn't matter who)', *n'importe quand* 'at any time (at all) (*lit.* it doesn't matter when)', e.g.:

> *N'importe qui vous dira où il habite*
> Anyone will tell you where he lives
>
> *Vous pouvez lui donner n'importe quoi*
> You can give him anything (you like)
>
> *n'importe lequel d'entre vous*
> any one of you
>
> *à n'importe quelle heure de la soirée*
> (at) any time in the evening
>
> *Vous pouvez les laisser n'importe où*
> You can leave them anywhere

Also *n'importe combien* 'any number', *n'importe comment* 'in any way at all'.

Do not expand the above by means of a relative clause, i.e. do not use them as equivalents for *qui que ce soit qui* 'whoever', *quoi que* 'whatever', *où que* 'wherever, no matter where', etc. (see 315).

302   *On* 'one'

On, meaning 'one' (as in 'One can understand the problem' – i.e. *not* as the equivalent of the numeral 'one') or 'you' or 'they' in a general sense (i.e. not referring to a specific person or persons), is used only as the subject of the verb, e.g.:

> *On peut s'amuser même quand on est seul*
> One can enjoy oneself even when one is alone
> You can enjoy yourself even when you are alone
>
> *On dit qu'on mange mieux à Dijon*
> They say you can eat better in Dijon

(*Vous* should not be used in this general sense – but see the end of this section for its use as the object of the verb.) *On* is, however, used much more extensively than English 'one' and, in particular, is frequently found where the passive is used in English, e.g.:

> *On parle allemand en Suisse aussi*
> German is spoken in Switzerland too

On m'en a parlé hier
I was told about it yesterday

On croit qu'il va démissionner
It is believed that he is going to resign

On dit qu'il est gravement malade
He is said to be seriously ill

On is frequently used, especially in speech, as the equivalent of any personal pronoun (particularly *nous* 'we'); in such cases, the verb is always in the third person singular, but adjectives and participles agree in gender and number with the person(s) concerned, e.g.:

On est bourgeois de Gand (Hugo) = *Je suis bourgeois de Gand*
I am a burgess of Ghent

On est fatiguée? = Tu es fatiguée?
Are you (fem. sing.) tired?

On a été contents de vous voir
We (masc.) were pleased to see you

On était heureuses à cette époque
We (fem.) were happy then

In the literary language *l'on* is frequently used for *on* after a word ending in a vowel, especially monosyllables such as *et, ou, où, qui, que, si,* and occasionally at the beginning of a sentence, e.g.:

et l'on y avait construit un monument
and a monument had been built there

C'est un endroit où l'on s'ennuie
It is a place where one gets bored

ceux à qui l'on doit tant
those to whom one owes so much

Si l'on avait su!
If we had known!

L'on is not used, however, after *dont* or before a word beginning with *l-* (to avoid the alliteration *l- . . . l-*), so could not be substituted for *on* in such contexts as the following:

un roman dont on parle   a novel that is talked about

si on lit son roman	if one reads his novel
quand on l'avait vu	when we had seen him

As has been said, *on* can be used only as the subject of a verb. As reflexive pronouns relating to *on*, *se* and *soi* are used, e.g.:

On se couche tard	One goes to bed late
On le ferait pour soi(-même)	One would do it for oneself

but this is not possible when 'one' is the object pronoun in English. In such cases, the object pronoun corresponding to 'one' is *nous* or, more frequently, *vous*, e.g.:

La musique vous calme quand on est agité
Music calms one when one is upset

Il est bon de parler de ce qui vous (or *nous*) *inquiète*
It is good to talk about what worries one

But sometimes there is nothing corresponding to English 'one', e.g.:

Cela donne à penser	That makes one think

303 *Pareil* and *tel* 'such'

Pareil and *tel* can both mean 'such' but, though there is some overlap between the two, there are also significant differences both in the way they are used and, to some extent, in meaning. It will be helpful to bear in mind that, basically, *pareil* means 'similar' and *tel* means 'of such a kind'.

(i) When it means 'such', *pareil* may either precede or follow the noun, e.g. *une pareille chose* or *une chose pareille* 'such a thing'. Before the noun it is not infrequently used without a determiner, especially after a verb in the negative, e.g. *Je n'ai jamais vu pareille chose* 'I have never seen such a thing', and in certain prepositional phrases, e.g. *en pareil cas* 'in such circumstances', *en pareille occasion* 'on such an occasion', *(hier) à pareille heure* '(yesterday) at the same hour'.

After *pareil*, 'as' cannot be translated by *que* (contrast the use of *que* with *tel*, see ii,b below): use the preposition *à* (i.e. 'similar to'), e.g. *une joie pareille à la vôtre* 'joy such as yours'.

Le pareil, la pareille can be used as nouns meaning 'the like (of someone, of something), etc.', e.g. *Il n'a pas son pareil* 'There is no one like him (to equal him)', *Cette soie me plaît beaucoup;*

où pourrais-je en trouver la pareille? 'I like this silk very much; where could I find some like it?' (The use of the feminine, however, is a little old-fashioned in speech – one would be more likely to say something like *Où pourrais-je trouver la même?*)

(ii) The following comments on *tel* do not aim to cover all its uses, some of which are now rare and characteristic only of a somewhat archaic literary style; for these, one of the major dictionaries referred to in the Preface to this grammar should be consulted.

(a) *Tel* is most frequently found as an adjectve, though it occasionally functions as a pronoun (see h below). Its primary meaning, like that of its English counterpart 'such', is a neutral one, viz. 'of such a kind', e.g. *de telles circonstances* 'such circumstances'. However, again like 'such', it very frequently has an exclamatory value which can be either positive or negative (cf. English 'I have never had such a meal before', which could suggest either that the meal was an especially good one or that it was a remarkably bad one).

When it accompanies a noun, *tel* precedes the noun and, in most circumstances (but see d below), is itself preceded by the indefinite article *un(e)* (note the difference in word-order between French *un(e) tel(le)* and English 'such a') or, in the plural, by *de* (see **44**), e.g.:

un tel bruit	such a noise
une telle chose	such a thing
de tels problèmes	such problems

(b) 'Such as (= like)' followed by a noun or pronoun is *tel que* (in speech one would be more likely to use *comme*), e.g.:

un savant tel que vous (= *un savant comme vous*)
a scholar like you

des poètes romantiques tels que Lamartine et Hugo
Romantic poets like Lamartine and Hugo

The same construction serves as the equivalent of English '(just) as' introducing a clause (and, in this case, is more usual than *comme* even in speech), e.g.:

Laissez-les tels qu'ils sont!
Leave them as they are!

le problème tel que je l'envisage
the problem as I see it

Vous ne verrez jamais cette église telle qu'elle était avant la guerre
You will never see this church as it was before the war

A different use of *tel . . . que* is that in which it expresses not a comparison ('such as') but a consequence ('such that'), e.g.:

Vous faites un tel bruit que vous allez réveiller les voisins
You are making such a noise that you will wake the neighbours

Son insolence est telle qu'il me met en colère
His insolence is such that he makes me angry

(c) Like English 'such', *tel* may precede the verb *être* 'to be', e.g.:

Amuser sans offenser, tel est le but de ce roman
To amuse without offending, such is the aim of this novel

Telle est son impatience qu'il refuse d'attendre plus longtemps
Such is his impatience that he refuses to wait any longer

(d) *Tel* (without a determiner) means 'such-and-such' (i.e. it refers to some unspecified example of a particular category), e.g.:

Il fut convenu que je prendrai le train tel jour, à telle heure, pour telle gare (O. Mirbeau)
It was agreed that I shall catch such-and-such a train, at such-and-such a time, for such-and-such a station

Similarly, *tel ou tel* (or, less frequently, *tel et tel*) means 'some . . . or other' or sometimes 'such-and-such', e.g.:

telle ou telle chose
something or other

J'ai dû le lire dans tel ou tel journal
I must have read it in some newspaper or other

Il se plaint toujours de l'attitude de tel ou tel collègue
He is always complaining about the attitude of some colleague or other

(e) In literary French, *tel* is also an alternative to *comme* in such contexts as the following:

Il se tenait là tel (or *telle*) *une statue de bronze*
He stood there like a bronze statue

Note that in such contexts *tel* may agree with either term of the comparison (i.e., in this example, either with *il*, masculine, or with *statue*, feminine).

In a few proverbial expressions, this use of *tel* is repeated, e.g. *Tel père, tel fils* 'Like father, like son'.

(f) *Comme tel* and, after certain verbs, *pour tel*, mean 'as such', e.g.:

> *Elle n'est pas sa femme même si elle se considère comme telle*
> She is not his wife even if she considers herself as such

> *Est-ce qu'il est médecin? Il se fait passer pour tel*
> Is he a doctor? He purports to be one

Likewise *en tant que tel* 'as such' in the more restricted sense of 'in that capacity', e.g.:

> *C'est lui le ministre et en tant que tel il devrait prendre la décision*
> He is the minister and, as such, he ought to take the decision

(g) Note the expression *tel quel* . . . 'as it is (was), as they are (were), etc.', in which both *tel* and *quel* agree with the noun or pronoun they refer to, e.g.:

> *Il a acheté la maison telle quelle*
> He bought the house as it was

> *Je vais le prendre tel quel*
> I shall take it as it is

> *Il faut laisser les choses telles quelles*
> Things must be left as they are

(h) The use of *tel* as a pronoun is largely confined to the literary language; note in particular such usages as the following (the last of which occurs only in proverbial expressions):

> *Si tel ou tel vous promet cela, faites attention* (cf. d above)
> If someone or other promises you that, take care

> *Tel consent à être trompé pourvu qu'on le lui dise, tel autre pourvu qu'on le lui cache* (Proust)
> Some agree to be deceived provided they are told, others provided it is concealed from them

> *Tel qui rit vendredi, dimanche pleurera*
> He who laughs on Friday will weep on Sunday

(iii) When 'such (a)' means no more than 'of this kind', it is often best translated by *de ce genre, de cette sorte*, e.g.:

J'ai chez moi un instrument de cette sorte
I have such an instrument at home

Il a écrit beaucoup de livres de ce genre
He has written many such books

(iv) 'Such (a)' with reference to adjectives is *si* or (particularly in speech) *tellement*, e.g.:

une si belle vue
such a beautiful view

une ville tellement historique
such an historic town

*des problèmes si (*or *tellement) difficiles*
such difficult problems

(v) When 'such' refers to quantity (= 'so much'), it is often best translated by *tant de* or *tellement de*, e.g.:

*Nous avons eu tant (*or *tellement) de difficulté*
We have had such difficulty

Il faisait tant de bruit
He was making such a noise

(but the difference in meaning between these sentences and . . . *une telle difficulté*, . . . *un tel bruit*, which characterize the difficulty and the noise in terms of quality – i.e. their intensity – rather than in terms of quantity, is only slight).

304 *Quelconque* 'some or other, any (one) at all'

Quelconque normally follows a noun introduced by an indefinite article, e.g.:

sous un prétexte quelconque
on some pretext or other

Soient deux droites quelconques
Let there be any two straight lines

(Note that *quelconque* has acquired the meaning of 'mediocre, poor' in such contexts as *C'est un vin quelconque*' 'It's a pretty ordinary sort of wine', *Ce film est tout à fait quelconque* 'This film isn't up to much'.)

305 The following indefinites (which will be discussed in the order given here) must be clearly distinguished as they are not in any way interchangeable:

(i) *quelque, quelques* (determiner) 'some' (see **306**)

(ii) *quelque* (invariable adverb) + numeral 'some, approximately' (see **307**)

(iii) *quel que* (variable) + *être* + noun or pronoun 'whatever (= of whatever kind)' (see **308**)

(iv) *quelque(s)* + noun + relative clause 'whatever (+ noun)' (see **309**)

(v) *quelque* (invariable adverb) + adjective + *que* 'however (+ adjective)' (see **310**).

306 *Quelque, quelques* 'some, a few'

Quelque(s) is an indefinite determiner whose meaning in the plural does not differ much from that of the indefinite or partitive article *des*, e.g.:

Nous avons eu quelque difficulté
We had some difficulty

Quelque imbécile m'a cassé les lunettes
Some idiot has broken my glasses for me

Je lui ai acheté quelques fleurs
I bought her some (a few) flowers

In questions or after *si* 'if', *quelque(s)* is sometimes translatable by 'any', e.g. *Avez-vous eu quelque difficulté?* 'Did you have any difficulty?', *Si vous avez quelque difficulté . . .* 'If you have any difficulty . . .'

Note *quelques-uns* (fem. *unes*) as a plural pronoun 'some, a few', e.g.:

Quelques-uns de mes amis sont venus
Some of my friends came

Vous avez perdu toutes vos photos? – Non, mais j'en ai perdu quelques-unes
Have you lost all your photos? – No, but I've lost some (a few) of them

See also *quelque chose* 'something' (**311**) and *quelqu'un* 'someone' (**312**).

307   *Quelque* (adverb) 'some, approximately, about'

Note that *quelque* before a numeral and meaning 'some, approximately, about, roughly' is an adverb and therefore invariable (i.e. it does *not* take a plural *-s*), e.g.:

J'ai acheté quelque deux cent cinquante timbres
I bought about 250 stamps

Il est mort il y a quelque cinquante ans
He did some fifty years ago

308   *Quel que* (variable) 'whatever (= of whatever kind)'

The equivalent of English 'whatever' + 'to be' + a noun or pronoun is *not* the pronoun *quoi que* (see **315**,ii) but *quel que* (in which *quel* agrees in gender and number with the noun or pronoun); the reason for the use of *quel que* rather than *quoi que* is that, in an expression such as 'whatever the difficulty may be', we are not really dealing with 'what' it is (a difficulty is a difficulty) but with 'what kind of' difficulty it is. Note too that the verb 'to be', which is regularly omitted in this construction in English ('whatever the difficulty' means the same thing as 'whatever the difficulty may be'), *must* be inserted (in the subjunctive) in French, e.g.:

quelle que soit la difficulté
whatever the difficulty

quelles que soient vos inquiétudes
whatever your worries (may be)

tous vos problèmes, quels qu'ils soient
all your problems, whatever they may be

Être in this construction may be preceded by *devoir* or *pouvoir*, e.g.:

quel que doive être le prix de cette noble liberté
(Montesquieu)
whatever the cost of this noble freedom may be

quel qu'il puisse être
whatever he may be

309   *Quelque(s)* (determiner) + noun + relative clause 'whatever'

'Whatever' (in the sense of 'whichever') before a noun qualified by a relative clause is *quelque* (sing.), *quelques* (plur.) (note that *quel-* does not vary for gender or number); the relative clause is almost always introduced by *que*, but a *qui*-clause is not impossible, e.g.:

> *quelques fautes que vous ayez commises*
> whatever mistakes you may have made

> *de quelque manière que l'on aborde ce problème*
> in whatever (whichever) way one approaches this problem

> *quelque lien qui pût nous unir* (Musset)
> whatever bond united us

310 *Quelque* (adverb) + adjective 'however'

(i) *Quelque* 'however', modifying an adjective + *que* and the subjunctive, is an adverb and is therefore invariable, e.g.:

> *quelque riches qu'ils soient*
> however rich they are

> *quelque grands que soient vos défauts*
> however great your faults (may be)

Note:

(a) that if the subject is a noun it follows the verb, as in the example just quoted

(b) that, though the verb is sometimes omitted in English when the subject is a noun (see the translation of the last example above), this is not possible in French (cf. **308**)

(c) that the verb is in most cases *être* but that the construction is also possible with such verbs as *sembler* 'to seem' and *paraître* 'to appear', and that any of these verbs may be preceded by a modal verb such as *devoir* or *pouvoir*, e.g.:

> *quelque difficile que cela puisse paraître*
> however difficult that may appear

This is primarily a literary construction. In speech, one of the following alternatives should be used:

> *si riche que soit mon père*
> *tout riche que soit mon père* ⎫ however rich my father
> *pour riche que soit mon père* ⎬ may be
> *aussi riche que soit mon père* ⎭

(The construction with *aussi* is sometimes frowned on, but it has been used by good modern writers.)

Tout may also be followed by the indicative, but with a slight difference in meaning in that the construction in question presents the situation as a fact, e.g. *tout riche qu'est mon père* 'rich though my father is'.

When the subject is a personal pronoun, an even greater range of constructions is available since, with *si* and *aussi*, the *que* may be omitted, in which case the pronoun subject follows the verb; we therefore have, for 'however rich he is' (and not including *tout riche qu'il est* 'rich though he is'), at least seven possibilities, viz.:

quelque riche qu'il soit
si riche qu'il soit   *si riche soit-il*
tout riche qu'il soit
pour riche qu'il soit
aussi riche qu'il soit   *aussi riche soit-il*

(What is more, the constructions *quelque riche soit-il, tout riche soit-il* and *pour riche soit-il* do occur, but only infrequently and should therefore be avoided.)

(ii) A similar but much less frequent construction is that in which *quelque* modifies another adverb, e.g. *quelque profondément que vous l'aimiez* 'however deeply you love her'. The most usual alternative in speech is *si*, e.g. *si profondément que vous l'aimiez*. However, *pour* is firmly established in the expression *pour peu que* 'however little, if in the slightest, etc.', e.g. *Pour peu que tu y réfléchisses, tu comprendras ce que cela veut dire* 'If you just think about it, you'll understand what it means'.

311   *Quelque chose* 'something'

Note that, though *la chose* 'thing' is feminine, *quelque chose* is masculine.

Note too that, with adjectives, we have the construction *quelque chose d'intéressant* 'something interesting' (see **667**,i) (but *autre chose* 'something else').

In questions or after *si* 'if', *quelque chose* may correspond to English 'anything' (see also **319**), e.g.:

Avez-vous quelque chose à déclarer?
Have you anything to declare?

s'il arrive quelque chose
if anything happens

312   *Quelqu'un* 'someone, somebody'

Quelqu'un is used in much the same way as its English counter-parts 'someone, somebody', e.g.:

Quelqu'un vous demande
Someone is asking for you

Je connais quelqu'un qui peut le faire
I know someone who can do it

Note with adjectives the construction with *de* (see **667**,i), e.g. *quelqu'un d'important* 'someone important', *quelqu'un d'autre* 'someone else'.

In questions or after *si* 'if', *quelqu'un* may correspond to English 'anyone' (see also **319**), e.g.:

Avez-vous vu quelqu'un?	Did you see anybody?
Il y a quelqu'un?	Anybody there?
si quelqu'un vient	if anyone comes

313   *Quiconque* 'whoever, anyone (who)'

Quiconque may be used as an indefinite relative pronoun meaning 'whoever, anyone who', in which case it can function at the same time as the direct or indirect object of one verb and the subject of another (see the second and third examples below), e.g.:

Quiconque a dit cela doit être fou
Whoever said that must be mad

La loi punit quiconque est coupable
The law punishes anyone who is guilty

Ils vont vendre leurs services à quiconque veut les employer
(Voltaire)
They will go and sell their services to anyone who will employ them

314   *Qui . . . qui . . .* 'some . . . some . . .'

Qui, repeated and with no verb, has a distributive value meaning 'some (did this), some (did that)' e.g.:

Les clients de l'hotel prenaient, qui du thé, qui du porto, qui un cocktail, qui un whisky au soda (P. Bourget)

Some of the hotel's guests took tea, some took port, some a cocktail, some a whisky and soda

Note that, though we have translated *qui . . . qui . . .* as 'some . . . some . . .', in fact, since *qui* does not vary for number, this construction does not specify whether each *qui* refers to only one or to more than one individual.

315 *Qui que (ce soit)* 'whoever', *quoi que (ce soit)* 'whatever', *où que* 'wherever', etc.

(i) 'Whoever'

(a) The form *qui que* remains only as the complement of *être*, e.g.:

qui que vous soyez	whoever you are
qui que ce soit	whoever it is

(b) As subject of the verb, the form *qui que ce soit qui* must be used, e.g. *qui que ce soit qui ait dit cela* 'whoever said that' (see also d below)

(c) As direct object, though the form *qui que* is still given in some grammars (e.g. *qui que vous cherchiez* 'whoever you are looking for'), in practice only *qui que ce soit que* is now in current use, e.g. *qui que ce soit que vous cherchiez* (see also d below).

(d) The constructions given in b and c above, i.e. *qui que ce soit* + a relative clause introduced by *qui* or *que*, themselves function as the subject or object of another verb, e.g.:

Qui que ce soit qui vienne sera obligé de repartir tout de suite
Whoever comes will have to leave again at once

Qui que ce soit que vous rencontriez pourra vous diriger
Anyone whom (whoever) you meet will be able to direct you

Si par hasard vous rencontriez qui que ce soit qui m'ait envoyé ce livre, vous pourriez peut-être le remercier de ma part
If you happened to meet whoever it was that sent me this book, you might perhaps thank him for me

(e) After prepositions, only *qui que ce soit que* is found, e.g.:

à qui que ce soit que vous ayez écrit
whoever (it is) you wrote to

avec qui que ce soit qu'il voyage
whoever he is travelling with

(f) When not followed by a subordinate clause, *qui que ce soit* means 'anyone at all', e.g.:

si vous voyez qui que ce soit
if you see anyone at all

Ne le dites pas à qui que ce soit
Don't tell anyone

Pour le reste du chemin vous n'avez qu'à demander à qui que ce soit
For the rest of the way you have only to ask anyone

(ii) 'Whatever'

(a) *Quoi que* serves as the complement of *être*, e.g.:

quoi que ce soit   whatever it is

(Note the difference between *quoi que ce soit* and *quoi qu'il en soit* 'however that may be, be that as it may, at all events'.)

(b) As subject of the verb, only *quoi que ce soit qui* is in current use (*quoi qui* occurs, but only very rarely and should not be copied), e.g.:

quoi que ce soit qui vous inquiète
whatever is worrying you

(c) As direct object, the most common form is *quoi que*, e.g. *quoi que vous fassiez* 'whatever you do', but *quoi que ce soit que* may also be used, e.g.:

quoi que ce soit que vous fassiez
whatever you do

Quoi que ce soit qu'on lui ait dit l'inquiète beaucoup
Whatever (it is that) he was told worries him a lot

(d) After prepositions, *quoi que ce soit que* must be used, e.g.:

sur quoi que ce soit que vous l'écriviez
whatever you write it on

(e) When not followed by a subordinate clause, *quoi que ce soit* means 'anything at all', e.g.:

Vous pouvez dire quoi que ce soit
You can say anything (at all)

si vous le soupçonnez de quoi que ce soit
if you suspect him of anything at all

(iii) 'Wherever'

(a) 'Wherever' in its strictly indefinite sense is *où que*, e.g.:

Où qu'il aille, il n'est jamais content
Wherever he goes, he is never satisfied

(b) Note, however, that, in English, 'wherever' followed by a relative clause is the equivalent of 'anywhere' or 'everywhere', and this must be expressed in French by *partout où* (literally 'everywhere where'), e.g.:

Partout où vous allez, moi je peux y aller aussi
Wherever (anywhere) you go I can go too

Vous pouvez me conduire partout où vous voudrez
You may take me wherever (anywhere) you like

(c) Note that 'somewhere' and, in questions or 'if' clauses, 'anywhere', are *quelque part*, e.g.:

Je l'ai vu quelque part
I saw him somewhere

L'avez-vous vu quelque part?
Have you seen him anywhere?

si vous le voyez quelque part
if you see him anywhere (somewhere)

Note too *n'importe où* 'anywhere at all' (see **301**).

(iv) 'Whenever'

(a) Note that there is no form based on *quand* corresponding to *où que* 'wherever'. When 'whenever' has a strictly indefinite value, i.e. that of 'at whatever time', it can be expressed by some such turn of phrase as *à quelque moment (qu'il arrive)* 'whenever (= at whatever time) (he arrives)', but in practice *quand* 'when' alone is usually adequate, e.g.:

Quand il arrivera, dites-lui de me téléphoner
Whenever he arrives, tell him to ring me

(b) Frequently, however, 'whenever' means 'each time that', in which case the French equivalent is *chaque fois que* or *toutes les fois que*, e.g.:

> *Chaque fois qu'elle va à Paris, elle achète beaucoup de vêtements*
> Whenever she goes to Paris, she buys a lot of clothes

(v) 'However'

(a) 'However' in the sense of 'in whatever way' is *de quelque façon que* or *de quelque manière que*, e.g.:

> *De quelque façon que vous vous y preniez, vous n'allez pas réussir*
> However you go about it, you won't succeed

(b) For 'however' with an adjective or an adverb (e.g. 'however difficult'), see **310**.

('However' meaning 'nevertheless' is *cependant, pourtant* or *toutefois*.)

316   *Tel* 'such'

See **303**, '*Pareil* and *tel*'.

317   *Tout* 'all, every, etc.'

(i) *Tout* may be a determiner (as in *tout enfant* 'every child') or a predeterminer (i.e. an element that comes before the determiner, as in *tous les enfants* 'all the children') (see ii below), a pronoun (see iii), a noun (see iv), or an adverb (see v).

As a determiner, predeterminer or pronoun, it has these forms:

	singular	plural
masc.	*tout*	*tous*
fem.	*toute*	*toutes*

Note that the masculine plural form, *tous*, is pronounced:

as a determiner or predeterminer	[tu]
as a pronoun	[tus]
	(except before *ceux*, see iii,b)

(ii) As a determiner or predeterminer

(a) In the singular only, *tout* 'every, any' has a meaning close to that of *chaque* 'each' (see **295**), with the slight but nevertheless real distinction that *tout* refers to 'each and every member of a group' whereas *chaque* refers to 'each member of a group considered separately', e.g.:

Tout Français serait d'accord
Every (*or* Any) Frenchman would agree

Toute ville a son histoire
Every town has its history

Entrée interdite à toute personne étrangère à l'établissement
Entry forbidden to any person (i.e. all persons) unconnected with the establishment (*or* Staff only)

(b) With the definite article or with a possessive or demonstrative determiner, *tout* means 'all (of), the whole (of)' in the singular and 'all (of) (the)' in the plural, e.g.:

tout le temps	all (of) the time, the whole time
toute la classe	all the class, the whole class
tous les membres du parti	all (of the) members of the party
tout mon temps	all (of) my time
toute cette forêt	all this forest, the whole of this forest
tous nos amis	all (of) our friends

If *tout* (singular or plural) refers to nouns of different gender, it must be repeated with each; otherwise, it need not be; e.g.:

toute son intelligence et tout son courage
all his intelligence and courage

toute son intelligence et sa détermination
all his intelligence and determination

(note the repetition of the possessive: see **224**).

Note that *tous les*, *toutes les* with reference to units of time or distance is used like English 'every' to mean 'X times per so many units', e.g.:

tous les deux jours	every other day, every two days
(une fois) tous les trois jours	(once) every three days, every third day
(deux fois) tous les six mois	(twice) every six months

toutes les vingt minutes	every twenty minutes
tous les cent mètres	every hundred metres

Note also the expression *Tous les combien?* 'How often?'

(c) With names of towns, which do not normally take an article, *tout* alone means 'all, the whole of', e.g. *tout Paris* 'all Paris' with reference either to the city itself (*J'ai visité tout Paris* 'I visited the whole of Paris') or to its inhabitants (*Tout Paris fêtait la Libération* 'The whole of Paris was celebrating the Liberation').

Note that, even if the name of the town is feminine (see 52), *tout* is invariable in the latter sense, i.e. with reference to the inhabitants (*Tout Rome était dans les rues* 'All Rome was in the streets'), but usually (though not always) agrees in gender when the reference is to the city itself (*J'ai visité toute Rome* 'I visited the whole of Rome').

(d) In the singular only, *tout(e) un(e)* means 'a whole', e.g.:

J'ai passé toute une journée à le chercher
I spent a whole day looking for it

Il y a tout un débat là-dessus
There's a whole debate going on about it

But note that *entier* 'whole, entire' is more usual with reference to concrete nouns and that, in the plural, *entier* and not *tout* (which would mean 'all') *must* be used, e.g.:

Une ville entière fut détruite
A whole (entire) town was destroyed

Des villes entières furent détruites
Whole (entire) towns were destroyed

(e) *Tout* can be used without any determiner as follows:

1. *Tout autre* 'any other'; *autre* may be either an adjective, e.g. *Toute autre réponse serait inacceptable* 'Any other reply would be unacceptable', or a pronoun, e.g. *tout autre que lui* 'anyone but he'.

2. In various fixed expressions, singular or plural, meaning 'every, all', e.g. *tout compte fait* 'all things considered', *tous feux éteints*, 'with all lights extinguished, with no lights on', *toutes proportions gardées* 'provided one keeps things in proportion', and a considerable number of prepositional expressions, e.g. *à toute allure* or *à toute vitesse* 'at full speed', *à tous égards* 'in all respects', *à toute*

heure 'at any hour', *à tout moment* 'at any moment', *à tout prix* 'at all costs', *contre toute attente* 'contrary to all expectations', *de tout cœur* 'with all one's heart', *en toutes lettres* '(written out) in full'.

Many such expressions may be written either in the singular or in the plural (the pronunciation would be the same in either case), e.g. *toute(s) sorte(s) de* 'all kinds of', *à tout venant* or *à tous venants* 'to all comers', *de tout côté* or *de tous côtés* 'on all sides', *de toute(s) façon(s)* 'anyway, at all events'.

3. After *pour*, the meaning of *tout* approximates to that of *seul* 'only' in contexts such as:

> *Pour toute réponse il me lança un regard furieux*
> His only reply was to glare at me

(cf. 'All I had was an apple' = 'I only had an apple').

(f) With the numerals up to *quatre* 'four' functioning as pronouns (i.e. not followed by a noun), *tous* may be used either with or without the definite article *les* (the omission of the article is a feature of literary rather than of spoken usage), e.g.:

> *Je les connais tous les deux* (or *tous deux*)
> I know them both (*or* both of them)

> *Elles sont parties toutes (les) quatre*
> They (*fem.*) have all left (All four of them have left)

With numerals above 'four', and with all numerals (including 'two', 'three' and 'four') followed by a noun, the article *must* be used, e.g.:

> *Je les connais tous les dix*
> I know all ten of them

> *Tous les trois enfants sont allés se coucher*
> All three children have gone to bed

(iii) As a pronoun:

(a) The singular pronoun *tout* means 'all, everything', e.g.:

Tout est prêt	Everything is ready
Il a tout perdu	He has lost everything
Il a pensé à tout	He has thought of everything

When *tout* is followed by a relative clause (see **262–269**), the pronoun *ce* must be inserted even though there is usually no equivalent (such as 'that (which)') in English, e.g.:

tout ce qui est dans la boîte
everything (that is) in the box

Il vous donnera tout ce que vous voulez
He will give you all (everything) you want

tout ce dont j'ai besoin
everything I need (*lit.* of which I have need)

(b) The plural pronouns *tous* (masc.) (pronounced [tus] except before *ceux*, see below), *toutes* (fem.), mean 'all', e.g.:

Tous étaient d'accord	All were in agreement
Ils sont tous partis	They have all left
Je les connais toutes	I know them (*fem.*) all

(note that in examples such as the last, the personal pronoun, i.e. *les*, is required, as in English, with reference to the direct object).

Note also *nous tous* 'all of us', *vous tous* 'all of you' – the two pronouns may be separated, e.g. *Nous le connaissons tous* 'We all know him'.

When *tous*, *toutes* are followed by a relative clause (see **262–269**), the appropriate demonstrative pronoun must be inserted whether or not there is any corresponding pronoun ('those' or 'the ones') in English, i.e. *tous ceux* (*qui*, etc.) (and note that, in this case, *tous* is pronounced ([tu]), *toutes celles* (*qui*, etc.), e.g.:

tous ceux qui y étaient
all (those) who were there

Cette maison est mieux construite que toutes celles que nous avons vues hier
This house is better built than all the ones we saw yesterday

(iv) As a noun, *le* or *un tout* means 'the, *or* a, whole', e.g.:

Le tout est plus grand que la somme de ses parties
The whole is greater than the sum of its parts

Trois tiers font un tout
Three thirds make one whole

or, occasionally, 'the whole (lot) (of something)', e.g.:

Je vends le tout	I'm selling the whole lot

Note the idiomatic use of *le tout* in such expressions as *Le tout est de réussir* 'The thing that matters is to succeed (success is everything)'.

'The whole (of)' + determiner + noun is translated either by the predeterminer *tout* or by the adjective *entier* (see ii,b and d above), e.g. *Il passe tout son temps à lire* 'he spends the whole of his time (= all his time) reading'.

(v) As an adverb, *tout* has a variety of functions; as an adverb, it would normally be expected to be (like other adverbs) invariable, i.e. not to take any agreement in gender or number, and, generally speaking, this is so – but see b below.

(a) Before another adverb, *tout* means 'quite' (except in the sense of 'fairly, rather' when *assez* should be used, e.g. *assez vite* 'quite quickly'), e.g.:

Il habite tout près
He lives quite near

Je vous dis tout simplement que ce n'est pas vrai
I am telling you quite simply that it is not true

(b) *Tout* also means 'quite, wholly, etc.' when used with an adjective or participle. Here, too, it is invariable *except*, curiously, *in the feminine singular or plural before a consonant* – i.e. it does not agree in the masculine plural or, before a vowel (or mute *h*), in the feminine singular or plural, e.g.:

Elle est tout heureuse	She is extremely happy
Elles sont tout heureuses	They (*fem.*) are extremely happy
Ils sont tout nus	They (*masc.*) are quite naked

but

Elle est toute pâle	She is completely pale
Elles étaient toutes nues	They (*fem.*) were quite naked

Consequently, *tout autre* does not agree when it means 'quite another, quite different', e.g. *C'est une tout autre question* 'That is quite a different matter' but, in accordance with ii,a above, it agrees when it means 'every other' or 'any other', e.g. *Il répondra à toute autre question mais pas à celle-là* 'He will answer any other question but not that one'.

For the construction *tout riche qu'il soit* 'however rich he is', see **310**,i.

(c) Adverbial *tout* occurs in a number of idiomatic expressions, e.g. *tout à coup*, *tout d'un coup* 'all at once', *tout à fait* 'quite, completely', *tout à l'heure* 'just now, a little while ago, in a little while', *tout au début* 'right at the beginning', *tout d'abord* 'first of all', *tout de même* 'all the same, nevertheless', *tout de suite* 'at once'.

318 The translation of 'one' as a pronoun

(i) 'One' is translated by *un, une* when it is used in the strictly numerical sense, e.g.:

J'en prends un (or *une*)	I'll take one (of them)
un de mes amis	one of my friends
une des plus belles villes de France	one of the most beautiful cities in France

Note that, particularly when the numeral is used on its own, *un(e) seul(e)* is often used, e.g.:

Combien de bouteilles voulez-vous? – Une seule
How many bottles do you want? – (Just) one

In the literary language, but not in everyday speech, *l'un, l'une* may be used for *un, une* before *de* (only rarely elsewhere), e.g. *l'un de vous* 'one of you', *l'un de ses prédécesseurs* 'one of his predecessors', *l'une des plus grandes victoires de Napoléon* 'one of Napoleon's greatest victories'.

(ii) As an indefinite pronoun, the usual equivalent of 'one' is *on* (see **302**).

(iii) When 'one' is followed by a relative clause, as in 'the one(s) I bought yesterday', the French equivalent is the demonstrative pronoun *celui*, etc. (see **245**,ii).

(iv) For *l'un . . . l'autre*, *les uns . . . les autres*, see **292**,iii; for *chacun*, see **295**; for *quelqu'un*, see **312**.

319 The translation of 'anyone', 'anything'

The problems encountered by English speakers in selecting the appropriate French equivalents for 'anyone' and 'anything' arise mainly from the fact that these pronouns have a number of different values in English. The first step in solving the problem in a given context is to decide on the value of the pronoun in that context.

(i) In many cases, there is no distinction in French comparable to those between 'anyone' and 'someone' (see *quelqu'un*, 312) and between 'anything' and 'something' (see *quelque chose*, 311). Note in particular that *quelqu'un* and *quelque chose* are normally the most appropriate equivalents for 'anyone' and 'anything' in direct or indirect questions and in hypothetical clauses introduced by 'if', e.g.:

Y a-t-il quelqu'un à la maison?
Is anyone in?

Avez-vous quelque chose à déclarer?
Have you anything to declare?

Savez-vous si quelqu'un est déjà parti?
Do you know if anyone has already left?

Si vous voyez quelqu'un, dites-le-moi
If you see anybody, tell me

Si j'avais quelque chose à lire, je resterais ici
If I had anything to read, I should stay here

(ii) If 'anyone' or 'anything' can be replaced in English by 'everyone' or 'everything' without significantly altering the meaning, the French equivalent is often *tout le monde* 'everyone' or *tout* 'everything' or, before a relative clause, *(tous) ceux (qui, que)* '(all) those (who(m))' or *tout ce (qui, que)* 'all (that)', e.g.:

Tout le monde peut faire ça
Anyone can do that

Tout est préférable au déshonneur
Anything is better than disgrace

Tous ceux qui ont visité Paris savent que c'est une très belle ville
Anyone who has been to Paris knows that it is a very beautiful city

Je vous donnerai tout ce que voulez
I'll give you anything you want

(iii) When used in a very general sense, 'anyone' may be rendered by *on* 'one' (see 302), e.g.:

Si on me demande, dites que je suis parti
If anyone asks for me, say I've left

(iv) For 'anyone, anything' in negative sentences (i.e. when 'not anyone' = 'no one' and 'not anything' = 'nothing'), see 551.

(v) For other possible values of 'anyone' and 'anything', see *je ne sais qui, quoi*, 299; *n'importe qui, quoi*, 301; *quelconque*, 304; *qui que ce soit, quoi que ce soit*, 315,i,f and ii,e.

Quantifiers

320   Quantifiers, as the name suggests, define various elements in the sentence in terms of quantity (e.g. how little or how much thereof, how few or how many thereof). Some items that could have been included here (such as 'some' and 'all') have already been dealt with under 'Indefinites', and others could equally well have been included under that heading.

For reasons of convenience, we shall consider together both pronominal and adverbial quantifiers.

321   (i) Note that in English such quantifiers as 'enough, (as, so, too, how) much, (as, so too, how) many, more, less, few, fewer' can, and usually do, qualify directly the noun that they govern, e.g. 'enough bread, many books, less time'. In French, *de* must be used in comparable contexts, e.g.:

assez de pain	enough bread
trop de voitures	too many cars
autant de difficulté	as much difficulty
tant de problèmes	so many problems
beaucoup de livres	many books
combien d'enfants?	how many children?
plus de temps	more time
moins de danger	less danger
peu d'amis	few friends

(ii) In comparable expressions with a personal pronoun, English either uses 'of' or omits the pronoun altogether, leaving it to be implied from the context; in French, the pronoun *en* 'of it, of them' (see 201), must not be omitted, e.g.:

Il en vend autant que vous
He sells as many (of them) as you

Et le pain? – Nous en avons déjà assez
What about the bread? – We have enough already

Combien en avez-vous acheté?
How much (how many) did you buy?

When 'of it, of them' are not implied, then there is no *en* in
French, e.g.:

Beaucoup ont disparu	Many have disappeared
Combien a-t-il perdu?	How much did he lose?

(iii) Note that when the quantifiers are followed by a definite
article in English, the same is true of French; so, we have, without
an article, *beaucoup d'étudiants* 'many students', *trop de bière*
'too much beer', *combien de papier?* 'how much paper?', but:

Beaucoup des étudiants de cette université sont Africains
Many of the students at this university are Africans

Il a bu trop de la bière que vous avez achetée
He has drunk too much of the beer that you bought

Combien du papier a été brûlé?
How much of the paper was burnt?

322 *Assez* 'enough' and *trop* 'too (much, many)'

(i) Modifying a noun or pronoun, e.g.:

Ils achètent assez de bonbons pour tous les enfants
They are buying enough sweets for all the children

A-t-il assez d'argent?
Has he enough money?

Nous n'en vendons pas assez
We don't sell enough (of it, of them)

Notre pays importe trop de voitures
Our country imports too many cars

Vous en prenez trop
You are taking too much (too many)

Note that, after a phrase introduced by *assez* or *trop*, a following
infinitive is preceded by *pour*, e.g.:

Nous avons assez de temps pour le faire
We have enough time to do it

Il a perdu trop d'argent pour être content
He has lost too much money to be satisfied

(ii) When *assez* and *trop* are the complement of *être*, *en* is not required, e.g. *C'est assez* 'It's enough', *Ça c'est trop* 'that's too much'; but note the idioms *C'en est assez!* 'Enough is enough!' and *C'en est trop!* 'That's going too far!'

(iii) *Assez* and *trop* modifying an adjective or an adverb mean 'enough, quite, rather' and 'too' respectively; as with *assez (trop) de* (see i above), a following infinitive is preceded by *pour*, e.g.:

C'est assez difficile
It's rather difficult

Il est assez intelligent pour comprendre
He is intelligent enough to understand

Il marche assez lentement
He walks rather slowly

Il vient assez souvent nous voir
He comes to see us quite often

Il est trop malade pour pouvoir sortir
He is too ill to be able to go out

Nous sommes restés trop longtemps
We stayed too long

(iv) Note that, whereas in English 'enough' follows adjectives ('easy enough') and occasionally follows nouns ('time enough' for 'enough time'), *assez* always precedes both adjectives and nouns (*assez facile*, *assez de temps*).

(v) When modifying verbs, *assez* means 'enough' and *trop* means 'too much', and are often enough in themselves where English uses some expanded phrase such as 'long enough' or 'too hard', e.g.:

Nous avons assez travaillé pour une journée
We have worked enough for one day

Ils se disputent trop
They argue too much

Avez-vous assez dormi?
Have you slept long enough?

Il travaille trop
He works too hard

As in i and iii above, a following infinitive is preceded by *pour*, e.g.:

> *Il parle trop pour être pris au sérieux*
> He talks too much to be taken seriously

323 *Autant* 'as much, as many' and *tant* 'so (as) much, so (as) many'

(i) *Autant* expresses a comparison of equality between nouns or pronouns or between verbs, as *aussi* does between adjectives or between adverbs (see **157**), e.g.:

> *Il mange autant de pain (autant de pommes) que vous*
> He eats as much bread (as many apples) as you (do)

> *Mon frère en vend autant que mon père*
> My brother sells as much (as many) as my father (does)

> *Je lis autant que mon frère*
> I read as much as my brother (does)

> *Je vous aiderai autant que je pourrai*
> I shall help you as much as I can

Occasionally, as an alternative to the usual construction *Il est aussi agréable qu'intelligent* 'He is as pleasant as (he is) intelligent' (see **157**), one finds the construction *Il est agréable autant qu'intelligent*, in which *autant* qualifies the verb *être* that is understood (= *Il est agréable autant qu'il est intelligent*).

(ii) In negative and interrogative clauses, both *autant* and *tant* are possible, e.g.:

> *Il n'a pas autant* (or *tant*) *de patience que vous*
> He hasn't as much patience as you (have)

> *Je ne mange pas autant* (or *tant*) *(de viande) que vous*
> I do not eat as much (meat) as you (do)

> *Vous y tenez autant* (or *tant*) *que ça?*
> Are you that keen on it?

(iii) On the optional insertion in English of a verb such as 'to be, to have, to do' after a comparative, where French normally has no such verb, see **157** and **173**, and various examples in i and ii above.

(iv) Although *tant* is not usually used to express the comparative of equality in affirmative clauses, it is sometimes so used with the verbs *pouvoir* and *vouloir*, e.g.:

> *Il pleut tant qu'il peut*
> It is raining as hard as it can

> *Je vous en donnerai tant que vous voudrez*
> I will give you as much as you want

(v) *Tant que* (but not *autant que*) also means '(for) as long as' in contexts such as the following:

> *Je vous aiderai tant que je pourrai*
> I shall help you (for) as long as I can

> *Tant que la grève durera, elle restera à Paris*
> (For) as long as the strike lasts, she will stay in Paris

(Note that *tant que* is *not* the equivalent of *aussi longtemps que*, which must be used when 'as long as' expresses a comparison, e.g. *J'y suis resté aussi longtemps que vous* 'I stayed there as long as you (did)'.)

(vi) *Tant . . . que* is also the equivalent of 'so much, so many' when the following clause expresses a result, e.g.:

> *Je le plains tant que je vais tout faire pour l'aider*
> I am so sorry for him that I am going to do all I can to help him

> *J'ai tant de travail que je ne sais où commencer*
> I have so much work that I don't know where to begin

> *Tant de gens sont partis que les hôtels sont presque vides*
> So many people have left that the hotels are almost empty

In this type of sentence, in which *tant* means 'so much, so many' and *que* means 'that' (not 'as'), *tant* can be replaced by *tellement* (e.g. *Je le plains tellement que . . ., J'ai tellement de travail que . . .*).

(vii) In what is, in reality, in both French and English, a truncated version of the construction dealt with in vi above, *tant*, like 'so much, so many', can have an exclamatory value, e.g.:

> *Je le plains tant!*
> I am so sorry for him!

> *Il a tant de problèmes!*
> He has so many problems!

(the implication being 'I am so sorry for him [that . . .]', 'He has so many problems [that . . .]', the result being unexpressed).

324 *Beaucoup*, etc. 'much, many'

(i) *Beaucoup* is by far the most widespread French equivalent for 'much, many, a lot of', e.g.:

> *Il n'a pas beaucoup de patience*
> He hasn't much (a lot of) patience

> *Ils vendent beaucoup de fleurs*
> They sell a lot of flowers

> *Avez-vous beaucoup d'amis?*
> Have you many friends?

> *Je n'en veux pas beaucoup*
> I don't want much (*or* many)

> *Il a beaucoup voyagé*
> He has travelled a great deal

(ii) (a) 'Much' or 'far' before a comparative is also rendered by *beaucoup*, e.g.:

> *Il est beaucoup plus* (or *moins*) *intelligent que son frère*
> He is much more (*or* less) intelligent than his brother

> *Elle y va beaucoup plus* (or *moins*) *souvent que l'an dernier*
> She goes there much more (*or* less) often than last year

(Before a comparative adjective, but not before an adverb, 'much' or 'far' is sometimes, but less commonly, rendered by *de beaucoup* – cf. b below; so the first of the above examples could have read *Il est de beaucoup plus (moins) intelligent que son frère*, but, since *souvent* is an adverb, *de beaucoup* could not be used in the second example.)

Likewise *beaucoup trop* 'much (far) too much, far too many', e.g.:

> *J'ai acheté beaucoup trop de timbres*
> I have bought far too many stamps

(b) *De beaucoup*, not *beaucoup* alone, *must* be used as the equivalent of 'much' or 'by far' when placed after a comparative, e.g.:

> *Il est plus fort de beaucoup que son ami*
> He is much stronger than his friend

or with a superlative, e.g.:

Il est de beaucoup le plus intelligent de leurs enfants
He is by far the most intelligent of their children

or when a comparative or superlative is implied but not expressed in full, e.g.:

Il est plus fort que moi, et de beaucoup
He is stronger than I am, and by a long way

(iii) *Beaucoup* can never be qualified by *très* (or any other word for 'very'), *trop* 'too', *aussi* 'as' or *si* 'so'. 'Very much, very many' are usually just *beaucoup*, though *beaucoup, beaucoup* can be used for emphasis, 'too much, too many' are translated by *trop* alone (see **322**), 'as much, as many' by *autant* or (in some circumstances) *tant* (see **323**), and 'so much, so many' by *tant* (see **323**).

(iv) For (*le*) *plus* as the comparative and superlative of *beaucoup*, see **165–168**.

(v) A frequent form in conversational French is *pas mal (de)* 'quite a lot of', e.g.:

J'ai eu pas mal de difficulté
I had quite a lot of difficulty

Il en vend pas mal
He sells quite a lot of them

Note that the verb is not preceded by *ne* (contrast *pas grand-chose*, vii below).

(vi) Note that *force* 'many' (and occasionally 'much'), which sometimes occurs in the literary language, is not followed by *de* (see also **397**,i,c), e.g. *avec force compliments* 'with many compliments'.

(vii) Note the form *grand-chose* which occurs widely in speech but only in the expression *pas grand-chose* 'not much' and which cannot be followed by a noun as a complement; the verb, if there is one, is preceded by *ne* (contrast *pas mal*, v above); e.g.:

Il n'a pas dit grand-chose
He didn't say much

Qu'est-ce que vous avez acheté? – Pas grand-chose
What have you bought? – Not much

(viii) In the literary language, *maint*, which has the following forms:

	sing.	plur.
masc.	*maint*	*maints*
fem.	*mainte*	*maintes*

when used in either the singular or the plural expresses a plural number, 'many a, many', e.g. *maint Anglais* 'many an Englishman', *maints Anglais* 'many Englishmen'. It is used especially in the expressions *maintes fois* 'many a time', *à mainte(s) reprise(s)* 'on numerous occasions'.

(ix) *Nombre de, quantité de* (with no article before them) can be used with plural nouns in the sense of 'a lot of, a number of', e.g.:

Nombre de députés ont voté contre
A number of MPs voted against

Quantité d'indications laissent supposer qu'il est mort
A number of indications lead one to think he is dead

325 *Bien du, bien de la, bien de l'* 'much', *bien des* 'many'
These expressions for 'much, many' are somewhat less objective than *beaucoup* and convey the idea of a measure of surprise, satisfaction, disapproval, or some other subjective reaction, e.g.:

Il a bien de l'argent
He has plenty of money

Elle vous donne bien de l'inquiétude
She causes you a lot of worry

Bien des gens me l'ont dit
Many people have told me so

Strictly speaking, *des* should be replaced by *de* when an adjective precedes the noun (see **44**), e.g. *bien de belles églises* 'many fine churches', but in practice this is rarely the case and the construction *bien des belles églises* is used to mean 'many fine churches' as well as 'many of the fine churches' (the context will usually take the meaning clear). Note, however, that the 'rule' does apply with *d'autres*, e.g.:

J'ai bien d'autres choses à faire
I have many other things to do

This also covers the frequently occurring construction in which *d'autres* has become a pronoun (see **292,i**), i.e. *bien d'autres* 'many others', e.g.:

> *Bien d'autres sont d'accord*
> Many others agree

326   *Combien?* 'how much? how many?'

(i) Direct questions, e.g.:

> *Combien de pain?*
> How much bread?
>
> *Combien d'Américains sont venus?*
> How many Americans came?
>
> *Combien en avez-vous?*
> How much (*or* how many) have you?
>
> *Combien sont partis?*
> How many have left?
>
> *Combien est-ce que vous pesez?*
> How much do you weigh?

(ii) Indirect questions, e.g.:

> *Je ne sais pas combien il en a acheté*
> I don't know how much he bought

(iii) Note the following construction in which *combien* corresponds to English 'how' (see also **153,i,b**):

> *Je ne m'étais pas rendu compte combien vous étiez inquiet*
> I had not realized how worried you were

327   *Davantage* 'more' and *moins* 'less' – see **330**.

328   *Peu* 'little, few', *un peu* 'a little'

(i) When 'little' means 'not much', it must be translated by *peu de* and not by *petit*, e.g.:

> *Nous avons eu peu de difficulté*
> We had little difficulty

Note the difference between this, which stresses the negative aspect ('not much'), and *un peu de* 'a little' (and again *petit* cannot be used) which stresses the positive aspect ('there is some'), e.g.:

Nous avons eu un peu de difficulté
We had some (*or* a little) difficulty

Note the expression *peu de chose* 'little, not much', as in *Cela compte pour peu de chose* 'That doesn't count for much'.

(ii) In the plural, *peu* means 'few', e.g. *Il a peu d'amis* 'He has few friends'. There is no plural equivalent of *un peu* (for 'a few' use *quelques*, e.g. *Il a quelques amis* 'He has a few friends', see **306**).

(iii) For *le peu* 'the little, the few', see **397**,ii.

(iv) For (*le*) *moins* as the comparative and superlative of *peu*, see **164**.

329   *La plupart* 'most, the greater part'

La plupart can be either plural, e.g.:

La plupart de mes amis sont étudiants
Most of my friends are students

La plupart sont déjà partis
Most have already left

or, occasionally, singular, e.g.:

La plupart de ce qu'il dit est faux
Most of what he says is untrue

In the singular, however, there is a tendency (except in the expression *la plupart du temps* 'most of the time') to substitute for *la plupart* some other expression such as *la plus grande partie*.

330   *Plus* 'more', *moins* 'less', etc.

(i) For the use of *plus* and *moins* to express the comparative and superlative of adjectives and adverbs, see **160–165** and **169–173**.

(ii) For (*le*) *plus* as the comparative and superlative of *beaucoup* and (*le*) *moins* as the comparative and superlative of *peu*, see **164–170**.

(iii) For (*ne* . . .) *plus* in negative clauses, see **552**.

(iv) *Davantage* 'more'

(a) *Davantage* generally qualifies only verbs, e.g.:

Vous devriez manger davantage
You ought to eat more

Rien ne pourrait lui plaire davantage
Nothing could please him more

Note its use with reference to the pronoun *le* standing for an adjective (though even here it really qualifies the verb *être*), e.g.:

Il est vrai que ma sœur est inquiète, mais mon frère l'est davantage
It is true that my sister is worried, but my brother is more so

(b) *Davantage que* and *davantage de* are often considered to be incorrect (even though both constructions occurred in Classical French and may still be found in good authors), and are best avoided. However, there is no objection to using *davantage* with the pronoun *en* 'of it, of them', e.g.:

Voulez-vous encore du thé? – Merci, je n'en veux pas davantage
Do you want any more tea? – No, thank you, I don't want any more

Nous n'en dirons pas davantage
We shall say no more about it

(c) In practice, *davantage* usually comes at the end of its clause, though not invariably (e.g. *J'aimerais pouvoir faire davantage pour vous* 'I should like to be able to do more for you').

(d) Note that *davantage* can never be used with numbers, in which case 'more than' is always *plus de* (see 167).

(v) For the use of *encore* meaning 'more', see 616,iii.

331   *Plusieurs* 'several'

The use of *plusieurs* is much like that of English 'several'; note that it has the same form for both genders, e.g. *plusieurs Anglais* 'several Englishmen', *plusieurs femmes* 'several women', *plusieurs de mes amis* 'several of my friends', *j'en ai vu plusieurs* 'I have seen several' (with reference to either masculine or feminine nouns).

332   *Presque* 'almost, nearly'

(i) *Presque* can modify adjectives, adverbs, certain indefinite pronouns, and verbs, e.g.:

Il est presque aveugle   He is almost blind

presque tous	almost all (of them)
presque personne (or *rien*)	almost nobody (*or* nothing)
presque immédiatement	almost immediately
Il pleurait presque	He was almost crying

In the above uses, the *-e* of *presque* is never elided before a vowel.

Note the use of *ou presque* 'or almost', expressing a kind of afterthought, e.g.:

C'est impossible, ou presque	It's impossible, or almost
Il pleurait, ou presque	He was crying, or nearly

(ii) Certain nouns may also be modified by *presque*; with the exception of the one word *une presqu'île* 'peninsula', the *-e* is not elided, nor is a hyphen used, e.g.:

J'en ai la presque certitude
I am practically certain of it

la presque totalité des habitants
almost all the inhabitants

être élu à la presque unanimité
to be elected almost unanimously

333 *Que de . . .!* 'what a lot of!'

Que de . . . meaning 'what a lot of' or sometimes 'how much, how many' is often used as a quantifier in exclamations, e.g.:

Que de peine pour rien!
What a lot of trouble for nothing!

Que de fois faut-il que je vous le dise!
How many times must I tell you!

The two parts can be divided, as in:

Que nous avons dû visiter de cathédrales!
What a lot of cathedrals we had to go and see!

334 *Si* 'so', *tant* 'so much, so many', *tellement* 'so, so much, so many'

(i) 'So' with an adjective or adverb is *si* or, especially in familiar

style, *tellement*; 'so . . . that' is *si* (or *tellement*) . . . *que* . . . ;
e.g.:

> *Ce problème est si difficile*
> This problem is so difficult

> *Elle est tellement jolie*
> She is so pretty

> *J'y suis allé si souvent*
> I have been there so often

> *Je me suis levé si tard que j'ai manqué le train*
> I got up so late that I missed the train

> *Il est si distingué que je ne le vois plus*
> He is so grand that I never see him now

This construction must not be confused with *si . . . que* 'as . . .
as' after a negative (see 157).

(ii) 'So much, so many' must be rendered by *tant* or *tellement* (see
323,vi) and not by *si*. Note that *si* qualifies only adjectives and
adverbs – it never qualifies a verb.

Tellement (not *si* or *tant*) also serves as the equivalent of 'so much,
(all) that much' before a comparative, e.g.:

> *C'est tellement plus difficile que je n'avais pensé*
> It is so much more difficult than I had thought

> *Il n'est pas tellement plus grand que vous*
> He is not all that much taller than you

(iii) For the construction *si riche qu'il soit* 'however rich he is',
see 310,i.

335   *Très*, etc. 'very'

(i) *Très* is used in much the same way as 'very' with reference to
adjectives, e.g. *Je suis très content* 'I am very pleased', and to
adverbs, e.g. *Il mange très lentement* 'He eats very slowly'. It is
also used much more widely than 'very' with past participles and
adverbial expressions, in which case English tends to use some
other intensifier, e.g. *un ministre très estimé* 'a highly esteemed
minister', *un discours très apprécié* 'a much (*or* greatly) appreciated speech', *un style très à la mode* 'a style that is very much in
fashion'.

In the spoken language, *très* may also be used (though less frequently than 'very') with reference to a previously expressed adjective or adverb that is understood but not repeated, e.g.:

Vous êtes inquiet? – Oui, très
Are you worried? – Yes, very

(In such circumstances, French often repeats the adjective or adverb, i.e., in the case in point, *Oui, très inquiet.*)

A construction that is widely used in speech, but that some purists object to in the written language, is the use of *très* with expressions of the type *avoir* or *faire* + noun, such as *avoir froid* 'to be cold', *faire attention* 'to be careful', e.g. *J'ai très froid* 'I am very cold', *Il a eu très peur* 'He was very frightened', *Il faut faire très attention* 'One must be very careful', *Cela m'a fait très peur* 'That frightened me a lot'. (The purists do not object to the use of *bien* – see ii below – instead of *très* in such contexts.)

(ii) Particularly in the literary language, but to some extent in speech also (though rarely in colloquial speech), *bien* and *fort* can be used for 'very' in much the same way as *très*, e.g. *Il sera bien content de vous voir* 'He will be very pleased to see you', *fort difficile* 'very difficult', *bien souvent* 'very often', *fort lentement* 'very slowly'. Note, however, that they cannot be used on their own (i.e. as the equivalent of *très* in *Oui, très* 'Yes, very' – see above) and that *fort* is avoided before another word beginning with *f-*, so *très loin, bien loin, fort loin* 'very far', but preferably only *très facile* or *bien facile* 'very easy'.

(iii) Note that none of these words for 'very' can qualify *beaucoup* – see **324,iii**.

(For 'very' as an adjective, translated by *même*, see **300,ii**.)

336 *Trop* 'too (much, many)' – see **322**.

337 Note that when the subject of the verb is a quantifier (or an expression introduced by a quantifier, such as *beaucoup de gens*) that can be either singular or plural, the number of the verb and the number and gender of any adjectives or participles depend on the sense of the quantifier and its complement if any, e.g.:

Beaucoup de ce qu'il dit est faux
Much of what he says is untrue

Beaucoup estiment que c'est trop tard
Many think it is too late

> *Combien de temps s'est écoulé?*
> How much time has elapsed?

> *Combien de personnes ont été tuées?*
> How many people were killed?

But note too that there is a tendency to avoid the use of such quantifiers (other than *beaucoup*) as a subject, especially when there is no *de*-phrase as a complement. Various procedures exist for rephrasing such sentences, e.g.:

> *Il y en a combien qui sont partis?*
> How many have left?

> *Il est survenu trop de difficultés*
> Too many difficulties arose

which avoid having *combien?* or *trop de difficultés* as the subject.

Verbs

Introduction

338   Verbs will be discussed according to the following plan:

A The conjugations

339 (i) The term 'conjugation' is used in two different but closely connected senses:

(a) It denotes the set of forms that a given verb takes to indicate different tenses, moods and persons – see, for example, **351**, the conjugation of the verb *donner* 'to give';

(b) It refers to a class of verbs having the same forms throughout their conjugation (in the sense given in a above); so, since the endings of such verbs as *aimer* 'to love', *chanter* 'to sing', *porter* 'to carry', and thousands of others, are the same as those of *donner*, these verbs are all said to belong to the same conjugation (known conventionally as the 'First Conjugation', see ii,a below). It is often convenient to extend the use of this term so as to group together verbs whose forms coincide only in certain specific circumstances; in this book, the basis for our classification of verbs into conjugations is the ending of the infinitive (*-er*, *-ir*, *-re* or *-oir*) (see ii below) though, as we shall see, each of these conjugations includes various subdivisions.

In the following paragraphs, 'conjugation' is used in both of the above senses, but it will always be clear from the context which sense is intended.

(ii) There is no generally accepted basis for classifying French verbs into conjugations. The classification adopted here is based solely on the ending of the infinitive, which may be *-er*, *-ir*, *-re* or *-oir*. However, within each of these 'conjugations' there are various patterns, and it is indeed questionable whether verbs in *-oir* form a conjugation at all – see d below.

(a) Verbs whose infinitive ends in *-er* (e.g. *donner* 'to give', see **351**), are generally known as 'First Conjugation' verbs. This conjugation contains over 90% of all verbs in the language (i.e. several thousand) and since, in practice (but see also b below), all new verbs entering the language (e.g. *cocoricoter* 'to go cock-a-doodle-do' and *festivaler* 'to attend a festival', both first recorded in 1985, or *enrucher* 'to put (bees) in a hive (*ruche*)' and *golfer* 'to play golf', both from 1986) follow this pattern, the First Conjugation is often referred to as a 'living' conjugation.

Most verbs in this conjugation are 'regular', i.e. they follow a set pattern, exemplified by that of *donner*; for exceptions, see 352–357.

(b) Verbs whose infinitive ends in *-ir* form the 'Second Conjugation', which numbers about 300 regular verbs (e.g. *finir* 'to finish', see 359), two small sub-groups (represented by *dormir* 'to sleep', see 363, and *cueillir* 'to gather', see 364), and a number of irregular verbs, i.e. verbs whose conjugation differs even more than that of *dormir* and *cueillir* from the basic pattern (see 377).

Many grammars consider the *finir* type as a second 'living' conjugation (cf. a above), but there seems very little justification for this. It is true that a very few new verbs in *-ir* have appeared in the course of the twentieth century, viz. *amerrir* 'to alight on the sea', dating from about 1910, *alunir* 'to land on the moon', about 1930 (and even *avénusir* 'to land on Venus' has been used but seems not to have caught on). However, these are quite clearly exceptions, formed specifically on the model of *atterrir* 'to land', and they are not enough to justify one in considering the Second Conjugation as 'living' in the same sense as the First.

(c) Verbs whose infinitive ends in *-re* (e.g. *vendre* 'to sell', see 367) belong to the 'Third Conjugation'; this contains only about 100 verbs, of which a great number are irregular and, since no new verbs have been created on this pattern for many centuries past, and it is virtually inconceivable that any could now be created, this is known as a 'dead' conjugation.

(d) About thirty verbs have an infinitive ending in *-oir*, but since, apart from one small group of seven (see 375), they differ widely in their forms, there is no case for considering them as a 'conjugation' in any but the most formal sense (i.e. the fact that they all end in *-oir*). It would certainly be out of the question to create new verbs in *-oir* and so this 'conjugation' (if it is one at all) is very definitely 'dead'.

B Names of moods and tenses

340   There is no completely standardized set of names, in either English or French, for the various tenses of the French verb. We

give below, in the first column, the names adopted in this grammar and, in the second column, the names most widely used in French; in two cases, we give in a third column alternative English names used in some other grammars (but note that some grammars adopt their own non-standard names for various tenses – none of these are listed here):

Indicative	*Indicatif*	
present	*présent*	
perfect	*passé composé*	
imperfect	*imparfait*	
pluperfect	*plus-que-parfait*	
preterite	*passé simple*	past historic
past anterior	*passé antérieur*	
double-compound past	*passé surcomposé*	
future	*futur*	
future perfect	*futur antérieur*	
Conditional	*Conditionnel*	
present	*présent* (or *futur dans le passé*)	
past	*passé* (or *futur antérieur du passé*)	
Subjunctive	*Subjonctif*	
present	*présent*	
perfect	*passé*	
imperfect	*imparfait*	past
pluperfect	*plus-que-parfait*	
Imperative	*Impératif*	

The tenses of the conditional are sometimes considered as tenses of the indicative, and there is a case for this. However, for the sake of convenience, the conditional is here (as in many other grammars) classified as a separate mood.

The tenses formed on the basis of a part of the verb *avoir* or *être* and the past participle (e.g. *j'ai parlé, il était venu*) are known as **compound tenses** (for a full list with examples, see **448**). For **double-compound tenses**, see **412**. All other tenses are known as **simple tenses**.

341 A form of the verb that shows tense and mood (i.e., as far as French is concerned, a form that has an ending corresponding

to one of the six persons of the verb – see **342**) is known as a 'finite verb'. The non-finite forms of the verb are the infinitive (see **425–438**), the present participle (see **439–446**), and the past participle (see **447–471**).

C The persons of the verb

342   The persons of the verb are associated with the following subject pronouns:

	sing.	plur.
first	*je* 'I'	*nous* 'we'
second	*tu* 'you'	*vous* 'you'
third (masc.)	*il* 'he, it'	*ils* 'they'
(fem.)	*elle* 'she, it'	*elles* 'they'

For further discussion, see **194–197**.

Impersonal verbs

343   (i) French has two fully impersonal verbs, i.e. verbs that can never take any subject other than the impersonal pronoun *il* 'it'; these are *neiger* 'to snow' (for other verbs referring to the weather, see ii,a, below) and *falloir* 'to be necessary', e.g.:

Il a neigé pendant la nuit
It has been snowing during the night

Il faut le faire
One must do it (*lit.* It is necessary to do it)

Il faudra qu'on le lui dise
He will have to be told (*lit.* It will be necessary for one to tell him)

(ii) Certain other verbs are, to varying extents, used either personally, i.e. with a subject other than impersonal *il*, or impersonally:

(a) Verbs having to do with the weather, other than *neiger* (see i above), fall into this category; some of these, e.g. *geler* 'to freeze' and *dégeler* 'to thaw', are quite currently used both personally and impersonally:

Je gèle	I'm freezing
Le lac dégèle	The lake is thawing
Il a gelé pendant la nuit	It froze during the night
Il dégèle	It is thawing

while others, such as *pleuvoir* 'to rain' and *tonner* 'to thunder', are normally used impersonally, e.g.:

Il va pleuvoir	It is going to rain
Il tonne	It is thundering

but can be used personally when they have a metaphorical meaning, e.g.:

Des coups pleuvaient sur lui
Blows were raining down on him

Robespierre tonnait contre ceux qui voulaient affamer le peuple (Brunot)
Robespierre fulminated against those who wanted to starve the people

The verb *grêler* is impersonal when intransitive (*il grêle* 'it is hailing') but personal when used transitively (e.g. *L'orage a grêlé les vignes* 'The hail-storm damaged the vines').

(b) Some verbs are used impersonally only in certain constructions, e.g.:

agir	*il s'agit de* it is a question of, a matter of, etc.
aller	*il y va de (sa vie, etc.)* (his life, *etc.*) is at stake
avoir	*il y a* there is, there are
convenir	*il convient de* it is as well (*or* advisable) to
faire	*il fait beau, chaud, froid*, etc. it is fine, hot, cold, etc.
	il fait du soleil, du vent, etc. it is sunny, windy, etc.

Être is used impersonally in a small number of expressions, in particular *il est*, which is a literary equivalent of *il y a* 'there is, there are', *il est temps de* (or *que*) 'it is time to (*or* that)', and *il est question de* 'it is a matter of, there is some question of, etc.', *il est question que* 'there is some question (talk, suggestion) that', e.g.:

Il était une fois une petite princesse
Once upon a time there was a little princess

Il est temps de commencer
It is time to begin

Il est temps que cette dispute soit réglée
It is time this dispute was settled

Il n'en est pas question
There is no question of it

Il n'est pas question de démissionner
There is no question of resigning

Il est question que nous partions demain
There is some question of our leaving tomorrow

(For the distinction between *c'est* and impersonal *il est*, see **253–256**.)

Sembler 'to seem' and *paraître* 'to appear' are used impersonally in similar but not identical ways to their English equivalents, e.g.:

il semble (paraît) que . . .
it seems (appears) that . . .

Il me semble l'avoir déjà vu quelque part
I have an idea I've seen him somewhere before

à ce qu'il paraît
apparently

(for further uses, consult a good dictionary).

Note too the impersonal use of *arriver* 'to happen' in such contexts as *Il m'arrive de ne pas le comprendre* 'Sometimes I don't understand him' (*lit.* 'It happens to me not to understand him'), *Il arriva que je le rencontrai* (Littré) 'I happened to meet him', *Il arrive souvent qu'il parte avant moi* 'He often leaves before me' (*lit.* 'It often happens that he leaves before me') (*il arrive que* is followed by the indicative with reference to past events but by the subjunctive with reference to the present or the future).

(c) Impersonal *il* not infrequently serves as a 'dummy' subject for a verb that has only a weak semantic value and serves primarily to lead into the 'real' subject, which in such circumstances follows the verb. This occurs particularly with verbs such as *arriver* 'to arrive, to happen', *se passer* 'to happen, to be going on', *rester* 'to remain', but is also found with many other verbs (cf. the example with *souffler* below). The construction can be used to make a stylistic distinction similar to the one that exists in English between 'Ten soldiers arrived' (in French *Dix soldats sont arrivés*) and 'There arrived ten soldiers' (see below); note, however, that in such cases (i) there is no equivalent of 'there' other than the impersonal *il*, and (ii) in French, the verb is in the singular even if the following 'real' subject is plural; e.g.:

Il se passe quelque chose
There is something going on

Il m'est arrivé une catastrophe
A catastrophe has happened to me

Le lendemain, il arriva dix soldats
The next day, there arrived ten soldiers

Il n'en reste que deux
There are only two left

Il soufflait un vent du nord
There was a north wind blowing

D Defective verbs

344 Defective verbs are verbs that exist only in certain tenses or even only in parts of tenses. In general, French defective verbs are not in widespread use and there is even uncertainty in some cases as to which forms actually occur other than as exceptionally rare forms that one author or another happens at some time to have used (and may in fact have invented). Defective verbs are all indicated as such in our tables (**377**) in which the forms given are those that are generally recognized as existing.

Defective verbs must not be confused with impersonal verbs (see **343**) which, by virtue of their meaning, exist only in the third person singular, having as their subject the impersonal pronoun *il*.

E The morphology (forms) of the verb

The endings

345   (i) The endings of the future are the same for all verbs without exception, and the endings of the imperfect indicative and the conditional of all verbs are identical; furthermore, apart from the exceptions indicated in a and b below, the endings of the present subjunctive and of the imperfect subjunctive respectively are the same in all verbs:

Future	-ai	-as	-a	-ons	-ez	-ont
Imperf. indic./Condit.	-ais	-ais	-ait	-ions	-iez	-aient
Pres. subjunct.	-e	-es	-e	-ions	-iez	-ent
Imperf. subjunct.	-sse	-sses	-^t	-ssions	-ssions	-ssent

(a) *Present subjunctive*; *avoir* 'to have' and *être* 'to be' do not follow the above pattern – see **349** and **350**.

(b) *Imperfect subjunctive*: whereas, in the third person singular, all other verbs have *-ât*, *-ît*, or *-ût*, the verbs *tenir* 'to hold' and *venir* 'to come' and their compounds (e.g. *contenir* 'to contain', *devenir* 'to become') have *tînt* (*contînt*, etc.) and *vînt* (*devînt*, etc.).

(ii) The stem and endings of the imperative are the same as those of the present indicative except:

(a) in the second person singular of *-er* verbs and verbs such as *cueillir*, *couvrir* that are conjugated like *-er* verbs in that tense (see **364**); these lose their *-s* except before *y* and *en*, e.g.:

	2nd sing. pres. indic.	2nd sing. imper.
penser	*tu penses*	*Pense à moi* Think of me
		Penses-y Think about it

donner	*tu donnes*	*Donne-le-moi*
		Give it to me
		Donnes-en à Jean
		Give John some

cf. too, for the verb *aller*, second person singular indicative *tu vas*, imperative *va* but *vas-y*;

(b) in the verbs *avoir*, *être*, *savoir* and *vouloir*; see the notes to these verbs in the tables.

Note that *pouvoir*, impersonal verbs, and certain defective verbs have no imperative; this fact is referred to in the notes to the verbs in question in the tables.

(iii) (a) Verbs whose past participle ends in *-i*, *-is* or *-it* have a preterite in *-is*, etc. (see for example *finir*, **359**).

(b) Many *irregular* verbs whose past participle ends in *-u* have a preterite in *-us*, etc. (e.g. *vouloir* 'to wish', past participle *voulu*, preterite *je voulus*); note that this does *not* apply to regular Third Conjugation verbs (e.g. *vendre* 'to sell', past participle *vendu*, preterite *je vendis* – see **367**), or to the almost regular Third Conjugation verbs *rompre* 'to break', *battre* 'to beat', *vaincre* 'to conquer' and their compounds (see **368–370**), or to the verbs *coudre* 'to sew' (*cousu, je cousis*), *tenir* 'to hold' (*tenu, je tins*), *venir* 'to come' (*venu, je vins*), *vêtir* 'to dress' (*vêtu, je vêtis*) and *voir* 'to see' (*vu, je vis*) and their compounds.

The stems

346 (i) Except for *aller*, *avoir*, *être*, *faire*, *pouvoir*, *savoir*, *valoir* and *vouloir*, and any impersonal or defective verbs that do not have a form for the third person plural present indicative, the third person plural present indicative provides the key to the stem of the present subjunctive, e.g.:

	3rd plur. pres. indic.	1st sing. pres. subjunct.
dire	*ils disent*	*je dise*
prendre	*ils prennent*	*je prenne*
recevoir	*ils reçoivent*	*je reçoive*

Note that *aller*, *valoir* and *vouloir*, like many other irregular verbs, have one stem in the first and second persons plural of the present subjunctive and a different one in the other persons, e.g. *j'aille, nous allions*. Note too that, apart from *avoir, être, faire, pouvoir* and *savoir*, the first and second persons plural of the present subjunctive are the same as those of the imperfect indicative, e.g. from *devoir, nous devions, vous deviez*.

(ii) On the stem of the imperative, see **345,ii**.

(iii) The stem of the future and conditional in regular *-er* and *-ir* verbs is the same as the infinitive (e.g. *finir, je finirai*); in all regular and irregular *-re* verbs except *être* and *faire*, it is the same as the infinitive without the final *-e* (e.g. *prendre, je prendrai*); in all verbs, however irregular the stem of the future may be in other respects, it always ends in *-r-* (e.g. *être, je serai; voir, je verrai*).

(iv) The stem of the imperfect subjunctive is the same as that of the preterite; the vowel of the ending (*-a-, -i-* or *-u-*) is also the same as that of the preterite; so, in regular First Conjugation verbs we have, for example, preterite *je chantai, tu chantas*, etc., imperfect subjunctive *je chantasse*, etc.; for other verbs, the first person singular imperfect subjunctive may be formed from the first person preterite by replacing the *-s* of the preterite by *-sse* (e.g. for the verbs *être, prendre, vivre* and *voir* we have preterite *je fus, je pris, je vécus, je vis*, etc., imperfect subjunctive *je fusse, prisse, vécusse, visse*, etc.). As this is true for all verbs (including *tenir* and *venir* – see below), the imperfect subjunctive is not listed in the tables of irregular verbs given in section **377**. (Note that, as is stated below, **496–505**, the imperfect subjunctive is in any case no longer used in ordinary speech and, even in literary usage, is avoided except with the verbs *avoir* and *être* and in the third person of other verbs – see **502**.)

The verbs *tenir* 'to hold' and *venir* 'to come' and their compounds have an irregular preterite, *je vins, je tins*, etc., but the principle that the imperfect subjunctive has the same stem as the preterite applies, *je tinsse, vinsse*, etc. – see **378** (25).

A note on the subjunctive

347   Some grammars of French give the forms of the subjunctive with an introductory *que* (e.g. *que je sois*, etc., for the present subjunctive of *être* rather than just *je sois*, etc.). This practice was also followed in previous editions of this grammar but in the present edition it has been abandoned as potentially misleading. It must not be assumed either that *que* always requires the subjunctive (in fact, *que* is more often followed by the indicative) or that the subjunctive cannot occur without *que* (for the subjunctive without *que*, see 476–478).

The verbs avoir and être

348 The two very common verbs *avoir* and *être* are highly irregular. The forms of each of them are, however, the same whether they are used:

(i) as full verbs with the meanings 'to have' and 'to be' respectively, or

(ii) as auxiliary verbs; in particular:

(a) *avoir* serves to form the compound tenses of the active voice of most verbs (e.g. *j'ai fini* 'I have finished')

(b) *être* serves to form the compound tenses of the active voice of reflexive verbs and a few others (e.g. *je me suis levé* 'I have got up', *je suis arrivé* 'I have arrived') (see 450, 452–454) and to form the passive (e.g. *il est soupçonné* 'he is suspected') (see 382–385).

Note that the active compound tenses both of *avoir* itself and of *être* are formed with *avoir*, e.g. *j'ai eu* 'I have had', *j'ai été* 'I have been'.

As these two verbs are so important, we list their forms in full (349–350) before those of the regular verbs.

349 *Avoir* 'to have'

		Infinitive		
pres.	*avoir*		past	*avoir eu*
		Participles		
pres.	*ayant*		past	*eu*
		Indicative		
pres.	*j'ai*		perf.	*j'ai eu*
	tu as			*tu as eu*
	il a			*il a eu*
	nous avons			*nous avons eu*
	vous avez			*vous avez eu*
	ils ont			*ils ont eu*

imperf.	*j'avais*	pluperf.	*j'avais eu*
	tu avais		*tu avais eu*
	il avait		*il avait eu*
	nous avions		*nous avions eu*
	vouz aviez		*vous aviez eu*
	ils avaient		*ils avaient eu*
pret.	*j'eus*	past ant.	*j'eus eu*
	tu eus		*tu eus eu*
	il eut		*il eut eu*
	nous eûmes		*nous eûmes eu*
	vous eûtes		*vous eûtes eu*
	ils eurent		*ils eurent eu*
fut.	*j'aurai*	fut. perf.	*j'aurai eu*
	tu auras		*tu auras eu*
	il aura		*il aura eu*
	nous aurons		*nous aurons eu*
	vous aurez		*vous aurez eu*
	ils auront		*ils auront eu*

Conditional

pres.	*j'aurais*	past	*j'aurais eu*
	tu aurais		*tu aurais eu*
	il aurait		*il aurait eu*
	nous aurions		*nous aurions eu*
	vous auriez		*vous auriez eu*
	ils auraient		*ils auraient eu*

Subjunctive

pres.	*j'aie*	perf.	*j'aie eu*
	tu aies		*tu aies eu*
	il ait		*il ait eu*
	nous ayons		*nous ayons eu*
	vous ayez		*vous ayez eu*
	ils aient		*ils aient eu*
imperf.	*j'eusse*	pluperf.	*j'eusse eu*
	tu eusses		*tu eusses eu*
	il eût		*il eût eu*
	nous eussions		*nous eussions eu*
	vous eussiez		*vous eussiez eu*
	ils eussent		*ils eussent eu*

Imperative

aie   ayons   ayez

Notes on *avoir*:

1 The compound *ravoir* 'to get back, recover' is used only in the infinitive.

2   The forms of the imperative are the same as those of the
present subjunctive except that the second person singular is
aie instead of *aies*.

3   Some idioms with *avoir* will be found in **539**.

350 *Être* 'to be'

		Infinitive		
pres.	*être*		past	*avoir été*

		Participles		
pres.	*étant*		past	*été*

		Indicative		
pres.	*je suis*		perf.	*j'ai été*
	tu es			*tu as été*
	il est			*il a été*
	nous sommes			*nous avons été*
	vous êtes			*vous avez été*
	ils sont			*ils ont été*
imperf.	*j'étais*		pluperf.	*j'avais été*
	tu étais			*tu avais été*
	il était			*il avait été*
	nous étions			*nous avions été*
	vous étiez			*vous aviez été*
	ils étaient			*ils avaient été*
pret.	*je fus*		past ant.	*j'eus été*
	tu fus			*tu eus été*
	il fut			*il eut été*
	nous fûmes			*nous eûmes été*
	vous fûtes			*vous eûtes été*
	ils furent			*ils eurent été*
fut.	*je serai*		fut. perf.	*j'aurai été*
	tu seras			*tu auras été*
	il sera			*il aura été*
	nous serons			*nous aurons été*
	vous serez			*vous aurez été*
	ils seront			*ils auront été*

		Conditional		
pres.	*je serais*		past	*j'aurais été*
	tu serais			*tu aurais été*
	il serait			*il aurait été*
	nous serions			*nous aurions été*
	vous seriez			*vous auriez été*
	ils seraient			*ils auraient été*

Subjunctive

pres.	je sois	perf.	j'aie été
	tu sois		tu aies été
	il soit		il ait été
	nous soyons		nous ayons été
	vous soyez		vous ayez été
	ils soient		ils aient été
imperf.	je fusse	pluperf.	j'eusse été
	tu fusses		tu eusses été
	il fût		il eût été
	nous fussions		nous eussions été
	vous fussiez		vous eussiez été
	ils fussent		ils eussent été

Imperative

sois   soyons   soyez

Notes on *être*:

1   The past participle *été* can never take an agreement in gender or number and its spelling therefore never changes.
2   The forms of the imperative are the same as those of the present subjunctive.
3   Some idioms with *être* will be found in **540**.

First Conjugation: verbs in -er

351   *Donner* 'to give'

Infinitive

pres.	donner	past	avoir donné

Participles

pres.	donnant	past	donné

Indicative

pres.	je donne	perf.	j'ai donné
	tu donnes		tu as donné
	il donne		il a donné
	nous donnons		nous avons donné
	vous donnez		vous avez donné
	ils donnent		ils ont donné
imperf.	je donnais	pluperf.	j'avais donné
	tu donnais		tu avais donné
	il donnait		il avait donné
	nous donnions		nous avions donné
	vous donniez		vous aviez donné
	ils donnaient		ils avaient donné

pret.	je donnai	past ant.	j'eus donné
	tu donnas		tu eus donné
	il donna		il eut donné
	nous donnâmes		nous eûmes donné
	vous donnâtes		vous eûtes donné
	ils donnèrent		ils eurent donné
fut.	je donnerai	fut. perf.	j'aurai donné
	tu donneras		tu auras donné
	il donnera		il aura donné
	nous donnerons		nous aurons donné
	vous donnerez		vous aurez donné
	ils donneront		ils auront donné

Conditional

pres.	je donnerais	past	j'aurais donné
	tu donnerais		tu aurais donné
	il donnerait		il aurait donné
	nous donnerions		nous aurions donné
	vous donneriez		vous auriez donné
	ils donneraient		ils auraient donné

Subjunctive

pres.	je donne	perf.	j'aie donné
	tu donnes		tu aies donné
	il donne		il ait donné
	nous donnions		nous ayons donné
	vous donniez		vous ayez donné
	ils donnent		ils aient donné
imperf.	je donnasse	pluperf.	j'eusse donné
	tu donnasses		tu eusses donné
	il donnât		il eût donné
	nous donnassions		nous eussions donné
	vous donnassiez		vous eussiez donné
	ils donnassent		ils eussent donné

Imperative

donne   donnons   donnez

Note on *donner*:

The second person singular imperative takes an *-s* before *en* or *y* (see **345**,ii), e.g. *Donnes-en à Jean* 'Give John some', *Parles-en à ta mère* 'Speak to your mother about it', *Penses-y* 'Think about it'.

Peculiarities of verbs in -*er*
Verbs in -*cer*, -*ger*

352 Since *c* and *g* are pronounced [k] and [g] respectively before a vowel other than *e* or *i*, verbs whose infinitive ends in -*cer* [se] or -*ger* [ʒe] take a cedilla under the *c* or an *e* after the *g* when (and *only* when) the ending begins with *a* or *o*, e.g. (from *commencer* 'to begin') *nous commençons, je commençais* and (from the verb *manger* 'to eat') *nous mangeons, je mangeais*.

Verbs with *é* or *e* [ə] in the penultimate syllable

353 A minor complication arises in the case of verbs such as *céder, espérer*, etc., which have -*é*-, pronounced [e], in the last syllable but one of the infinitive. In those parts of the verb in which there is no ending in pronunciation (final -*e*, -*es* and -*ent* being unpronounced), the corresponding syllable is pronounced [ɛ] and written -*è*- (i.e. with a grave accent instead of the acute accent of the infinitive). This affects only the following parts of the verb:

(a) in the present indicative and subjunctive, the three persons singular (*je, tu, il/elle*) and the third person plural (*ils/elles*)

(b) in the imperative, the second person singular (corresponding to *tu*).

In the first and second persons plural of these tenses and in all persons of all other tenses, and in the present and past participles, all of which have pronounced endings, the *é* is kept.

The present indicative and subjunctive and the imperative of *céder* 'to yield' are therefore as follows:

pres. indic.	pres. subjunct.	imper.
je cède	*je cède*	
tu cèdes	*tu cèdes*	*cède*
il cède	*il cède*	
nous cédons	*nous cédions*	*cédons*
vous cédez	*vous cédiez*	*cédez*
ils cèdent	*ils cèdent*	

But *cédant, cédé*, future *je céderai*, etc., conditional *je céderais*, etc., imperfect indicative *je cédais*, etc., preterite *je cédai*, etc., imperfect subjunctive *il cédât*, etc.

Like céder are *altérer* 'to impair' (*j'altère*, etc.), *compléter* 'to complete', *espérer* 'to hope', *léguer* 'to bequeath', *protéger* 'to protect', *régner* 'to reign', *refléter* 'to reflect'. Note that, in the case of verbs having *é* in two successive syllables, it is only the second that is affected, e.g. *répéter* 'to repeat' (*je répète*, etc.), *pénétrer* 'to penetrate', *persévérer* 'to persevere', *préférer* 'to prefer', *révéler* 'to reveal'. Note too that verbs such as *agréer* 'to accept' and *créer* 'to create', in which there is no consonant between the *é* and the ending, are not affected by this rule, e.g. *j'agrée, ils créent* (see **358**).

354 A similar, but greater, complication arises in the case of verbs such as *mener* [məne], *acheter* [aʃte], that have a so-called mute *e* [ə] (either pronounced as in *mener*, or unpronounced as in *acheter*) immediately before the final consonant of the stem (i.e. the consonant preceding the *-er* of the infinitive). Some verbs in *-eler* or *-eter* (for those that behave differently, see **355**) and all other verbs in this category (e.g. *mener* 'to lead', *semer* 'to sow', *lever* 'to raise', *peser* 'to weigh', and compounds thereof such as *amener* 'to bring', *emmener* 'to take away', *enlever* 'to remove', *soupeser* 'to feel the weight of') have *è* [ɛ] in the parts of the verb listed in **353** a and b, *and also throughout the future and conditional tenses*. Elsewhere, the *e* is kept, e.g. (from *geler* 'to freeze' and *acheter* 'to buy'):

pres. indic.	pres. subjunct.	imper.
je gèle	*je gèle*	
tu gèles	*tu gèles*	*gèle*
il gèle	*il gèle*	
nous gelons	*nous gelions*	*gelons*
vous gelez	*vous geliez*	*gelez*
ils gèlent	*ils gèlent*	
j'achète	*j'achète*	
tu achètes	*tu achètes*	*achète*
il achète	*il achète*	
nous achetons	*nous achetions*	*achetons*
vouz achetez	*vous achetiez*	*achetez*
ils achètent	*ils achètent*	

Future *je gèlerai, tu gèleras, il gèlera, nous gèlerons, vous gèlerez, ils gèleront, j'achèterai*, etc.; conditional *je gèlerais, j'achèterais*, etc.; but imperfect indicative *je gelais, j'achetais*, etc.; preterite *je gelai, j'achetai*, etc.; imperfect subjunctive *il gelât, il achetât*, etc.; present participle, *gelant, achetant*; past participle *gelé, acheté*.

Similarly *je mène, nous menons, je mènerai*, etc.; *je sème, nous semons, je sèmerai*, etc.; *je lève, nous levons, je lèverai*, etc.; *je pèse, nous pesons, je pèserai*, etc.

Like *geler* are *celer* 'to conceal', *ciseler* 'to chisel', *congeler* 'to (deep-)freeze', *déceler* 'to detect, reveal', *écarteler* 'to tear apart', *modeler* 'to model', *peler* 'to peel'. Like *acheter* are *crocheter* 'to pick (a lock, etc.)', *haleter* 'to pant', *racheter* 'to buy back, redeem'. For other verbs in *-eler, -eter*, see **355** and **356** below.

355 Most other verbs in *-eler, -eter*, double the *l* or the *t* in those forms where *geler, acheter*, etc., take a grave accent, e.g. (from *appeler* 'to call', *jeter* 'to throw'):

> pres. indic.

j'appelle	*je jette*
tu appelles	*tu jettes*
il appelle	*il jette*
nous appelons	*nous jetons*
vous appelez	*vous jetez*
ils appellent	*ils jettent*

and similarly in the present subjunctive and the imperative. Future *j'appellerai, je jetterai*, etc.; conditional *j'appellerais, je jetterais*, etc.; but imperfect indicative *j'appelais, je jetais*, etc.; preterite *j'appelai, je jetai*, etc.; imperfect subjunctive *il appelât, il jetât*, etc.; present participle *appelant, jetant*; past participle *appelé, jeté*.

The following verbs (and various other highly uncommon ones) are like *appeler* and *jeter*:

> *amonceler*, to heap up
> *atteler*, to harness
> *chanceler*, to totter
> *ensorceler*, to bewitch
> *épeler*, to spell
> *étinceler*, to sparkle
> *ficeler*, to tie up
> *grommeler*, to mutter
> *niveler*, to level
> *rappeler*, to recall

renouveler, to renew
ruisseler, to stream
cacheter, to seal
caqueter, to cackle, gossip
colleter, to seize by the collar
décacheter, to unseal
épousseter, to dust
étiqueter, to label
feuilleter, to leaf through (a book, etc.)
moucheter, to speckle, fleck
projeter, to project, plan
rejeter, to reject

356 The verb *harceler* 'to harass' can be either like *geler* (e.g. *je harcèle*) or like *appeler* (e.g. *je harcelle*). A few (relatively uncommon) verbs in *-eter* can be treated either like *acheter* or like *jeter*; they include *becqueter* 'to peck' (e.g. *il becquète* or *becquette*), *breveter* 'to patent', and *fureter* 'to ferret about, pry, rummage'.

Verbs in *-yer*

357 Verbs whose infinitive ends in *-oyer* (except *(r)envoyer*, see below) or *-uyer* take *i* instead of *y* in those parts of the verb listed in **353** a and b and throughout the future and conditional, e.g. *employer* 'to use', *j'emploie, j'emploierai*, etc.; *nettoyer* 'to clean', *il nettoie, il nettoierait*, etc.; *s'ennuyer* 'to get bored', *ils s'ennuient, vous vous ennuierez*, etc. In the same circumstances, verbs in *-ayer* take either *i* or *y*, e.g. *payer* 'to pay', *je paie* or *je paye, je paierai* or *je payerai*.

The verb *grasseyer* 'speak with a guttural *r*' keeps the *y* throughout, e.g. *il grasseye*.

Envoyer 'to send' and its compound *renvoyer* 'to send back, to send away' follow the pattern of *employer* except that their future and conditional are irregular, *j'enverrai, j'enverrais, il renverra, il renverrait*, etc.

Other verbs in *-voyer*, such as *convoyer* 'to escort', *fourvoyer* 'to lead astray', follow the same pattern as *employer* throughout.

Verbs in *-éer, -ier*

358   Verbs in *-éer* and *-ier* are entirely regular (i.e. they are conjugated throughout like *donner*, see **351**); note in particular the succession of vowels *ééе* in the feminine past participle of verbs in *-éer*. Examples (from *créer* 'to create' and *crier* 'to shout'):

past part.	*créé, créée, créés, créées*	*crié, criée, criés, criées*
pres. indic.	*je crée*	*je crie*
	nous créons	*nous crions*
imp. indic.	*je créais*	*je criais*
	nous créions	*nous criions*
fut. indic.	*je créerai*	*je crierai*
	nous créerons	*nous crierons*

Second Conjugation: verbs in -ir

359   *Finir* 'to finish'

Infinitive

pres.	*finir*	past	*avoir fini*

Participles

pres.	*finissant*	past	*fini*

Indicative

pres.	*je finis*	perf.	*j'ai fini*
	tu finis		*tu as fini*
	il finit		*il a fini*
	nous finissons		*nous avons fini*
	vous finissez		*vous avez fini*
	ils finissent		*ils ont fini*
imperf.	*je finissais*	pluperf.	*j'avais fini*
	tu finissais		*tu avais fini*
	il finissait		*il avait fini*
	nous finissions		*nous avions fini*
	vous finissiez		*vous aviez fini*
	ils finissaient		*ils avaient fini*
pret.	*je finis*	past. ant.	*j'eus fini*
	tu finis		*tu eus fini*
	il finit		*il eut fini*
	nous finîmes		*nous eûmes fini*
	vous finîtes		*vous eûtes fini*
	ils finirent		*ils eurent fini*

fut.	je finirai	fut. perf.	j'aurai fini
	tu finiras		tu auras fini
	il finira		il aura fini
	nous finirons		nous aurons fini
	vous finirez		vous aurez fini
	ils finiront		ils auront fini

Conditional

pres.	je finirais	past	j'aurais fini
	tu finirais		tu aurais fini
	il finirait		il aurait fini
	nous finirions		nous aurions fini
	vous finiriez		vous auriez fini
	ils finiraient		ils auraient fini

Subjunctive

pres.	je finisse	perf.	j'aie fini
	tu finisses		tu aies fini
	il finisse		il ait fini
	nous finissions		nous ayons fini
	vous finissiez		vous ayez fini
	ils finissent		ils aient fini
imperf.	je finisse	pluperf.	j'eusse fini
	tu finisses		tu eusses fini
	il finît		il eût fini
	nous finissions		nous eussions fini
	vous finissiez		vous eussiez fini
	ils finissent		ils eussent fini

Imperative

finis   finissons   finissez

360   The verbs *fleurir* 'to blossom, to come into flower' and *bénir* 'to bless' are completely regular, e.g. *fleurissant* 'blossoming', *les arbres fleurissaient* 'The trees were coming into flower', *L'évêque l'a béni* 'The bishop has blessed him'.

Note however that:

(a) when it means 'to flourish, to prosper', *fleurir* has the present participle *florissant* and the imperfect indicative *je florissais*, etc. (but is regular in other tenses)

(b) an old form of the past participle of *bénir*, viz. *bénit*, survives as an adjective meaning 'consecrated, holy', e.g. *du pain bénit* 'consecrated bread', *de l'eau bénite* 'holy water'.

361   *Haïr* 'to hate' (note the *tréma* – *ï* not *i*) is irregular in the singular of the present indicative, *je hais, tu hais, il hait,* and the second singular of the imperative, *hais* – these forms have no *tréma* and are pronounced [ɛ]. In all other forms, the verb is regular except for the *tréma*, which indicates that the group *-ai-* is pronounced as two syllables, [ai], not as [ɛ], e.g. *nous haïssons, je haïssais, il haïra, j'ai haï*, etc., and, in the preterite and imperfect subjunctive where the *tréma* takes the place of the usual circumflex accent (but in fact these tenses of *haïr* are almost never used even in the literary language), *nous haïmes, vous haïtes, qu'il haït*.

Two sub-classes of *-ir* verbs

362 Two important sub-classes of *-ir* verbs, viz. *dormir*, etc. (see **363**) and *cueillir, couvrir*, etc. (see **364**), are regular in certain tenses but irregular in others. The two sub-classes have in common the fact that they have no *-iss-* (except of course in the imperfect subjunctive, *je dormisse, je couvrisse*, etc.).

363 The following verbs and most of their compounds (for exceptions see the end of this section) not only have no *-iss-* but are also irregular in the singular of the present indicative and imperative (they drop the last letter, *-m-*, *-v-*, or *-t-*, of the stem before the endings *-s*, *-s*, *-t*):

dormir, to sleep	*se repentir*, to repent
servir, to serve	*sentir*, to feel
mentir, to lie, tell lies	*sortir*, to come out, go out
partir, to leave, go away	

Examples:

pres. part.	pres. indic.	imperf. indic.	pres. subjunct.	imper.
dormant	*je dors*	*je dormais*	*je dorme*	
	tu dors			*dors*
	il dort			
	nous dormons			*dormons*
	vous dormez			*dormez*
	ils dorment			
servant	*je sers*	*je servais*	*je serve*	
	tu sers			*sers*
	il sert			
	nous servons			*servons*
	vous servez			*servez*
	ils servent			

mentant	*je mens*	*je mentais*	*je mente*
	tu mens		*mens*
	il ment		
	nous mentons		*mentons*
	vous mentez		*mentez*
	ils mentent		

Compounds conjugated in the same way include *s'endormir* 'to go to sleep', *desservir* '(of buses, trains, etc.) to serve (a certain place)', *démentir* 'to deny', *repartir* 'to go away again', *ressentir* 'to feel', *ressortir* 'to go out again'. Note, however, that the following are conjugated like *finir*: *asservir* 'to subjugate', *impartir* 'to assign', *répartir* 'to share out', *assortir* 'to match', *ressortir à* 'to come under the jurisdiction of', e.g. *Vous assortissez toujours la couleur de votre robe à celle de vos yeux* 'You always match the colour of your dress to that of your eyes', *L'affaire ressortit (ressortissait) à la Cour suprême* 'The affair comes (came) under the jurisdiction of the High Court'.

364   The following verbs not only have no *-iss-* but are irregular in the present indicative and subjunctive and the imperative, where they are conjugated like *-er* verbs, and, in some cases (see below), in the future and conditional or in the past participle:

cueillir, to gather	*découvrir*, to discover
accueillir, to welcome	*recouvrir*, to re-cover
recueillir, to gather	*offrir*, to offer
assaillir, to assail	*ouvrir*, to open
tressaillir, to shudder	*rouvrir*, to re-open
couvrir, to cover	*souffrir*, to suffer

Examples:

Pres. part. *cueillant, assaillant, couvrant*, etc.

Pres. indic.:

je cueille	*j'assaille*	*je couvre*
tu cueilles	*tu assailles*	*tu couvres*
il cueille	*il assaille*	*il couvre*
nous cueillons	*nous assaillons*	*nous couvrons*
vous cueillez	*vous assaillez*	*vous couvrez*
ils cueillent	*ils assaillent*	*ils couvrent*

Imper.: *cueille, cueillons, cueillez; ouvre, ouvrons, ouvrez*, etc.

Pres. subjunct.: *je cueille, tu assailles, nous couvrions*, etc.

Imperf. indic.: *je recueillais, tu tressaillais, il offrait*, etc.

Pret.: *je cueillis*, etc.

Imperf. subjunct.: *j'offrisse*, etc.

Note also the following irregularities:

(a) *cueillir* and its compounds change *-ir-* to *-er-* in the future and conditional: *je cueillerai, il accueillera, nous recueillerions*, etc. (but all the others are regular, e.g. *je tressaillirai, il ouvrira*)

(b) *couvrir* and its compounds, and *offrir, (r)ouvrir* and *souffrir* form their past participles in *-ert: couvert, découvert, recouvert, offert, ouvert, rouvert, souffert.*

365   The verb *défaillir* 'to faint, weaken, etc.', is defective (see **344**). It is conjugated like *assaillir* but, in practice, occurs only in the plural of the present indicative (*nous défaillons, vous défaillez, ils défaillent*), the imperfect indicative (*je défaillais*, etc.), the preterite (*je défaillis*, etc.), the infinitive, and the participles (*défaillant, défailli*). (Other parts of the verb occur very rarely, and there is much uncertainty as to the correct forms.) *Faillir* is both irregular and defective (see **377** below).

The verb *saillir* is also defective, occurring in practice only in the third persons singular and plural of various tenses, the infinitive, and the participles. When meaning 'to jut out, protrude' (i.e. when indicating state, not movement), it is conjugated like *assaillir* (*il saille, ils saillent, il saillait*, etc., *saillant, sailli*). With the meaning 'to gush out, spurt', it is conjugated like *finir*, but it is now rarely used in this sense.

366   Many other verbs in *-ir* are irregular in various respects and are listed among the irregular verbs in **377** below.

Third Conjugation: verbs in -re

367   *Vendre* 'to sell'

	Infinitive		
pres.	*vendre*	past	*avoir vendu*
	Participles		
pres.	*vendant*	past	*vendu*

Indicative

pres.	*je vends*	perf.	*j'ai vendu*
	tu vends		*tu as vendu*
	il vend		*il a vendu*
	nous vendons		*nous avons vendu*
	vous vendez		*vous avez vendu*
	ils vendent		*ils ont vendu*
imperf.	*je vendais*	pluperf.	*j'avais vendu*
	tu vendais		etc.
	il vendait		
	nous vendions		
	vous vendiez		
	ils vendaient		
pret.	*je vendis*	past ant.	*j'eus vendu*
	tu vendis		etc.
	il vendit		
	nous vendîmes		
	vous vendîtes		
	ils vendirent		
fut.	*je vendrai*	fut. perf.	*j'aurai vendu*
	tu vendras		etc.
	il vendra		
	nous vendrons		
	vous vendrez		
	ils vendront		

Conditional

pres.	*je vendrais*	past	*j'aurais vendu*
	tu vendrais		etc.
	il vendrait		
	nous vendrions		
	vous vendriez		
	ils vendraient		

Subjunctive

pres.	*je vende*	perf.	*j'aie vendu*
	tu vendes		etc.
	il vende		
	nous vendions		
	vous vendiez		
	ils vendent		
imperf.	*je vendisse*	pluperf.	*j'eusse vendu*
	tu vendisses		etc.
	il vendît		
	nous vendissions		
	vous vendissiez		
	ils vendissent		

Imperative

vends   vendons   vendez

There are under thirty verbs that conform entirely to the above pattern. They include: *attendre* 'to wait (for)', *confondre* 'to confuse', *défendre* 'to defend, forbid', *dépendre* 'to depend', *descendre* 'to come or go down', *détendre* 'to slacken' (*se détendre* 'to relax'), *distendre* 'to distend', *entendre* 'to hear', *épandre* (literary) 'to shed', *étendre* 'to spread', *fendre* 'to split', *fondre* 'to melt', *mordre* 'to bite', *pendre* 'to hang', *perdre* 'to lose', *pondre* 'to lay (eggs)', *prétendre* 'to claim', *rendre* 'to give back', *répandre* 'to spread, scatter', *répondre* 'to answer', *tendre* 'to stretch, offer', *tondre* 'to shear', *tordre* 'to twist', *vendre* 'to sell', and compounds of a few of them in *re-*, e.g. *revendre* 'to resell'.

Note:

(a) that a few verbs not ending in *-dre* deviate only slightly from the above pattern; they are *battre* (see **369**), *rompre* (see **368**) and *vaincre* (see **370**) and their compounds.

(b) that very many verbs that do end in *-dre* are irregular, in particular *craindre, peindre, joindre*, etc. (see **372**) and *prendre* and its compounds *apprendre, comprendre*, etc. (see **377**, under *prendre*).

368   *Rompre* 'to break' and its compounds *corrompre* 'to corrupt' and *interrompre* 'to interrupt' are similar to *vendre* but have a *-t* in the third person singular of the present indicative:

je romps
tu romps
il rompt
nous rompons
vous rompez
ils rompent

369   *Battre* 'to beat, hit' and its compounds *abattre* 'to fell', *combattre* 'to fight, oppose', *débattre* 'to debate', *rabattre* 'to pull down (e.g. a lid)', etc., and *rebattre* 'to shuffle (cards)' are regular apart from the fact that there is only one *-t-* in the singular of the present indicative and imperative:

je bats
tu bats
il bat
nous battons
vous battez
ils battent

370   *Vaincre* 'to win, conquer', and its compound *convaincre* 'to convince', are regular apart from one purely orthographical feature, namely the fact that *-c-* is replaced by *-qu-* in the plural of the present indicative and imperative and throughout the present subjunctive, imperfect indicative, preterite, imperfect subjunctive, and in the present participle:

Pres. part.: *vainquant*

Past part.: *vaincu*

Pres. indic.: *je vaincs, tu vaincs, il vainc, nous vainquons, vous vainquez, ils vainquent*

Imper.: *vaincs, vainquons, vainquez*

Pres. subjunct.: *je vainque,* etc.

Imperf. indic.: *je vainquais,* etc.

Pret.: *je vainquis,* etc.

Imperf. subjunct.: *je vainquisse,* etc.

Fut.: *je vaincrai,* etc.

Condit.: *je vaincrais,* etc.

Note the *-t-* in the interrogative of the third person singular of the present indicative, *vainc-t-il?* etc. (see **388**,iii).

371   Other verbs in *-re* are irregular. Most of these are listed in **377**, but three groups each contain enough verbs to justify separate treatment here (**372–374**).

372   Verbs ending in *-aindre, -eindre, -oindre*

The only verbs in this group that occur at all frequently are *atteindre* 'to reach, attain', *contraindre* 'to compel', *craindre* 'to fear', *éteindre* 'to extinguish', *étreindre* 'to hug', *joindre* 'to join' (and its compounds *adjoindre, conjoindre, disjoindre, enjoindre, rejoindre*), *peindre* 'to paint', *plaindre* 'to pity', and *restreindre* 'to restrain'. Other verbs in this group are *astreindre* 'to compel', *ceindre* 'to gird', *dépeindre* 'to depict', *déteindre* 'to run (of colours), to fade', *enceindre* 'to surround', *enfreindre* 'to infringe', *feindre* 'to feign', *geindre* 'to moan', and *teindre* 'to dye'.

The little-used verbs *oindre* 'to anoint' and *poindre* 'to dawn' technically form part of this group, but both are defective (see **344**). *Oindre* now occurs in practice only in the infinitive and the past participle (*oint*) and *poindre* only in the infinitive and the third person singular of the present indicative (*il point*) and of the future (*il poindra*) (its present participle also remains, but only as an adjective, *poignant* 'poignant').

The special features of these verbs are (a) that the past participle ends in -*t*, and (b) that -*nd*- changes to -*gn*- when a vowel follows.

Examples:

Pres. part.: *craignant, atteignant, joignant*, etc.

Past. part.: *craint, atteint, joint*, etc.

Pres. indic.:

je crains	*j'atteins*	*je joins*
tu crains	*tu atteins*	*tu joins*
il craint	*il atteint*	*il joint*
nous craignons	*nous atteignons*	*nous joignons*
vous craignez	*vous atteignez*	*vous joignez*
ils craignent	*ils atteignent*	*ils joignent*

Imper.: *crains, craignons, craignez*, etc.

Pres. subjunct.: *je craigne, il atteigne, nous joignions*, etc.

Imperf. indic.: *je craignais, il atteignait, jous joignions*, etc.

Pret.: *je craignis, il atteignit, nous joignîmes*, etc.

Imperf. subjunct.: *je craignisse, il atteignît*, etc.

Fut.: *je craindrai, tu atteindras*, etc.

Condit.: *je craindrais*, etc.

373 Verbs ending in -*aître*, -*oître*

(i) The main verbs in this group are *connaître* 'to know' and its compounds *méconnaître* 'to misjudge' and *reconnaître* 'to recognize', and *paraître* 'to appear' and its compounds *apparaître* 'to appear' and *disparaître* 'to disappear'. There are also the verbs *accroître* 'to increase' and *décroître* 'to decrease' (for the simple verb *croître* see ii below) and the very uncommon verb *repaître* 'to feed'. The verb *paître* 'to graze' also falls within this group but is defective (see **344**); it has no preterite or imperfect subjunctive, and its past participle, *pu*, is not in normal use so, in effect, it has no compound tenses either.

Note that the stem of these verbs has -*î*- (with a circumflex accent) before -*t*, but -*i*- (without an accent) elsewhere (e.g. *connaît* but *connais*).

Examples:

Pres. part.: *connaissant, paraissant, accroissant,* etc.

Past part.: *connu, paru, accru, décru,* etc.

Pres. indic.:

je connais	*je parais*	*j'accrois*
tu connais	*tu parais*	*tu accrois*
il connaît	*il paraît*	*il accroît*
nous connaissons	*nous paraissons*	*nous accroissons*
vous connaissez	*vous paraissez*	*vous accroissez*
ils connaissent	*ils paraissent*	*ils accroissent*

Imper.: *connais, connaissons, connaissez,* etc.

Pres. subjunct.: *je connaisse, il paraisse, nous accroissions,* etc.

Imperf. indic.: *je connaissais, il paraissait, nous accroissions,* etc.

Pret.: *je connus, il parut, nous accrûmes,* etc.

Imperf. subjunct.: *je connusse, il parût,* etc.

Fut.: *je connaîtrai, il accroîtra,* etc.

Condit.: *je paraîtrais,* etc.

(ii) The verb *croître* 'to grow' is conjugated like *accroître* and *décroître* except that it has a circumflex accent in all three forms of the singular of the present indicative, in the 2nd sing. imperative, in all forms of the preterite, and, in the masculine singular only, in the past participle. The circumflex is all that distinguishes these forms from the corresponding forms of the verb *croire* 'to believe' (which, however, also has *crûmes, crûtes* in the preterite). For purposes of comparison, the forms of both verbs are given below:

	Croître	*Croire*
Pres. part.	*croissant*	*croyant*
Past part.	*crû, crue, crus, crues*	*cru, crue, crus, crues*

Indicative

pres.	*je croîs*	*je crois*
	tu croîs	*tu crois*
	il croît	*il croit*
	nous croissons	*nous croyons*
	vous croissez	*vous croyez*
	ils croissent	*ils croient*
imperf.	*je croissais*	*je croyais*
	tu croissais	*tu croyais*
	il croissait	*il croyait*
	nous croissions	*nous croyions*
	vous croissiez	*vous croyiez*
	ils croissaient	*ils croyaient*
pret.	*je crûs*	*je crus*
	tu crûs	*tu crus*
	il crût	*il crut*
	nous crûmes	*nous crûmes*
	vous crûtes	*vous crûtes*
	ils crûrent	*ils crurent*
fut.	*je croîtrai*, etc.	*je croirai*, etc.
condit.	*je croîtrais*, etc.	*je croirais*, etc.

Subjunctive

pres.	*je croisse*	*je croie*
	tu croisses	*tu croies*
	il croisse	*il croie*
	nous croissions	*nous croyions*
	vous croissiez	*vous croyiez*
	ils croissent	*ils croient*
imperf.	*je crusse*, etc.	*je crusse*, etc.

Imperative

croîs   croissons   croissez   *crois   croyons   croyez*

374   Verbs ending in -*uire*

(i) The main verbs in this group are *construire* 'to build', *cuire* 'to cook (intransitive)', *détruire* 'to destroy', *instruire* 'to teach', and a number of compounds of the obsolete verb *duire* 'to lead', viz. *conduire* 'to lead', *déduire* 'to deduce', *enduire* 'to coat', *introduire* 'to introduce', *produire* 'to produce', *réduire* 'to reduce', *séduire* 'to charm, seduce', and *traduire* 'to translate'.

Examples:

Pres. part.: *construisant, cuisant, traduisant*, etc.

Past part.: *construit, cuit, traduit*, etc.

Pres. indic.:

je construis	*je traduis*
tu construis	*tu traduis*
il construit	*il traduit*
nous construisons	*nous traduisons*
vous construisez	*vous traduisez*
ils construisent	*ils traduisent*

Imper.: *traduis, traduisons, traduisez*, etc.

Pres. subjunct.: *je construise, nous traduisions*, etc.

Imperf. indic.: *je construisais, il traduisait*, etc.

Pret.: *je construisis, nous traduisîmes*, etc.

Imperf. subjunct.: *je conduisisse, il traduisît*, etc.

Fut.: *je construirai, il traduira*, etc.

Condit.: *je construirais*, etc.

(ii) The verbs *luire* 'to shine', *reluire* 'to gleam', *nuire* 'to harm', are similarly conjugated except that (a) their past participles are *lui, relui, nui*, and (b) the preterite and the imperfect subjunctive of *luire* and *reluire* do not normally occur (and, in practice, these two verbs are more or less restricted to the third persons singular and plural even in other tenses).

Verbs in -oir

375 As already stated (see **339**), all verbs in *-oir* are irregular. However, the fact that one sub-group, namely that of verbs ending in *-evoir*, contains as many as seven verbs is grounds enough for giving it separate treatment. The verbs in question are *devoir* 'to owe, to have to' and its compound *redevoir* 'to owe a balance (when part of a debt has been paid)', and five verbs in *-cevoir*, viz. *apercevoir* 'to notice', *concevoir* 'to conceive', *décevoir* 'to disappoint', *percevoir* 'to perceive, collect (taxes, etc.)', *recevoir* 'to receive'. (Note (a) that the past participles of *devoir* and *redevoir* take a circumflex accent in the masculine singular *only*, and (b) that, quite regularly, the -c- of verbs in *-cevoir* takes a cedilla when it is immediately followed by *o* or *u*.)

Examples:

Pres. part.: *devant, recevant*

Past part.: *dû, due, dus, dues, reçu*

Pres. indic.:

je dois	*je reçois*
tu dois	*tu reçois*
il doit	*il reçoit*
nous devons	*nous recevons*
vous devez	*vous recevez*
ils doivent	*ils reçoivent*

Imper.: *dois, devons, devez, reçois, recevons, recevez*

Pres. subjunct.:

je doive	*je reçoive*
tu doives	*tu reçoives*
il doive	*il reçoive*
nous devions	*nous recevions*
vous deviez	*vous receviez*
ils doivent	*ils reçoivent*

Imperf. indic.: *je devais, il recevait, nous apercevions*, etc.

Pret.: *je dus, il reçut, nous aperçûmes*, etc.

Imperf. subjunct.: *je dusse, il reçût*, etc.

Fut.: *je devrai, il recevra, nous apercevrons*, etc.

Condit.: *je devrais, il recevrait, nous apercevrions*, etc.

Irregular verbs

376 The following points should be noted:

(1) The forms given below for a simple verb are also correct, unless otherwise stated, for all verbs formed from it. Note in particular the following:

(i) like *acquérir* are *conquérir* 'to conquer', *s'enquérir* 'to enquire', *requérir* 'to require'; the simple verb *quérir* 'to look for' now occurs (and then only rarely) in the infinitive in the expressions *aller quérir* 'to go and fetch', *envoyer quérir* 'to send for', *venir quérir* 'to come for'

(ii) like *courir* are *accourir* 'to rush up', *concourir* 'to compete', *discourir* 'to hold forth', *encourir* 'to incur', *parcourir* 'to travel through', *recourir* 'to have recourse (to)'

(iii) like *écrire* are *décrire* 'to describe', and verbs in *-scrire* such as *inscrire* 'to inscribe', *prescrire* 'to prescribe', *proscrire* 'to ban, proscribe', *souscrire* 'to subscribe', *transcrire* 'to transcribe', etc.

(iv) like *faire* are its compounds *défaire* 'to undo', *contrefaire* 'to imitate', *satisfaire* 'to satisfy', etc.; *parfaire* 'to perfect' is defective, having a past participle (*parfait*) and compound tenses, but no simple tenses

(v) like *mettre* are *admettre* 'to admit', *commettre* 'to commit', *compromettre* 'to compromise', *émettre* 'to emit, transmit, etc.', *omettre* 'to omit', *permettre* 'to permit', *promettre* 'to promise', *soumettre* 'to submit, subject', *transmettre* 'to transmit, pass on', etc.

(vi) like *prendre* are *apprendre* 'to learn', *comprendre* 'to understand', *entreprendre* 'to undertake', *surprendre* 'to surprise', etc.

(vii) like *tenir* are *s'abstenir* 'to abstain', *appartenir* 'to belong', *contenir* 'to contain', *maintenir* 'to maintain', *obtenir* 'to obtain', *retenir* 'to hold back, retain', *soutenir* 'to support', etc.

(viii) like *traire* are *abstraire* 'to abstract', *distraire* 'to entertain, distract', *extraire* 'to extract', *soustraire* 'to subtract, remove'

(ix) like *venir* are *convenir* 'to agree, suit', *devenir* 'to become', *intervenir* 'to intervene', *parvenir* 'to manage', *se souvenir (de)* 'to remember', etc.

(2) Not listed here are verbs of the following types that are discussed fully above:

(i) *-er* and *-ir* verbs having minor irregularities (see **352–358** and **360–362**)

(ii) *dormir, servir, sortir*, etc., and their compounds (see **363**)

(iii) *cueillir, assaillir, couvrir*, and other verbs similarly conjugated (see **364**)

(iv) verbs in *-aindre, -eindre, -oindre, aître, -oître, -uire* (see **372–374**)

(v) *(re)devoir* and *recevoir* and other verbs in *-cevoir* (see **375**).

(3) In all verbs, the conditional has the same stem as the future, and the imperfect subjunctive has the same stem as the preterite

(e.g. from *savoir* and *voir*, future *je saurai, je verrai*, so conditional *je saurais, je verrais*; preterite *je sus, je vis*, so imperfect subjunctive *je susse, je visse*); the conditional and the imperfect subjunctive are therefore not listed below.

(4) Unless otherwise stated in a note, the imperative is the same as the second person singular and the first and second persons plural of the present indicative (e.g. from *dire*, present indicative *tu dis, nous disons, vous dites*, imperative *dis, disons, dites*). If these forms do not exist, then neither does the imperative.

(5) Compound tenses are formed in the same way as in regular verbs.

(6) Defective verbs (see **344**) are indicated by †. A dash (—) indicates that the forms in question do not exist (or, in some cases, that they are so exceptionally rare as to be virtually non-existent in present-day French).

Irregular verbs:
principal forms

377   Irregular verbs: principal forms
A number after the infinitive or other part of a verb refers to the notes in 378 below.

infinitive	participles	present indicative	
(1) †*absoudre*[1] 'absolve'	*absolvant* *absous* (fem. *absoute*)	*j'absous* *tu absous* *il absout*	*nous absolvons* *vous absolvez* *ils absolvent*
(2) *acquérir* 'acquire'	*acquérant* *acquis*	*j'acquiers* *tu acquiers* *il acquiert*	*nous acquérons* *vous acquérez* *ils acquièrent*
(3) *aller* 'go'	*allant* *allé*	*je vais* *tu vas*[2] *il va*	*nous allons* *vous allez* *ils vont*
(4) *s'asseoir*[3] 'sit down'	*s'asseyant* *assis*	*je m'assieds* *tu t'assieds* *il s'assied*	*nous nous asseyons* *vous vous asseyez* *ils s'asseyent*
(5) *avoir* 'have' – see **349**			
(6) *boire* 'drink'	*buvant* *bu*	*je bois* *tu bois* *il boit*	*nous buvons* *vous buvez* *ils boivent*
(7) *bouillir*[4] 'boil'	*bouillant* *bouilli*	*je bous* *tu bous* *il bout*	*nous bouillons* *vous bouillez* *ils bouillent*
(8) †*braire*[5] 'bray'	*brayant* —	*il brait*	*ils braient*
(9) †*bruire* 'rustle', etc.	—	*il bruit*	*ils bruissent*
(10) †*choir*[6] 'fall'	— *chu*	*je chois* *tu chois* *il choit*	— — *ils choient*
(11) †*clore*[7] 'close'	— *clos*	*je clos* *tu clos* *il clôt*	— — *ils closent*
(12) *conclure*[8] 'conclude'	*concluant* *conclu*	*je conclus* *tu conclus* *il conclut*	*nous concluons* *vous concluez* *ils concluent*
(13) *confire* 'preserve (fruit, etc.)'	*confisant* *confit*	*je confis* *tu confis* *il confit*	*nous confisons* *vous confisez* *ils confisent*

pret.	fut. and imperf. indic.	present subjunct.	
—	*j'absoudrai* *j'absolvais*	*j'absolve* *tu absolves* *il absolve*	*nous absolvions* *vous absolviez* *ils absolvent*
j'acquis	*j'acquerrai* *j'acquérais*	*j'acquière* *tu acquières* *il acquière*	*nous acquérions* *vous acquériez* *ils acquièrent*
j'allai	*j'irai* *j'allais*	*j'aille* *tu ailles* *il aille*	*nous allions* *vous alliez* *ils aillent*
je m'assis	*je m'assiérai* *je m'asseyais*	*je m'asseye* *tu t'asseyes* *il s'asseye*	*nous nous asseyions* *vous vous asseyiez* *ils s'asseyent*
je bus	*je boirai* *je buvais*	*je boive* *tu boives* *il boive*	*nous buvions* *vous buviez* *ils boivent*
je bouillis	*je bouillirai* *je bouillais*	*je bouille* *tu bouilles* *il bouille*	*nous bouillions* *vous bouilliez* *ils bouillent*
—	*il braira* *il brayait*	—	—
—	*il bruira* *il bruissait*	—	—
il chut	— —	—	—
—	*je clorai* —	*je close* *tu closes* *il close*	*nous closions* *vous closiez* *ils closent*
je conclus	*je conclurai* *je concluais*	*je conclue* *tu conclues* *il conclue*	*nous concluions* *vous concluiez* *ils concluent*
je confis	*je confirai* *je confisais*	*je confise* *tu confises* *il confise*	*nous confisions* *vous confisiez* *ils confisent*

infinitive	participles		present indicative

(14) *contredire* 'contradict' – see note 11 (on *dire*)

(15) *coudre*	*cousant*	*je couds*	*nous cousons*
'sew'	*cousu*	*tu couds*	*vouz cousez*
		il coud	*ils cousent*

(16) *courir*[9]	*courant*	*je cours*	*nous courons*
'run'	*couru*	*tu cours*	*vous courez*
		il court	*ils courent*

(17) *croire* 'believe, think' – see 373,ii

(18) †*déchoir*[10]	—	*je déchois*	*nous déchoyons*
'decline'	*déchu*	*tu déchois*	*vous déchoyez*
		il déchoit	*ils déchoient*

(19) *devoir* 'owe', have to' – see 375

(20) *dire*[11]	*disant*	*je dis*	*nous disons*
'say'	*dit*	*tu dis*	*vous dites*
		il dit	*ils disent*

(21) †*dissoudre* 'dissolve' – like *absoudre*

(22) †*échoir*[12] 'fall due, expire'

(23) †*éclore*	—	*il éclot*	*ils éclosent*
'to hatch,	*éclos*		
open out'			

(24) *écrire*	*écrivant*	*j'écris*	*nous écrivons*
'write'	*écrit*	*tu écris*	*vous écrivez*
		il écrit	*ils écrivent*

(25) *élire* 'elect' – like *lire*

(26) *émouvoir* 'move, upset' – like *mouvoir* (but see note 13)

(27) †*s'ensuivre*[14] 'ensue'

(28) *entrevoir* 'glimpse' – like *voir*

(29) *envoyer* 'send' – see 357

(30) *être* 'be' – see 350

(31) *exclure* 'exclude' – like *conclure*

(32) *faillir*[15]	—	—	—
'almost	*failli*		
(do)'			

(33) *faire*	*faisant*	*je fais*	*nous faisons*
'do, make'	*fait*	*tu fais*	*vous faites*
		il fait	*ils font*

(34) *falloir*[16]	—	*il faut*	
'be	*fallu*		
necessary'			

(35) †*frire*[17]	—	*je fris*	—
'fry'	*frit*	*tu fris*	—
		il frit	—

(36) *fuir*	*fuyant*	*je fuis*	*nous fuyons*
'flee'	*fui*	*tu fuis*	*vous fuyez*
		il fuit	*ils fuient*

pret.	fut. and imperf. indic.	present subjunct.	
je cousis	je coudrai je cousais	je couse tu couses il couse	nous cousions vous cousiez ils cousent
je courus	je courrai je courais	je coure tu coures il coure	nous courions vous couriez ils courent
je déchus	je déchoirai —	je déchoie — il déchoie	nous déchoyions — ils déchoient
je dis	je dirai je disais	je dise tu dises il dise	nous disions vous disiez ils disent
—	il éclora —	il éclose	ils éclosent
j'écrivis	j'écrirai j'écrivais	j'écrive tu écrives il écrive	nous écrivions vous écriviez ils écrivent
je faillis	je faillirai —	—	—
je fis	je ferai je faisais	je fasse tu fasses il fasse	nous fassions vous fassiez ils fassent
il fallut	il faudra il fallait	il faille	
—	je frirai —	—	—
je fuis	je fuirai je fuyais	je fuie tu fuies il fuie	nous fuyions vous fuyiez ils fuient

infinitive	participles	present indicative	

(37) †*gésir*[18] *gisant*   *je gis*   *nous gisons*
     'lie'   —   *tu gis*   *vous gisez*
                           il gît   *ils gisent*

(38) *inclure* 'include' – see note 8 (to *conclure*)

(39) *interdire* 'forbid' – see note 11 (on *dire*)

(40) *lire*   *lisant*   *je lis*   *nous lisons*
     'read'   *lu*   *tu lis*   *vous lisez*
                           il lit   *ils lisent*

(41) *maudire* *maudissant* *je maudis*   *nous maudissons*
     'curse'   *maudit*   *tu maudis*   *vous maudissez*
                           il maudit   *ils maudissent*

(42) *médire* 'speak ill of' – see note 11 (on *dire*)

(43) *mettre*   *mettant*   *je mets*   *nous mettons*
     'put'   *mis*   *tu mets*   *vous mettez*
                           il met   *ils mettent*

(44) *moudre*   *moulant*   *je mouds*   *nous moulons*
     'grind'   *moulu*   *tu mouds*   *vous moulez*
                           il moud   *ils moulent*

(45) *mourir*   *mourant*   *je meurs*   *nous mourons*
     'die'   *mort*   *tu meurs*   *vous mourez*
                           il meurt   *ils meurent*

(46) *mouvoir* *mouvant*   *je meus*   *mous mouvons*
     'move'   *mû*[19]   *tu meus*   *vous mouvez*
                           il meut   *ils meuvent*

(47) *naître*   *naissant*   *je nais*   *nous naissons*
     'be born' *né*   *tu nais*   *vous naissez*
                           il naît   *ils naissent*

(48) †*ouïr*   —   —   —
     'hear'   *ouï*

(49) *plaire*   *plaisant*   *je plais*   *nous plaisons*
     'please' *plu*   *tu plais*   *vous plaisez*
                           il plaît   *ils plaisent*

(50) *pleuvoir*[20] *pleuvant* *il pleut*
     'rain'   *plu*

(51) *poursuivre* 'pursue' – like *suivre*

(52) *pourvoir* 'provide' – see note 28 (on *voir*)

(53) *pouvoir*[21] *pouvant*   *je peux, je* *nous pouvons*
     'can, be *pu*   *puis*[22]
     able'   *tu peux*   *vous pouvez*
                           il peut   *ils peuvent*

pret.	fut. and imperf. indic.	present subjunct.	
—	— —	—	
	je gisais		
je lus	*je lirai*	*je lise*	*nous lisions*
	je lisais	*tu lises*	*vous lisiez*
		il lise	*ils lisent*
je maudis	*je maudirai*	*je maudisse*	*nous maudissions*
	je maudissais	*tu maudisses*	*vous maudissiez*
		il maudisse	*ils maudissent*
je mis	*je mettrai*	*je mette*	*nous mettions*
	je mettais	*tu mettes*	*vous mettiez*
		il mette	*ils mettent*
je moulus	*je moudrai*	*je moule*	*nous moulions*
	je moulais	*tu moules*	*vous mouliez*
		il moule	*ils moulent*
je mourus	*je mourrai*	*je meure*	*nous mourions*
	je mourais	*tu meures*	*vous mouriez*
		il meure	*ils meurent*
je mus	*je mouvrai*	*je meuve*	*nous mouvions*
	je mouvais	*tu meuves*	*vous mouviez*
		il meuve	*ils meuvent*
je naquis	*je naîtrai*	*je naisse*	*nous naissions*
	je naissais	*tu naisses*	*vous naissiez*
		il naisse	*ils naissent*
—	— —	—	—
je plus	*je plairai*	*je plaise*	*nous plaisions*
	je plaisais	*tu plaises*	*vous plaisiez*
		il plaise	*ils plaisent*
il plut	*il pleuvra*	*il pleuve*	
	il pleuvait		
je pus	*je pourrai*	*je puisse*	*nous puissions*
	je pouvais	*tu puisses*	*vous puissiez*
		il puisse	*ils puissent*

infinitive	participles	present indicative	

(54) *prédire* 'foretell' – see note 11 (on *dire*)

(55) *prendre*   *prenant*   *je prends*   *nous prenons*
    'take'   *pris*   *tu prends*   *vous prenez*
                  il prend   *ils prennent*

(56) *prévaloir* 'prevail' – see note 26 (on *valoir*)

(57) *prévoir* 'foresee' – see note 28 (on *voir*)

(58) †*promouvoir*   *promouvant*   —   —
    'promote'   *promu*

(59) †*résoudre* 'resolve' – see note 1 (on *absoudre*)

(60) *rire*   *riant*   *je ris*   *nous rions*
    'laugh'   *ri*   *tu ris*   *vous riez*
              il rit   *ils rient*

(61) *savoir*[23]   *sachant*   *je sais*   *nous savons*
    'know'   *su*   *tu sais*   *vous savez*
              il sait   *ils savent*

(62) *seoir* 'be situated, suit' – see note 3 (on *s'asseoir*)

(63) *sourire* 'smile' – like *rire*

(64) *suffire*   *suffisant*   *je suffis*   *nous suffisons*
    'suffice'   *suffi*   *tu suffis*   *vous suffisez*
              il suffit   *ils suffisent*

(65) *suivre*   *suivant*   *je suis*   *nous suivons*
    'follow'   *suivi*   *tu suis*   *vous suivez*
              il suit   *ils suivent*

(66) *surseoir*   *sursoyant*   *je sursois*   *nous sursoyons*
    'postpone'   *sursis*   *tu sursois*   *vous sursoyez*
              il sursoit   *ils sursoient*

(67) *survivre* 'survive' – like *vivre*

(68) *taire*[24]   *taisant*   *je tais*   *nous taisons*
    'hush up'   *tu*   *tu tais*   *vous taisez*
              il tait   *ils taisent*

(69) *tenir*[25]   *tenant*   *je tiens*   *nous tenons*
    'hold'   *tenu*   *tu tiens*   *vous tenez*
              il tient   *ils tiennent*

(70) †*traire*   *trayant*   *je trais*   *nous trayons*
    'milk'   *trait*   *tu trais*   *vous trayez*
              il trait   *ils traient*

(71) *vaincre* 'conquer' – see **370**

(72) *valoir*[26]   *valant*   *je vaux*   *nous valons*
    'be worth'   *valu*   *tu vaux*   *vous valez*
              il vaut   *ils valent*

pret.	fut. and imperf. indic.	present subjunct.	
je pris	je prendrai	je prenne	nous prenions
	je prenais	tu prennes	vous preniez
		il prenne	ils prennent
je ris	je rirai	je rie	nous riions
	je riais	tu ries	vous riiez
		il rie	ils rient
je sus	je saurai	je sache	nous sachions
	je savais	tu saches	vous sachiez
		il sache	ils sachent
je suffis	je suffirai	je suffise	nous suffisions
	je suffisais	tu suffises	vous suffisiez
		il suffise	ils suffisent
je suivis	je suivrai	je suive	nous suivions
	je suivais	tu suives	vous suiviez
		il suive	ils suivent
je sursis	je surseoirai	je sursoie	nous sursoyions
	je sursoyais	tu sursoies	vous sursoyiez
		il sursoie	ils sursoient
je tus	je tairai	je taise	nous taisions
	je taisais	tu taises	vous taisiez
		il taise	ils taisent
je tins	je tiendrai	je tienne	nous tenions
	je tenais	tu tiennes	vous teniez
		il tienne	ils tiennent
—	je trairai	je traie	nous trayions
	je trayais	tu traies	vous trayiez
		il traie	ils traient
je valus	je vaudrai	je vaille	nous valions
	je valais	tu vailles	vous valiez
		il vaille	ils vaillent

infinitive	participles	present indicative	
(73) *venir* 'come'	*venant* *venu*	*je viens* *tu viens* *il vient*	*nous venons* *vous venez* *ils viennent*
(74) *vêtir* 'clothe'	*vêtant* *vêtu*	*je vêts* *tu vêts* *il vêt*	*nous vêtons* *vous vêtez* *ils vêtent*
(75) *vivre* 'live'	*vivant* *vécu*	*je vis* *tu vis* *il vit*	*nous vivons* *vous vivez* *ils vivent*
(76) *voir*[28] 'see'	*voyant* *vu*	*je vois* *tu vois* *il voit*	*nous voyons* *vous voyez* *ils voient*
(77) *vouloir*[29] 'wish'	*voulant* *voulu*	*je veux* *tu veux* *il veut*	*nous voulons* *vous voulez* *ils veulent*

	fut. and imperf.		
pret.	indic.	present subjunct.	
je vins[27]	*je viendrai*	*je vienne*	*nous venions*
	je venais	*tu viennes*	*vous veniez*
		il vienne	*ils viennent*
je vêtis	*je vêtirai*	*je vête*	*nous vêtions*
	je vêtais	*tu vêtes*	*vous vêtiez*
		il vête	*ils vêtent*
je vécus	*je vivrai*	*je vive*	*nous vivions*
	je vivais	*tu vives*	*vous viviez*
		il vive	*ils vivent*
je vis	*je verrai*	*je voie*	*nous voyions*
	je voyais	*tu voies*	*vous voyiez*
		il voie	*ils voient*
je voulus	*je voudrai*	*je veuille*	*nous voulions*
	je voulais	*tu veuilles*	*vous vouliez*
		il veuille	*ils veuillent*

378   Notes on irregular verbs

(1) *Absoudre* and *dissoudre* are not usually classified as defective, but strictly speaking they are since they lack the preterite and the imperfect subjunctive. *Résoudre* 'to solve, resolve' is like *absoudre* but usually has the past participle *résolu*.

(2) The second person singular imperative is *va* (but note the special case *vas-y*).

(3) *S'asseoir* may also be conjugated throughout like *surseoir* (i.e. present participle *s'assoyant*, present indicative *je m'assois, nous nous assoyons*, etc., imperfect indicative *je m'assoyais*, etc., imperative *assois-toi, assoyons-nous, assoyez-vous*), but with a difference of spelling in the future and conditional (*je m'assoirai*, etc., but *je surseoirai*, etc.) and the present subjunctive (*je m'assoie*, etc., but *je surseoie*, etc.). However, the forms listed above (i.e. *je m'assieds*, etc.) are more usual. *Asseoir* is occasionally used non-reflexively meaning 'to put someone (child, invalid, etc.) in a chair'. More often it has a technical sense, e.g. 'to impose (a tax), lay (a foundation), base (an opinion), etc.' However, it is most frequently used reflexively. It must be remembered that *s'asseoir* means literally 'to seat oneself', and so 'to sit down'. The past participle *assis* 'seated' is therefore equivalent to the English present participle 'sitting'. *S'asseyant* means 'taking one's seat'. 'I was sitting in the garden all the morning' is *j'étais assis toute la matinée au jardin*, not *je m'asseyais*, which could only mean 'I spent the whole morning taking my seat'. *M'étant assis* means 'having taken my seat, having sat down'.

The simple verb *seoir* in its original sense of 'to sit' remains in legal language in the participles *séant* (e.g. *un tribunal séant à Rouen* 'a tribunal sitting at Rouen') and *sis* 'situated' (e.g. *une maison sise à Versailles* 'a house situated at Versailles'). In the sense of 'suit, be becoming' it has present participle *seyant*, third person singular and third person plural of present indicative, *il sied, ils siéent*, present subjunctive (rare) *il siée, ils siéent*, imperfect indicative *il seyait, ils seyaient*, future *il siéra, ils siéront*, conditional *il siérait, ils siéraient*, but the verb in general is somewhat archaic and none of these forms is widely used.

(4) *Bouillir* is intransitive, e.g. *l'eau bout* 'the water is boiling'; for the transitive, *faire bouillir* must be used, e.g. *Je ferai bouillir de l'eau* 'I will boil some water'.

(5) Although other forms are very occasionally found, in general

braire occurs only in the third persons singular and plural of the tenses indicated (and some of these are rare). No imperative.

(6) Little used, even in literary style, other than in the infinitive (such expressions as *faire choir* 'to knock over', *laisser choir* 'to drop'). No imperfect subjunctive or imperative.

(7) Little used, even in literary style, other than in the infinitive and past participle.

(8) *Exclure* 'to exclude' is like *conclure*. *Inclure* 'to include' is hardly ever used except in the past participle, *inclus(e)* (contrast *conclu*), and then usually in the form *ci-inclus*, e.g. *la lettre ci-incluse* 'the enclosed letter'.

(9) An old form *courre* survives in a few phrases, e.g. *courre le cerf* 'to hung stag', *laisser courre les chiens* 'to lay the hounds on', *la chasse à courre* 'hunting' when it is wanted to distinguish hunting from *la chausse au fusil* 'shooting'.

(10) No imperative.

(11) In the compounds of *dire* the second person plural present indicative and second person plural imperative vary:

> *redire* 'to repeat' has *redites*; *contredire* 'to contradict', *interdire* 'to forbid', *prédire* 'to foretell', *médire* 'to speak ill of', have *contredisez, interdisez, prédisez, médisez*.

Otherwise, these verbs are conjugated exactly like *dire*. Note, however, that *maudire* 'to curse' is conjugated differently (like *finir*, in fact) and so is listed separately.

(12) Used only in the infinitive, the participles, and in the third persons singular and (even less frequently) plural of the tenses indicated and of the conditional (not imperfect subjunctive).

(13) But the past participle, *ému*, has no accent on the -*u*.

(14) Like *suivre* but used only in the infinitive and the third persons singular and plural (of simple and compound tensese).

(15) No imperfect subjunctive. *Faillir* is constructed with an infinitive, e.g. *J'ai failli tomber* 'I nearly fell'. In the earlier meaning of 'to fail', which is still occasionally found but only as an archaism, some forms occur in addition to those we list, e.g. *Le cœur me faut* 'My heart fails me'.

(16) An impersonal verb and so used with impersonal *il* as its subject; no present participle or imperative, but not usually considered defective.

(17) Imperative has second person singular, *fris*, only; future is little used. The missing tenses are supplied by the locution *faire frire*, e.g. *il faisait frire des pommes de terre* 'he was frying potatoes'. *Faire frire* is also widely used in those simple and compound tenses for which forms of *frire* do exist, e.g. *J'ai frit* or *j'ai fait frire des pommes de terre* 'I have fried some potatoes'. But *faire frire* has no passive – use *être* and the past part. *frit*, e.g. *Le poisson avait été frit* 'The fish had been fried'.

(18) Rarely used other than in the expressions (on tombstones) *ci-gît* 'here lies', *ci-gisent* 'here lie'.

(19) The past participle has no accent in the feminine singular (*mue*) and in the plural (*mus, mues*).

(20) Usually impersonal and so used in third person singular only. However, other persons occasionally occur in metaphorical uses, e.g. *Eau, quand donc pleuvras-tu?* (Baudelaire) 'Water, when will you rain?', *Des coups pleuvent (pleuvaient) sur son dos* 'Blows rain (rained) on his back'.

(21) No imperative.

(22) *Puis* is now rarely used except in inversion (questions, etc.), when it *must* be used (i.e. *peux* cannot be used), e.g. *Que puis-je dire?* 'What can I say?', *Peut-être puis-je vous aider* 'Perhaps I can help you'.

(23) Imperative: *sache, sachons, sachez*.

(24) Most frequently used reflexively, *se taire* 'to be silent'.

(25) Note that *tenir* 'to hold' and *venir* 'to come' are conjugated in exactly the same way in all simple tenses. The forms of the preterite and the imperfect subjunctive of these two verbs are so unusual that these tenses are given in full below:

pret.		imperf. subjunct.	
je tins	*je vins*	*je tinsse*	*je vinsse*
tu tins	*tu vins*	*tu tinsses*	*tu vinsses*
il tint	*il vint*	*il tînt*	*il vînt*
nous tînmes	*nous vînmes*	*nous tinssions*	*nous vinssions*
vous tîntes	*vous vîntes*	*vous tinssiez*	*vous vinssiez*
ils tinrent	*ils vinrent*	*ils tinssent*	*ils vinssent*

(26) *Prévaloir* 'to prevail' is conjugated like *valoir* except in the present subjunctive, which keeps -*val*- throughout:

    je prévale   *tu prévales*

il prévale   *vous prévaliez*
nous prévalions   *ils prévalent*

(27) For the full preterite and imperfect subjunctive of *venir*, see note 25, on *tenir*.

(28) *Entrevoir* 'to glimpse', and *revoir* 'to see again, revise' are conjugated like *voir* throughout. *Pourvoir* 'to provide' and *prévoir* 'to foresee' are conjugated like *voir* except that (a) both verbs have their future and conditional in *-voir-*, viz. *je pourvoirai, je pourvoirais, je prévoirai, je prévoirais*, etc., and (b) *pourvoir* has the preterite *je pourvus* and the imperfect subjunctive *je pourvusse*, etc. (but *je prévis, je prévisse*, etc.).

(29) The usual forms of the imperative are *veuille, veuillons, veuillez*, but with the expression *en vouloir à quelqu'un* 'to have (hold) something against someone' the more usual forms of the imperative (and, in practice, this is always in the negative) are *veux, voulons, voulez*, e.g. *Ne m'en veux pas, ne m'en voulez pas* 'Don't hold it against me', *Ne lui en voulons pas* 'Let's not hold it against him' (though *Ne m'en veuillez pas*, etc., also occur).

F Reflexive verbs

379 Strictly speaking, the term **reflexive verb** ought to refer only to verbs whose direct or indirect object, expressed by one or other of the conjunctive pronouns *me, te, se, nous* or *vous* (see **198–199**), refers to the subject of the same verb, e.g. *Jacques se lave* 'James is washing (himself)'. However, in practice the term also covers **reciprocal** verbs, i.e. those expressing actions that the various individuals included in the subject do to one another, e.g. *nous nous aimons* 'we love one another', *ils s'écrivent souvent* 'they often write to each other'.

A number of verbs are used only reflexively, and in some of these the reflexive pronoun is virtually meaningless and untranslatable in English. Among such verbs are:

s'abstenir, abstain, refrain
s'accouder, lean on one's elbows[2]
s'accroupir, crouch[2]

s'adonner (à), devote oneself to, etc.[2]
s'arroger, lay claim to
se blottir, huddle (up)[2]
se démener, fling oneself (about)
se désister, stand down
s'écrier, cry out
s'écrouler, collapse[2]
s'efforcer, strive, endeavour
s'emparer (de), seize
s'empresser, hasten, bustle[2]
s'en aller, go away
s'enquérir, inquire
s'éprendre (de), fall in love with[2]
s'evader, escape
s'évanouir, faint[2]
s'évertuer, strive
s'extasier, go into ecstasies
s'ingénier, contrive
se méfier (de), mistrust
se méprendre, be mistaken
se moquer (de), make fun of[1]
s'opiniâtrer, persist
se raviser, change one's mind
se rebeller, rebel
se récrier, cry out
se réfugier, take refuge
se rengorger, puff oneself up
se repentir, repent[2]
se souvenir (de), remember

Notes

1 Although *se moquer de* is included in this list, the non-reflexive form *moquer* 'to mock' still sometimes occurs in a somewhat archaic literary usage and more generally in the passive, *être moqué* 'to be mocked'.

2 Note the following past participles:

(a) *adonné à* 'addicted to', *blotti* 'huddled (up)', *écroulé* 'collapsed, tumbledown', *épris de* 'enamoured of, in love with', *évanoui* 'unconscious, in a faint'

(b) corresponding to English present participles: *accoudé* 'leaning (on one's elbows)', *accroupi* 'crouching'

(c) used in an active sense: *empressé* 'attentive, assiduous', *repenti* 'penitent, repentant'.

380 Reflexive verbs form their compound tenses with *être*. The past participle agrees with the reflexive pronoun if this serves as the direct object, but not if it serves as the indirect object. Take, for example, the verbs *se blesser* 'to injure oneself' in which *se* is the direct object, and *se nuire* 'to do harm to oneself' in which *se* is the indirect object: in the perfect tense we have *elle s'est blessée* (*blessée* is feminine to agree with *se* 'herself') but *elle s'est nui* (*nui* does not agree because *se* is the indirect object). See further on this, **461**.

381 Example of the conjugation of a reflexive verb:

se laver 'to wash (oneself)'

Infinitive

pres.	*se laver*	past	*s'être lavé/lavée/lavés/lavées*

Participles

pres.	*se lavant*	past	*lavé*

Indicative

pres.	*je me lave*	perf.	*je me suis lavé(e)*
	tu te laves		*tu t'es lavé(e)*
	il se lave		*il s'est lavé*
	elle se lave		*elle s'est lavée*
	nous nous lavons		*nous nous sommes lavé(e)s*
	vous vous lavez		*vous vous êtes lavé(e)(s)*
	ils se lavent		*ils se sont lavés*
	elles se lavent		*elles se sont lavées*
imperf.	*je me lavais*, etc.	pluperf.	*je m'étais lavé*, etc.
pret.	*je me lavai*, etc.	past ant.	*je me fus lavé*, etc.
fut.	*je me laverai*, etc.	fut. perf.	*je me serai lavé*, etc.

Conditional

pres.	*je me laverais*, etc.	past	*je me serais lavé*, etc.

Subjunctive

pres.	*je me lave*, etc.	pref.	*je me sois lavé*, etc.
imperf.	*je me lavasse*, etc.	pluperf.	*je me fusse lavé*, etc.

Imperative

lave-toi   *lavons-nous*   *lavez-vous*

G The passive

382 The French passive is formed in exactly the same way as the English passive, i.e. with the verb *être* 'to be' and the past participle, e.g. *Il sera tué* 'He will be killed'. The past participle varies, agreeing in gender and number with the subject, e.g. *Elle sera tuée* 'She will be killed' (but note that, in the compound tenses, *été* does not change, e.g. *Elle a été tuée* 'She has been killed'), *Elles ont peur d'être blessées* 'They are afraid of being hurt'.

383 Example of the passive conjugaton: *être blessé* 'to be hurt or wounded' (passive of *blesser* 'to hurt, to wound'):

	Infinitive		
pres.	*être blessé* (or *-és, -ée, -ées*) to be hurt	past	*avoir été blessé*, etc., to have been hurt
	Participles		
pres.	*étant blessé*, etc., being hurt	past	*blessé*, etc., hurt, or having been hurt
	Indicative		
pres.	*je suis blessé* (or *-ée*) I am hurt	perf.	*j'ai été blessé*, etc., I have been hurt
	tu es blessé (or *-ée*)		*tu as été blessé*, etc.
	il est blessé		*il a été blessé*
	elle est blessée		*elle a été blessée*
	nous sommes blessés (or *ées*)		*nous avons été blessés*, etc.
	vous êtes blessé (or *-ée, -és, -ées*)		*vous avez été blessé*, etc.
	ils sont blessés		*ils ont été blessés*
	elles sont blessées		*elles ont été blessées*

Only the masculine form of the past participle is shown in the rest of the conjugation below:

imperf.	*j'étais blessé* I was hurt		pluperf.	*j'avais été blessé* I had been hurt
pret.	*Je fus blessé* I was hurt		past ant.	*j'eus été blessé* I had been hurt
fut.	*je serai blessé* I shall be hurt		fut. perf.	*j'aurai été blessé* I shall have been hurt

Conditional

pres.	*je serais blessé* I should be hurt	past	*j'aurais été blessé* I should have been hurt

Subjunctive

pres.	*je sois blessé* I am (may be) hurt	perf.	*j'aie été blessé* I (may) have been hurt
imperf.	*je fusse blessé* that I was (might be) hurt	pluperf.	*j'eusse été blessé* I had (might have) been hurt

Imperative

sois blessé be hurt	*soyons blessés* let us be hurt	*soyez blessé* be hurt

384 French frequently uses other constructions where English uses the passive. Note in particular:

(1) the fact that *on* (see **302**) is much more extensively used than its English equivalent, 'one', e.g. *On dit que* . . ., literally 'One says that . . .', where English would normally say 'It is said that', *On lui a rendu son argent* 'His money was given back to him'

(2) the widespread use of the reflexive as an equivalent of the English passive, e.g. *Cela se comprend* 'That is understood'

(3) the fact that word-for-word equivalents of the English passive with a direct object, e.g. 'He was given a book', do not exist in French – but the view one sometimes sees expressed, that French has *no* equivalent construction, is mistaken (see **385**).

385 An English sentence such as 'The teacher gave the boy a book' can be turned into a passive by taking as the subject either the original direct object, 'A book was given to the boy (by the teacher)', or the original indirect object, 'The boy was given a book (by the teacher)'. French has a word-for-word equivalent of the first of these, viz. *Un livre fut donné au garçon (par le professeur)*, but not of the second. However, although many grammars fail to mention the fact, a construction in which the original indirect object is the subject, i.e. a passive in which the original direct object remains the direct object, **is** possible in French and, though less common than its English equivalent, is in widespread use, particularly but by no means exclusively in journalistic usage. It involves the verb *voir* 'to see', as in:

Les mineurs se voient déjà offrir plus de 16% (Le Monde)
The miners are already being offered more than 16%

Je me suis vu refuser un visa par le consulat américain
I have been refused a visa by the American consulate

The construction can occur even when the subject is inanimate and so cannot 'see' the action that is performed, e.g.:

'Le Voyage au bout de la nuit' se vit décerner le prix Théophraste Renaudot par 6 voix sur 10 (J. A. Ducourneau)
(The novel) *Le Voyage au bout de la nuit* was awarded the Théophraste Renaudot prize by 6 votes out of 10

On the other hand, when the main verb is a verb of saying, the passive auxiliary is usually *entendre* 'to hear' rather than *voir*, e.g.:

C'est plutôt rare qu'une femme de ménage s'entende dire ça
(Simenon)
It's not often a cleaning lady is told that

H Negative and interrogative conjugations

386 Negation and interrogation (questions) are dealt with more fully below in **542–580** and **581–593** respectively. Here, we are concerned only with the basic forms involved.

387 (i) The following table illustrates, from one simple tense (the present) and one compound tense (the perfect), the difference between verbs conjugated affirmatively and those conjugated negatively, or interrogatively, or both:

affirmative ('I speak', etc.)	interrogative ('Do I speak?', etc.)
je parle	(See **389**)
tu parles	*parles-tu?*
il parle	*parle-t-il?*
elle parle	*parle-t-elle?*
nous parlons	*parlons-nous?*
vous parlez	*parlez-vous?*

ils parlent	*parlent-ils?*
elles parlent	*parlent-elles?*
j'ai parlé	*ai-je parlé?*
tu as parlé	*as-tu parlé?*
il a parlé	*a-t-il parlé?*
elle a parlé	*a-t-elle parlé?*
nous avons parlé	*avons-nous parlé?*
vous avez parlé	*avez-vous parlé?*
ils ont parlé	*ont-ils parlé?*
elles ont parlé	*ont-elles parlé?*
negative	negative-interrogative
('I do not speak', etc.)	('Do I not speak?', etc.)
je ne parle pas	(See **389**)
tu ne parles pas	*ne parles-tu pas?*
il ne parle pas	*ne parle-t-il pas?*
elle ne parle pas	*ne parle-t-elle pas?*
nous ne parlons pas	*ne parlons-nous pas?*
vous ne parlez pas	*ne parlez-vous pas?*
ils ne parlent pas	*ne parlent-ils pas?*
elles ne parlent pas	*ne parlent-elles pas?*
je n'ai pas parlé	*n'ai-je pas parlé?*
tu n'as pas parlé	*n'as-tu pas parlé?*
il n'a pas parlé	*n'a-t-il pas parlé?*
elle n'a pas parlé	*n'a-t-elle pas parlé?*
nous n'avons pas parlé	*n'avons-nous pas parlé?*
vous n'avez pas parlé	*n'avez-vous pas parlé?*
ils n'ont pas parlé	*n'ont-ils pas parlé?*
elles n'ont pas parlé	*n'ont-elles pas parlé?*

(ii) Note:

(a) that in the interrogative form, the subject pronoun stands after the verb, and in a compound tense stands after the auxiliary, to which it is linked by a hyphen; for important exceptions, see **388** and **389**

(b) that in the negative form, *ne* and *pas* respectively precede and follow the verb or the auxiliary

(c) that in the negative-interrogative form, *ne* precedes the verb and *pas* follows the pronoun

(d) that the only elements that can come between *ne* and the verb are the conjunctive pronouns (including *y* and *en*) (see 198–201), e.g. *il ne me les donne pas* 'he does not give them to me', *nous n'en parlons pas* 'we do not talk about it', *ne lui avez-vous pas parlé?* 'haven't you spoken to him?'

(iii) Other verbs and tenses are treated in the same way, e.g.:

vous finissez 'you finish', *finissez-vous? vous ne finissez pas, ne finissez-vous pas?*

tu vends 'you sell', *vends-tu? tu ne vends pas, ne vends-tu pas?*

il viendra 'he will come', *viendra-t-il? il ne viendra pas, ne viendra-t-il pas?*

ils sont partis 'they have left', *sont-ils partis? ils ne sont pas partis, ne sont-ils pas partis?*

nous avions vu 'we had seen', *avions-nous vu? nous n'avions pas vu, n'avions-nous pas vu?*

388 (i) Note that, if the verb ends in a vowel, *-t-* is inserted before *il* or *elle* in the interrogative and negative-interrogative forms, e.g. *parle-t-il? n'a-t-elle pas parlé? viendra-t-il? viendra-t-elle?*

(ii) There is no *-t-* when the verb ends in a consonant, e.g. *est-il?* 'is he?', *voit-elle?* 'does she see?', *vend-il?* 'does he sell?', *avait-il fini?* 'had he finished?' In such circumstances, the final *-t* and the final *-d* are both pronounced as a [t], e.g. *Que répond-il?* [kə repɔ̃til] 'What does he reply?'

(iii) The only exception to (ii) above is the present tense of *vaincre* and *convaincre* (see 370), e.g. *vainc-t-il? convainc-t-elle?*

(iv) Note that this *-t-* also occurs with the pronoun *on* 'one', e.g. *Où va-t-on?* 'Where are we going?' (*lit.* 'Where is one going?'), *Que cherche-t-on?* 'What are they looking for?' (*lit.* 'What is one looking for?').

389 (i) In the present indicative, it is normally only with a few common monosyllabic verbs that *je* is inverted (placed after the verb), in particular *ai-je? dis-je? dois-je? puis-je?* (as the interrogative of *je peux*), *sais-je? suis-je?* and, with a following infinitive, *vais-je?*, e.g.:

Ai-je bien compris?
Have I understood aright?

Que dois-je répondre?
What am I to reply?

Puis-je vous aider?
May I help you?

Où vais-je le cacher?
Where am I going to hide it?

Je fais and *je vois* may also be inverted, but even less commonly so than the above, which are themselves characteristic of a slightly formal style rather than of everyday spoken usage.

(ii) In the present indicative of first conjugation verbs, many grammars list forms like *parlé-je?* (note the acute accent – but the pronunciation is [parlɛ:ʒ]), etc. These certainly do exist, but nowadays only rarely occur even in the written language. They should never be used in speech and are best avoided even in writing. (Note that, in any case, this form does not occur with verbs whose stem ends in [ʒ], like *je mange* and *je voyage*.)

(iii) *Je* is **never** inverted in the present indicative of other verbs (e.g. *je finis, je vends, je dors, j'écris*).

(iv) Normally, the interrogative of the *je* form of the present indicative (and frequently of other tenses too) is expressed either by intonation (see **586**) or by *est-ce que?* (see **585**), *qu'est-ce que?* 'what?' (see **283**), etc.; so, an alternative form for the sentences quoted in i above would be *Est-ce que j'ai bien compris? Qu'est-ce que je dois répondre? Est-ce que je peux vous aider? Où est-ce que je vais le cacher?*

I Person and number

Introduction

390 A verb agrees in person and number with its subject, i.e. a first person singular subject (*je*) takes a first person singular verb, a second person plural subject (*vous*) takes a second person plural verb, etc., e.g.:

Je sais où vous habitez
I know where you live

If the subject is a noun, or a pronoun other than a first or second person pronoun, the verb is in the third person (singular or plural depending on the subject), e.g.:

Mon frère arrivera demain
My brother will arrive tomorrow

Ces livres-ci m'intéressent mais ceux-là ne valent rien
These books interest me but those are worthless

Où travaillent-elles?
Where do they work?

Generally speaking, this agreement should pose no problems. Some cases that may not be quite straightforward are dealt with in the following sections.

Coordinate subjects

391 (i) When a coordinate subject (i.e. a subject consisting of two or more elements, usually linked by *et* 'and') consists solely of nouns and/or pronouns *other than first or second person pronouns*, the verb is in the third person plural (but see iii below), e.g.:

Jean et Pierre habitaient ici
John and Peter used to live here

Celui-ci et celui-là sont tout à fait pareils
This one and that one are exactly alike

Son père et lui sont déjà partis
His father and he have already left

Lui et elle se détestent
He and she hate one another

(ii) When the elements of a coordinate subject taken together are the equivalent of 'we' (in which case one element will necessarily be *moi* 'I' or *nous* 'we'), the verb is in the first person plural, e.g.:

Mon frère et moi nous partons demain
My brother and I are leaving tomorrow

Vous et moi, nous n'avons jamais dit cela
You and I have never said that

Similarly, when the elements of a coordinate subject are the equivalent of 'you' (in which case one element will necessarily be either *toi* or *vous* 'you'), the verb is in the second person plural, e.g.:

Ton frère et toi, vous faites énormément de bruit
Your brother and you are making an awful lot of noise

Qu'est-ce que vous faites demain, vous et vos amis?
What are you and your friends doing tomorrow?

(For the use or non-use of the conjunctive pronoun in such contexts, see 216,ii.)

(iii) When coordinate subjects are linked by *ou* 'either' or *ni* 'neither', the verb in French is normally in the plural (whereas in equivalent sentences in English it may well be in the singular), e.g.:

Un homme de génie ou un intrigant seuls se disent: 'J'ai eu tort' (Balzac)
Only a genius or a schemer can say: 'I was wrong'

Je suis sûr que ni Pierre ni Jean ne le connaissent
I am sure that neither Peter nor John knows him

However, the singular can occur after *ou* when 'either . . . or' means 'one or other but not both', e.g.:

Ou M. Dupont ou M. Lambert sera élu président
Either M. Dupont or M. Lambert will be elected president

The singular can also occur after *ni . . . ni* 'neither . . . nor' when one of the elements refers to a category that includes the other; this is particularly so when French uses *personne* 'nobody' where English uses 'nor anyone else', e.g.:

Ni lui ni personne ne saura vous le dire
Neither he nor anyone else will be able to tell you

(the justification for the singular being that, if 'no one' can tell you, then 'he' is included in the category of those who cannot tell you).

(iv) For the agreement of the verb with *l'un et l'autre, l'un ou l'autre, ni l'un ni l'autre*, see 292,iv.

392 Note:

(a) that *chacun* 'each', even when followed by *de nous* or *de vous*, takes a third person singular verb, e.g.:

Chacun de vous recevra une récompense
Each of you will receive a reward

(b) that *certains d'entre nous* (or *vous*) 'some of us (*or* you)' and *plusieurs d'entre nous* (or *vous*) 'several of us (*or* you)' take a third person plural verb, e.g.:

Certains d'entre nous le savent déjà
Some of us know already

Plusieurs d'entre vous seront obligés de partir
Several of you will be obliged to leave

393 Note that when two nouns and/or pronouns are linked not by *et* 'and' but by some such expression as *ainsi que, aussi bien que, de même que* 'as well as, together with', the two nouns and/or pronouns are not coordinate and the verb agrees with the first (cf. the agreement of adjectives, **129**), e.g.:

Son frère, ainsi que ses parents, est furieux
His brother, together with his parents, is furious

The same is true when two nouns and/or pronouns are linked by a negative adverb such as *non* or by some expression containing an implied negation, such as *plutôt que* 'rather than', e.g.:

Je crois que lui et non (or *plutôt que*) *sa sœur répondra à ta lettre*
I think he, not (*or* rather than) his sister, will answer your letter

Collective nouns

394 A further problem may arise when the subject is a collective noun, i.e. a noun referring to a group of individuals that collectively form some kind of whole, e.g. 'committee', 'crowd', 'government', 'team'. In British English (much more so than in American English), such nouns, although grammatically singular, often take a plural verb, e.g.: 'The committee are (*or* is) meeting now', 'The crowd were (*or* was) cheering', 'The government do (*or* does) not agree', 'The team have (*or* has) already left'. Theoretically, and to some extent in reality, the distinction between singular and plural depends on whether the noun is interpreted as denoting one collective entity ('The government has decided') or as a group of individuals ('The government have decided'); this distinction, however, seems not to be always observed in practice.

In French, there is some degree of comparable flexibility when a collective noun is followed by *de* and a plural noun (see **396**), but not otherwise (see **395**).

395 When a collective noun stands on its own, i.e. when it is not accompanied by *de* + plural noun (see **396**), the verb must be in the singular, e.g.:

Le comité se réunit aujourd'hui
The committee is (*or* are) meeting today

La foule applaudissait
The crowd were (*or* was) applauding

Le gouvernment a démissioné
The government has (*or* have) resigned

Le parti socialiste n'accepte pas cette proposition
The socialist party do (*or* does) not accept this proposal

L'équipe anglaise est déjà partie
The English team have (*or* has) already left

– and likewise with such words as *l'armée* 'the army', *la classe* 'the class', *la compagnie* 'the company', *la famille* 'the family', *le ministère* 'the ministry', *le peuple (français)* 'the (French) people', *le troupeau* 'the flock', *l'université* 'the university'.

Note in particular that *tout le monde* 'everybody' always takes a singular verb, e.g. *Tout le monde est parti* 'Everybody has left'.

396 (i) When a collective noun is followed by *de* + a plural noun, the agreement may be:

(a) with the (singular) collective noun, when the idea of the collective entity is dominant, e.g.:

Un bataillon de soldats défilait dans les rues
A battalion of soldiers was marching through the streets

Une troupe d'oies sauvages traversa le ciel (Bazin)
A flock of wild geese flew across the sky

or, (b) with the plural noun, when the emphasis is on the individuals making up the collective entity, e.g.:

Une foule de gens sont venus nous voir
A crowd of people came to see us

Une multitude de villes ont été détruites (Bernardin de Saint-Pierre)
A multitude of cities have been destroyed

Une nuée d'oiseaux s'élevaient des arbres (Bosco)
A cloud of birds rose from the trees

(ii) Similar considerations apply to numerals expressing round numbers such as *une douzaine* 'a dozen' (see **185**,b) and fractions like *la moitié* 'half', *un tiers* 'a third', *un quart* 'a quarter', e.g.:

(a) (verb in the singular)

Une douzaine d'œufs suffira
A dozen eggs will be enough

La moitié des sénateurs a voté pour le projet de loi
Half the Senators voted for the bill

(b) (verb in the plural)

Une douzaine de personnes sont déjà parties
A dozen people have already left

La moitié de nos étudiants sont âgés de plus de vingt ans
Half our students are aged over twenty

397 The agreement of the verb with indefinites and quantifiers generally follows the principle that, if the overall sense of the subject is plural, then the verb is plural. Note in particular the following:

(i) A plural verb is used:

(a) with *beaucoup* 'many' (not, of course, when it means 'much', see **45**) and *la plupart* 'the majority, most', whether or not they are followed by *de*, e.g.:

La plupart de mes amis habitent près de Paris
Most of my friends live near Paris

La plupart (or *Beaucoup*) *sont déjà partis*
Most (*or* Many) have already left

(b) with *nombre de, quantité de* 'a number of', *bon nombre de* 'a good number of', and usually (though not invariably) with other expressions based on *nombre* or *quantité* such as *un grand* (or *petit*) *nombre (de)* 'a large (*or* small) number (of)', *un certain nombre (de)* 'most (of)', *une (grande) quantité (de)* 'a great quantity (of)', e.g.:

Nombre de personnes me l'ont dit
A lot of people have told me so

Un certain nombre de difficultés surgissent
A certain number of difficulties arise

Un grand nombre de nos étudiants sont américains
A great number of our students are Americans

Le plus grand nombre sont déjà partis
Most have already left

(c) The archaic quantifier *force* (no *de*) 'many', takes a plural verb, e.g.:

Force gens croient être plaisants, qui ne sont que ridicules
Many people think they are amusing when they are merely ridiculous

(ii) *Le peu (de)* followed by a singular noun, i.e. when it means 'the little (= small amount) (of)', necessarily takes a singular verb, e.g.:

Le peu d'argent qui me reste me suffira
The little money I have left will be enough for me

whereas, when followed by a plural noun, i.e. when it means 'the few', the verb is normally plural if the emphasis is on the number (small though it may be) of individual persons or things denoted by the noun, e.g.:

Le peu de troupes qu'il avait rassemblées ont tenu ferme
The small number of troops he had gathered together stood firm

(It can however happen, though infrequently, that *le peu de* + a plural noun emphasizes the smallness of the quantity, e.g. *Le peu de gens qui nous suit n'y suffira pas* 'The fewness of our followers will not suffice for the purpose'.)

(iii) Despite what mathematics might suggest, *plus d'un* 'more than one' usually takes a singular verb, e.g.:

> *Plus d'un se rappela des matinées pareilles* (Flaubert)
> More than one remembered mornings like that

while *moins de* 'less than' + a numeral (even *moins de deux* 'less than two') takes a plural verb, e.g.:

> *Moins de deux mois se sont écoulés*
> Less than two months have elapsed

(iv) Note that when 'the rest' means 'the others' rather than 'what remains' (as in *le reste de son argent* 'the rest of his money'), it is best translated by *les autres* which, of course, takes a plural verb, e.g. *Cette lettre est pour moi mais les autres sont pour toi* 'This letter is for me but the rest (the others) are for you'.

J Tenses

Introduction

398 There are many similarities but also some fundamental differences between the tense systems of English and French. Among the main differences are the following:

399 (i) The English distinction between simple forms and continuous forms (constructed with the verb 'to be' and the present participle) is not paralleled in French. When it is desired to stress the fact that the action was in progress, French can certainly do so, by using the expression *être en train de* 'to be in the process of' + the infinitive, e.g.:

> *Il ne faut pas le déranger, il est en train de réfléchir*
> We mustn't disturb him, he's thinking
>
> *Il était en train de téléphoner à sa femme quand je suis arrivé*
> He was telephoning his wife when I arrived

but this construction should be used only sparingly and not be regarded as an all-purpose equivalent of the English continuous forms. The following will illustrate some of the forms that correspond in the two languages:

I write	I am writing	*j'écris*
I lived	I was living	*j'habitais*
I have worked	I have been working	*j'ai travaillé*

Nor does French have a special form corresponding to the English 'habitual past' expressed by 'used to' – e.g. the normal equivalent of 'I used to work' is just *je travaillais*.

400 (ii) The English preterite or simple past (e.g. 'I wrote, he came') has a number of different values which in French are expressed by different tenses (see **405–410**).

On the other hand, the French perfect (e.g. *j'ai chanté*) may correspond either to the English perfect ('I have sung') or, very frequently, to the English preterite ('I sang') (see **410**).

401 Note too (though this is not a matter of tense) that French does not use *faire* as English uses 'to do' as a mere auxiliary verb in the negative and interrogative conjugations (e.g. 'I do not sing', 'Do you sing?'), or for the purpose of emphasizing the verb (e.g. 'I do find my work hard') (in such contexts, French uses some such expression as *en fait* 'indeed' or *il est vrai que* 'it is true that').

402 In sections **404–424** we consider some problems relating to the use of particular tenses of the indicative. For tenses of the subjunctive, see **496–506**.

403 English allows the repetition of an auxiliary verb such as 'be', 'have', 'do', 'shall', 'will', 'let', by way of confirmation or contradiction (particularly but not exclusively in answer to a question), e.g.:

Are you coming – Yes, I am / No, I'm not
Have you finished? – Yes, I have
Do you speak German? – I do
I think he's written to you already – He has / No, he hasn't
Will they be coming? – (Yes,) they will / (No,) they won't
Let's go now – Yes, let's

Nothing comparable is possible in French. In such contexts, French uses 'yes' or 'no' and/or repeats the verb and/or introduces some other expression by way of emphasis. So, the above examples could be rendered as follows, among many other possibilities:

> *Tu viens? – Oui, oui, (je viens) / Non, non, (je ne viens pas)*
> *Avez-vous fini? – Oui, (j'ai fini)*
> *Vous parlez allemand? – Oui, (je parle allemand)*
> *Je crois qu'il vous a déjà écrit – Ah, oui! / Pas du tout*
> *Ils vont venir? – Bien sûr / Sûrement pas*
> *Partons maintenant. – Oui, partons*

The 'historic present'

404 The 'historic present', i.e. the present tense as a narrative and descriptive tense with reference to the past, is very much more widely used in French than in English, e.g.:

> *Le lendemain matin, un homme muni d'un appareil photo*
> *pénètre dans la salle à manger de mon hôtel. Il se plante à*
> *quelques mètres de moi et, calmement, déclenche son flash*
> (Sylviane Stein in *L'Express*)
> The next morning a man with a camera made his way into the dining-room of my hotel. He planted himself a few yards from me and, calmly, took a flash photo.

The imperfect, the preterite, and the perfect

405 The preterite is no longer in normal use in spoken French though it survives in the written language (except in an informal style influenced by the spoken language). In discussing the use of these three past tenses, we must therefore distinguish between (i) the written language (see **406–408**) and (ii) the spoken language (see **409–410**).

(i) The written language

406   The imperfect is used:

(a) to refer to a past event regarded as continuous or as being in progress, i.e. it corresponds to the English 'was (were) + . . . ing' which can always be translated by the French imperfect; note, however, that English sometimes uses the preterite in such contexts, e.g.:

Il pleuvait lorsque Jean partit
It was raining when John left

Pendant que mon père travaillait, mon frère dormait
While my father was working, my brother was sleeping
While my father worked, my brother slept

(b) for descriptions in the past (including descriptions of states of mind, etc.), e.g.:

Sous l'Empire les Romains étaient très civilisés
Under the Empire the Romans were very civilized

Elle ne voulait pas sortir
She did not wish to go out

Le sentier descendait vers un pont qui traversait un petit ruisseau
The path sloped down towards a bridge that crossed a little stream

(c) with reference to habitual actions in the past, i.e. it corresponds to English 'used to do' which can always be translated by the French imperfect; note, however, that English very often uses the preterite in such contexts whereas French does not; e.g.:

Lorsqu'il voyageait beaucoup, il m'écrivait chaque semaine
When he used to travel a lot, he used to write to me every week
When he travelled a lot, he wrote to me every week

Quand nous étions à Paris, nous allions tous les jours au Bois de Boulogne
When we were in Paris we went (*or* we used to go) to the Bois de Boulogne every day

Note that the important thing is that the action is regarded as **habitual, not merely as frequent or repeated** (in which case the preterite or the perfect is used – see also 407,a), e.g.:

Pendant les vacances, il lui téléphonait régulièrement
During the holidays, he rang (*or* used to ring) her regularly

Pendant les vacances, il lui téléphona plusieurs fois
During the holidays, he rang her several times

Il lui a déjà téléphoné dix fois
He has already rung her ten times

(d) The imperfect can also be used for various stylistic effects; this is particularly true of what has been termed the 'picturesque imperfect', i.e. the use of the imperfect where the preterite or the perfect would normally be expected (see **407** and **410**) with reference to a completed action in the past, and often with a precise indication of time or date, e.g.:

Louis XIV se remariait deux ans après (É. Faguet)
Louis XIV remarried two years afterwards

Il y a six ans, l'armée française débarquait sur les côtes de Provence (France-Illustration)
Six years ago the French army landed on the coast of Provence

Since one role of the imperfect is to present the action as in progress (see a above), the effect of using it instead of the preterite or perfect is to present the action as unfolding before our eyes, so to speak, and hence to heighten the effect. But this construction should only be used sparingly and with care and is best avoided by learners.

407 The preterite refers to events regarded as completed (i.e. not as continuous or habitual – see **406**) in the past, e.g.:

L'accord fut signé mardi
The agreement was signed on Tuesday

Les alliés débarquèrent en Normandie en 1944
The allies landed in Normandy in 1944

It is frequently used as a narrative tense, expressing successive events in the story, e.g.:

Giuseppa embrassa son fils et rentra en pleurant dans sa cabane. Elle se jeta à genoux devant une image de la Vierge, et pria avec ferveur. Cependant Falcone marcha quelque deux cents pas dans le sentier et ne s'arrêta que dans un petit ravin où il descendit. L'endroit lui parut convenable pour son dessein. (Mérimée)

Giuseppa kissed her son and went back into the hut in tears. She fell upon her knees before an image of the Virgin, and prayed fervently. Meanwhile Falcone walked some two hundred paces along the path, and did not stop till he came to a little gully into which he descended. The place seemed to him suitable for carrying out his plan.

Note:

(a) that while habitual actions are expressed by the imperfect, actions that are merely presented as repeated can be in the preterite (see also **406**,c), e.g.:

Il visita Paris quatre fois pendant les années 50
He visited Paris four times during the 50s

(b) that the length of time taken by the action is irrelevant – an event that lasted years, or centuries, or millions of years, is expressed by the preterite if it is regarded as a completed event in the past, e.g.:

Voltaire vécut 84 ans
Voltaire lived for 84 years

L'ère tertiaire dura cinquante millions d'années
The tertiary era lasted fifty million years

408   The use of the perfect corresponds closely to that of the English perfect; it implies some kind of link between the past event and present time, e.g. that the action has taken place in a period of time (the same day, the same century, someone's lifetime, etc.) that still continues, or that the consequences of the action continue into the present, e.g.:

Je n'ai jamais visité Versailles
I have never visited Versailles (i.e. in the course of my life, which continues)

as contrasted with:

Je passai trois ans à Paris mais je ne visitai jamais Versailles
I spent three years in Paris but I never visited Versailles (i.e. during the three years in question, which are now over)

The difference between the preterite and the perfect is well illustrated by the following example in which they both occur:

Nous nous adressâmes la parole quelques jours plus tard, un dimanche matin, en des circonstances dont j'ai bien gardé la mémoire (Lacretelle)
We spoke to one another a few days later, one Sunday morning, in circumstances that have remained clearly in my memory

(ii) The spoken language

409   The use of the imperfect in speech is the same as in the written language (see **406**).

410   The preterite is no longer in normal use in speech, in which its functions as a narrative past tense have been taken over entirely by the perfect, e.g.:

J'ai visité Paris pour la première fois en 1948
I visited Paris for the first time in 1948

La guerre a éclaté en 1939
War broke out in 1939

This use of the perfect, as a substitute for the preterite, is increasingly found not only in speech but in writing, especially in journalism and in a narrative style that is modelled on spoken usage, e.g.:

Jeter l'Angleterre à genoux en l'atteignant par les Indes, jamais Napoléon n'a perdu de vue cet objectif. Il l'a poursuivi par toutes les voies
To beat England to her knees by striking at her through India – this was the objective that Napoleon never lost sight of. He tried every road that might lead to its attainment

Note examples such as the following in which the French corresponds once to the English preterite and once to the English perfect:

Je l'ai vu il y a dix ans et je ne l'ai jamais revu
I saw him ten years ago and I have never seen him since

The pluperfect and the past anterior

411 (i) The pluperfect is used as in English, e.g.:

Je croyais qu'il avait terminé son travail
I thought he had finished his work

Note however that, in sentences such as the following in which English can use a preterite instead of the pluperfect that, strictly speaking, the sense requires, the pluperfect **must** be used in French:

Il prétendait que son frère lui avait écrit la semaine précédente
He claimed that his brother wrote (*or* had written) to him the week before

(ii) The past anterior, like the preterite, is practically unknown in conversation. It is a literary form used principally:

(a) with temporal conjunctions, such as *quand, lorsque* 'when', *après que* 'after', *dès que, aussitôt que* 'as soon as', when the main verb is preterite, and similarly after *à peine* 'scarcely' followed by a *que*-clause, to indicate that one thing happened immediately after something else had happened, e.g.:

Dès qu'ils eurent mis le nez dehors, l'orage éclata
The storm burst the instant they put their noses outside

A peine eurent-ils mis le nez dehors que l'orage éclata
Hardly had they put their noses outside when the storm burst

(b) occasionally, in a main clause, with an expression of time such as *bientôt* 'soon', *vite* 'quickly', *en un instant* 'in a moment', to express the speed with which something happened, e.g.:

Cependant il eut bien vite deviné que . . . (Hugo)
However, he had very quickly guessed that . . .

Ils eurent rejoint la chasse en un instant (Mérimée)
In a moment they had caught up with the hunt

The 'double-compound' tenses

412   (i) The past anterior is, of course, based on the preterite, e.g. *(il) eut (fini), (il) fut (parti)*. As we have seen (410), the preterite is replaced in speech, and often in writing, by the perfect. If we now substitute the perfect of *avoir* or *être* for the preterite in *il eut fini*, etc., we get the so-called 'double-compound' tense known in French as the *passé surcomposé*, viz. *il a eu fini, il a été parti*. Although not all grammars refer to them, such forms as these have been in use for many centuries and they are well established as substitutes for the past anterior in those spoken and written styles that avoid the preterite, e.g.:

> *Dès que je l'ai eu vu, il s'est mis à courir*
> The moment I saw him, he started to run

> *Je l'ai démêlé après que Monsieur a été parti* (Marivaux)
> I sorted it out after you had left, sir

(ii) Other 'double-compound' tenses formed on the basis of compound tenses of the auxiliaries (e.g. *j'aurai eu fait, j'aurais eu fait, j'avais eu fait*) also exist but in practice rarely occur with the exception (itself by no means common) of the type *j'avais eu fait*, e.g.:

> *Ils avaient eu vite tourné le câble autour des bittes* (R. Vercel)
> They had quickly got the cable wound round the bollards

> *A peine les avais-je eu quittés qu'ils s'étaient reformés* (Proust)
> Scarcely had I left them than they had formed up again

Tenses with depuis (que), il y a (voici, voilà) . . . que

413   (i) The use of tenses with *depuis que* and *il y a (voici, voilà)* . . . *que* often causes difficulty.

(ii) *Depuis que* has two meanings:

(a) It refers to a specific event, i.e. to a specific point in time, in which case it is translated as 'since' or sometimes 'after' and takes the same tense as in English (allowing that the French perfect is often the equivalent of the English preterite – see 410), e.g.:

Je ne le vois plus depuis qu'il s'est marié
I no longer see him since he got married

Depuis qu'il s'est établi à la campagne je le vois presque tous les jours
I see him nearly every day since he settled in the country

Je le voyais souvent depuis qu'il s'était établi à Paris
I used to see him often after he had settled in Paris

– but note that, in examples such as this last one in which English has the option of using the preterite as an alternative to the pluperfect ('. . . after he settled in Paris'), French insists on the pluperfect (see 411,i).

(b) It introduces a verb that relates not to a past event but to a continuing state of affairs, i.e. it expresses duration; in this case, the two languages use different constructions (see iv below).

(iii) (a) When used with expressions of time, *il y a, voici* and *voilà* serve to express the meaning 'ago', *Je l'ai vu il y a (voici, voilà) dix minutes* 'I saw him ten minutes ago'. When followed by a *que*-clause, they express the meaning of 'since', e.g. *Voilà dix ans qu'il est parti* 'It is ten years since he left'. In such sentences as these, then, French uses the same tense as English (cf. ii,a above).

(b) However, when *il y a* etc. . . . *que* are followed by a verb expressing the duration of a continuing state of affairs, the two languages use different tenses (see iv below).

(iv) When *depuis que, il y a (voici, voilà)* . . . *que* are followed by a verb that refers not to a past event, i.e. not to a point in time, but to a continuing state of affairs, i.e. to duration, French uses

(a) the present tense where English uses the perfect

(b) the imperfect tense where English uses the pluperfect.

Examples:

Il y a
Voici } *dix ans que je le connais*
Voilà

I have known him for ten years (and still know him)

$$\left.\begin{array}{l} \textit{Il y avait} \\ \textit{Voici} \\ \textit{Voilà} \end{array}\right\} \quad \textit{dix ans que je le connaissais}$$

I had known him for ten years (and still knew him)

Similarly, French uses the present or the imperfect (corresponding to the perfect or the pluperfect in English) to express duration in a main clause that includes the preposition *depuis*, or is preceded or followed by a clause introduced by *depuis que*, and in questions introduced by *depuis quand?* or *depuis combien de temps?* 'since when? (for) how long?', e.g.:

Je le connais depuis dix ans
I have known him for ten years

Je le connaissais depuis dix ans
I had known him for ten years

Je le connais depuis 1970
I have known him since 1970

Je le connais depuis qu'il est arrivé à Paris
I have known him since he arrived in Paris

The future, aller faire, etc.

414 (i) The future tense is used in much the same way in French as in English, e.g.:

Je le ferai demain
I shall do it tomorrow

(ii) The present tense is used even more frequently than in English with reference to future time, especially when the future event is regarded as in some way influenced by past or present events (such as the fact that a decision to do something in the future has been taken), e.g.:

Je pars demain
I am leaving tomorrow

Note also the use of the present tense in such contexts as *Je vous aide?* 'Shall I help you?'

(iii) Whereas English uses the present tense with reference to future time after such conjunctions as 'when', 'as soon as', 'after', the future tense *must* be used in French in corresponding contexts, i.e. after conjunctions such as *quand, lorsque,* 'when', *dès que, aussitôt que* 'as soon as', *après que* 'after', e.g.:

Je le verrai quand il viendra (not *vient*)
I shall see him when he comes

Aussitôt qu'il arrivera, dites-lui ce qui s'est passé
As soon as he arrives, tell him what has happened

and, likewise, French uses the future perfect where English uses the perfect, e.g.:

Quand (or *Aussitôt que*) *vous aurez fini, nous pourrons partir*
As soon as you have finished, we can leave

Je vous écrirai après qu'il sera parti
I'll write to you after he has left

Note, however, that the subjunctive is used after *avant que* 'before' and *jusqu'à ce que* 'until' and, increasingly, after *après que* 'after' (see **488**).

Note that this rule applies *only* when reference is to future time – French, like English, uses the present tense in such contexts as *Quand je vais à Paris, je vais toujours au théâtre* 'When (i.e. whenever) I go to Paris, I always go to the theatre'.

Note also that the same does not apply to *si* 'if', after which French uses the present tense where it would be used in English (e.g. *s'il arrive demain* 'if he comes tomorrow') – see **419**.

(iv) The future of *être* and (though less frequently) *avoir* may be used, like that of the corresponding English verbs, to indicate that the state of affairs referred to is assumed to exist (the explanation for the use of the future tense is perhaps that the truth of this assumption will be demonstrated later), e.g.:

Il sera déjà à Paris
He will be in Paris by now

Likewise, the future perfect (which is, of course, formed on the basis of the future of *avoir* or *être*), e.g.:

Je suis sûr qu'il vient – ma mère lui aura écrit
I'm sure he's coming – my mother will have written to him

(v) Contrary to what some grammars state, the construction *aller faire* does not (or not necessarily) express a *futur proche* or immediate future. It indicates that the future event (which may be a long way in the future) is in some way linked to the present, e.g. as being inevitable or as arising out of the present situation or as depending on some decision or intention already known, e.g.:

> *Tôt ou tard, nous allons tous mourir*
> Sooner or later, we are all going to die
>
> *Dans dix ans, je vais prendre ma retraite*
> In ten years time I am going to retire

(vi) For the use of the future as an imperative, see **517**.

The conditional

415   As in English, the so-called 'conditional' tense in French has two quite distinct values:

(i) It expresses a future-in-the-past, e.g.:

> *Il a dit qu'il viendrait*
> He said he would come

– at the time of speaking (*il a dit*), the action of coming was in the future (he presumably said something like *Je viendrai* 'I shall come'), hence the term 'future-in-the-past'; with reference to this use, the term 'conditional' is not really appropriate.

(ii) It is used in conditional sentences proper, i.e. in sentences containing (or at least implying) a subordinate clause introduced by *si* and expressing a condition (but note that the conditional is **not** used in the *si*-clause itself), e.g.:

> *Il viendrait s'il savait que vous étiez ici*
> He would come if he knew you were here
>
> *Dans ce cas-là, je vous écrirais*
> In that case (i.e. if that were so), I should write to you

For fuller discussion of the use of tenses after *si*, see **418–422**.

416   Note the following constructions where French uses a conditional and English does not:

(i) In relative clauses, temporal clauses and after *comme* where English uses (or can use) the past tense, but the conditional in the main clause, e.g.:

> *Un homme qui dirait cela serait tout à fait irresponsable*
> A man who said (*or* would say) that would be quite irresponsible
>
> *On le surveillerait à partir du moment où il débarquerait*
> He would be watched from the moment he landed
>
> *Vous feriez comme vous voudriez*
> You would do as you liked

(ii) to indicate that one does not vouch for the truth of a statement that one is reporting, e.g.:

> *A en croire le 'Figaro' la guerre serait inévitable*
> According to the *Figaro* war is inevitable
>
> *Le premier ministre partirait demain pour Washington*
> It is reported (rumoured, believed) that the Prime Minister will be leaving tomorrow for Washington

(On the use of the conditional in a main clause or a subordinate clause as the equivalent of an 'if'-clause, see **422** and **701**.)

417 Note on the other hand that when, as is occasionally the case, English 'would' is the equivalent of 'used to', the imperfect and not the conditional must be used in French, e.g.:

> When we were children, we would spend our holidays every year at the sea-side
> *Quand nous étions enfants, nous passions nos vacances tous les ans au bord de la mer*

Tenses in conditional sentences with si 'if'

418 The use of tenses in conditional clauses in which the subordinate clause is introduced by *si* 'if' is similar in the two languages. It must, however, be noted that, where English has a past tense in the 'if'-clause (which may, in the case of the verb 'to be', be a subjunctive, as in 'if he were here'), French uses the *imperfect indicative*, e.g.:

Il serait très content si vous lui écriviez
He would be very happy if you wrote to him

S'il était ici, je le saurais
If he were here, I should know

Note:

(a) that it is important to be sure of this use of the imperfect, since experience shows that students have a tendency to use the conditional instead (even though the conditional is not used in English either); the conditional is never used after *si* in this type of sentence (the conditional after *si* meaning 'whether' is a different matter – see **594**).

(b) that the preterite is never used in this type of sentence; the only time the preterite can be used after *si* in conditional sentences (and even then only rarely) is when the *si*-clause in reality expresses a fact, e.g. *S'il quitta la ville en toute hâte, on ne peut pas l'en blâmer* 'If he left the town in a hurry, one cannot blame him for it' (the implication is that he did leave the town in a hurry).

For the use of the imperfect of *devoir* as an equivalent of 'should' or 'were to' in 'if'-clauses, see **512**,ii.

419 Whereas French uses the future or future perfect after *quand* 'when', etc., where English uses the present or the perfect (see **414**,iii), after *si* 'if' (except when it means 'whether' – see **594**) the present and perfect are used as in English, e.g.:

S'il arrive (not *arrivera*) *demain, vous le verrez*
If he arrives tomorrow, you will see him

Est-ce qu'il viendra si je ne lui écris pas?
Will he come if I don't write to him?

Si vous avez déjà fini au moment où il arrivera, nous pourrons partir ensemble
If you have finished by the time he arrives, we can leave together

Likewise with the perfect tense, e.g.:

S'il a reçu ma lettre, il n'y a pas répondu
If he (has) received my letter, he hasn't answered it

S'il a reçu ma lettre, il téléphonera demain
If he has received my letter, he will phone tomorrow

420 The pluperfect indicative in the 'if'-clause and the past conditional in the main clause are used as in English, e.g.:

S'il en avait reçu, il vous les aurait montrés
If he had received any, he would have shown them to you

(The pluperfect subjunctive is sometimes used in either clause, e.g. *S'il en eût reçu, il vous les eût montrés*, but this is a literary archaism that should not be imitated; see also **478,c**.)

421 Miscellaneous points

(i) *Si* with the imperfect can correspond to English 'Suppose' or 'What about . . .?', as in:

Si nous partions maintenant?
Suppose we left now? What about leaving now?

(ii) 'If (only)' is often rendered by *si (seulement)* and the appropriate tense (imperfect or pluperfect), e.g.:

Si seulement nous pouvions y aller!
If only we could go!

Si (seulement) j'avais su!
If (only) I had known!

(iii) On *que* for 'if' when repeated, see **702**.

(iv) On *si* meaning 'if, whether' (e.g. *Je ne sais pas s'il viendra* 'I don't know if (whether) he'll come'), see **594**.

422 'Even if' may be rendered quite literally by *même si* which takes the tenses normally used after *si*, e.g.:

Même s'il le jure, je ne le croirai pas
Even if he swears it, I shall not believe it

Même s'il le jurait, je ne le croirais pas
Even if he swore it, I should not believe it

Alternatively, *quand même* (or sometimes *quand* alone or *quand bien même*) is used with the tense normally used after *quand*, i.e. the present with reference to present time, the future with reference to the future (see **414,iii**), the conditional in such contexts as the following:

Quand même il le jurerait, je ne le croirais pas
Even if he swore it, I should not believe it

See also **423** and **424**.

423 Another construction, which can mean either 'if' or 'even if', is the following, in which what would otherwise be the subordinate clause (the 'if'-clause) in a conditional sentence becomes the main clause and what would otherwise be the main clause becomes the subordinate clause, introduced by *que*, with the conditional or past conditional tense in both clauses:

Il le jurerait que je ne le croirais pas
Even if he swore it, I should not believe it

Vous seriez parti que je ne m'en serais pas aperçu
If you had left I should not have noticed

A similar construction exists, and is frequent in speech, in which there is no subordinating conjunction, e.g. (to take the equivalents of the last two examples):

Il le jurerait, je ne le croirais pas
Vous seriez parti, je ne m'en serais pas aperçu

424 We note, *for recognition purposes only*, the existence in the literary language (but not in everyday speech) of conditional clauses in which the order of the verb and a pronominal subject (personal pronoun, *ce* or *on*) is inverted, as in English 'had I known' for 'if I had known'; the verb is either in the conditional or past conditional or in the imperfect or pluperfect subjunctive; the meaning is either 'if' or 'even if'; e.g.:

L'aurait-il essayé, il n'aurait pu choisir (Genevoix)
Had he tried, he could not have chosen

Dût-il en mourir, il n'y consentirait jamais
Even if he were to die for it, he would never agree

Eût-elle parlé, elle eût crié (Genevoix)
Had she spoken, she would have screamed

Il se serait retiré, n'eût-il pas pensé qu'il se ferait remarquer
He would have withdrawn had he not thought he would attract attention

(On the possible omission of *pas* in this last example see **561**,i.)

K The infinitive

425 The infinitive is the form, ending in *-er*, *-ir*, *-re* or *-oir*, under which verbs are normally listed in dictionaries. Generally speaking, it corresponds to the English infinitive (sometimes referred to as the 'base form'), with or without 'to', e.g.:

Il veut partir	He wants to leave
Pouvez-vous marcher?	Can you walk?

Sometimes, however, as will be seen in succeeding paragraphs, it is used where English uses the present participle (i.e. the form in *-ing*).

Except after *en*, the infinitive is the only form of a French verb that can be used after a preposition (see **649**).

426 Although part of the verb, the infinitive can also function as a noun to the extent that it can serve as the subject of a verb or as the complement of the verb *être* 'to be', e.g.:

Penser à vous sera ma seule consolation
Thinking (to think) of you will be my only consolation

Voir, c'est croire
Seeing is believing

Consentir n'est pas approuver
To consent is not to approve

Mieux vaut les garder
Better keep them (i.e. to keep them would be better)

For the use of *c'est* when both subject and complement are positive infinitives, see **258**,iii.

In Classical French and occasionally still in literary usage, the infinitive subject may be preceded by *de*, e.g. *De penser à toi me soutiendra* (Gide) 'Thinking of you will sustain me'; this *de* is required when the infinitive follows the verb, e.g.:

Ma seule consolation sera de penser à vous
My only consolation will be to think of you

Ça m'agace de l'écouter
It irritates me to listen to him

In such cases, the infinitive may also be introduced by *que de*, e.g.:

C'est une honte que de dire cela
It is shameful to say that

427 (i) After verbs of saying and thinking, the infinitive may often be used as an alternative to a *que*-clause when the subject of both verbs is the same, e.g.:

J'ai cru rêver (or *J'ai cru que je rêvais*)
I thought I was dreaming

Il reconnaissait avoir écrit (or *qu'il avait écrit*) *la lettre*
He admitted writing (having written, that he had written) the letter

It is not possible to tie this down to strict rules – for example, while *Il disait avoir faim* seems entirely acceptable as an equivalent of *Il disait qu'il avait faim* 'He said he was hungry', the infinitive construction would be somewhat unlikely as an alternative to the corresponding statement in the present tense, *Il dit qu'il a faim* 'He says he is hungry'. In case of doubt, it is safer to use a *que*-clause.

(ii) The infinitive is also used after a verb of saying or thinking introduced by a relative pronoun that is the object of the verb of saying or thinking and whose antecedent is the subject of the infinitive (as in *L'homme qu'ils croyaient être malade* 'The man they thought to be ill', in which *que* is the object of *croyaient* and its antecedent, *l'homme*, is the subject of *être*, i.e. '(They thought that) he was ill'), e.g.:

La reine qu'on croyait ne rien savoir
The queen who they thought knew nothing

Le danger qu'on affirmait être imaginaire
The danger which was declared to be imaginary

An alternative construction (see **268**,ii) would be:

La reine dont on croyait qu'elle ne savait rien
Le danger dont on affirmait qu'il était imaginaire

428 After verbs such as *être*, *y avoir*, *rester*, when English uses a passive infinitive to express a possible, desirable or necessary course of action, French uses *à* and the active infinitive, e.g.:

Toutes ces fenêtres sont à réparer
All these windows are to be repaired

Il n'y a rien à faire
There is nothing to be done

Cela reste à décider
That remains to be decided

In such sentences, the grammatical subject is, according to the sense, the object of the infinitive, i.e. what the above sentences express is that 'one needs to repair these windows', 'one can do nothing', and 'one has still to decide that'.

The same construction occurs in expressions such as *appartement à louer* 'flat to let' and *terrain à vendre* 'plot (of land) for sale'. It also underlies the construction *Cela laisse à désirer* 'That leaves something to be desired'.

429 Note the following circumstances in which French uses the infinitive but English does not:

(i) in elliptical interrogative clauses, which often (but not necessarily) have an exclamatory value, e.g.:

Que dire? (for something like *Que peut-on dire?*)
What can one say? What is there to be said?

Où aller? (for something like *Où faut-il aller?*)
Where are we (was he, etc.) to go?

(This is possible in English with 'why (not)?', e.g. *Pourquoi ne pas le dire?* 'Why not say so?')

(ii) in generalized instructions, e.g.:

Tenir au frais	Keep in a cool place
Tenir la main courante	Hold on to the handrail
Ne pas se pencher en dehors	Do not lean out
Voir chapitre dix	See chapter 10

The infinitive with **faire, laisser,** *and verbs of the senses*

430 After *faire* 'to make', *laisser* 'to let', and verbs of the senses (*écouter* 'to listen to', *entendre* 'to hear', *regarder* 'to look at', *sentir* 'to feel', *voir* 'to see'), French uses an active infinitive where English may, according to circumstances, use either an active or a passive infinitive, a present participle, or a past participle. There are both close similarities and important differences between the two languages in this respect.

Two fundamentally different constructions are involved. In one, a noun or pronoun serves both as the object of *faire*, etc., and as the subject of the infinitive (or, in English, the present participle) (see **431**). In the other, a noun or pronoun is the object (in French) of the infinitive (English uses a very different construction – see **432**).

The remarks in **431** and **432** apply to nouns and to such pronouns as possessives (e.g. *le mien*) and demonstratives (e.g. *ceux-ci*), but further problems arise in the case of personal pronouns (see **436** and **437**).

431 The noun serves both as the object of *faire, laisser*, or a verb of the senses and as the subject of the following infinitive:

(i) With *faire*, the noun follows the infinitive whereas it precedes it in English (see also **435**,i), e.g.:

> *Vous faites aboyer les chiens*
> You are making the dogs bark

(ii) With *laisser* and verbs of the senses, the noun may (with exceptions – see **435**,i) either precede or follow the infinitive, e.g.:

> *Je laisse Pierre venir*
> *Je laisse venir Pierre*
> I am letting Peter come
>
> *J'ai regardé décoller l'avion*
> *J'ai regardé l'avion décoller*
> I watched the plane take off (*or* taking off – see below)

Note that French makes no distinction comparable to the difference that exists in English with verbs of the senses (but not with 'to let') between the use of the present participle (e.g. 'I heard the children shouting' *J'ai entendu crier les enfants*), which presents the action as something in process, and the infinitive (e.g. 'I heard my brother shout' *J'ai entendu crier mon frère*), which presents the action as a completed event. (In case of possible ambiguity, the distinction can be made by using a relative clause with the appropriate tense, e.g. *J'ai entendu mon frère qui criait* 'I heard my brother shouting'.)

432 The noun serves as the direct object of the infinitive, whereas English uses a past participle (sometimes preceded by 'be' or 'being') (see examples below). The direct object, if a noun (on personal pronouns, see **436** and **437**), always follows the infinitive (contrast the construction discussed in **431**,ii), e.g.:

Il fait construire un garage
He is having a garage built

Nous ne laisserons pas intimider nos amis
We shall not let our friends be intimidated

Je regardais abattre les arbres
I was watching the trees being cut down

Il a vu tuer son ami
He saw his friend killed

The French construction may perhaps be more easily understood if it is appreciated that what we have here is a type of context in which there is an unspecified direct object of *faire*, etc., which also serves as the unexpressed subject of the infinitive. If this element is expressed as 'someone, anyone', it can be seen that the above examples are, in fact, the equivalent of 'He is making (someone) build a garage', 'We shall not let (anyone) intimidate our friends', 'I was watching (someone) cut(ting) down the trees', 'He saw (someone) kill his friend'.

This is also the construction that occurs in expressions such as *envoyer chercher* 'to send for' (*lit* 'to send (someone) to look for'), as in *J'ai envoyé chercher le médecin* 'I've sent for the doctor'.

433 A further complication arises when, according to the sense and to English grammar, each verb, i.e. (a) *faire, laisser* or the verb of the senses and (b) the infinitive, has a direct object as, for example, in 'I saw the boy catch a fish' in which 'the boy' is the object of 'saw' and 'a fish' is the object of 'catch'. In such circumstances:

(i) the direct object of *faire* is treated grammatically as an *indirect* object, e.g.:

Faites descendre les bagages au porteur
Get the porter to bring down the luggage

Je lui ferai abandonner cette idée
I will make him give up that idea

(Contrast these with the examples with *faire* given in 431,i and 436,i in which the infinitive has no object and so *faire* takes a direct object.)

(ii) the direct object of *laisser* or a verb of the senses may be treated grammatically as either a direct or an indirect object, e.g.:

J'ai laissé mon fils choisir le métier qu'il préfère
J'ai laissé choisir le métier qu'il préfère à mon fils
I have let my son choose the occupation he prefers

Je l'ai (or *lui ai*) *entendu dire beaucoup de bêtises*
I have heard him say a lot of silly things

Nous les (or *leur*) *regardions brûler des documents importants*
We were watching them burn(ing) important documents

(Even with *faire*, both objects are sometimes treated as direct objects if that of *faire* is a personal pronoun, e.g. *Je le ferai abandonner cette idée*, but this is not the usual construction and so is best avoided.)

As an alternative to the construction with an indirect object, a construction with *par* 'by' may be used, e.g.:

Il a fait exécuter ses ordres à ses hommes (or *par ses hommes*)
He made his men carry out his order (*or* had his orders carried out by his men)

434 The situation referred to in **433** also arises when the direct object of the infinitive is not a noun or a pronoun but a subordinate clause, e.g.:

J'ai fait entendre à Pierre $\begin{cases} qu'il\ ne\ devait\ pas\ agir\ de\ la\ sorte \\ en\ quoi\ il\ avait\ eu\ tort \end{cases}$

I made Peter understand $\begin{cases} \text{that he must not behave like that} \\ \text{in what respect he had been wrong} \end{cases}$

J'ai entendu dire à quelqu'un que le danger était passé
I heard someone say that the danger was over

In cases of possible ambiguity, as in the second example above which in certain contexts might just mean 'I heard someone told that . . ., I heard it said to someone that . . .', an alternative construction should be used, e.g. *J'ai entendu quelqu'un dire que* . . .

435 (i) A noun serving as the direct object of *faire* and the subject of the infinitive follows the infinitive, e.g. *Il a fait partir mon frère* 'He made my brother leave' (the implied sentence is 'my brother leaves' – 'my brother' is the subject). But with *laisser* and verbs of the senses, such a noun may come either before or after the infinitive; the choice may be determined either by considerations of meaning, e.g.:

(a) *Je laisse Pierre venir* } I am letting Peter come
(b) *Je laisse venir Pierre*

– (a) is a neutral statement with no implications, whereas (b) may suggest that there are others that I am not letting come (in this case, 'Peter' would be slightly stressed in English); or by stylistic factors, for example, in the case of a lengthy direct object, e.g.:

Je regardais jouer tous les petits enfants du village
I was watching all the little children in the village playing

or, even more so, when the infinitive is accompanied by a complement and the noun phrase is relatively short, e.g.:

J'ai vu votre fils partir de la maison
I saw your son leave the house

In the kinds of circumstances illustrated by these last two examples it would not normally be acceptable to put the longer element before the shorter one. Elsewhere, however, the two constructions are more or less interchangeable.

(ii) When the construction with *à* or *par* + a noun is used, the infinitive follows *faire*, etc., immediately and the direct object follows the infinitive, e.g.:

Il fait construire sa maison à (or *par*) *un architecte remarquable*
He is having his house built by a remarkable architect

(for another example, see the end of **433**).

436 The following remarks on the position of object pronouns do not apply to reflexive verbs (see **437**).

(i) When there is only one direct object conjunctive pronoun, whether it is, according to the sense, the object of *faire*, *laisser*, or of the infinitive, it is treated grammatically as the object of *faire*, etc., e.g.:

(a) (object of *faire*, *laisser*, etc.)

> *Je les ferai descendre*
> I'll get them to come down (object of *faire*)
>
> *Je l'ai vu courir*
> I saw him running (object of *voir*)

(b) (object of the infinitive)

> *Je les ferai descendre*
> I will have them brought down (= I will make [someone] bring them down)
>
> *Je l'ai vu tuer*
> I saw him killed (= I saw [someone] kill him)

(ii) When both *faire, laisser* or a verb of the senses and the following infinitive each have, according to the meaning, a direct object pronoun, a variety of constructions occur. The following observations cover the most usual of them (note that a and b do not refer to the positive imperative (see **207** and **514**) which is dealt with in c):

(a) The object of *faire*, etc., may be treated grammatically as an indirect object (cf. **433**), in which case both pronouns come before *faire*, etc., e.g.:

> *Il te le fera répéter*
> He will make you repeat it
>
> *Ne me les laissez pas oublier*
> Don't let me forget them
>
> *Je les lui ai vu écrire*
> I saw him writing them
>
> *Je les lui regardais brûler*
> I was watching her burn(ing) them

Except with *faire*, this is a literary construction that should be avoided in conversational French.

(b) Each pronoun may function grammatically as the direct object of its own verb, e.g.:

Elle m'a fait la quitter (Léautaud)
She made me leave her

Ne me laissez pas les oublier
Don't let me forget them

Je la regardais les brûler
I was watching her burn(ing) them

This is the usual construction in speech, especially with verbs other than *faire*.

This construction *must* be used:

(1) when the object of *laisser* or a verb of the senses is a 3rd person pronoun (*le, la, les*) and the object of the other verb is a 1st or 2nd person pronoun, e.g.:

Tu les laisses m'insulter (Mauriac)
You are letting them insult me

(note that *Tu me les laisses insulter* can only mean 'You are letting me insult them' – cf. a above); or

(2) when both objects are 1st or 2nd person pronouns, e.g.:

Cette décision me fait vous respecter
This decision makes me respect you

(type a is impossible since *me* and *vous* cannot function as objects of the same verb – see **206**, a)

(c) With a positive imperative, the usual construction with *faire* is that both pronouns are grammatically objects of *faire* (i.e., as in a above), e.g.:

Faites-le-leur répéter
Make them repeat it

but, with other verbs, each pronoun usually functions grammatically as the object of its own verb (as in b above), e.g.:

Laissez-la les jeter!
Let her throw them away!

Laisse-les te flatter!
Let them flatter you!

Regardez-moi l'écrire
Watch me writing it

(iii) With *envoyer chercher* 'to send for (*lit.* to send to look for) [someone]', two constructions are possible:

Nous l'enverrons chercher
Nous enverrons le chercher
We shall send for him

However, with *envoyer dire à quelqu'un* 'to send word to (*lit.* to send to tell) someone', only one construction is possible:

Nous le lui enverrons dire
We shall send him (*or* her) word of it

437 When *faire* or, though less frequently, *laisser, envoyer, mener* or *emmener*, is followed by the infinitive of a reflexive verb, the reflexive pronoun may be omitted, e.g.:

Nous les ferons taire or *Nous les ferons se taire*
We shall make them be quiet

Ils vous en feront repentir or *Ils vous en feront vous repentir*
They will make you regret it

This does not apply to the reflexive infinitive after verbs of the senses, after which the reflexive pronoun must be used, e.g.:

Je les entendais se plaindre
I could hear them complaining

Even with *faire*, the reflexive pronoun must be used with the infinitive if the sentence could otherwise be ambiguous, e.g.:

Ils l'ont fait se tuer
They made him kill himself

Il nous fera nous arrêter
He will make us stop

In such contexts, the construction omitting the reflexive pronoun is debarred because *Ils l'ont fait tuer* and *Il nous fera arrêter* would be interpreted as 'They had him killed' and 'He will have us arrested' respectively.

Note the following construction in which the reflexive pronoun is grammatically the object of *faire* but, according to the sense, is the object of the following infinitive:

Il s'est fait arrêter
He got himself arrested

Vous vous ferez écraser
You'll get run over

which, more literally but quite unidiomatically, could be interpreted as 'He caused [someone] to arrest him' and 'You will cause [someone] to run over you'.

438 Out of context, such utterances as the following could be ambiguous:

Faites-le expliquer
Make him explain
or Have it explained

Nous lui avons vu jouer un mauvais tour
We saw him play a dirty trick
or We saw a dirty trick played on him

L'homme que j'ai vu peindre
The man I saw painting
or The man I saw being painted (= 'having his portrait painted')

The problem, however, is little more than a theoretical one. In practice, such forms are rarely ambiguous, i.e. the context is sufficient to disambiguate them or, if not, some other construction can be used, e.g. *Demandez-lui une explication* 'Ask him for an explanation', *Nous l'avons vu jouer un mauvais tour* 'We saw him play a dirty trick'.

L The present participle

439 The present participle corresponds, broadly speaking, to the English present participle in '-ing' (on some differences in the way the participle is used in the two languages, see following paragraphs).

The present participle of all verbs ends in *-ant*, and in all regular verbs and all but a handful of irregular verbs the stem is the same as that of the first person plural of the present indicative, e.g.

from *donner* 'to give', *finir* 'to finish', *vendre* 'to sell', *boire* 'to drink', *connaître* 'to know', *craindre* 'to fear', *dire* 'to say', *prendre* 'to take', we have *donnant* 'giving', *finissant* 'finishing', *vendant* 'selling', *buvant* 'drinking', *connaissant* 'knowing', *craignant* 'fearing', *disant* 'saying', *prenant* 'taking', corresponding to (*nous*) *donnons, finissons, vendons, buvons, connaissons, craignons, disons, prenons*.

Apart from a few defective verbs and verbs used impersonally and which have no first person plural forms (for these, see **377**), the only exceptions are the present participles of the verbs *avoir* 'to have' (*ayant*), *être* 'to be' (*étant*), and *savoir* 'to know' (*sachant*).

440 (i) Like its English equivalent, the French present participle can be used as an adjective (but see also **446**), in which case it agrees in gender and number with its noun just like any other adjective, e.g.:

une obscurité terrifiante
terrifying darkness

des femmes charmantes
charming women

Leurs cris étaient assourdissants
Their cries were deafening

(ii) The verb *être* 'to be' + the present participle, as in the last example in i above, can of course be used *only* when the meaning of the English participle is strictly adjectival. When the English construction 'to be' + present participle functions as a progressive form of the verb (as in 'She is singing', 'They were working'), the appropriate tense of the verb (or, occasionally, *être en train de* + infinitive) must be used in French (see **399**,i), e.g.:

Il terrifie les enfants
He is terrifying the children

Leurs cris m'assourdissaient
Their cries were deafening me

(iii) The adjectival value can still dominate over the verbal value (i.e. the participle can agree) even when the participle is modified by a phrase introduced by *de*, e.g.:

*La petite cour . . . était divisée en deux parties: l'une ruissel-
ante de soleil, l'autre envahie par l'ombre du bâtiment*
(Simenon)
The little courtyard was divided into two parts: one shim-
mering with sunlight, the other shaded by the building

Elle arrive, mourante de soif, à un vieux puits garni de lierre
(P. Devoluy)
She arrives, dying of thirst, at an old ivy-covered well

(iv) On differences in spelling between some present participles
and corresponding adjectives or nouns, see **446**.

441 When the participle is *not* an adjective (see **440**), it is
invariable, i.e. it does *not* agree in gender or number, e.g.:

(a) (referring to the subject of the verb)

Réfléchissant à cette question, elle décida de lui écrire
Thinking about this question, she decided to write to him

Ils se sont approchés de moi, souriant et me tendant les bras
They came towards me, smiling and stretching out their
arms to me

J'ai acheté ce dictionnaire ne sachant pas qu'il était mauvais
I bought this dictionary not knowing that it was a poor one

Étant satisfaites de notre réponse, elles sont parties
Being satisfied with our reply, they left

Ayant terminé leurs études, ils rentrent chez eux
Having finished their studies, they are going home

Not infrequently, as in the last three examples, the participle
expresses cause ('because I did not know . . .', 'because they were
satisfied . . .', 'because they have finished . . .').

(b) (referring to the object of the verb)

Il l'a aperçue lisant ma lettre
He noticed her reading my letter

Vous allez les rencontrer, souriant et vous tendant les bras
You will meet them smiling and stretching out their arms to
you

(c) (with *voici* 'here is, are' and *voilà* 'there is, are')

Les voilà, travaillant comme toujours
There they are, working as always

Note that *soi-disant* 'so-called' is invariable (see **136**,iii), e.g. *la soi-disant princesse* 'the so-called princess', *nos soi-disant chefs* 'our so-called leaders'.

Note, for recognition purposes, the literary construction *aller* or *s'en aller* + present participle to indicate the progressive nature of the action expressed by the verb, e.g. *La situation va s'aggravant* 'The situation is steadily getting worse'.

442   Where English uses a present participle with reference to a preceding noun or pronoun, French frequently uses a relative clause, especially after verbs of the senses, e.g.:

> *J'entendais des chiens qui aboyaient toute la nuit*
> I could hear dogs barking all night
>
> *Je le vois qui tâche d'ouvrir la porte*
> I can see him trying to open the door

443   The present participle can also be used absolutely (cf. the absolute use of the past participle, **457**), e.g.:

> *Les choses ne s'arrangeant pas à son gré, il fut forcé de quitter la France*
> Things not going as he wanted, he had to leave France
>
> *Son chapeau étant perdu, il s'en alla nu-tête*
> His hat being lost, he went away bareheaded

444   There are many circumstances in which the French present participle cannot be used as the equivalent of the English present participle. In particular:

(i) It cannot be used with the verb *être* 'to be' to form a 'progressive' tense (cf. English 'He is working', 'I have been writing a letter') – see **399**.

(ii) When English uses the present participle to express an action that *precedes* (i.e. is not simultaneous with) the action expressed by the verb, French uses the present participle of *avoir* or *être* (with verbs that form their compound tenses with *être* – see **451–456**) + the past participle, e.g. *ayant répondu* 'having replied', *étant descendu* 'having come down', or else a subordinate clause, e.g.:

> Hurriedly paying his bill, he rushed out of the shop
> *Ayant réglé son compte à la hâte, il quitta précipitamment le magasin*

Jumping on his horse, he galloped away
Il sauta sur son cheval et s'en alla au galop

The same is often true of contexts in which English uses 'on' or 'by' with a participle, e.g.:

By leaving home late he missed his train
Étant parti trop tard de chez lui, il a raté son train

On receiving his letter, I decided to leave at once
Ayant reçu sa lettre, j'ai décidé de partir tout de suite
Quand j'ai reçu sa lettre, j'ai décidé de partir tout de suite

(On the use of the French gerund in similar but nevertheless different circumstances, see 445,ii,b.)

(iii) When English uses 'by' + participle after a verb of beginning or ending, French uses *par* + infinitive (see also 649,iii), e.g.:

I shall begin by explaining how things stand at present
Je vais commencer par expliquer où en sont les choses

They ended by agreeing with one another
Ils ont fini par se mettre d'accord

(iv) Where English uses the present participle to refer to bodily posture, French in most cases uses a past participle; among the most common of such participles are *accoudé* 'leaning (on one's elbow(s))', *adossé* 'leaning (with one's back against)', *agenouillé* 'kneeling', *appuyé* 'leaning', *assis* 'sitting' (but see also 378, n. 3), *couché* 'lying', e.g.:

Il était adossé contre le mur
He was leaning against (with his back against) the wall

Elle est couchée sur le sable
She is lying on the sand

(Note, however, that 'standing' is *debout*, which is an adverb not an adjective, and therefore does not agree, e.g. *Elle était debout* 'She was standing'.)

445 (i) When preceded by the preposition *en* (which is the only preposition that can precede it), e.g. *en chantant*, the form in *-ant* is often referred to as the 'gerund' (in French, *le gérondif*).

(ii) The primary function of the gerund is to indicate that two actions, i.e. the one expressed by the gerund itself and the one expressed by the verb of its clause, are simultaneous, e.g.:

Il flânait le long de la rue en regardant dans toutes les vitrines
He strolled along the street looking in all the shop windows

En l'écoutant chanter, je pense toujours à Maria Callas
Listening to her sing, I always think of Maria Callas

This covers cases in which the two actions are only partly simultaneous. These include:

(a) cases in which the main verb expresses something that takes place at some point during the time when the action expressed by the gerund is going on, e.g.:

En sortant de l'église, il glissa et se cassa la jambe
Coming out of church, he slipped and broke his leg

(b) cases in which the action expressed by the gerund is simultaneous only with the onset of the action expressed by the verb, or even slightly precedes it but gives rise to the action expressed by the verb, e.g.:

En entendant sa voix, je me suis précipité dehors
On hearing her voice, I rushed outside

This must be distinguished from the construction referred to at the end of section 444,ii.

(iii) Various secondary functions derive from the function of expressing simultaneity. In particular, the gerund can express such values as the following (which sometimes overlap with that of simultaneity or with one another):

(a) means or manner, e.g.:

Il a exprimé sa désapprobation en donnant sa démission
He expressed his disapproval by resigning

(b) cause, e.g.:

En glissant, il se cassa la jambe
By slipping he broke his leg (i.e. he broke his leg because he slipped)

(c) condition, e.g.:

En refusant son invitation, vous pourriez le rendre furieux
By refusing his invitation (i.e. If you were to refuse his invitation), you could infuriate him

En faisant un très grand effort, vous pourrez toujours réussir
By making a great effort, you can still succeed

(In this last example, the functions of cause and condition are combined, i.e. it contains the ideas of 'By reason of making a great effort' and of 'If you make a great effort'.)

The gerund can also have a concessive value (i.e. 'although'), but in this case it is usually preceded by *tout* – see iv,b below.

(iv) The gerund is frequently preceded by *tout*, particularly:

(a) to emphasize the simultaneity of the two actions, e.g.:

Il travaille tout en souriant
He works while smiling all the time

(b) with a concessive value, i.e. to express the idea of 'although' (cf. the use of 'while' in English), e.g.:

Tout en se déclarant satisfaite de son explication, elle continue à le critiquer
While claiming to be satisfied (i.e. Although she claims to be satisfied) with his explanation, she continues to criticize him

(v) As in all the above examples, the gerund normally refers to the subject of its clause. However, where no ambiguity can arise, it is occasionally used more loosely, e.g.:

En le voyant, une sorte de choc électrique secoua Sally (Maurois)
When she saw him (*lit.* On seeing him), a kind of electric shock shook Sally

This construction should be avoided except in the case of a few fixed expressions such as *en attendant* 'meanwhile', *en passant* 'in passing, *en passant*'.

(vi) The modern language retains as fixed expressions a few examples of an earlier stage in its history in which the participle, although functioning as a gerund, was not preceded by *en*, e.g. *ce disant* 'so saying (*lit.* saying this)', *chemin faisant* 'on the way' (i.e. 'while making one's way'), *généralement parlant* 'generally speaking', *payer argent comptant* 'to pay cash' (i.e. 'to pay by counting out one's money').

446   As the result of a totally unnecessary quirk of French spelling, some present participles in *-guant* or *-quant* are not used as adjectives but are replaced in this function by forms in *-gant*, *-cant*; note in particular the following:

infinitive	participle	adjective
communiquer 'to communicate'	*communiquant*	*communicant* 'communicating'
convaincre 'to convince'	*convainquant*	*convaincant* 'convincing'
fatiguer 'to tire'	*fatiguant*	*fatigant* 'tiring'
provoquer 'to provoke'	*provoquant*	*provocant* 'provocative'
suffoquer 'to suffocate'	*suffoquant*	*suffocant* 'suffocating'

e.g. *Convainquant son père de sa sincérité, il réussit à le calmer* 'Convincing his father of his sincerity, he succeeded in calming him down', but *des arguments convaincants* 'convincing arguments'; *En le provoquant comme ça, vous allez le mettre en colère* 'By provoking him like that you'll make him angry', but *une manière provocante* 'a provocative manner'; likewise *des pièces communicantes* 'communicating rooms', *un voyage fatigant* 'a tiring journey', *une chaleur suffocante* 'a stifling heat'.

Note too, corresponding to the verbs *intriguer* 'to scheme', *naviguer* 'to sail, navigate', the forms *intrigant* 'scheming' (as an adjective) or (as a noun) 'schemer, intriguer' and *navigant*, used especially in the term *le personnel navigant* 'seagoing personnel, flying personnel', and, corresponding to the verb *fabriquer* 'to manufacture', *le fabricant* 'manufacturer' (used as a noun only) – contrast the present participles *intriguant*, *naviguant*, *fabriquant*.

This does not apply to other verbs in *-quer*, e.g., corresponding to *attaquer* 'to attack' and *piquer* 'to sting', *un attaquant* 'attacker', *une réplique piquante* 'a stinging rejoinder'.

M The past participle

Introduction

447 The past participle is used (i) to form the perfect and other compound tenses (see **448**), (ii) to form the passive (see

382–385), (iii) in certain absolute constructions (see 457–458), and (iv) as an adjective, in which case it agrees with its noun in gender and number in the same way as other adjectives (see 127–130), e.g. *une expression détendue* 'a relaxed expression', *des verres cassés* 'broken glasses'.

448   As a participle it is used with *avoir* and *être* to form the compound tenses, i.e. the perfect (e.g. *j'ai fini, je suis parti*), the pluperfect (*j'avais fini, j'étais parti*), the past anterior (*j'eus fini, je fus parti*), the future perfect (*j'aurai fini, je serai parti*), the past conditional (*j'aurais fini, je serais parti*), the perfect subjunctive (*j'aie fini, je sois parti*), the imperfect subjunctive (*j'eusse fini, je fusse parti*) and the double-compound tenses (see 412).

Compound tenses with avoir

449   With *avoir*, the past participle forms the compound tenses of the active voice of all transitive verbs except reflexive verbs (see 379–381), and of all intransitive verbs (including *être*) except those listed in 451–456, e.g.:

J'ai fini
I have finished

Avez-vous lu ce livre?
Have you read this book?

Nous avions marché pendant trois heures
We had walked for three hours

Jean n'aura pas vendu sa maison
John will not have sold his house

Qui l'aurait cru?
Who would have believed it?

Compound tenses with être

450   With *être*, the past participle forms the compound tenses of:

(a) all reflexive verbs (see 380–381), e.g.:

Il s'est cassé le bras
He has broken his arm

Ne s'était-elle pas levée?
Hadn't she got up?

Ils se seraient blessés
They would have hurt themselves

(b) the following verbs when used intransitively (for the transitive use of some of these verbs, see **451**):

aller, go
arriver, arrive, happen
décéder, die
descendre, come or go down
devenir, become
entrer, enter, go in
monter, come or go up (but see also **455**)
mourir, die
naître, be born
partir, go away, leave
rentrer, come back, come home
rester, remain stay
retourner, go back, return
sortir, come or go out
tomber, fall
venir, come

and intransitive compounds of *partir*, *sortir* and *venir*, except *convenir à* 'to suit' which takes *avoir*. (*Prévenir* 'to warn' is transitive and therefore takes *avoir*.)

Examples:

Ils sont devenus tristes
They became sad

Elle n'était pas descendue
She had not come down

Il sera parti
He will have left

Seraient-elles venues?
Would they have come?

For verbs that are sometimes compounded with *avoir* and sometimes with *être*, see 452–456.

451   Some of the verbs discussed in **450** may also be used transitively, with a different meaning, in which case, like all other transitive verbs, they form their compound tenses with *avoir*; the only such verbs that are widely so used are:

descendre	(1) descend (ladder, hill, etc.)
	(2) take (bring) down
monter	(1) climb, ascend
	(2) take up
remonter	wind up
rentrer	bring in
retourner	to turn (something) over (etc.)
sortir	take out

Examples:

Elle a descendu l'escalier
She came down the stairs

J'ai monté les bagages
I have brought the luggage up

J'ai remonté ma montre
I have wound up my watch

Il a sorti sa voiture du garage
He took his car out of the garage

Entrer and *tomber* are occasionally transitive in such expressions as *entrer un meuble dans une pièce* 'to get a piece of furniture into a room', *tomber sa veste* 'to take off one's jacket', *tomber quelqu'un* 'to throw someone' (in wrestling), and then they too are compounded with *avoir*.

Verbs compounded with avoir or être

452   With two verbs only, viz. *accourir* 'to run, rush (up)' and *apparaître* 'to appear, come to light', either *avoir* or *être* may be used with no difference in meaning, e.g.:

Elle a accouru (or *est accourue*) *vers son fils*
She ran towards her son

Soudain les étoiles ont apparu (or *sont apparues*)
Suddenly the stars appeared

453 *Demeurer* takes *avoir* when it means 'to dwell, live (at)',
but *être* when it is the equivalent of *rester* 'to remain', e.g.:

Avant mon mariage, j'ai demeuré à Paris
Before my marriage I lived in Paris

Il est toujours demeuré fidèle
He has always remained faithful

454 *Passer* takes *avoir* in the expression *passer pour* 'to pass as,
be taken for', e.g.:

Il avait passé pour un homme intelligent
He had passed as (been taken for) an intelligent man

but in other intransitive senses now usually takes *être*, though
avoir is also possible, e.g.:

Nous sommes passés (or *avons passé*) *sous le pont*
We passed under the bridge

Ils sont passés (or *ont passé*) *à l'ennemi*
They have gone over to the enemy

Le facteur n'est pas (or *n'a pas*) *encore passé*
The postman hasn't been yet

Elle est passée (or *a passé*) *plusieurs fois à la télé*
She has been on TV several times

455 Although *monter* 'to rise, go up' as an intransitive verb
usually takes *être*, it often takes *avoir* when it refers to the fact
that the level of something has risen (either literally or
figuratively), e.g.:

Le fleuve a monté de deux mètres
The (level of the) river has gone up by two metres

Le baromètre a monté
The barometer has risen

Tous les prix ont monté
All the prices have gone up

Il est très malade – la fièvre a encore monté
He's very ill – his temperature has gone up again

(Note that the opposite of *monter* in this sense is not *descendre* but *baisser*, which always takes *avoir*, e.g. *Les prix ont baissé* 'The prices have gone down'.)

456   Note that the compound tenses of verbs such as *changer* 'to change', *disparaître* 'to disappear', *grandir* 'to grow (bigger)', *vieillir* 'to age, to grow old(er)', whose past participles may well be found with the verb *être*, are in fact *always* formed with *avoir*, e.g.:

La ville a beaucoup changé ces dernières années
The town has changed a lot these last few years

Il a dit que le bateau avait disparu la veille
He said that the boat had disappeared the previous day

Vos enfants ont grandi depuis l'an dernier
Your children have grown since last year

Vous n'avez pas vieilli du tout
You haven't aged at all

When the past participle of such a verb is found with *être*, the reason is that it is then being used strictly as an adjective, referring to the state resulting from the process expressed by the verb, e.g.:

Elle est complètement changée
She is completely changed (different)

Ils sont disparus
They are missing (nowhere to be seen)

The absolute use of the past participle

457   French makes rather more use than English of absolute participial constructions, i.e. clauses consisting of a noun or pronoun and a present or past participle with no introductory conjunction and no personal form of the verb, e.g. 'Weather permitting' = 'if the weather permits', 'that being so' = 'if (*or*) since that is so', 'The Christmas cards written, he went to bed' = 'When he had written the Christmas cards, . . .' e.g.:

cela dit
that said

Réflexion faite, il décida de partir
On reflection, he decided to leave

Toutes choses considérées, je crois qu'il faut accepter cette proposition
All things considered, I think we must accept this proposal

Ses dettes payées, il quitta la ville
His debts (having been) paid, he left town

This construction is also used introduced by *une fois* 'once' in a way that is not possible in English, e.g.:

Une fois la décision prise, la réunion prit fin
Once the decision had been taken (*or* The decision once taken), the meeting came to an end

458   On the absolute use of *excepté, vu, y compris*, and other participles, see **134**.

The agreement of the past participle

459   (i) When forming part of a compound tense, the past participle can vary for gender and number, e.g.:

arrivé	*arrivée*	*arrivés*	*arrivées*
écrit	*écrite*	*écrits*	*écrites*

according to the following rules (which apply to **all** compound tenses):

(a) the participle compounded with *avoir* agrees with a preceding direct object (see **460**); otherwise it is invariable

(b) the participle of a reflexive verb, even though compounded with *être*, also agrees with a preceding direct object (see **461**)

(c) the participle of other verbs compounded with *être* (see **450**, b, and **452–456**) agrees with the subject (see **462**).

(ii) In the passive, the participle always agrees with the subject, e.g.:

Ma sœur a été retenue par un petit accident
My sister has been delayed by a slight accident

Les livres avaient été vendus
The books had been sold

Elles seront punies
They (*fem.*) will be punished

(Note that *été* never agrees.)

460   The past participle compounded with *avoir* agrees only with a preceding direct object, i.e. with a direct object coming before the verb; this does not mean that the object must necessarily come immediately before the verb – the two are often separated by a number of other elements.

The only words that can come before the verb as its direct object and so cause agreement of the participle are:

(a) the interrogatives *quel, lequel* and *combien de* (see also the notes below)

(b) the exclamatory *que de* 'what a lot of' (see **333**)

(c) the relative pronouns *que* and *lequel*

(d) the conjunctive pronouns *me, te, nous vous, le, la, les* (for *se* see **461**).

Examples:

Quelle maison a-t-il achetée? (agreement with *quelle maison*)
Which house has he bought?

Je ne sais pas laquelle il a achetée (agreement with *laquelle*)
I don't know which one he has bought

Combien de lettres avez-vous écrites? (agreement with *combien de lettres*)
How many letters have you written?

Que de problèmes il a rencontrés! (agreement with *que de problèmes*)
What a lot of problems he encountered!

Voilà la maison que j'ai achetée (agreement with *que = la maison*)
There is the house I have bought

– Il ne m'a pas vue, dit-elle (agreement with *me*, feminine)
"He didn't see me," she said

Elle ne les avait pas vendus (agreement with *les*)
She had not sold them

(iii) Note the following points:

(a) *combien de* and *que de* take their gender and number from the noun they govern (e.g. *combien de glace?* is feminine singular, *que de difficultés* is feminine plural)

(b) grammarians differ as to whether, and if so when, the participle should agree with *combien* accompanied by the pronoun *en* 'of it, of them', e.g.:

> *Combien en a-t-il vendu* (or *vendus*)?
> How many of them has he sold?

It is safest never to make the participle agree in this case. The same applies to the infrequent instances where other quantifiers such as *plus* or *moins* + *en* precede the verb, e.g. *Plus il a acheté de livres, plus il en a vendu(s)* 'The more books he bought, the more he sold'.

(c) *que* takes its gender and number from its antecedent, e.g. in *les lettres que j'ai écrites* 'the letters that I have written', *que*, standing for *les lettres* (fem. plur.), is itself feminine plural.

(d) *qui?* 'whom?' is always treated as masculine singular, even in contexts in which it might be supposed to relate to a female or to more than one person, so, when functioning as the preceding direct object of a verb in a compound tense, it never leads to any agreement other than the masculine singular, e.g. *Qui avez-vous vu?* 'Whom did you see?'

(e) *me, te, nous* and *les* can be masculine or feminine, while *vous* can be masculine or feminine, singular or plural.

(iv) For some less straightforward cases, see **463–471**.

461 The participle of a reflexive verb also agrees with the preceding direct object. If this is the reflexive pronoun itself, it takes its gender and number from the subject (which it refers back to), e.g.:

> *Elle s'est blessée*
> She has hurt herself

> *Ils se sont blessés*
> They have hurt themselves

> *Je me suis blessé* (the speaker is male)
> *Je me suis blessée* (the speaker is female)
> I have hurt myself

Vous vous êtes blessé (one male addressee)
You have hurt yourself

Vous vous êtes blessées (more than one female addressee)
You have hurt yourselves

Note:

(a) that when the reflexive pronoun represents an indirect object, it does not of course bring about agreement, e.g.:

Elle s'est nui (nuire à quelqu'un)
She has harmed herself (i.e. her interests)

Elle s'est blessé le doigt
She has hurt her finger (*lit*. She has hurt the finger to herself)

Ils se sont écrit
They have written to one another

(b) that some other element than the reflexive pronoun may be the direct object, e.g.:

J'ai lu les lettres qu'ils se sont écrites
I have read the letters they wrote to one another

in which *écrites* agrees with the preceding direct object *que* whose antecedent is *les lettres* and which is therefore feminine plural.

462   The participle of other verbs compounded with *être* agrees with the subject, e.g.:

Votre sœur est-elle arrivée?
Has your sister arrived?

Jean et Pierre sont déjà partis
John and Peter have already left

The past participle with an infinitive

463   When a compound tense of *faire, laisser* or a verb of the senses such as *voir, entendre*, etc. is followed by an infinitive (see 430), the following rules apply:

464   *faire*

The past participle of *faire* remains invariable, e.g.:

Quels livres avez-vous fait venir?
What books have you had sent?

Voilà la maison que nous avons fait construire
There is the house that we have had built

465 *laisser*

The past participle of *laisser*, like that of *faire*, may be treated as invariable, but, more usually, it agrees with a preceding direct object whether that object is, according to the sense, the object of *laisser* (as in *Il la laisse entrer* 'He lets her come in') or the object of the infinitive (as in *Ils se laissent prendre* 'They let themselves be caught', *lit.* 'They let [someone] catch them'), e.g.:

Il l'a laissée (or *laissé*) *entrer*
He has let her come in

Ils se sont laissés (or *laissé*) *prendre*
They have let themselves be caught

466 Verbs of the senses

In the case of a verb of the senses such as *entendre* 'to hear', *voir* 'to see', etc. (see **430**), the participle agrees with a preceding direct object (see **460**), provided that, according to the meaning, it is the object of the verb of the senses and not the object of the infinitive (in which case there is no agreement). A little thought will usually clear up any difficulty there may be in deciding. For example, in *Quels acteurs avez-vous vus jouer?* 'Which actors did you see act(ing)?', *acteurs* is the object of *voir* 'to see' and the subject of *jouer* 'to act' ('One sees the actors': 'The actors act') and so the past participle *vus* agrees, whereas in *Quelles pièces avez-vous vu jouer?* 'Which plays did you see performed?' (i.e. 'Which plays did you see [someone] perform?') *pièces* is the object of *jouer* 'to perform' ('One performs plays') and there is therefore no agreement of the past participle *vu*.

Note that the two constructions are in fact clearly distinguished in English (though in a very different way from in French). If a noun or pronoun (see the examples below with relative or personal pronouns) is the object of the verb of the senses, English uses *the infinitive or the present participle* of the other verb (and in French the past participle agrees), e.g.:

les acteurs que nous avons vus jouer
the actors we saw act (*or* acting)

Je l'ai entendue chanter
I have heard her sing (*or* singing)

But if, in French, the noun or pronoun is the object of the infinitive (in which case the past participle does not agree), English uses a totally different construction in which the noun or pronoun is still the object of the verb of the senses and the other verb is represented by a *past participle*, e.g.:

les pièces que nous avons vu jouer
the plays (which) we saw performed

Je connais cette chanson: je l'ai souvent entendu chanter
I know that song: I have often heard it sung

467   A similar situation exists with a verb governed by *à* or *de*, in which case again the direct object may be the object either of the main verb (and the participle agrees) or of the infinitive (and the participle does not agree). Note, however, that, in this case, English uses the infinitive (and never the present participle or the past participle) of the other verb, e.g.:

Les rapports que je leur ai donnés à écrire sont assez longs
The reports that I gave them to write out are rather long

(*donnés*, because 'I gave them the reports' so, according to the sense, *les rapports* is the object of *donner*)

Les raisons que j'ai essayé de leur expliquer
The reasons that I tried to explain to them

(*essayé* – no agreement – because 'I tried to explain the reasons' so, according to the sense, *les raisons* is the object of *expliquer* not of *essayer*).

468   Similar problems to those presented by *faire, laisser* and verbs of the senses might seem to be presented by modal verbs (e.g. *devoir, pouvoir*) and certain other verbs that are followed by an infinitive without *à* or *de*. In fact, there is no real problem. The participle of such verbs is invariable whether the infinitive is expressed or merely understood since, if there is a direct object, it is in all cases the object of the infinitive not of the other verb.
Among the most widely used of such verbs are:

aimer mieux, prefer
compter, expect

désirer, wish
devoir, have to (etc.)
espérer, hope
oser, dare
paraître, appear
pouvoir, be able
préférer, prefer
savoir, know how to, be able
sembler, seem
souhaiter, wish
vouloir, wish

Examples:

Il y avait tant de choses que nous avions espéré voir
There were so many things which we had hoped to see

Nous avons fait tous les préparatifs que nous avons pu (faire
is understood)
We have made all the preparations we could

Je vais vous montrer la maison qu'il avait désiré acheter
I'll show you the house that he had wanted to buy

Problematic cases not connected with the infinitive

469   *courir, coûter, marcher, peser, valoir*
The participles of these verbs are invariable when they are followed by an expression of amount, time or distance. The reason
is that, in sentences such as *Ce paquet pèse trois kilos* 'This
parcel weighs three kilos', *J'ai couru huit kilomètres* 'I ran eight
kilometres', *J'ai marché deux heures* 'I walked (for) two hours',
the expressions *trois kilos, huit kilomètres, deux heures* are not
really direct objects but adverbial expressions of amount, distance
or time, and so the relative pronoun *que* standing for them is not
a direct object either and so, in a compound tense, does not cause
agreement. Note, however, that *courir, coûter, peser* and *valoir*
do take a direct object (and so the participle takes agreement)
when they are used metaphorically, and that *peser* in the sense
of 'to weigh (an object)' also has a normal direct object.

Examples:

Malgré les huit kilomètres qu'il avait couru, il n'était guère essoufflé
In spite of the eight kilometres he had run, he was hardly out of breath

Malgré les dangers qu'il avait courus, il n'était guère ému
In spite of the dangers he had run, he was almost unmoved

les cent cinquante francs que ce livre m'a coûté
the 150 francs that this book cost me

les soucis que sa conduite m'a coûtés
the worries that his behaviour has cost me

les vingt kilos que le paquet avait pesé
the twenty kilos that the parcel had weighed

les pommes qu'il avait pesées
the apples that he had weighed

les cinquante mille francs que le tableau avait valu
the fifty thousand francs that the picture had been worth

les félicitations que son courage lui a values
the congratulations that his courage earned him

470   Expressions denoting duration of time, as in 'The strike lasted three months', 'I have been waiting two hours', are adverbial expressions and must not be interpreted as direct objects – as is clearly indicated by the alternative English formulation 'The strike lasted for three months', 'I have been waiting for two hours'. Consequently, in such examples as the following *que* is not a direct object and the past participle is therefore invariable:

J'ai perdu les deux heures que j'ai attendu
I have wasted the two hours I have been waiting

Combien d'heures avez-vous dormi?
How many hours did you sleep (have you slept)?

les trois mois que la grève a duré
the three months that the strike lasted

471   Note, however, that *passer* 'to spend (time)' does take a direct object and that there is therefore agreement of the past participle in such examples as the following:

Combien d'années a-t-il passées à Paris?
How many years has he spent in Paris?

les dix heures que nous avons passées sur le bateau
the ten hours we spent on the boat

N The moods

472 There is so little agreement among grammars of French as to just how many 'moods' French has that we shall not attempt to define the term 'mood' but shall concentrate on discussing the ways in which each so-called mood is used.

The moods recognized by some though, as we have said, not all grammars are the following (of which the first three are agreed by everyone to be moods):

(i) The indicative – for a brief general discussion of the difference between the indicative and the subjunctive, see **473**; the tenses of the indicative are discussed above, under 'J: The tenses'

(ii) The subjunctive – discussed at length below, **474–506**

(iii) The imperative – see **514–517**

(iv) The conditional – discussed above under 'Tenses', see **415–424**

(v) The infinitive – see **425–438**

(vi) The participles – see **439–471**

(vii) The gerund – here included under the present participle (see **445**)

O The subjunctive

Introduction

473 If one thing is certain about the use of the subjunctive in Modern French, it is that it cannot be reduced to a few easy rules. It is true that, in many cases, one can give precise guidance, i.e. one can say that in certain circumstances one **must** use the subjunctive (and, in others, that one **must** use the indicative).

But there are other circumstances that allow the use of either the indicative or the subjunctive. Often the choice is a meaningful one, each mood having a real and distinctive, if not always easily definable, expressive value. But sometimes the distinction is merely stylistic – the literary language, for example, may still prefer the subjunctive where in speech, and even in educated speech, the indicative is well established.

With these reservations, it is not too much of a simplification to say that, in general, the indicative presents an event as a fact, whereas the subjunctive expresses it as, for example, a possibility or an aim, or calls it into doubt or denies its reality, or expresses a judgement on it.

474 Many errors made by students in the use of the subjunctive can be avoided if one remembers that, with the exception of a few fixed expressions and certain constructions in which its use is little more than a relic of an earlier stage of the language (see 476–478), the subjunctive occurs **only**:

(i) in clauses introduced by *que* or conjunctions ending in *que* (e.g. *quoique* 'although') (see **486–491**) – but *most clauses* introduced by *que* have the indicative, and

(ii) in certain types of relative clauses (see **492–495**) – but, again, *most* relative clauses have the indicative.

475 We shall discuss first the exceptional cases referred to above. These are of three types:

(i) fixed expressions, i.e. expressions that cannot be varied in any way (476)

(ii) constructions allowing a slight amount of variation, but only within very strict limits (477)

(iii) constructions allowing a greater degree of variation than those referred to under (ii) (478).

(i) Fixed expressions

476 The subjunctive without *que* occurs in a small number of fixed expressions (many of them having religious associations), e.g.:

advienne que pourra	come what may
grand bien vous fasse	much good may it do you
ainsi soit-il (after a prayer)	amen (*lit.* so be it)
soit dit entre nous	between you and me (*lit.* let it be said between us)
coûte que coûte	at all costs (*lit.* let it cost what it costs)
n'en déplaise à . . . (ne vous en déplaise, etc.)	with all due respect to . . ., if you have no objection
fasse le ciel que . . .	Heaven (God) grant that . . .
Dieu vous bénisse!	(when someone sneezes) (God) bless you!
Dieu soit loué!	God be praised!
A Dieu ne plaise!	God forbid! (*lit.* May it not please God)

Note that the English equivalents are in some cases also fixed expressions involving the subjunctive, *Come what may, God be praised, God forbid,* etc.

(ii) *Constructions allowing a minimum of variation*

477 The subjunctive without *que* occurs in the following constructions, all of them other than (a) and (b) being characteristic of literary rather than of spoken usage:

(a) with *vivre* 'to live': *Vive la France!* 'Long live France!', *Vivent les Belges!* 'Long live the Belgians!' – occurs only when the subject is a noun (which may, however, be any noun that makes sense in the context)

(b) with *venir* 'to come': *vienne la fin du mois* 'come the end of the month', *viennent les beaux jours* 'when the fine weather comes' – the subject is usually a noun referring to a point in time

(c) with *pouvoir* 'may': *Puisse-t-il arriver à temps!* 'May he arrive (= if only he can arrive) in time!', *Puissiez-vous réussir* 'May you succeed', *Puissent vos beaux yeux ne jamais pleurer* (Vigny) 'May your lovely eyes never weep' – can occur with all persons of the verb (note the form *puisse-jé*)

(d) with *être* 'to be': *Soit un triangle ABC* 'Let there be a triangle ABC', and similar expressions used in geometry

(e) with *savoir* 'to know': *je ne sache pas que* . . . 'I am not aware that . . .' (with a subjunctive in the following clause) – normally found only with *je* or *on* (e.g. *On ne sache pas qu'il ait jamais fait de grands efforts* 'It is not known that he has ever made any great effort'); similarly *Je ne sache rien de plus agréable* 'I know of nothing more pleasant', and comparable expressions with *ne* . . . *personne* 'no one', *ne* . . . *guère* 'scarcely', etc.

(iii) Constructions allowing a greater degree of variation

478   (a) *The imperfect subjunctive in conditional clauses*, e.g. *fût-il du sang des dieux aussi bien que des rois* (Corneille) 'were he of the blood of gods as well as of kings', *dût-il* (*dussiez-vous*, etc.) *en mourir* 'had he, were he (you, etc.) to die because of it (i.e. even if . . .)', *dussent mille dangers me menacer* 'were a thousand dangers to threaten me', *voulût-il le faire* 'even if he wanted to do so' – the subject may be a personal pronoun (note the forms *fussé-je, dussé-je*), or *ce*, or *on*, or a noun, but note that, if it is a noun, complex inversion (see **596**) is obligatory in the case of *être* and *vouloir*, e.g. *la situation fût-elle encore plus grave* 'were the situation even more serious', but not in the case of *devoir*

(b) *The pluperfect subjunctive with inversion of the subject in 'if'-clauses*, e.g. *Pierre Louis m'eût-il encouragé* (Gide) 'had Pierre Louis encouraged me'; this highly literary construction is the equivalent of the usual *si Pierre Louis m'avait encouragé*

(c) *The pluperfect subjunctive in both parts of conditional sentences*. In constructions of the type *S'il avait parlé, j'aurais répondu* 'If he had spoken, I should have replied', the pluperfect indicative in the *si* clause and the past conditional in the main clause (or, sometimes, one of the two but not both) may be replaced by the pluperfect subjunctive, *S'il eût parlé, j'eusse répondu*; similarly, with verbs taking *être*, one may find *si elle fût partie*, etc., for *si elle était partie* 'if she had left', etc.

Note (1) that this construction occurs *only* as the equivalent of the pluperfect and the past conditional and that no parallel construction exists as the equivalent of the construction *S'il parlait, je répondrais* 'If she spoke, I should reply', and (2) that it is in any case a highly literary and even somewhat archaic construction and should not be imitated.

(d) As an alternative to the construction *si (quelque . . . , aussi . . ., tout . . ., pour . . .) riche qu'il soit* 'however rich he may be' (see **310**) one sometimes finds the construction *si riche soit-il* 'however rich he is (may be)', but only when the subject is *il, elle, ils* or *elles*.

The subjunctive introduced by que

479 We shall divide the clauses introduced by *que* and taking the subjunctive into three categories, viz.:

(i) those in which the *que*-clause is not dependent on some preceding verb, adjective, noun, or adverb (**480**)

(ii) those in which the *que*-clause *is* dependent on a preceding verb, adjective, noun, etc. (**481–485**)

(iii) those in which *que* is part of a conjunction (the majority of which are in fact what in French are known as *locutions conjonctives*, i.e. compound conjunctions such as *à moins que* 'unless', *en sorte que* 'so that', *pourvu que* 'provided that') (**486–491**).

(The distinction between (ii) and (iii) is sometimes uncertain – for example, *de crainte que* 'for fear that, lest', could well fit into either category.)

The subjunctive in independent clauses

480 The subjunctive occurs in the following types of clauses in which *que* is not dependent upon a preceding element (verb, noun, etc.):

(i) In clauses expressing an order (a kind of third person imperative) or an exhortation; these can often be rendered in

English by 'Let X do so-and-so', though in practice some other equivalent usually occurs, e.g. *Qu'il vienne me voir demain* 'Let him come and see me (He can come and see me, Tell him to come and see me) tomorrow', *Qu'elles rentrent avant minuit* 'Let them be back (They'd better be back) by midnight', *Qu'ils fassent bien attention* 'Let them (They'd better) take care', *Que tout le monde sorte* '(Let) everybody leave'.

(ii) The subjunctive is usual when *que* introduces a noun-clause (i.e. a clause functioning as a noun in relation to some other clause) placed at the beginning of the sentence; the noun-clause may function as the subject of another clause, e.g. *Qu'il soit mécontent est certain* 'That he is displeased is certain' (*qu'il soit mécontent* is the subject of *est*), or stand in some other relation to the other clause, e.g. *Qu'il puisse partir demain, tout le monde le sait* 'That he may leave tomorrow everybody knows', *Que vous ayez raison, j'en suis certain* 'That you are right I am sure of'. (The indicative can occur when the factual nature of the statement is stressed, e.g. *Que Louis XVIII ne l'aimait pas (. . .), cela, il le savait* (Aragon) 'That Louis XVIII did not like him, that he knew'.)

(iii) In certain types of hypothetical (conditional) clause, in particular:

(a) in a *que*-clause as the equivalent of a *si*-clause at the beginning of the sentence, e.g. *Qu'il fasse beau demain (= S'il fait beau demain), (et) j'irai à la pêche* 'If (provided) it's fine tomorrow, I shall go fishing' (note that the following clause is often introduced by *et*); *Que l'ennemi vienne, le lâche s'enfuit* 'Should the enemy come, the coward runs away'

(b) as the equivalent of *si* introducing a second hypothetical clause (but see also 702,i), e.g. *s'il fait beau et qu'il ne fasse pas trop chaud . . . (= s'il ne fait pas trop chaud)* 'if it's fine and if it's not too hot . . .'

(c) after *soit que . . . soit que* or *soit que . . . ou que* 'whether . . . or (whether)', e.g. *Soit qu'il ne comprenne pas, soit qu'il* (or *ou qu'il*) *ne veuille pas comprendre, il est de tout façon très entêté* 'Whether he does not understand, or whether he does not wish to understand, he is at all events very stubborn'

(d) in the construction *que . . . ou que* (or *ou non*) 'whether . . . or whether (or not)', e.g. *Qu'il fasse beau ou qu'il pleuve (Qu'il fasse beau ou non), j'irai à la pêche* 'Whether it's fine or whether it rains (Whether it's fine or not), I shall go fishing'.

The subjunctive in dependent que-clauses

481 Broadly speaking, *que*-clauses involving the subjunctive fall into four categories, each expressing – if sometimes rather vaguely – a particular value which is something other than a mere factual statement. The following indications (and in many cases they *are* indications rather than rules) are not exhaustive, and there are frequent exceptions, i.e. instances where the indicative occurs when the subjunctive might be expected, and vice versa. The four categories in question are the following (in each case, we use the term 'event' to indicate the action or idea expressed by the verb):

(i) clauses in which the event is presented as something to be accomplished (**482**)

(ii) clauses in which the event is presented as merely possible, or is called into doubt (**483**)

(iii) clauses in which the reality of the event is denied (**484**)

(iv) clauses expressing a judgement on or reaction to the event (**485**).

The *que*-clause may be dependent on a verb or an adjective or, occasionally, on a noun or an adverb.

482 (i) **The event is presented as something to be accomplished**
(a) After verbs expressing a wish, a request, an order, an expectation, permission, etc.; these include:

vouloir que	to wish, want	*insister pour que*	to insist
souhaiter que	to wish	*tenir à ce que*	to insist, be keen
désirer que	to wish, desire	*veiller à ce que*	to take care, see to it
demander que	to ask	*attendre que*	to wait (until)
exiger que	to demand, require	*s'attendre à ce que*	to expect
ordonner que	to order	*permettre que*	to allow
recommander que	to recommend	*consentir à ce que*	to agree, consent

e.g. *Je veux qu'il parte* 'I want him to leave', *Il a demandé que toutes les lettres soient brûlées* 'He asked that all the letters be burnt', *Nous insistons pour que vous veniez nous voir* 'We insist that you come and see us', *Mon frère veillera à ce que ce soit fait* 'My brother will see that it is done', *Attendons que le courrier arrive* 'Let's wait until the mail arrives (for the mail to arrive)'.

Note that other verbs, such as *dire* 'to say', *crier* 'to shout', may sometimes express an order and so take a subjunctive, e.g. *Dites-lui qu'il parte tout de suite* 'Tell him to leave at once', *Ils crient qu'on les serve* 'They are shouting to be served'.

With most of the above verbs, the infinitive **must** be used instead of a *que*-clause when the subject of both verbs is the same, e.g. *Je veux le faire* 'I want to do it', *Il a demandé à descendre* 'He asked to get down', *Mon frère insiste pour vous voir* 'My brother insists on seeing you', *Nous nous attendons à partir demain* 'We expect to leave tomorrow'. On these and other infinitive constructions (e.g. *Dites-lui, permettez-lui de partir* 'Tell him, allow him, to leave') see **529–537**.

(b) After the following impersonal verbs:

il convient que, it is advisable
il faut que, it is necessary
il importe que, it is important
il suffit que, it is enough
it vaut mieux que, it is better

e.g. *Il faut que vous partiez maintenant* 'It is necessary that you leave (You must leave) now', *Il suffit que je le dise* 'It is enough that I say so (for me to say so)', *Il vaut mieux qu'il le sache* 'It is better that he should know (for him to know)'.

(c) After such adjectives as:

essentiel, essential	*nécessaire*, necessary
important	*préférable*
indispensable	*utile*, useful

e.g. *Il est nécessaire que vous achetiez ce livre* 'It is necessary for you to buy this book'.

(d) After nouns such as *besoin* 'need', e.g. *Nous avons besoin que vous nous aidiez* 'We need you to help us', *avoir soin que* 'to take care that'.

(e) In the construction *assez X pour que*, where 'X' is an adjective or an adverb, e.g. *Ce livre est assez simple pour qu'un enfant le comprenne* 'This book is easy enough for a child to understand', *Il parle assez lentement pour que tout le monde comprenne* 'He is speaking slowly enough for everyone to understand'.

483   (ii)   The event is presented as doubtful or as merely possible

(a) After *douter que* 'to doubt that (whether)', and *il se peut que* 'it is possible that', e.g. *Je doute que ce soit vrai* 'I doubt whether it is true'. But the indicative (or the conditional) may be used instead of the subjunctive after *douter* in the interrogative or negative, when the reality of the event is stressed, e.g.:

$$Il\ ne\ faut\ pas\ douter\ qu'il\ \begin{Bmatrix} fera \\ ferait \end{Bmatrix}\ ce\ qu'il \begin{Bmatrix} pourra \\ pourrait \end{Bmatrix}$$

$$\text{It cannot be doubted that he } \begin{Bmatrix} \text{will} \\ \text{would} \end{Bmatrix} \text{ do all he } \begin{Bmatrix} \text{can} \\ \text{could} \end{Bmatrix}$$

(b) After verbs of thinking and saying *in the negative or interrogative*, in particular:

croire que, to think, believe
penser que, to think
trouver que, to be of the opinion that
espérer que, to hope that
affirmer que, to assert
déclarer que, to declare
dire que, to say

e.g. *Je ne crois pas qu'il l'ait fait* 'I don't think he did it', *Trouvez-vous qu'elle soit jolie?* 'Do you think she's pretty?', *Est-ce qu'il espère que j'y aille?* 'Does he hope that I shall go there?', *Je ne dis pas qu'il m'écrive souvent* 'I don't say he writes to me often'. Likewise with other verbs when they express a similar idea, e.g. *Je ne vois pas qu'il puisse arriver à temps* 'I don't see that (how) he can arrive in time'.

The indicative is used after such verbs when they are neither negative nor interrogative, e.g. *Je crois qu'il viendra* 'I think he will come', *Nous espérons qu'il recevra demain notre lettre* 'We hope he will receive our letter tomorrow'. The indicative may also occur even after a negative or interrogative if one is stressing the reality or virtual certainty of the event, e.g. *Je ne crois pas qu'il pleuvra* 'I don't think it will rain' (i.e. in effect, 'I think, I feel sure, it won't rain').

(c) Verbs like *sembler, paraître*, are followed by the indicative or the subjunctive depending on the degree of certainty or doubt it is intended to convey, e.g. *Il semble qu'ils sont malades* 'It seems they are ill' (i.e. the speaker accepts that they are ill), *Il semble qu'ils soient malades* 'It seems they are ill' (the speaker is not vouching for the fact). In practice, the indicative is usually found when it is stated that 'it seems *to someone* that . . .', e.g. *Il me semble (Il me paraît) que vous avez raison* 'It seems (appears) to me that you're right'. When the verbs in question are in the negative or the interrogative, the subjunctive is usual, e.g. *Il ne (me) semble pas qu'on puisse partir aujourd'hui* 'It doesn't seem (to me) that we can leave today'.

(d) After adjectives such as *douteux* 'doubtful', *possible, rare*, e.g. *Il est possible que mon père aille à Paris* 'It is possible that my father may go to Paris', *Il est rare qu'un Français comprenne le gallois* 'It is rare for a Frenchman to understand Welsh'.

Also after *peu probable* 'improbable, unlikely', and (usually though not invariably) after the adjectives *certain, sûr* 'sure', *vrai* 'true', in negative and interrogative constructions, *Il est peu probable que, il n'est pas certain (sûr, vrai) que mon père ait reçu la lettre* 'It is unlikely, not certain (true) that my father has received the letter', *Est-il vrai que vous soyez malade?* 'Is it true that you are ill?' – but *Il est probable, certain, vrai, que mon père a reçu la lettre* 'It is probable, certain, true, that my father has received the letter'.

(e) The subjunctive is frequently (but not invariably) used in miscellaneous constructions (here admittedly grouped somewhat uneasily together) in which the event seems to be envisaged as a possibility rather than as a fact, e.g.:

(1) After

il arrive que	it happens that
ignorer que	to be unaware that
l'idée que	the idea that

e.g. *Il arrive que nous nous trompions* 'It (sometimes) happens that we are wrong', *L'idée qu'il revienne m'effraie* 'The idea that he is coming (might come) back frightens me', *J'ignorais qu'il fût arrivé* 'I did not know that he had come'.

(2) After verbs such as *admettre* 'to admit', *comprendre* 'to understand', *s'expliquer* 'to understand', *supposer* 'to suppose', which

take the indicative when the event is presented as a fact (or, at least, as a supposed fact), e.g. *J'admets que vous avez raison* 'I admit that you are right', *Je comprends que cela vous est difficile* 'I understand that that is difficult for you', *Je suppose que vous avez été à Paris* 'I assume you have been to Paris', but the subjunctive when the event is merely envisaged as a possibility, e.g. *Admettons (supposons) que vous ayez raison* 'Let us admit, suppose (i.e. for the sake of argument) that you are right', *Je comprends que vous en soyez mécontent* 'I understand (how it is) that you are displeased about it', *Je m'explique mal qu'il soit déjà parti* 'I find it difficult to understand that he has already left'. Similarly after some other verbs such as *se souvenir* 'to remember' in the negative or interrogative, e.g. *Vous souvenez-vous qu'il a écrit* (indicative) *à son frère?* 'Do you remember [the fact] that he has written to his brother?', but *Vous souvenez-vous qu'il ait écrit* (subjunctive) *à son frère?* 'Do you recall whether he has written to his brother?'

(3) After *si* (*tellement, tant*) . . . *que* interrogative or imperative clauses, or clauses containing a suggestion of obligation or duty, e.g. *Est-ce que vous habitez si (tellement) loin qu'on soit obligé de prendre un taxi?* 'Do you live so far out that one has to take a taxi?', *A-t-il tant de travail qu'il soit toujours fatigué?* 'Has he so much work to do that he is always tired?', *Parlez* (or *Il faut parler*) *si éloquemment qu'on ne puisse rien vous refuser* 'Speak (*or* You must speak) so eloquently that no one can refuse you anything', *Faites-vous tant aimer qu'on ne puisse* . . . (etc.) 'Make yourself so much loved that no one can . . . (etc.)'.

For the subjunctive after these adverbs in negative clauses, see **484**,d.

484   (iii)   The reality of the event is denied

(a) After such verbs as:

> *nier que*, to deny
> *défendre que*, to forbid
> *interdire que*, to forbid
> *éviter que*, to avoid
> *empêcher que*, to prevent
> *s'opposer à ce que*, to oppose, object

e.g. *Je nie que ce soit vrai* 'I deny that it is true', *Évitez (empêchez) qu'il ne vienne* (note the *ne*) 'Avoid having him come, prevent him from coming', *Il s'oppose à ce que vous y alliez* 'He is opposed to (is against) your going there'.

Nier in the negative is followed either by the subjunctive (*Je ne nie pas que vous ayez raison* 'I don't deny that you are right') or, if the reality of the event is being stressed, by the indicative (*Je ne nie pas qu'il m'a écrit* 'I don't deny that he wrote to me').

(b) After expressions such as *ce n'est pas que* . . ., e.g. *Ce n'est pas que je me sente malade* 'It is not that I feel ill', *il s'en faut de beaucoup que* . . ., e.g. *Il s'en faut de beaucoup qu'elle soit belle* 'She's far from being beautiful'.

(c) After adjectival expressions like *il est impossible que* . . ., *il n'est pas possible (vrai) que* . . . 'it is impossible, not possible, not true, that . . .'.

(d) After *trop X pour que* . . . (where X is an adjective or an adverb), e.g. *Il est trop jeune pour que vous lui donniez du vin* 'He's too young for you to give him wine', *Il est trop tard pour qu'elle arrive ce soir* 'It's too late for her to arrive this evening', and after *si (tellement)* . . . *que, tant* . . . *que*, in a negative or interrogative clause, e.g. *Il n'est pas si riche* (or *tellement riche*) *qu'il puisse s'offrir une Rolls-Royce* 'He's not so rich that he can afford a Rolls-Royce' (for the subjunctive after these adverbs in interrogative clauses, see **483,e,3**). Cf. also the subjective after *bien loin que*, e.g. *Bien loin qu'il vous pardonne, il est toujours fâché* 'Far from forgiving you, he's still cross'.

(e) After a variety of negative constructions in which *que* depends on a noun, e.g. *ce n'est pas la peine que* 'it is not worth', *il n'y a aucune chance que* 'there is no chance that', *il n'y a pas de danger que* 'there is no fear (risk, danger) that', e.g. *Ce n'est pas la peine que tu lui écrives* 'It's not worth (while) your writing to him'.

(f) In surprised or indignant exclamations, where the *que*-clause may appear to be an independent clause but is not really so, as the main clause is understood, e.g.:

Moi, que je trahisse mon pays!
I betray my country!

where some such idea as 'Do you think that I would . . .?' is understood.

485 (iv) **The clause expresses a judgement on or reaction to the event**

(a) Expressions of acceptance, approval or pleasure, including verbs like

> *accepter que*, to accept
> *approuver que*, to approve
> *aimer mieux que*, to prefer
> *préférer que*, to prefer
> *se réjouir que*, to be delighted

adjectives like *content* 'pleased', *heureux* 'happy', *fier* 'proud', *ravi* 'delighted', *satisfait* 'satisfied'; impersonal expressions of the type *il est bon* 'it is good', *inévitable, juste* 'fair, right', *logique* 'logical', *naturel* 'natural', *normal* 'normal, natural', *préférable* 'preferable', e.g. *Je préfère que vous restiez* 'I prefer you to stay', *Elle est fière que son fils ait appris à nager* 'She is proud that her son has learned how to swim', *Il est juste qu'il soit puni* 'It is right that he (should) be punished'.

(b) Expressions of curiosity or surprise, including *s'étonner que* 'to be amazed that', *être étonné, surpris que* 'to be amazed, surprised that', *il est bizarre, curieux, extraordinaire que* 'it is odd, curious, extraordinary that'.

(c) Expressions of indifference, annoyance, anger, or sorrow, e.g. verbs like

> *ennuyer que*, to bother   *se plaindre que*, to complain
> *se fâcher que*, to be annoyed   *regretter que*, to regret

the impersonal verb *peu (m') importe que* 'it matters little (I don't mind, etc.)', adjectives like *désolé* 'upset', *fâché* 'annoyed', *furieux* 'angry', *triste* 'sad', e.g. *Cela m'ennuie que tu sois triste* 'It bothers, upsets, me that you are sad', *Peu m'importe qu'il soit déjà parti* 'I don't care if he has gone already'.

(d) Expressions of fear, including *avoir peur* 'to be afraid', *craindre* 'to fear', *de crainte que, de peur que* 'for fear, lest'; in the literary language, these are usually followed by a redundant *ne* (see **564**), e.g. *Je crains que ce ne soit trop tard* 'I fear it is too late', *de peur qu'il ne nous voie* 'for fear, lest, he (should) see us'.

The subjunctive after conjunctions formed on the basis of que

486   As in the case of dependent *que*-clauses in the subjunctive (**481–485**), these clauses usually express something other than a mere factual statement of the event. The commonest conjunctions taking the subjunctive are discussed in sections **487–491** – others are listed in **697**.

487   Conjunctions meaning 'although', of which the commonest are *quoique* (note that this is written as one word) and *bien que*, e.g.:

Il le fera bien que ce soit défendu
He will do it although it is forbidden

Quoique mon frère ait reçu ma lettre, il ne vient pas
Although my brother has received my letter, he is not coming

(The reality of the event may well be accepted, but it is discounted – e.g., in the second of these examples it is accepted that the letter has been received, but *in spite of that fact*, the brother is not coming.)

Bien que and *quoique* occasionally take the indicative or conditional when 'though' is almost the same as 'but', e.g.:

Il nous faut le faire, bien que nous n'y gagnerons rien

We must do it, $\left\{ \begin{array}{l} \text{though} \\ \text{but} \end{array} \right\}$ we shall gain nothing by it

But, generally speaking, the subjunctive should be used.

Other conjunctions meaning 'although' and taking the subjunctive are *encore que* (exclusively literary) and *malgré que* (familiar, and frowned on by some grammarians – see **698**).

Note that *alors que* and *tandis que*, both meaning 'whereas', always take the indicative.

488   The conjunctions *avant que* 'before' and *jusqu'à ce que* and *en attendant que* 'until', e.g.:

Nous le verrons avant qu'il parte
We shall see him before he leaves

Restons ici jusqu'à ce qu'il vienne (*en attendant qu'il vienne*)
Let's wait here until he comes

Note that, when 'not . . . until' is the equivalent of 'not . . . before', *avant que* must be used, e.g.:

Je ne partirai pas avant qu'il vienne
I shall not leave until he comes (= before he comes)

but

Je n'attendrai pas jusqu'à ce qu'il vienne (or *qu'il vienne* without *jusqu'à ce*)
I shall not wait until he comes ('before he comes' does not make sense)

Note too that comparable expressions based not on *que* but on *où* 'when', in particular *avant le moment où* 'before (the time when)', *jusqu'au moment où, en attendant le moment où* 'until (the time when)', always take the indicative. (Even *jusqu'à ce que* occasionally takes the indicative, but it is safer to stick to the subjunctive which is always correct.)

Other conjunctions relating to time, e.g. *aussitôt que* 'as soon as', *pendant que* 'while' (for a full list, see **693–695**), take the indicative. But note that, whereas according to strict grammar *après que* 'after' takes the indicative, there is an increasing tendency to use the subjunctive (presumably by analogy with *avant que*); those whose French is not at a really advanced level are advised to stick to the indicative.

489 Conjunctions meaning 'in order that, so that' (i.e., conjunctions expressing purpose, introducing what are often known as 'final' clauses – Latin *finis* and French *la fin* mean 'purpose' as well as 'end'); these include *afin que* and *pour que*, e.g.:

J'ai brulé la lettre afin que personne ne la lise
I burnt the letter so that no one should read it
Je vous le dis pour que vous le sachiez
I am telling you so that (in order that) you may know

Like English 'so that', the following are both final (i.e. expressing purpose) and consecutive (i.e. expressing consequence, result):

de (telle) façon que	
de (telle) manière que	so that, in such a way that
de (telle) sorte que	
en sorte que	

They take the subjunctive when any idea of purpose is implied, e.g.:

Le professeur expérimenté s'exprime de (telle) sorte que sa classe puisse le comprendre
An experienced teacher expresses himself in such a way that his class can understand him

Il parle toujours de (telle) façon que tout le monde l'entende
He always speaks so that (in such a way that) everyone may hear him

or when they express a result that is to be avoided (this too implies purpose), e.g.:

Je ne veux pas agir de (telle) sorte (façon, manière) qu'on me déteste
I do not want to act in such a way as to get myself disliked

But when they express a result that is merely stated as a fact, they take the indicative, e.g.:

Il parle toujours de (telle) façon que tout le monde l'entend
He always speaks in such a way that everybody hears him

Il a agi de telle sorte qu'il s'est fait détester
He acted in such a way that he got himself disliked

Note that *de façon à ce que* and *de manière à ce que* 'so that' have only a final value and so always take the subjunctive.

This use of the subjunctive is extended to *si . . . que* and *tant que* when the main clause

(i) is imperative, or suggests a duty or obligation, as with *il faut, devoir*, e.g.:

Agissez ⎫
Il faut agir ⎬ *si vite qu'on ne sache pas ce que vous faites*

You must act so quickly that no one can know what you are doing

(ii) contains a negative, or an interrogative suggesting a negative sense, e.g.:

Vous n'êtes pas si essoufflé que vous ne puissiez dire quelques mots
You are not so much out of breath that you cannot say a few words

Es-tu si stupide que tu veuilles partir tout de suite?
Are you so stupid that you want to leave straight away?

490   Certain conjunctions expressing conditions, hypotheses or suppositions, including:

à moins que (usually with *ne*, see **566**)	unless
pour peu que	if only, if ever, etc.
pourvu que	provided that
à supposer que, supposé que	supposing
si tant est que	so long as, provided that

Examples:

A moins que tu ne partes tout de suite
Unless you leave at once

Pour peu que vous répondiez à sa lettre, il consentira à rester
You've only got to answer his letter and he'll agree to stay

A supposer qu'il ne vienne pas, qu'allez-vous faire?
Supposing he doesn't come, what are you going to do?

Note that *à (la) condition que, sous (la) condition que* 'on condition that' may take either (a) the subjunctive or (b) the future indicative or the conditional (but **not** other indicative tenses), e.g. *Vous pouvez rester à (la) condition que vous vous taisiez* (or *tairez*) 'You can stay on condition that you keep quiet'.

Autant que and *pour autant que* 'as far as' can take either the indicative or the subjunctive depending on the degree of certainty or uncertainty the clause is intended to express, e.g.:

(pour) autant que je peux (or *puisse*) *en juger*
as far as I can judge

491   Conjunctions that deny the reality of the event, e.g.:

non que, non pas que	not that
loin que	far from (. . . ing)
sans que	without (. . . ing)

Examples:

> *non (pas) qu'il ait peur*
> not that he's afraid
>
> *Loin qu'il puisse m'aider, il ne comprend même pas le problème*
> Far from being able to help me, he doesn't even understand the problem
>
> *Il est parti sans que nous le sachions*
> He left without our knowing

de peur que, de crainte que (usually with *ne*, see **564**) 'lest, for fear', e.g.:

> *Partons tout de suite de peur qu'il (ne) nous voie*
> Let's leave at once for fear (in case) he sees us

The subjunctive in relative clauses

492   The subjunctive can occur in three types of relative clause:

(i) when the relative clause relates not to an actual individual or individuals but to a possible member or members of a class (**493**)

(ii) when the antecedent is qualified by a superlative or equivalent expression (**494**)

(iii) after the so-called 'indefinite relatives' (the equivalent of English 'whoever', 'whatever', 'wherever', etc.) (**495**).

493   The subjunctive in relative clauses relating to a possible member or members of a class. (This is sometimes known as the 'generic subjunctive' – *generic*: 'relating to a class or group'.)

An example will help to make this clear. If I ask someone: 'Could you show me the road that leads to the station?', the relative clause 'that leads . . . etc.' describes a particular road that I know (or, at any rate, that I assume) actually exists – the French equivalent has the indicative, *Pourriez-vous m'indiquer le chemin qui conduit à la gare?* Likewise, if I say: 'I am looking for a road [i.e. a road that I know exists and that I am describing] that leads to the station', the French equivalent is: *Je cherche un chemin qui conduit à la gare.* But if I ask: 'Could you show me a road that leads to the station?' (i.e. I am in fact enquiring whether any such road exists), or if I say: 'I am looking for a road that [if such a road exists] leads to the station', the relative clause rather than describing a particular road indicates the *type* of road that I want, i.e. it relates to any members of the class (which may or may not exist) of 'roads leading to the station'. In such cases, French has the subjunctive, viz. *Pourriez-vous m'indiquer un chemin qui conduise à la gare?*, or *Je cherche un chemin qui conduise à la gare*. Likewise, the subjunctive is of course used when the existence of the class in question is represented as hypothetical, as in 'If you know a road that leads to the station', *Si vous connaissez un chemin qui conduise à la gare*, or is denied (cf. **484**), as in 'There is no road that leads to the station', *Il n'y a pas de chemin qui conduise à la gare*. For similar reasons, a relative clause depending on *peu* 'little, few, not many' (see **328**) requires the subjunctive. Examples:

Pouvez-vous me montrer une dame qui soit mieux habillée que moi?
Can you show me a lady who is better dressed than I am?

Il lui faut un ami qui lui écrive régulièrement
He needs a friend who will write to him regularly

J'attends
Je désire } *une explication qui soit du moins raisonnable*

I am waiting for
I want } an explanation which is at least reasonable

Il n'y a personne qui veuille m'aider
There is no one who is willing to help me

Il n'y a rien que vous puissiez lui dire
There is nothing you can say to him

Je voudrais une chambre où l'on n'entende pas ce bruit
I should like a room where you can't hear that noise

Donnez-moi une plume avec laquelle je puisse écrire
Give me a pen I can write with

Il y a ici peu de gens que je connaisse
There are not many people I know here

Contrast these with the following, in which the relative clause relates to an actual and not a possible or hypothetical member of a class and so takes the indicative:

Pouvez-vous me montrer la dame qui est mieux habillée que moi?
Can you show me the lady who is better dressed than I am?

Il a un ami qui lui écrit régulièrement
He has a friend who writes to him regularly

J'ai une chambre où l'on n'entend pas ce bruit
I have a room where you can't hear that noise

Voilà une plume avec laquelle je peux écrire
Here is a pen I can write with

494   The subjunctive in relative clauses after a superlative

When the antecedent of the relative pronoun *qui* or *que* is qualified by a superlative adjective (*le plus beau*, etc.), or by one of the adjectives *premier* 'first', *dernier* 'last', *seul* 'only', or *unique* 'only', which are in some respects the equivalent of a superlative, the relative clause frequently takes the subjunctive, e.g.:

Elle est la seule personne qui puisse m'aider
She is the only person who can help me

C'est l'histoire la plus fascinante qu'on puisse imaginer
It is the most fascinating story one can imagine

Pierre est le meilleur ami que nous ayons
Peter is the best friend we have

The indicative occurs, however, when the strictly factual nature of the superlative is being emphasized, e.g. *C'est le dernier livre que j'écrirai* 'It's the last book I shall write', *les seules distractions que je prenais alors* (Nodier) 'the only leisure activities I engaged in at that time'. In general, the indicative is more likely to occur in familiar style (e.g. conversational speech or informal letters) than in literary usage.

Note that after expressions such as *la première (dernière) fois que* the indicative **must** be used, e.g. *C'est la première (dernière) fois que ça m'est arrivé* 'It's the first (last) time that that has happened to me'. (Beware of sentences in which the superlative is followed by a genitive plural, e.g. 'It is the best of the books I have read', which do *not* come under the above rule since the meaning is either 'The book I have read is the best one', i.e. *C'est le meilleur des livres que j'ai lu*, or 'Of those books that I have read it is the best', i.e. *C'est le meilleur des livres que j'ai lus*.)

495   The subjunctive after indefinite relatives

(i) The subjunctive **must** be used after:

(a) *qui que ce soit qui* 'whoever' (subject), *quoi que ce soit qui* 'whatever' (subject), e.g. *qui que ce soit qui le dise* 'whoever says so'

(b) *qui que ce soit que* 'whoever' (object), *quoi que, quoi que ce soit que* 'whatever' (object), e.g. *qui que ce soit que vous voyiez* 'whoever you see', *quoi (que ce soit) qu'il fasse, . . . qu'il ait fait* 'whatever he does, . . . he has done'

(c) *où que* 'wherever', e.g. *où que j'aille* 'wherever I go'

(d) *quelque(s)* + noun, 'whatever', e.g. *Quelques fautes que vous ayez commises, vous faites tout de même des progrès* 'Whatever mistakes you (may) have made, you are making progress all the same'.

(ii) Note that with the verb *être* (used alone or preceded by *pouvoir* or *devoir*), the construction *quel* (variable) + *que* + verb in the subjunctive + noun is used (see 308), e.g. *quels que soient les problèmes* 'whatever the problems', *quelle qu'ait pu être sa conduite* 'whatever his behaviour may have been'. A variant on this is the construction *Les difficultés, quelles qu'elles soient, ne sont pas insurmontables* 'The difficulties, whatever they are, are not insurmountable'.

(iii) Note the use of *quelque* or *si* + adjective or adverb, meaning 'however' (see 310), e.g. *quelque intelligents qu'ils soient, si intelligents qu'ils soient* 'however intelligent they are' (note that *quelque* here is an adverb and does not vary for gender or number), *quelque heureuse, si heureuse qu'elle puisse paraître* 'however happy she may appear', *Quelque* (or *Si*) *lentement que nous parlions, il ne comprend pas* 'However slowly we speak, he doesn't understand'.

Aussi, tout or *pour* can occur in place of *quelque* or *si*, e.g. *aussi riche, tout riche, pour riche qu'il soit* 'however rich he is'; *tout* may also take the indicative when the factual nature of the statement is stressed, e.g. *tout riche qu'il est* 'rich though he is'; for the agreement of *tout* see 317,v. On the alternative construction *si riche soit-il*, etc., see 310,i.

The tenses of the subjunctive

496 The French subjunctive has only four tenses, viz. two simple tenses:

the present   the imperfect

and two compound tenses:

the perfect   the pluperfect

The imperfect and pluperfect subjunctive are virtually never used now in speech and there is an increasing tendency to avoid them even in writing. The rules that we give in **497–499** should therefore be regarded as characteristic only of a very conservative literary style. In practice, the principles set out in sections **500–506** should be followed.

497 The subjunctive in independent clauses (see **476, 477** and **480**) is normally in the present or the perfect tense, as the meaning requires; for constructions taking the imperfect or the pluperfect subjunctive, see **478**.

498 (i) In a conservative literary style (see **496**), the choice of tense of the subjunctive is determined in most cases (for exceptions see **499**) by a 'rule for the sequence of tenses' that can be simply stated. (Note that, in what follows, the verb of the clause on which the subjunctive clause depends is referred to as the 'main verb' – e.g. in *Je ne crois pas qu'il soit malade* 'I don't think he is ill', *crois* is the main verb; strictly, this 'main verb' is sometimes itself a subordinate verb, as in *Elle dit qu'elle ne croit pas qu'il soit malade* 'She says that she doesn't think that he is ill', but this is of little practical consequence for our present purpose and, having now drawn attention to the matter, we shall not refer to it any more.)

(ii) The 'rule for the sequence of tenses' runs as follows:

If the main verb is:	the subjunctive is:
present future perfect imperative	present or perfect

If the main verb is:	the subjunctive is:
preterite	
imperfect	
pluperfect	imperfect or pluperfect
conditional	
past conditional	

(iii) The present or imperfect is used when the event expressed by the verb in the subjunctive is considered to take place at the same time as or later than that of the main verb – note therefore that there is normally no distinction between present and future (but see **506**). The perfect or pluperfect is used when the event expressed by the verb in the subjunctive is considered to have taken place before that of the main verb.

The application of the rule can be illustrated thus:

Je ne crois pas	
Je ne croirai pas	(a) *qu'il vienne*
Je n'ai jamais cru	(b) *qu'il soit venu*
Ne croyez pas	

I do not believe	
I shall not believe	(a) that he is coming, that he will come
I have never believed	(b) that he has come
Do not believe	

Je ne crus pas	
Je ne croyais pas	
Je n'avais pas cru	(a) *qu'il vînt*
Je ne croirais pas	(b) *qu'il fût venu*
Je n'aurais pas cru	

I did not believe	
I did not believe	(a) that he was coming, that he would come
I had not believed	
I should not believe	(b) that he had come
I should not have believed	

499 The sequence of tenses given in **498** should not be applied too mechanically. Sometimes the sense requires us to depart from it, as when, for example, a main verb in the present is followed by a verb that, in the indicative, would be in the imperfect, e.g. corresponding to *il était heureux* 'he was happy':

On ne peut pas croire qu'il fût heureux
One cannot believe that he was happy

or when a main verb in the past is followed by a verb referring to an event that is present or future at the time of speaking, e.g.:

Il n'avait pas voulu croire que mon frère vienne demain
He had not wanted to believe that my brother is coming tomorrow

500   Even in literary French, the sequence of tenses is frequently not followed when the main verb is in the conditional, which is treated as a member of the first rather than of the second group of tenses given in **498**,ii, e.g. *Je ne croirais pas qu'il vienne* rather than *Je ne croirais pas qu'il vînt* 'I should not believe that he would come'.

501   As is mentioned in section **496** above, the imperfect and pluperfect subjunctive are no longer used in ordinary speech and are indeed increasingly avoided in writing. The following principles should therefore be followed as far as possible:

502   In writing, the imperfect subjunctive may still be used:

(i) with the verbs *avoir* and *être*

(ii) in the third person singular of other verbs (e.g. *qu'il chantât*).
   Otherwise, it should be avoided so, for example, such forms as *que je vinsse, que nous chantassions, qu'ils écrivissent* should **never** be used.
   Two possible ways of avoiding the imperfect subjunctive, both of them widely used, not only when that tense really must be avoided but when its use is still tolerated in a literary style, i.e. in the circumstances stated in (i) and (ii) above, are:

(a) to recast the sentence in such a way as to avoid the subjunctive altogether; for example, instead of:

Les propriétaires n'avaient jamais permis que nous y entrassions
The owners had never allowed us to go in

Il ordonna qu'on déposât les armes
He ordered them to lay down their arms

one could write:

Les propriétaires ne nous avaient jamais permis d'y entrer
L'ordre fut donné de déposer les armes

(b) to use the present subjunctive instead of the imperfect, as in the following examples from literary texts:

Il fallait que Lucienne réponde (A. Orain)
It was essential that Lucienne should answer

Il n'aurait jamais dû permettre que sa femme s'en aille seule
(Maurois)
He ought never to have allowed his wife to go away alone

Il suffisait que je regarde le banc, la lampe, le tas de poussier,
pour que je sente que j'allais mourir (Sartre)
I only had to look at the seat, the lamp, the heap of coal-dust, to feel that I was going to die

Nous avions passé une semaine angoissée côte à côte avant
que je ne reparte pour l'été chez mes parents (Sagan)
We had spent an agonized week side by side before I left for my parents' place for the summer

503   The pluperfect subjunctive, based as it is on the imperfect subjunctive of *avoir* or *être* (see **502**,i), e.g. *qu'il eût fini, qu'ils fussent partis*, is still in use in a literary style, but, on the other hand, is frequently replaced by the perfect subjunctive.

504   In speech, the imperfect and pluperfect subjunctive should **always** be either (i) avoided (cf. **502**,a) or (ii) replaced by the present or the perfect subjunctive respectively, e.g.:

Ma femme voulait que j'aille voir (Simenon)
My wife wanted me to go and see

Je craignais qu'il soit déjà parti
I was afraid he had already left

505   Where the use of the present subjunctive in place of the imperfect could cause ambiguity, the perfect may be used instead; for example, corresponding to the indicative *Il travaillait jeudi* 'He was working on Thursday', we could have *Je ne crois pas qu'il ait travaillé jeudi* 'I don't think he was working on Thursday', since *Je ne crois pas qu'il travaille jeudi* would mean 'I don't think he is working (*or* will be working) on Thursday'.

506 Where the use of the present subjunctive as the equivalent of a future indicative could cause ambiguity, the subjunctive of *devoir* and the infinitive may be used to form a kind of future subjunctive, e.g. *Je ne crois pas qu'il doive le faire* 'I don't think he will do so' in contexts in which *Je ne crois pas qu'il le fasse* would be likely to be interpreted as 'I don't think he is doing so'.

P 'May, might, must, ought, should, would'

507 It is important to be aware that, though English 'may, might, should, would' often correspond to a subjunctive in French, very often they do not. These particular modal verbs in English correspond in reality to a number of different constructions in French and great care must be taken in translating these forms, and the closely related modals 'must' and 'ought'. Note in particular the constructions dealt with below.

508 May

'May'

(i) corresponds to the French subjunctive expressing purpose, after *pour que* or *afin que* or sometimes *que* alone, e.g.:

Pour que vous compreniez, je vais vous expliquer ce que cela veut dire
So that you may understand, I am going to explain what that means

(ii) corresponds to the French subjunctive, expressing a wish, e.g.:

(Que) Dieu vous bénisse!   May God bless you!

(iii) corresponds to the French subjunctive in a variety of other contexts, e.g.:

J'y vais de peur qu'il ne soit inquiet
I'm going for fear he may be worried

quelque riche qu'il soit
however rich he may be

(iv) expresses possibility, in which case French uses either the verb *pouvoir*, e.g.:

Cela peut être vrai	That may be true
Il a pu le faire	He may have done it

(in this last example, note that French uses the perfect of *pouvoir* and the present infinitive where English uses the present of 'may' and the past infinitive – cf. 510,ii); or *il est possible que* or *il se peut que* 'it is possible that' followed by a subjunctive clause, e.g.:

Il est possible que ⎫
Il se peut que ⎬ *ce soit vrai*　It may be true

or *peut-être* 'perhaps', e.g.:

Il viendra peut-être demain　He may come tomorrow

(v) expresses permission, in which case French uses *pouvoir* and not the subjunctive, e.g.:

Vous pouvez vous asseoir si vous voulez
You may sit down if you wish

Peut-on entrer?
May we come in?

509　Might

'Might'

(i) is used (somewhat loosely) in English as an alternative to 'may' in contexts such as those dealt with in 508,i, iii and iv

(ii) in its strict usage is the past tense of 'may' and so corresponds to the French imperfect subjunctive in such contexts as the following (corresponding to the use of the present subjunctive as in 508,i, iii and v):

Je lui écrivis afin qu'il ne fût plus inquiet
I wrote to him so that he might no longer be worried

J'y allai de peur qu'il ne fût inquiet
I went for fear he might be worried

Il était possible que ce fût vrai
It was possible that it might be true

(For restrictions on the use of the imperfect subjunctive in French, see 500–504.)

(iii) is used much like 'may' in 508,ii, but suggests less hope of fulfilment, e.g.:

Oh, que ce fût vrai!
Oh, that it might be true!

(iv) expresses a possibility (often a slight possibility) (cf. 508,iv):

Ça pourrait être vrai, mais j'en doute
That might be true, but I doubt it

(v) is used to request permission (cf. 508,v), e.g.:

Pourrais-je vous suggérer que c'est idiot?
Might I suggest that this is idiotic?

510 Must

'Must'

(i) expresses a moral certainty, something that is regarded as being inevitably so, in which case the usual equivalent is *devoir*, e.g.:

Cela doit être vrai
That must be true

Vous devez croire que je suis bête
You must think that I am stupid

Note that, where English uses 'must' and the past infinitive, French usually has a compound tense of *devoir* and the present infinitive (cf. 508,iv), e.g.:

Il a dû partir
He must have left

Je supposais qu'il avait dû partir la veille
I assumed he must have left the day before

(ii) expresses obligation – note that in this case *devoir* is not strong enough and that some such expression as *il faut que* or *il est nécessaire que* 'it is necessary that' has to be used, e.g.:

Il faut que nous partions tout de suite
We must leave at once

511 Ought

'Ought' is translated by the conditional of *devoir*, e.g.:

Je devrais y aller   I ought to go

or, when English has 'ought to have' and the past participle, by the past conditional of *devoir* and the infinitive, e.g.:

> *J'aurais dû y aller*   I ought to have gone

512 Should

'Should'

(i) is often the expression of the conditional (see 415–423) in the first persons singular and plural, e.g.:

> *Je ne vous le dirais pas, même si je le savais*
> I should not tell you, even if I knew

(ii) is sometimes the equivalent of 'were to' in 'if'-clauses; in such cases, it must **not** be translated by the French conditional but by the imperfect of *devoir* and the infinitive, e.g.:

> *S'il devait arriver ce soir, donnez-moi un coup de fil*
> If he should arrive (were to arrive) this evening, give me a ring

(iii) is sometimes the equivalent of 'ought to', in which case it must be translated as in 511, e.g.:

> *Vous devriez y aller*
> You should go (= You ought to go)

(iv) is sometimes used with verbs of believing or doubting as a less categorical assertion than would be the case if the present tense were used, e.g. 'I should think he will come', 'I should doubt whether he will come'; in such contexts, French would usually use the present indicative, i.e. *Je crois qu'il viendra, Je doute qu'il vienne*, or some kind of circumlocution, e.g. *Je suis porté à croire qu'il viendra* 'I am inclined to think he will come'.

513 Would

'Would'

(i) is very frequently the expression of the conditional (see 415–423), e.g.:

> *Ils ne vous le diraient pas, même s'ils le savaient*
> They would not tell you even if they knew

(ii) expresses determination, in which case it is usually stressed in English and should be rendered in French by *vouloir* 'to wish' or *tenir à* 'to insist on (doing)', which are often strengthened by an adverb, e.g.:

Il voulait (absolument) y aller ⎫
Il tenait (absolument) à y aller ⎬ He *would* go

(iii) in 'would that', expresses a wish and is rendered in French by a *si*-clause, e.g.:

Si j'étais (j'avais été) plus jeune
Would that I were (had been) younger

(iv) occasionally expresses a habitual action or state in the past, in which case French uses the imperfect indicative (see **417**), e.g.:

Un jour il était insensé de fureur; le lendemain il oubliait ses griefs et devenait l'ami de tout le monde
One day he would be beside himself with rage; the next he would forget his grievances and make friends with everybody

Q The imperative

514   Generally speaking, the imperative is used to express commands in French in much the same way as in English. Note however:

(i) that, whereas it is possible in English to use the subject pronoun 'you' with the imperative for purposes of emphasis, this is not possible in French which instead uses, depending on the precise type of emphasis required, either the appropriate form for 'yourself' or 'yourselves', e.g.:

Fais-le toi-même! ⎫
Faites-le vous-même! ⎬ *You* do it!
Faites-le vous-mêmes! ⎭

or some such circumlocution as *Il faut que toi tu le fasses* 'You must do it (= *You* do it)', or *Vous pourriez peut-être le lui dire* 'You might perhaps tell him (= *You* tell him, please)'

(ii) that French has a first person plural imperative corresponding to 'Let us (do something)' and that neither the verb *laisser* nor *que* and the subjunctive (as in 515) must be used, e.g.:

Partons tout de suite   Let's leave at once

515 A kind of third person imperative can be expressed by means of *que* and the subjunctive, e.g. *Qu'il attende* 'Let him wait' (see also **480**,i).

516 For the use of the infinitive as the equivalent of an imperative in general instructions, etc., see **429**,ii.

517 The future tense may be used as a polite imperative, i.e. to express a request rather than a command, e.g.:

Quand il arrivera, vous me le direz, s'il vous plaît
When he comes, please let me know

R The complement of verbs

518 Linking verbs

A certain number of verbs, in particular *être* 'to be' but also *devenir* 'to become', *sembler* 'to seem', *paraître* 'to appear', *rester* 'to remain' and a few others, can function as 'linking verbs'. This means that they take as their complement (i.e. complete their sense with) not a direct or indirect object but a noun (or noun phrase) or adjective (or adjectival phrase) relating to the subject, e.g. 'Peter is a doctor', 'She is becoming a very attractive girl', 'These books seem too difficult'.

The main differences between English and French in their treatment of the complement of linking verbs are the following:

(i) in French, the adjective has to agree with the subject (see **127–130**), e.g.:

Il est petit
He is small

Elle en est devenue furieuse
She became angry at it

Vos sœurs paraissent intelligentes
Your sisters seem intelligent

Ils sont restés calmes
They remained calm

(ii) in English, one might hesitate in the case of personal pronouns between the more formal 'It is I', 'It was he', etc., and the more informal 'It's me', 'It was him', etc.; in French there is no problem since the disjunctive pronoun must always be used, e.g. *C'est moi, C'était lui.*

Verbs other than linking verbs

519   Verbs other than linking verbs (see **518**) may, in appropriate circumstances, take as their complement(s) one or more of the following (though it is not necessarily the case that any particular one of these complements can occur with any given verb):

(i) a direct object (otherwise referred to as an object in the *accusative* – see **17**), e.g. *Il a acheté ce livre* 'He bought this book', *Je les connais* 'I know them' (for direct object personal pronouns, see **198–199**)

(ii) a noun or pronoun introduced by the preposition *à*, or one or other of the dative conjunctive pronouns *me, te, nous, vous, se, lui, leur* or *y* (see **198–200**)

(iii) a noun or pronoun introduced by the preposition *de* (see **19**), or the genitive conjunctive pronoun *en* 'of it, of them, etc.' (see **201**)

(iv) a noun or pronoun preceded by some other preposition – e.g. *avec, dans, en, sur*

(v) an infinitive alone without a preposition

(vi) an infinitive introduced by *de*

(vii) an infinitive introduced by *à*

(viii) an infinitive introduced by some other preposition – e.g. *après, par, pour, sans*

(ix) a present participle introduced by the preposition *en*

(x) a clause introduced by a conjunction or by some interrogative word.

520   The complement(s) that can occur with a given French verb are not necessarily the same as those that occur with the equivalent verb in English – for example, in English 'one plays the piano' and 'one plays football' (direct object in each case) whereas in French *on joue du piano* (complement introduced by *de*) and *on joue au football* (complement introduced by *à*), and, on the other hand, in English 'one listens to the music' (complement introduced by 'to') whereas in French *on écoute la musique* (direct object).

Some of the main differences that occur in this respect are classified in the following sections. For the terms *accusative*, *dative* and *genitive*, see **17–19** and **519**,i–iii.

521 Verbs taking a direct object in English but in French taking a noun or pronoun introduced by *à* or one of the dative conjunctive pronouns *me, te, nous, vous, se, lui, leur* or *y* (see **198–200**):

(a) The following verbs, among others, take a direct object in English and an indirect object in French:

> *convenir à*, suit
> *déplaire à*, displease
> *désobéir à*, disobey
> *grimper à*, climb[1]
> *jouer à*, play (a game)
> *nuire à*, harm
> *obéir à*, obey
> *obvier à*, obviate
> *parvenir à*, reach, attain
> *plaire à*, please
> *remédier à*, remedy, make good
> *renoncer à*, renounce, abandon, give up
> *répondre à*, answer
> *résister à*, resist
> *ressembler à*, resemble, be like, look like
> *succéder à*, follow, succeed
> *survivre à*, survive

Examples:

> *Il joue au football*
> He plays football
> *Je vais obéir à vos ordres*
> I shall obey your orders
> *J'y ai renoncé*
> I've given it up
> *Il ne ressemble pas du tout à son frère*
> He is not at all like his brother

Note

1 *Grimper* can also take *dans* or *sur* when the sense allows, e.g. *grimper à l'échelle, aux arbres* 'to climb the ladder, to climb trees', *grimper dans un arbre* 'to climb up into a tree', *grimper sur le toit* 'to climb on to the roof'.

(b) The following verbs always take a direct object in English but in French take either a direct object or an indirect object depending on the meaning:

insulter 'to insult' takes a direct object with reference to a person (*insulter quelqu'un* 'to insult someone') but otherwise an indirect object (eg. *insulter à l'intelligence de quelqu'un* 'to insult someone's intelligence'); *toucher* takes a direct object when it merely means 'to touch' physically (e.g. *toucher le mur* 'to touch the wall', *toucher quelqu'un à l'épaule* 'to touch someone on the shoulder'), but an indirect object when it conveys the idea of 'meddling with' (e.g. *Ne touchez pas à mes papiers* 'Don't touch my papers') and in certain other cases (e.g. *Il n'a pas touché à son petit déjeuner* 'He hasn't touched his breakfast (i.e. he hasn't eaten any of it)', *toucher à une question* 'to touch on a question') – consult a good dictionary.

(c) Note that in English 'one asks or forgives someone for something' whereas in French *on demande ou on pardonne quelque chose à quelqu'un*, e.g.:

J'ai demandé cent francs à mon frère
I asked my brother for a hundred francs

Je lui pardonnerai son absence
I shall forgive him for his absence

(d) Verbs such as *défendre* 'to forbid', *dire* 'to tell', *offrir* 'to offer', *ordonner* 'to order', *permettre* 'to allow, permit', *promettre* 'to promise', *raconter* 'to tell', *refuser* 'to refuse' and others of similar meaning that can have both a direct and an indirect object have the same construction in both languages, but whereas in English the indirect object is often identical in form with the direct object, i.e. it is not accompanied by the preposition 'to' (e.g. 'to promise *somebody* something' = 'to promise something *to somebody*'), in French the indirect object must always be expressed by a dative pronoun or by *à* + a noun phrase, e.g.:

Il faudra le dire à Pierre
We shall have to tell Peter

Voulez-vous permettre aux enfants de sortir?
Will you allow the children to go out?

Je lui ai promis cent francs
I promised him a hundred francs

Le consulat leur refuse un visa
The consulate refuses them a visa

522   Verbs taking a direct object in English but in French taking a noun or pronoun introduced by *de* or the genitive pronoun *en* (see **201**):

abuser de, misuse, exploit
s'apercevoir de, notice
douter de, doubt
se douter de, suspect
s'emparer de, seize
hériter de, inherit[1]
jouer de, play (an instrument)[2]
jouir de, enjoy
médire de, malign, speak ill of
se tromper de, get wrong, make a mistake about
user de, use (with direct object = 'wear out')

Examples:

Je ne m'en suis pas aperçu
I didn't notice (it)

Je doute de sa sincérité
I doubt his sincerity

Il joue du piano
He plays the piano

Dans un grand nombre de cas, posséder un objet, c'est pouvoir en user (Sartre)
In many cases, to possess an object is to be able to use it

Il s'est trompé de date
He got the date wrong

Notes
1   *Hériter* is used in three ways, viz. *hériter d'une fortune* 'to

inherit a fortune', *hériter une fortune de quelqu'un* 'to inherit a fortune from someone', *hériter de quelqu'un* 'to be someone's heir'.

2 *Jouer d'un instrument* but *jouer à* with reference to games, e.g. *jouer au football* 'to play football'.

523 Among commonly used verbs that take a prepositional complement (introduced by 'of', 'for', 'at', 'to' or 'with') in English but a direct object in French are:

approuver, approve of
attendre, wait for
chercher, look for
demander, ask for
écouter, listen to
espérer, hope for
fournir, supply with (see also **526**)
habiter, live in[1]
payer, pay for
regarder, look at
reprocher, reproach for[2]
viser, aim at

Examples:

Attendons le bus
Let's wait for the bus

Je n'ai pas écouté son discours
I didn't listen to his speech

Il lui fournit une grande somme d'argent
He supplied him with a large sum of money

Qui a payé les billets?
Who paid for the tickets?

Notes
1 *Habiter* with an accusative is used of the house, room, town, etc., in which one lives, e.g.:

Il habite la maison en face
He lives in the house opposite

It can also be used absolutely, e.g.:

Il habite depuis quelques mois en Italie
He has been living for a few months in Italy

Il habite près de Paris
He lives near Paris

2   *Reprocher*: in English one reproaches someone for something, in French *on reproche quelque chose à quelqu'un*, e.g.:

Il reprocha au garçon ses fautes
He reproached the boy for his mistakes

524   With a number of verbs, of which the following are the most frequent, French uses the preposition *à* or one of the dative conjunctive pronouns (see **18** and **198**) *me, te, lui, nous, vous, leur*, with the somewhat unusual value of 'from':

cacher à, hide from
dérober à, steal from, hide from
échapper à, escape (from)[1]
emprunter à, borrow from
enlever à ⎫
ôter à ⎭   take away from
louer à, rent, hire from
prendre à, take from (also *dans*, **659**,iii; *sur*, **685**)
retirer à, remove from
soustraire à, abstract from (maths, subtract, *de*)
se soustraire à, withdraw from (intrans.)
voler à, steal from[2]

Examples:

Il cacha son dessein à ses amis
He hid his plan from his friends

Je vais emprunter mille francs à mon frère
I am going to borrow a thousand francs from my brother

On lui a volé sa montre
Someone has stolen his watch from him

Notes

1   *Échapper à* implies 'not being caught' and so is usually to be translated 'to escape' (with a direct object) rather than 'to escape from', e.g. *Il a échappé à la police* 'He escaped the police' (i.e. 'He avoided being caught'), *échapper au gibet* 'to escape the gallows'; 'to escape from' in the sense of 'to get out of' is *s'échapper de* (as in *Il y a de l'eau qui s'échappe de*

ce tuyau 'There is water escaping from this pipe') or, particularly in the sense of escaping from prison, etc., *s'évader de.*

2 *Voler* meaning 'to rob (a person)', when the thing stolen is not mentioned, takes a direct object, e.g. *voler ses clients* 'to rob one's clients', *On l'a volé* 'They have robbed him' or 'He has been robbed'.

525 English uses a much wider range of prepositions than French in introducing prepositional complements. After the following verbs, French uses *à* (or the conjunctive pronoun *y* – see **200,i**) where English uses 'at', 'by', 'in', 'for', 'on', 'of', 'about', 'over', 'upon' or 'to' (for a similar variety of prepositions corresponding to French *de*, see **527**):

assister à, be present at, attend[1]
connaître à, know by[2]
croire à or *en*, believe in[3]
mêler à, mix, involve in
pendre à, hang on (trans. or intrans.)
penser à, think of, about[4]
pourvoir à, provide for
présider à, preside over (also with direct object)
reconnaître à, recognize by[5]
réfléchir à, think of, about, reflect on, upon (also *sur*)
réserver à, reserve for
songer à, think of, about, over
suspendre à, hang on (intrans.)
veiller à, attend to, see to (things)[6]

Examples:

Il va assister à la réunion
He is going to attend (be present at) the meeting

Ils veulent me mêler à leur entreprise
They want to involve me in their venture

J'y pense souvent
I often think about it

Vous le reconnaîtrez à sa cicatrice
You will recognize him by his scar

Cette salle est réservée à nos clients
This room is reserved for our customers

Notes

1 *Assister* meaning 'to help' takes a direct object.

2 'To know someone by name, by repute, by sight' is *connaître quelqu'un de nom, de réputation, de vue*. 'To be known by' in the sense of 'known to' is *être connu de*, e.g. *Il est connu de tout le monde* 'He is known by (to) everyone'.

3 *Croire* sometimes takes a direct object, sometimes *à* or *en*, e.g. *Croyez-vous cette histoire ?* 'Do you believe that story?', *Je vous crois* 'I believe you', *Je ne crois pas aux miracles* 'I do not believe in miracles', *croire au Saint-Esprit, au diable, aux fées* 'to believe in the Holy Spirit, in the devil, in fairies' (but *croire en* with names, e.g. *croire en Dieu, en Jésus-Christ* 'to believe in God, in Jesus Christ'), *Je crois en mes amis* 'I believe in (i.e. I have confidence in) my friends'. For other uses of *croire* with *à* or *en*, consult a good dictionary.

4 *Penser à* 'think of' in the sense of 'have in mind, keep in mind, remember, reflect on', e.g.:

A quoi pensez-vous?
What are you thinking about?

penser de 'think of' in the sense of 'have an opinion about, form a judgement on', e.g.:

Que pensez-vous de ces gens?
What do you think of these people?

5 'To be recognized by a person' is *être reconnu par*, e.g. *Il fut reconnu par la police* 'He was recognized by the police'.

6 *Veiller à*, as in *veiller à l'ordre public* 'to see to it that public order is maintained'. *Veiller sur* is 'to watch over, keep an eye on (people)', e.g. *Il me faut veiller sur ces enfants* 'I have to keep an eye on these children'. *Veiller* in the sense of 'to sit up with (a sick person or a dead body)' takes a direct object.

526 (i) After the following verbs (among many others – and see also ii below), French uses *de* whereas English uses 'with' (for verbs after which English uses either 'with' or some other preposition, see **527**):

accabler de, overwhelm with
armer de, arm with
charger de, load with, entrust with
combler de, shower with, fill with

faire de, do with
fourmiller de, swarm with
fournir de, supply with[1] (see also 523)
menacer de, threaten with
munir de, provide with
orner de, decorate with, adorn with
pourvoir de, provide with
remplir de, fill with
trembler de, tremble with

Examples:

Cette nouvelle m'accable de honte
This news overwhelms me with shame

Il m'a chargé de cette responsabilité
He has entrusted me with this responsibility

Qu'avez-vous fait de mon livre?
What have you done with my book?

Le gazon fourmille d'insectes
The turf is swarming with insects

menacer quelqu'un de mort
to threaten someone with death

L'enfant tremblait de peur
The child was trembling with fear

Note
1 *Fournir* takes either *de* or, more usually nowadays, *en*, e.g.
fournir quelqu'un de viande or *en viande* 'to supply someone
with meat'.

(ii) With many such verbs, *de* = 'with' is found particularly (but
not exclusively) in the passive, e.g.:

Il fut criblé de balles
He was riddled with bullets

or when the past participle is used adjectivally, e.g.:

La salle est ornée de tapisseries
The room is adorned with tapestries

(and likewise *armé de* 'armed with', *couronné de* 'crowned with',
planté de 'planted with', *semé de* 'strewn with', *taché de* 'stained
with', etc.).

527 Like *à* (see **525**), *de* may correspond to any one of a variety of prepositions in English including, as the following list shows, 'in', 'from', 'by', 'at', 'on', 'for', 'after', 'over' or 'about' (and, in some cases, as an alternative to one of these, 'with' – for other verbs taking 'with', see **526**):

> *s'abriter de*, to shelter (take shelter) from
> *s'alarmer de*, to become alarmed by, at
> *couvrir de*, cover in, with
> *débarrasser de*, free from, rid of (*se débarrasser de*, get rid of)
> *délivrer de*, deliver from, free from
> *dépendre de*, depend on
> *dîner de*, dine on
> *envelopper de*, wrap (up) in, envelop in
> *se moquer de*, laugh at, make fun of
> *se nourrir de*, feed on
> *répondre de*, answer for, guarantee
> *rire de*, laugh at
> *rougir de*, blush for, with
> *tenir de*, take after
> *triompher de*, triumph over
> *vivre de*, live on

Examples:

> *La voiture était couverte de boue*
> The car was covered in mud
>
> *Cela dépend de vous*
> That depends on you
>
> *Vous vous moquez de moi*
> You are making fun of me
>
> *Il triomphe toujours de ses ennemis*
> He always triumphs over his enemies

Infinitive complements

528 Sections **529–537** classify verbs on the basis of the construction they take when their complement, or one of their complements, is an infinitive.

529 Certain categories of verbs are followed directly by the infinitive, i.e. there is no linking preposition. These are:

(i) The modal verbs:

devoir, be (due) to, have to, must
pouvoir, be able, can
savoir, know how to, be able, can
vouloir, wish

Examples:

Vous devez être fatigué
You must be tired

Savez-vous nager?
Can you swim?

Note that *vouloir* only takes the infinitive when the subject of both verbs is the same, e.g. *Je veux le faire*, 'I want to do it'; otherwise *que* and the subjunctive must be used, e.g. *Je veux que vous le fassiez* 'I want you to do it'.

(ii) The following verbs of the senses (see also **430–438**):

écouter, listen to
entendre, hear
regarder, look at, watch
sentir, feel
voir, see

Examples:

Il écoutait chanter les oiseaux
He was listening to the birds sing(ing)

Je le vois venir
I can see him coming

(iii) Most verbs of 'saying' and 'thinking' when the subject of both verbs is the same, e.g.:

Il prétendait la connaître
He claimed to know her (i.e., that he knew her)

Je crois la connaître
I think I know her

which could also be expressed as follows:

Il prétendait qu'il la connaissait
Je crois que je la connais

Among the verbs in this category are:

affirmer, maintain, assert
avouer, admit
croire, believe, think
déclarer, declare, state
dire, say
nier, deny
penser, think
prétendre, claim, maintain
reconnaître, acknowledge, admit

In some cases, the construction with an infinitive is also possible with the corresponding verb in English (see the first example above, with 'to claim') but in other cases it is not (see the second example above, with 'to think').

Note that, if the subject of both verbs is not the same, the construction with *que* must be used, e.g.:

Je crois que vous la connaissez
I think you know her

(iv) Certain verbs of motion, in which case the construction verb + infinitive expresses purpose, e.g.:

Il accourut m'annoncer l'heureuse nouvelle
He came running to tell me the good news

Je suis venu vous féliciter de votre succès
I have come to congratulate you on your success

Among the verbs in this category are:

accourir, run up, rush
aller, go
courir, run
descendre, come (*or* go) down (and *redescendre*)
monter, come (*or* go) up (and *remonter*)
partir, to go (away)
retourner, return
venir, come (and *revenir*)

(v) The following verbs:

adorer, adore, love
aimer autant (see example below)[1]

aimer mieux, prefer[1]
amener, bring (and *ramener*)
compter, intend, expect
daigner, deign
désirer, wish
détester, hate, detest (also with *de*)
emmener, take
envoyer, send
espérer, hope
faillir (see example below)
faire (see example below and **430–438**)
falloir (impersonal), be necessary
se figurer, imagine
s'imaginer, imagine
laisser, let, allow (and see **430–438**)
oser, dare
paraître, appear, seem
préférer, prefer[1]
sembler, seem
souhaiter, wish (also with *de*)
valoir autant (impersonal), be just as well[1]
valoir mieux (impersonal), be better[1]

Examples:

J'adore jouer au tennis
I love playing tennis

J'aime autant partir tout de suite
I'd just as soon leave immediately

Je compte y arriver demain
I expect to get there tomorrow

Il m'a emmené voir ses roses
He took me to see his roses

J'espère vous revoir bientôt
I hope to see you again soon

Il faut le faire
One must (It is necessary to) do it

J'ai failli tomber
I nearly fell

Il fait bon se promener sur la plage
It's nice going for a walk on the beach

Laissez-moi finir!
Let me finish!

Je n'ai pas osé le lui dire
I didn't dare tell him

Elle semble être contente
She seems to be pleased

Il vaudrait mieux lui écrire
It would be better to write to him

Note the idioms *envoyer chercher quelqu'un* 'to send for someone', *envoyer dire à quelqu'un* 'to send word to someone'.

Note

1 In a comparison after *aimer autant, aimer mieux, valoir autant, valoir mieux* and usually also after *préférer*, a second infinitive (introduced by *que* 'than') is preceded by *de*, e.g.:

J'aimerais autant
J'aime mieux (Je préfère) } *partir maintenant que*
Autant vaut   *d'attendre*
Il vaut mieux

I would just as soon leave now as }
I prefer to leave now rather than } wait
We might as well leave now as   }
It's better to leave now than   }

530 The following verbs (and a few other relatively infrequent ones) take *à* before a following infinitive (this list does not include verbs that also take a direct object (see **531**) or an indirect object (see **532**) or reflexive verbs (see **533**)):

aimer à, like to[1]
apprendre à, learn to
aspirer à, aspire to
avoir à, have to
chercher à, try to
commencer à, begin to (also *de*) (and *recommencer à, de*)
concourir à, combine to
condescendre à, condescend to
consentir à, consent to

consister à, consist in . . .-ing
conspirer à, conspire to
continuer à, continue to (also *de*)
contribuer à, contribute to
demander à, ask to[2]
exceller à, excel in . . . -ing
hésiter à, hesitate to
incliner à, incline to
parvenir à, manage to, succeed in . . .-ing
persister à, persist in . . .-ing
renoncer à, give up . . .-ing
répugner à, detest, loathe . . .-ing[3]
réussir à, succeed in . . .-ing
songer à, think of . . .-ing
suffire à, be enough to (also *pour*)[4]
tendre à, tend to
tenir à, be anxious, eager, keen to
viser à, aim to

Examples:

Je cherche à vous aider
I am trying to help you

Pourquoi ne veut-il pas renoncer à fumer?
Why doesn't he want to give up smoking?

Notes

1 *Aimer* is also used without a preposition, e.g. *J'aime voyager* 'I like travelling'; this is the most usual construction in speech and it must always be used with *aimer autant*, e.g. *J'aimerais autant partir tout de suite* 'I would just as soon leave right away', and *aimer mieux* 'to prefer'. *Aimer de* is archaic and should not be used.

2 For *demander à* or *demander de* + infinitive, see **536**, note 1.

3 Though *répugner* when used personally takes *à*, e.g. *Je répugne à suivre ses conseils* 'I am reluctant to take his advice', it is more often used impersonally, in which case it takes *de*, e.g. *Il me répugne de le faire* 'I hate doing it, it is repugnant to me to do it'.

4 *Suffire*, whether used personally or impersonally, takes *à* or *pour* when the infinitive expresses what something or other is sufficient for, e.g. *Cette somme suffira à* (or *pour*) *payer ses*

dettes 'That sum will be enough to pay his debts', or, impersonally, *Il a suffi de trois jours pour achever le travail* 'Three days were enough to complete the work'. But when the impersonal *il suffit* introduces an infinitive expressing what it is that is sufficient, the infinitive is preceded by *de*, e.g. *Il suffira de lui écrire* 'It will be enough to write to him' (i.e. 'Writing to him is all that will be necessary').

531 The following verbs (and a few other relatively infrequent ones) can take both a direct object and an infinitive introduced by *à*:

accoutumer à, accustom
aider à, help
amener à, induce, persuade
appeler à, summon
astreindre à, compel
autoriser à, authorize
condamner à, condemn
conduire à, lead, induce
convier à, invite
destiner à, destine[1]
déterminer à, decide (someone) to
disposer à, induce
employer à, employ
encourager à, encourage
engager à, urge
exciter à, incite
exercer à, train
exhorter à, exhort
exposer à, expose
forcer à, force[2]
habituer à, accustom
inciter à, incite
incliner à, lead, incline, make inclined
inviter à, invite
mettre à, set someone to work at
obliger à, oblige[2]
passer à, spend (time) in
porter à, induce, cause
pousser à, urge
préparer à, prepare

provoquer à, provoke
réduire à, reduce[1]

Examples:

Vous ne l'amènerez jamais à avouer sa faute
You will never induce him to admit his mistake

Je les ai encouragés à persévérer
I encouraged them to persevere

Je vais le pousser à se raviser
I shall urge him to reconsider his decision

Notes

1   *Destiner* and *réduire* + *à* + infinitive are found particularly in the passive, *être destiné (réduit) à*, e.g. *destiné à disparaître*, 'doomed to disappear', *J'en ai été réduit à boire de l'eau* 'I was reduced to drinking water'.

2   In the passive, *être forcé* and *être obligé* take *de*, e.g. *J'ai été obligé de partir* 'I was obliged to leave'.

532   The following verbs take an indirect object and an infinitive introduced by *à*:

apprendre à quelqu'un à, to teach someone (how) to[1]
enseigner à quelqu'un à, to teach someone (how) to[2]
montrer à quelqu'un à, to show someone how to

Examples:

Je lui apprends à jouer du piano
I am teaching him to play the piano

Il montre aux plus hardis à braver le danger
He shows the bravest how to face danger

Notes

1   With a direct object only, *apprendre* means 'to learn', e.g. *J'apprends l'allemand* 'I am learning German'. With a direct object and an indirect object, it means 'to teach something to someone', e.g. *Je lui apprends l'allemand* 'I am teaching him German'.

2   With a direct object only, *enseigner* means 'to teach (a subject)', e.g. *J'enseigne l'allemand* 'I teach German'. With a direct object and an indirect object, it means 'to teach something to someone', e.g. *J'enseigne l'allemand à mes étudiants* 'I teach my students German'.

533 The following reflexive verbs (among others) take *à* before a following infinitive:

s'abaisser à, condescend to
s'accoutumer à, be accustomed to
s'acharner à, persist in, be bent on
s'amuser à, enjoy
s'appliquer à, apply oneself to
s'apprêter à, get ready to
s'astreindre à, force oneself to
s'attacher à, be intent on
s'attendre à, expect to
se borner à, confine onself to
se complaire à, take pleasure in
se disposer à, arrange to, prepare to
s'égayer à, be highly amused at
s'employer à, apply oneself to
s'engager à, undertake to
s'entêter à, persist in
s'essayer à, try one's hand at
s'évertuer à, strive to
se fatiguer à, wear oneself out by
s'habituer à, get used to
se hasarder à, risk
se mettre à, begin to
s'obstiner à, persist in
s'occuper à, busy oneself with[1]
s'offrir à, offer to
se plaire à, delight in
se refuser à, refuse to
se résigner à, resign oneself to
se résoudre à, resolve to

Examples:

Je ne m'attendais pas à réussir
I wasn't expecting to succeed

Je m'habitue à me coucher de bonne heure
I am getting used to going to bed early

Il s'est mis à pleurer
He began to cry

Note
1 There is a distinction between *s'occuper à* + infinitive (which
   is in any case somewhat old-fashioned) 'to busy oneself with',
   e.g. *Il s'occupe à faire des traductions* 'He busies himself with
   doing translations', and *s'occuper de* + infinitive 'to deal with,
   see about', e.g. *Il s'occupe de prendre les billets* 'He is seeing
   about getting the tickets'.

534 The following verbs (among others) take *de* before a following infinitive (this list does not include verbs that also take a
direct object (see **535**) or an indirect object (see **536**), or reflexive
verbs (see **537**)):

achever de, finish . . .-ing
affecter de, pretend to
ambitionner de, aspire to
brûler de, long to
cesser de, cease to
choisir de, choose to
commencer de, begin to (also *à*) (also *recommencer*)
continuer de, continue to (also *à*)
craindre de, fear to
décider de, decide to
dédaigner de, disdain to
désespérer de, despair of . . .-ing
détester de, detest (see also **529**,v)
discontinuer de, leave off
enrager de, be infuriated by, loathe
entreprendre de, undertake to
essayer de, try to
éviter de, avoid
feindre de, pretend to
finir de, finish . . .-ing
jurer de, swear to
ne pas manquer de, not to fail to[1] (etc.)
mériter de, deserve to
négliger de, neglect to
obtenir de, get leave to
offrir de, offer to
omettre de, omit to
oublier de, forget to
projeter de, plan to

promettre de, promise to
refuser de, refuse to
regretter de, regret to
risquer de, risk
rougir de, blush, be ashamed to
souffrir de, be grieved to
souhaiter de, wish to (see also 529,v)
supporter de, bear to
tâcher de, try to
tenter de, try to

Examples:

Il a choisi d'y demeurer
He has chosen to live there

Il a décidé de vendre sa maison
He has decided to sell his house

J'essaie de comprendre
I am trying to understand

Il avait juré de nous aider
He had sworn to help us

Voulez-vous me promettre de ne plus y aller?
Will you promise me not to go there again?

Note
1 *Ne pas manquer de* is used *only* in the negative, e.g. *Je ne manquerai pas de vous écrire* 'I shall not fail to write to you'.

535 The following verbs (and a few other relatively infrequent ones) can take both a direct object and an infinitive introduced by *de*:

accuser de, accuse of
applaudir de, applaud for
avertir de, warn to
blâmer de, blame for
charger de, make responsible for
conjurer de, implore, beg to
défier de, challenge
dégoûter de, disgust with, deter from
détourner de, divert from
dispenser de, exempt from, let off

dissuader de, dissuade from
empêcher de, prevent from
excuser de, excuse for
féliciter de, congratulate on
gronder de, scold for
louer de, praise for
persuader de, persuade to[1]
plaindre de, pity for
presser de, press to, urge to
prier de, beg to
punir de, punish for
remercier de, thank for
reprendre de, reprove for
sommer de, summon to
soupçonner de, suspect of
supplier de, entreat, beg to

Examples:

Il m'accuse d'avoir volé son crayon
He accuses me of stealing his pencil

Cela ne m'empêchera pas d'y aller
That won't prevent me from going there

Je vous supplie de me croire
I beg you to believe me

Note
1   *Persuader* takes either a direct or an indirect object, i.e. either *persuader quelqu'un de faire quelque chose* or, more usually nowadays, *persuader à quelqu'un de faire quelque chose* 'to persuade someone to do something'.

536   The following verbs can take both an indirect object and an infinitive introduced by *de*:

commander de, command
conseiller de, advise
crier de, shout to
défendre de, forbid
demander de, ask[1]
déplaire de, displease[3]
dire de, tell
écrire de, write to

enjoindre de, enjoin upon
jurer de, swear to
offrir de, offer
ordonner de, order
pardonner de, pardon for
permettre de, allow
persuader de, persuade[2]
plaire de, please[3]
prescrire de, prescribe, ordain
promettre de, promise
proposer de, propose
recommander de, urge
reprocher de, reproach for
répugner de, be repugnant, disgust[3]
suggérer de, suggest

Examples:

Il lui a conseillé de ne pas le faire
He advised him not to do it

Il leur demanda (permit) de s'en aller
He asked (allowed) them to go away

Je lui ai dit de rester
I told him to stay

Il répugne à une mère de voir sa fille mal habillée
A mother hates (*lit.* It disgusts a mother) to see her daughter
badly dressed

Notes

1 'To ask someone (else) to do something' is *demander à
quelqu'un de faire quelque chose*, but 'to ask to (be allowed
to) do something (oneself)' is *demander à faire quelque chose*,
e.g. *Il a demandé à partir* 'He asked to (be allowed to) leave'.

2 For *persuader* + direct or indirect object + infinitive, see **535**,
note 1.

3 *Déplaire, plaire* and *répugner* (see **530**, note 3) are followed
by *de* and an infinitive only when used impersonally, e.g. *Il
me plaît de vous écouter* 'I like listening to you (*lit.* It pleases
me to listen to you)'.

537 The following reflexive verbs (and a few other relatively
infrequent ones) take *de* before a following infinitive:

il s'agit de, it is a question of
s'arrêter de, stop
s'attrister de, regret to
s'aviser de, take it into one's head to
se charger de, undertake to
se contenter de, be content with, put up with
se dépêcher de, hasten to
se désaccoutumer de ⎫
se déshabituer de ⎬ get out of the habit of
s'efforcer de, struggle to
s'empresser de, hasten to
s'ennuyer de, be bored with
s'enorgueillir de, pride oneself on
s'étonner de, be surprised to
s'excuser de, apologize for
se flatter de, flatter oneself on
se garder de, take care not to
se hâter de, hasten to
s'impatienter de, long to, be dying to
s'inquiéter de, be anxious about, care for
s'irriter de, be angry at
s'occuper de, deal with[1]
s'offenser de, be offended at
se passer de, do without
se piquer de, pride oneself on
se plaindre de, complain of
se presser de, hurry to
se réjouir de, rejoice at, be glad to
se repentir de, regret, be sorry for
se soucier de, care for, or about
se souvenir de, remember
se vanter de, boast of

Examples:

Il s'est arrêté de travailler
He has stopped working

Il s'excuse d'être en retard
He apologizes for being late

Je me hâte de répondre à votre lettre
I hasten to reply to your letter

Note

1   For *s'occuper* with *à* or *de*, see 533, note 1.

538   Miscellaneous verbs

The following verbs are used in a variety of constructions and with a variety of meanings:

approcher

1   Transitive

(a) 'bring near (*or* nearer) to' (*de* 'to'), e.g.:

> *Approchez la table de la fenêtre*
> Bring the table near (*or* nearer to) the window

(b) 'approach, come near', e.g.:

> *Ne m'approchez pas!*
> Don't come near me!

2   Intransitive

'come, get near (*or* nearer)' (*de* 'to'), either literally or figuratively, e.g.:

> *L'hiver approche*
> Winter is coming (*or* will soon be here)

> *Nous approchons de Paris*
> We are getting near Paris

> *Il approchait de la cinquantaine*
> He was approaching (getting on for) fifty

3   Reflexive

s'approcher (de), 'come, draw near', usually (but not exclusively) in a literal sense, e.g.:

> *Approchez-vous!*
> Come closer!

> *Il s'approcha de la porte*
> He walked towards the door

> *Elle s'approcha de moi*
> She came up to me

Whereas *approcher (de)* (see 2 above) refers only to the fact of drawing near(er), *s'approcher (de)* usually implies an intention to do so.

changer

Changer has many meanings, including the following (for others, consult a good dictionary):

1   Transitive

(a) 'change, alter, modify', e.g.:

> *Il a changé le début de son roman*
> He has changed the beginning of his novel
>
> *Il a changé ses habitudes*
> He has changed his habits

(b) 'change, exchange (one thing for another)', e.g.:

> *Aves-vous changé les draps?*
> Have you changed the sheets?
>
> *Il a changé deux mille francs*
> He changed two thousand francs

(c) 'change (one thing into another), transform' (*en* 'into'), e.g.:

> *Les alchimistes cherchaient à changer les métaux vils en or*
> The alchemists tried to change base metals into gold

(d) 'move' (followed by *de*), e.g.:

> *changer les meubles de place*
> to move the furniture around
>
> *changer quelqu'un de poste*
> to move someone to another job

2   Intransitive

(a) 'change (i.e. become different)', e.g.:

> *Le temps va changer*
> The weather is going to change
>
> *Vous n'avez pas changé du tout*
> You haven't changed at all

(b) 'change (trains, etc.)', e.g.:

> *Il faut changer à Dijon*
> You have to change at Dijon

(c) 'to change' in the sense of 'to exchange one item for another of the same type' is *changer de*, e.g.:

changer d'avis	to change one's mind
changer de train	to change (trains)
changer de place	to change one's seat
changer de coiffure	to change one's hair-style

3   Reflexive

(a) 'to change, turn into', e.g.:

Les souris de Cendrillon se sont changées en chevaux
Cinderella's mice turned into horses

(In this sense, *se transformer* is very often used.)

(b) 'to change' (one's clothes)', e.g.:

Il faut que je me change avant de sortir
I must change before I go out

convenir

1   Personal, with an indirect object, 'suit, be fitting, agree with', e.g.:

Ses vêtements conviennent à sa position
His clothes suit (are in keeping with) his position

Ce climat ne leur convient pas
This climate does not suit them (agree with them)

2   Impersonal followed by *de* and an infinitive, 'to be fitting, appropriate, advisable', e.g.:

Il convient de ne pas trop en parler
It is advisable not to say too much about it

3   *Convenir de* 'to agree'

(a) with an infinitive, e.g.:

Nous avons convenu d'y être à midi
We have agreed to be there at noon

(b) with a noun or pronoun (including *en* 'of it, of them' – see 201), e.g.:

Nous allons convenir du prix
We are going to agree on the price

(c) note *être convenu de* with either an infinitive or a noun or pronoun, 'to be in agreement', e.g.:

Nous sommes convenus de nous taire
We are in agreement to say nothing

Nous sommes convenus du prix
We are agreed on the price

4   *Convenir de* with a noun or pronoun (including *en* – see **201**),
'to acknowledge, recognize, admit', e.g.:

Il a convenu de son erreur
He has acknowledged his mistake

J'ai eu tort – j'en conviens
I was wrong – I admit it

décider 'decide, induce, etc.'
1   Transitive
(a) 'decide (on)', e.g.:

La compagnie a décidé la fermeture de cette usine
The company has decided on the closure of this factory

(b) 'induce, make (someone) decide' (*quelqu'un à faire quelque
chose* 'someone to do something'), e.g.:

La mort de son fils l'a décidé à partir
The death of his son made him decide to leave

2   Intransitive
(a) 'decide, take a decision (decisions), etc.', e.g.:

C'est moi qui décide ici
I take the decisions here

(b) *décider de* (*quelque chose*) 'decide about (something)', e.g.:

Le gouvernement a décidé de l'avenir du projet
The government has decided on the future of the project

Le comité en décidera
The committee will decide about it

3   Reflexive
(a) *se décider* (= passive) 'to be decided', e.g.:

La question se décidera aujourd'hui
The question will be decided today

(b) *se décider à* + infinitive 'to decide to (do something)', e.g.:

Elle s'est decidée à partir
She has decided to leave

4   Passive

être décidé à quelque chose, à faire quelque chose 'to be determined on something, to do something', e.g.:

J'y suis décidé
I am determined on it

Nous sommes décidés à partir
We are determined to leave

devoir
1   'Owe', e.g.:

Je lui dois mille francs
I owe him a thousand francs

2   In simple tenses (other than the conditional – see 3 below),
when followed by an infinitive, 'be to', or 'have to', or, sometimes,
'must' (but see also **510**), e.g.:

Je dois y aller demain
I am to (have to) go there tomorrow

Cela doit être vrai
That must be true

Il devait partir le lendemain
He was to leave the next day

Je devrai lui écrire
I shall have to write to him

Je dus y aller
I had to go there

3   In the conditional when followed by an infinitive, 'ought' or
'should' (expressing obligation) – see **511** and **512**,iii

4   In compound tenses when followed by an infinitive, two quite
distinct meanings (see also **510**,i):

Il a dû écrire à son frère
(a) He had to write to his brother
(b) He must have written to his brother

Je supposais qu'il avait dû le faire
(a) I supposed that he had had to do it
(b) I supposed that he must have done it

5   For *devoir* and an infinitive as the equivalent of a future subjunctive, see **506**.

manquer
Manquer is used in a variety of constructions and with a number of different meanings of which the following are the most important (for the whole range of meanings, consult a good dictionary):

1   Transitive, 'miss, fail in, etc.', e.g.:

manquer un train	to miss a train
manquer une classe	to miss a class
Je les ai manqués à la gare	I missed them at the station
Il a manqué son coup	He failed in his attempt

2   Intransitive

(a) 'fail' (*échouer* is more usual in this sense), e.g.:

L'expérience a manqué	The experiment failed

(b) 'be lacking, missing', with, when necessary, *à* = 'from' and/or *de* and an infinitive, e.g.:

La première page manque à ce livre
The first page is missing from this book
Rien ne manque
Nothing is missing
Les occasions ne m'ont pas manqué de visiter Paris
I haven't lacked opportunities to visit Paris

(c) *manquer à* 'fail (someone), fail in (something)', etc., e.g.:

Les mots me manquent	Words fail me
manquer à son devoir	to fail in one's duty
manquer à sa promesse	to break one's promise

Note the idiom *A manque à B* = 'B misses A' (i.e. 'regrets his *or* her absence'), e.g.:

Elle me manque beaucoup
I miss her a lot

(d) *manquer de* 'lack (= not have any of, or enough of)', e.g.:

Il manque de patience
He lacks patience

Je manque de temps pour le faire
I haven't (enough) time to do it

3 *Manquer* followed by an infinitive

(a) *manquer de faire* or *manquer faire* translated by 'nearly', e.g.:

J'ai manqué (de) tomber
I nearly fell

(*Faillir* is more usual in this sense, e.g. *J'ai failli tomber*.)

(b) *ne pas manquer de faire* 'not to fail to do', e.g.:

Ne manquez pas de nous écrire
Don't fail to write to us (*or* Mind you write to us)

Je ne manquerai pas de vous le dire
I shan't fail to tell you

In the negative (as in the above examples), this construction is still in current use. In the affirmative, however, *manquer de faire* and its alternative *manquer à faire* are now characteristic only of a somewhat archaic literary usage; *négliger de* 'to neglect to' or *omettre de* 'to omit to' should be used instead for 'to fail to do something' in the sense of 'not to do', e.g.:

Il a négligé de répondre à ma lettre
He failed to answer my letter

4 Impersonal 'be missing, lacking', with, when necessary, *à* = 'from', e.g.:

Il ne manque pas de candidats
There is no shortage of candidates

Il manque vingt pages à ce livre
There are twenty pages missing from this book

Il nous manque cent francs
We are a hundred francs short

rester

1 'Remain, stay', e.g.:

J'y suis, j'y reste
Here I am and here I stay

Elle y est restée dix jours
She stayed there for ten days

2   'Remain, be left (over)' e.g.:

tout ce qui reste
all that remains

les quelques amis qui lui restaient
the few friends who remained to him (that he had left)

With reference to precise amounts remaining, the impersonal construction (see 3 below) is more usual.

Note the construction in which the verb comes first and is translated into English as 'there remain(s), there remained', etc., e.g.:

Restait le problème des pays en voie de développement
There remained the problem of the developing countries

Restent deux solutions
There remain two solutions

3   Impersonal, 'to be left', with an indirect object of the person, e.g.:

Il ne leur restait que cent francs
They had only a hundred francs left (*lit.* There remained to them only a hundred francs)

4   Impersonal with *à* and the infinitive, 'it remains to', e.g.:

Il ne me reste qu'à vous remercier de votre bonté
It only remains for me to thank you for your kindness

Reste à voir
It remains to be seen

servir
1   Transitive, 'serve' in a wide range of contexts, including the following:

(a) 'be of service to (a person, a cause)', e.g.:

servir le roi	to serve the king
servir un client	to serve a customer
servir la cause de la paix	to serve the cause of peace

(b) with a thing as direct object, e.g.:

servir la balle	to serve the ball (at tennis)
servir un repas	to serve a meal

2 Intransitive, in various senses, e.g.:

J'ai servi pendant la guerre
I served in the war

Il sert dans un café
He serves (i.e. He is a waiter) in a café

C'est à vous de servir
It is you to serve (*or* your service) (at tennis)

3 *Servir à* 'be of use to or for, be for', with a noun or pronoun or with an infinitive (N.B. an infinitive representing the subject is introduced by *de*), e.g.:

Cela ne sert à rien
That is (of) no use

Mes paroles ne servaient qu'à l'irriter
My words only served to annoy him

Une pelle sert à creuser des trous
A spade is for digging holes

A quoi sert de pleurer?
What is the use of crying? (i.e. What purpose does crying serve?)

4 *Servir de* 'serve as, act as', e.g.:

Je lui ai servi d'interprète
I acted as interpreter for him

Cette pièce sert de salle à manger
This room serves as a dining-room

5 *Se servir*

(a) 'help oneself (to food)', e.g.:

Servez-vous (de légumes)
Help yourself (to (some) vegetables)

Je me suis servi de poisson
I've taken some fish

(b) *se servir de* 'use, make use of', e.g.:

Il vaut mieux vous servir d'un dictionnaire
You had better use a dictionary

tarder

1 'Delay, linger, be a long time (doing)', with *à* and an infinitive where necessary, e.g.:

Vous avez tardé à venir
You have been a long time coming

Il ne va pas tarder
He won't be long

Je suis venu sans tarder
I came without delay

2 Impersonal, 'long to, be impatient to', with dative of the person and *de* with the infinitive, e.g.:

Il lui tarde de partir
He is longing to start

traiter

1 'To treat (a person)' – 'as' is either *comme (un)* or *en*, e.g.:

Il me traitait durement
He used to treat me harshly

traiter un malade
to treat a patient

Traitez-moi comme (un) ami
Treat me as a friend

traiter quelqu'un en enfant
to treat someone as a child

2 *Traiter quelqu'un de* 'call someone something', e.g.:

Il nous a traités d'imbéciles
He called us fools

3 *Traiter un sujet* and *traiter d'un sujet*, 'deal with'

Traiter un sujet implies a systematic treatment of a subject, whereas *traiter d'un sujet* implies no more than that the subject is dealt with in the book, article, etc., in question, perhaps even only incidentally, e.g.:

Ce rapport traite le problème de l'énergie nucléaire
This report deals with the problem of nuclear energy

Tous ses romans traitent du problème des relations entre parents et enfants
All his novels deal with the problem of relations between parents and children

venir

1 'Come (and)' – *venir* and infinitive, i.e. no word for 'and' and no preposition, e.g.:

Venez me voir demain	Come and see me tomorrow
Il est venu me remercier	He came to thank me

2 *Venir de* 'to have just', e.g.:

Je viens de lui écrire	I have just written to him
Il venait de les voir	He had just seen them

This construction does not occur with tenses other than the present (for 'have just, has just') and the imperfect (for 'had just').

3 *Venir à* with an infinitive, 'happen to', e.g.:

Un de mes amis vint à passer
One of my friends happened to pass

Si vous veniez à le voir
If you happened to see him

4 *En venir à* with a noun or an infinitive, 'come to, turn to, be reduced to, etc.', e.g.:

J'en viens maintenant au problème principal
I now come (*or* turn) to the main problem

Il en était venu à mendier
He had been reduced to begging

5 For the difference between *Il vient à moi* 'He comes to me', etc., and *L'idée me vient que . . .* 'The idea comes to me that . . .', etc., see **220,b**.

S Idioms with *avoir, être, faire*

539 Idioms with *avoir*
(a) In a number of idioms, French uses *avoir* + a noun (without an article) where English uses 'to be' + an adjective:

avoir faim, to be hungry
avoir soif, to be thirsty
avoir froid, to be cold
avoir chaud, to be hot
avoir dix ans, to be ten years old
avoir raison, to be right
avoir tort, to be wrong
avoir honte, to be ashamed
avoir peur, to be frightened
avoir sommeil, to be sleepy

Other idioms in which French uses *avoir* + a noun without an article include:

avoir affaire à, to have . . . to deal with, be faced with
avoir besoin de, to need
avoir envie de, to want (something, to do something)
avoir pitié de, to pity, take pity on
avoir soin de, to look after, take care of

(b) In expressions of age, French uses the construction *avoir X ans, mois*, etc., where English uses the construction 'to be X years, months, etc., old', e.g.:

Elle a trente ans
She is thirty years old

Le bébé n'avait que six mois
The baby was only six months old

Note that, although it is possible in English to omit the words 'years old', the word *ans* cannot be omitted in French, e.g.:

Ma fille a vingt-neuf ans
My daughter is twenty-nine

except when the conjunctive pronoun *en* 'of them' stands in for it, e.g.:

Il aura bientôt cinquante ans mais sa femme n'en a que trente
He will soon be fifty but his wife is only thirty (*lit.* 'has only thirty of them (i.e. years)')

Likewise, 'How old . . .?' is *Quel âge . . .?* + *avoir*, e.g.:

Quel âge avez-vous?
How old are you?

(c) *avoir* + a noun sometimes (and particularly in the perfect and preterite tenses) expresses a physical reaction, e.g.:

Il a eu un mouvement de colère
He made an angry gesture

Il eut un murmure de satisfaction en apercevant la cuisine (Simenon)
He murmured with satisfaction on noticing the kitchen

La jeune femme près de lui eut un petit rire (Simenon)
The young woman near him gave a little laugh

(d) *en avoir pour* expresses the amount of time or money that has to be expended in achieving a certain end, e.g.:

Nous en avons pour une demi-heure
It will take us half an hour

Je n'en ai pas pour longtemps
It won't take me long (I shan't be long about it)

Je lui ai dit que j'en avais pour le reste de la journée
I told him it would take me the rest of the day (that I should be at it for the rest of the day)

Il en a pour mille francs
It will cost him a thousand francs

(Note that the French construction uses the present or imperfect tenses where the corresponding English constructions take the future or the conditional.)

(e) With *avoir l'air* + adjective 'to look, seem, appear', the adjective may agree either with *l'air* (as, strictly speaking, it should since the literal meaning of *Il a l'air heureux* 'He looks happy' is 'He has a happy appearance', cf. *Il a les yeux bleus* 'He has blue eyes') or (as is more usual nowadays) with the subject, e.g.:

Elle a l'air heureux (agreement with *air*)
Elle a l'air heureuse (agreement with *elle*)
She looks happy

(f) Note the idiom *Qu'est-ce que vous avez?* 'What is the matter (with you)?', *Qu'est-ce qu'il avait?* 'What was the matter with him?', etc., and, similarly, *Qu'est-ce qu'il y a?* 'What's the matter?'

540   Idioms with *être*

(a) *y être*, as well as having its literal meaning of 'to be there' (e.g. *Il y est déjà* 'He is there already'), is used in the expression *J'y suis, j'y reste* 'Here I am and here I stay' and can also have the meaning of 'to understand, to get the point', e.g.:

J'y suis maintenant
Now I get it (I understand)

(b) *en être* can have the meaning of 'to have reached a certain point', e.g.:

Où en étions-nous?
How far had we got? (e.g. in a discussion or a course of lessons)

J'en suis au chapitre douze
I am up to (I have got as far as) chapter twelve

Ils en étaient à mourir de faim
They had reached starvation point

(c) In the literary language only, and only in the preterite and very occasionally in the imperfect subjunctive, *être* is used reflexively (with *en*) as the equivalent of *s'en aller* 'to go (away)', e.g.:

Patrice s'en fut au jardin (Duhamel)
Patrick went (out, off) into the garden

Il s'en fut la chercher
He went off to look for her

(d) Forms of *être* occur in a considerable number of other idiomatic expressions, including:

C'en est trop!	That's going too far
cela étant	that being so
ainsi soit-il	1. so be it; 2. amen
Nous sommes le 7 avril	It is the 7th of April
toujours est-il que . . .	the fact remains that . . .
il n'est que de . . .	the best thing is to
en être pour sa peine	to have wasted one's efforts

For others, consult a good dictionary.

541   Idioms with *faire*

Faire is used in a great variety of idioms of which the following are some:

(a) *faire* alone, like the English 'does', 'have', etc., is used as a substitute for a verb which would otherwise have to be repeated, e.g.:

> *Il mange des escargots comme le font les Français*
> He eats snails as the French do

> *Il est merveilleux qu'ils aient tenu bon comme ils l'ont fait*
> It is wonderful that they have held out as they have

This is not possible when the substitute verb is stressed in English, in which case various corresponding expressions are found in French, e.g.:

> She sings well. – Yes, she does
> *Elle chante bien. – Oui, en effet* (or *c'est vrai*)

> He doesn't like cheese. – Yes he does!
> *Il n'aime pas le fromage. – Mais si!*

(b) *faire* + an adjective is used in a number of expressions referring to the weather and the like, e.g.:

il fait beau	it is fine
il fait chaud	it is hot
il fait froid	it is cold
il fait lourd	it (*or* the weather) is close
il fair noir	it is dark
il fait sombre	it is dull

Also *il fait bon* 'it is nice' (e.g. *Il fait bon se promener à la campagne* 'It's nice going for walks in the country') and, with nouns, *il fait jour* 'it is daylight' and *il fait nuit* 'it is dark (i.e. night-time)'.

(c) Many idioms are based on the construction *faire* + noun (with no article), e.g., among many others:

faire attention	to take care
faire face (à)	to face (up to), be opposite
faire honte à	to make (someone) feel ashamed
faire horreur à	to disgust, be repugnant to
faire part à quelqu'un de quelque chose	to inform someone of something
faire peur à	to frighten, scare,

faire plaisir à	to please, give pleasure to
faire semblant (de faire quelque chose)	to pretend (to do something)
faire signe (à)	to beckon, signal (to)
faire tort à	to wrong

(d) *se faire* + an adjective or adverb can have the meaning of 'to get, become', e.g.:

Il se fait vieux
He is getting old

Le beurre se faisait rare
Butter was getting scarce

Il se fait tard
It is getting late

(e) *se faire* + an infinitive serves the same function as English 'to get' + a past participle or some other equivalent construction meaning 'to undergo a certain process' (particularly an unpleasant one), e.g.:

Si tu ne fais pas attention, tu te feras tuer
If you don't take care, you'll get (yourself) killed

Il s'est fait gronder
He got scolded, ticked off

and likewise *se faire agresser* 'to be (get) assaulted, mugged', *se faire arrêter* 'to get arrested', *se faire écraser* 'to get run over', *se faire opérer* 'to have an operation', *se faire voler* 'to get (be) robbed'.

(f) Note that, though *faire quelque chose de quelque chose* is one equivalent of English 'to make something (out) of something (else)', e.g.:

Il va faire de sa pelouse un jardin potager
He is going to make a vegetable garden (out) of his lawn

'to make' + an adjective, meaning 'to cause someone or something to be what they were not before', is expressed by *rendre*, not by *faire*, e.g.:

La guerre l'a rendu pauvre
The war has made him poor

Son premier roman l'avait rendu célèbre
His first novel had made him famous

*Le comité rendra publique la décision qu'il doit prendre
demain*
The committee will make public the decision it is to take
tomorrow

For other idioms involving *faire*, consult a good dictionary.

The Structure of the Sentence

Negation

Introduction

542 We shall discuss negation under the following headings:
  A: Negation with a verb
  B: The negative conjunction *ni* 'neither, nor'
  C: Negation of an element other than a verb

A Negation with a verb

Introduction

543 Negation with a verb is expressed by the use of *ne* (or *n'*
before a vowel or mute *h*) before the verb and, in most cases, of
another element which may be a determiner (*aucun, nul* 'no, not
any'), a pronoun (*personne* 'nobody', *rien* 'nothing', *aucun, nul*),
an adverb (*aucunement, nullement*, 'in no way, not at all', *guère*
'hardly, scarcely', *jamais* 'never', *plus* '(no) longer', *que* 'only',
and what are often termed the negative particles *pas* and *point*

'not'). Some of these elements always follow the verb, others may either precede or follow depending on meaning or on the degree of emphasis they carry. All are discussed at greater length below.

Note that *faire* must not be used as the equivalent of 'do' in negative constructions, e.g.:

> *Ils ne parlent pas français*
> They do not speak French

For the use of *ne* alone, see **559–567**.

Ne and another element

ne . . . pas, ne . . . point *'not'*

544 (i) The normal way of making a verb negative is to use *ne* . . . *pas*. *Pas* comes immediately after the verb or, in compound tenses, after the auxiliary (but see also ii below), e.g.:

> *Je ne viens pas*
> I am not coming
>
> *Il n'est pas venu*
> He has not come
>
> *Mon frère ne la connaissait pas*
> My brother did not know her

However, *ne pas* come together before an infinitive, e.g.:

> *Je préfère ne pas le voir*
> I prefer not to see him
>
> *Je suis content de ne pas le lui avoir dit*
> I am glad not to have told him

(The construction *ne* + infinitive + *pas* exists but is archaic and should not be imitated.)

(ii) Nothing can come between the verb (or auxiliary) and *pas* except the subject pronoun in a negative-interrogative clause or certain adverbs, mainly adverbs of affirmation or doubt (see **627–628**), such as *certainement* 'certainly', *même* 'even', *peut-être* 'perhaps', *probablement* 'probably', *sûrement* 'certainly' and the adverbial phrase *sans doute* 'doubtless', e.g.:

> *Ne vient-il pas?*
> Isn't he coming?

Ne vous l'avais-je pas dit?
Had I not told you?

Il ne viendra certainement pas
He certainly won't come

Il ne m'a même pas regardé
He did not even look at me

Vous ne l'avez peut-être pas vu
Perhaps you did not see him

Il ne la connaissait probablement pas
He probably didn't know her

The only items that can come between *ne* and the verb are the conjunctive personal pronouns, *me, le, vous,* etc. – see 387,ii,d, and some of the examples quoted above.

(iii) The only case in which *pas* can precede the verb is when it forms part of the expression *pas un (seul)* 'not (a single) one' as subject of the verb, e.g.:

De tous mes amis, pas un (seul) n'a voulu m'aider
Of all my friends, not one was willing to help me

Pas un oiseau ne chantait dans la forêt
Not a single bird was singing in the forest

545 Some grammars state that *point* expresses a 'stronger' negation than *pas* (some, indeed, go so far as to translate it as 'not at all'). **This is not so.** For 'not at all', some such expression as *pas du tout* or *absolument pas* must be used. *Point* nowadays is used mainly by writers who wish to give a slightly archaic or a provincial flavour to their French. Many modern writers never use it and foreigners are well advised to avoid it altogether.

Note that, although (subject to the above remarks) *point* could replace *pas* in any of the examples given in 544,i and ii, it cannot be substituted for *pas* in *pas un* – see 544,iii.

546 *aucun* 'no, not any, etc.'

Aucun is used:

(i) In the singular only, as a pronoun, e.g.:

Aucun de mes amis n'est venu
Not one of my friends came

Aucune de ces raisons n'est valable
None of these reasons is valid

De tous mes amis, aucun ne m'a aidé
Of all my friends, not one helped me

In compound tenses it follows the past participle, e.g.:

Je n'en ai acheté aucun
I did not buy one (any) of them

(ii) As a determiner, e.g.:

Aucun exemple ne me vient à l'esprit
No example comes to my mind

Je n'ai aucune intention d'y aller
I have no intention of going there

As a determiner, *aucun* is not used in the plural except sometimes with nouns that have no singular (e.g. *aucuns frais* 'no expenditure') or are used in the plural with a meaning they do not have in the singular (e.g. *aucuns gages* 'no wages').

547   *nul* 'no, not any, etc.'

(i) *Nul* is characteristic of the literary rather than of the spoken language.

(ii) As a pronoun it is used, usually only in the singular and only as the subject of the verb:

(a) with reference to some person or thing already mentioned (in which case the conversational equivalent is *aucun*), e.g.:

De toutes les maisons que je connais, nulle n'est plus agréable que la vôtre
Of all the houses I know, none is more pleasant than yours

(b) meaning 'nobody' (in this sense *personne*, not *aucun*, is used in speech), e.g.:

Nul ne sait ce qu'il est devenu
Nobody knows what has happened to him

(iii) As a determiner, *nul* is used in the literary language, mainly in the singular but occasionally (though this should not be imitated) in the plural, as the equivalent of *aucun*, e.g.:

Je n'ai nulle envie de la faire
I have no desire to do so

548   *aucunement, nullement* 'not at all'

Aucunement and, especially in the literary language, *nullement* serve to negate the verb more emphatically than *pas*; they follow the verb (or the auxiliary, or the infinitive if the sense requires it), e.g.:

Je n'en suis aucunement (or *nullement*) *froissé*
I am in no way (*or* not at all) put out about it

Je ne crains nullement (or *aucunement*) *la mort*
I am not in the least afraid of death

Il semble ne vouloir aucunement y aller
He seems to be by no means anxious to go there

549   *ne . . . guère* 'hardly, scarcely'

Ne . . . guère is used both as an adverb, e.g.:

Cela n'est guère probable
That is hardly likely

Je ne comprends guère ce qu'il dit
I scarcely understand what he says

and as a quantifier, e.g.:

Je n'ai guère d'argent   I have hardly any money

In compound tenses it precedes the past participle, e.g.:

Je ne l'aurais guère cru
I should hardly have believed it

550   *ne . . . jamais* 'never'

Jamais usually follows the verb or the auxiliary, e.g.:

Je ne bois jamais de vin   I never drink wine
Il n'a jamais dit ça   He never said that

but it comes before the infinitive, e.g.:

Il décida de ne jamais revenir
He decided never to come back

For emphasis, it may be placed first, e.g.:

Jamais je ne dirais ça!   I would *never* say that!

551 *ne . . . personne* 'nobody', *ne . . . rien* 'nothing'

Personne and *rien* can serve either as the subject or as the object of a verb or as the complement of a preposition, e.g.:

Personne n'arrivera ce soir
Nobody will arrive this evening

Rien ne le satisfait
Nothing satisfies him

Je ne vois personne
I can't see anyone

Je ne dirai rien
I shall say nothing

Je ne travaillais avec personne
I wasn't working with anybody

Je ne pensais à rien
I wasn't thinking of anything

Note that, in compound tenses, *rien* follows the auxiliary but *personne* follows the past participle, e.g.:

Je n'ai rien vu
I saw nothing (I haven't seen anything)

Je n'ai vu personne
I saw no one (I haven't seen anyone)

Nous n'avions rien fait d'intéressant
We hadn't done anything interesting

(*Rien*, however, sometimes follows the participle if it is qualified, e.g. *Je n'ai trouvé rien qui vaille la peine* 'I found nothing worthwhile'.)

Likewise, *rien* goes before and *personne* after the infinitive, e.g.:

Il a décidé de ne rien faire
He decided to do nothing

Il a décidé de n'accepter personne
He decided to accept nobody

552 *ne . . . plus* 'no longer, not any more'

Ne . . . plus means 'no more' **only** in the sense of 'no longer, not any more', e.g.:

Je n'y travaille plus
I don't work there any more, I no longer work there

Nous n'avons plus de pain
We have no more bread (i.e. no bread left)

('No more' in a strictly comparative or quantitative sense is *ne
. . . pas plus*, e.g. *Ce livre n'est pas plus intelligible que l'autre*
'This book is no more intelligible than the other one', *Je n'ai pas
plus de temps que vous* 'I have no more time than you'.)

Plus follows the verb or auxiliary, but precedes the infinitive,
e.g.:

Je n'y suis plus allé
I never went there any more

J'ai décidé de ne plus y aller
I have decided not to go there any more

553   *ne . . . que . . .* 'only'

(i) Whereas in unaffected English (as distinct from pedantic
English) 'only' can go before the verb even when it relates to
something else, provided the meaning is clear from the context
(e.g. 'He only works on Saturdays' = 'He works only on
Saturdays'), the *que* of *ne . . . que . . .* always goes immediately
before the element it relates to, e.g.:

Je n'en ai que trois
I only have three

Il ne travaille que le samedi
He only works (= works only) on Saturdays

Je ne l'ai dit qu'à mon frère
I only told (told only) my brother

(ii) As *que* must also follow the verb, there might seem to be a
problem when 'only' relates to the verb itself, as in 'She only
laughed' or 'On Saturdays he only works' (i.e. 'All he does on
Saturdays is work'); what happens in French is that the verb *faire*
'to do' is used to express the relevant person, tense and mood,
which *que* can then follow while at the same time preceding the
infinitive of the verb it relates to, e.g.:

Je ne faisais que plaisanter
I was only joking

Elle n'a fait que rire
She only laughed

Le samedi il ne fait que travailler
On Saturdays he only works
All he does on Saturdays is work

Il ne fera que te gronder
He'll only scold you

(iii) Though the use of *ne . . . pas que . . .* to mean 'not only' is frowned on by some purists, it is well established in literary as well as spoken usage and there is no good reason to avoid it, e.g.:

Ne pensez pas qu'à vous (A. France)
Don't only think of yourself

Il ne négligea pas que l'église (Mauriac)
It was not only the church he neglected

Il n'y a pas que l'argent qui compte
It is not only money that counts (i.e. Money isn't everything)

554 'Fossilized' negative complements

In a few idioms, *goutte* and *mot* replace *rien*. *Goutte* occurs only with *voir* 'to see', *comprendre* 'to understand', and *entendre* in the sense of 'to understand' (not in the sense of 'to hear') and usually with *y* before the verb or, failing that, *à* + a noun, e.g.:

La lune est cachée, on n'y voit goutte (Mauriac)
The moon is hidden, one cannot see a thing

L'électeur moyen n'y comprend goutte (Le Monde)
The average voter understands nothing about it

Ils ne comprennent goutte à ma conduite (Flaubert)
They completely fail to understand my behaviour

Mot still retains its meaning of 'word' and occurs only with *dire* 'to say', *répondre* 'to answer' and in the idioms *ne (pas) sonner mot* and *ne (pas) souffler mot* 'not to utter a word', e.g.:

Le curé souriait . . . mais ne disait mot (Mauriac)
The priest smiled but said nothing

Il n'en souffle mot à personne (P.-J. Hélias)
He says nothing about it to anyone

555 Multiple negative complements

Pas and *point* cannot be combined with any of the other negative complements discussed in **546–554** (except in the expression *ne . . . pas que*, see **553**,iii). Various combinations of other complements are, however, possible, e.g.:

Personne n'a rien dit
Nobody said anything

Personne ne peut plus le supporter
Nobody can stand him any more

Il n'a jamais blessé personne
He has never hurt anyone

Nous n'avons jamais eu aucun problème
We never had any problem

Cela ne me regarde plus guère
That hardly concerns me any more

Il se décida à ne jamais plus rien supporter de la sorte
He decided never to put up with anything of the kind again

556 In colloquial usage, *ne* is very frequently omitted and the negation is expressed by *pas*, *rien*, *jamais*, etc., alone, e.g.:

Je veux pas y aller	I don't want to go (there)
Dis pas ça!	Don't say that!
J'ai rien acheté	I haven't bought anything
Tu viens jamais me voir	You never come and see me

This is so widespread, even in educated speech, that it cannot be considered unacceptable. However, foreigners should not adopt this construction until they have reached the stage of speaking French fluently and correctly and at a normal conversational speed.

The feature in question is sometimes found in print in plays, novels, etc., that aim to represent spoken usage; the following examples are from Sartre's play *Les Mains sales*:

C'est pas vrai	It isn't true
Touche pas	Don't touch
Je crois pas	I don't think so

It should not, however, be used in writing in other circumstances.

Negation without *ne*

557 *pas* without *ne*

When the verb of a negative clause is dropped, the *ne* of course drops with it and *pas* alone expresses the negation; for example, in answer to the question *Est-il arrivé?* 'Has he arrived?', instead of the complete sentence *Il n'est pas encore arrivé* 'He has not yet arrived', one is likely to find simply the expression *Pas encore* 'Not yet'. This is a construction one constantly comes across. Further examples:

> *Est-ce que vous l'admirez? – Pas du tout* (or even *Du tout*)
> Do you admire him? – Not at all
>
> *Tu viens? – Pas tout de suite*
> Are you coming? – Not immediately
>
> *Qu'est-ce que je dois prendre? – Pas ça!*
> What am I to take? – Not that!
>
> *Qui l'a dit? – Pas moi, de toute façon*
> Who said so? – Not me, at any rate

Likewise *certainement pas* 'certainly not', *pourquoi pas?* 'why not?', *pas là!* 'not there!', etc.

For other negative complements without *ne*, see **558**,iii.

558

| *aucun,* | *jamais,* | *personne,* | *plus,* | *rien* | without *ne* |
| any | ever | anybody | more | anything | |

(i) As *sans* 'without' implies a negative, these five words may be used after *sans* or *sans que* 'without', e.g.:

> *sans aucune raison, sans raison aucune*
> without any reason
>
> *sans jamais le dire*
> without ever saying so
>
> *sans voir personne*
> without seeing anyone
>
> *sans plus tarder*
> without delaying any more, without further delay
>
> *sans rien dire*
> without saying anything, saying nothing

Il est parti sans rien
He left without anything

Elle est partie sans que personne le sache
She left without anyone knowing

sans que rien soit fait
without anything being done

(ii) The five words in question originally had a positive value and this survives in questions and comparisons and after *si* 'if', e.g.:

Y a-t-il aucune raison pour ça?
Is there any reason for that?

Je le respecte plus qu'aucun autre homme
I respect him more than any other man

Vous le savez mieux que personne
You know better than anyone

Avez-vous jamais rien entendu de si absurde?
Have you ever heard anything so absurd?

Si jamais vous le voyez, dites-le-moi
If ever you see him, tell me

On *jamais*, see also **618**.

Plus retains a positive value generally, not just in the circumstances mentioned above – see **159–173**.

(iii) As is explained in **557**, *pas* retains a negative value when the verb (and hence the *ne*) of a negative clause is dropped. The same is true of *aucun, jamais, personne, plus* and *rien*. Each of these originally had a positive value but, through their constant association with negative constructions, they have themselves acquired a negative value in the circumstances in question, e.g.:

Y a-t-il aucune raison pour ça? – Aucune
Is there any reason for that? – None

Le lui avez-vous jamais montré? – Jamais
Have you ever shown it to him? – Never

Qui vous l'a dit? – Personne
Who told you so? – Nobody

Plus de discussions!
No more arguing!

Qu'est-ce qu'il t'a dit – Rien de très intéressant
What did he tell you? – Nothing very interesting

Ne alone

559   In medieval French, *ne* was frequently used on its own (i.e. without *pas* or any other complement, though these were in fact already in use) to negate a verb, e.g. *Ne m'oci!* 'Don't kill me!' There are relics of this in modern French, falling into three categories, viz.:

(i) Fixed expressions and proverbs (560)

(ii) Constructions in which *ne* is a literary alternative to *ne . . . pas* (561)

(iii) Constructions in which *ne* is superfluous (and where English has no negative at all) (562–567)

(i) Ne *on its own in fixed expressions and proverbs*

560   *Ne* is used on its own:

(a) In a number of fixed expressions, including:

> *A Dieu ne plaise!*
> God forbid!
>
> *N'ayez crainte!*
> Fear not! Never fear!
>
> *N'importe* or *Il n'importe*
> It doesn't matter
>
> *Qu'à cela ne tienne!*
> Never mind that! No problem!

(b) A few constructions that can vary slightly in respect of their subject and/or tense and/or complement, and mainly involving one or other of the verbs *avoir* and *être*, e.g.:

> *n'avoir cure de*
> not to be concerned about
>
> *n'avoir (pas) de cesse que . . .*
> not to rest until . . .
>
> *n'avoir garde de (faire)*
> to take good care not to

n'avoir que faire de (+ noun)
to have no need of, no use for, to manage very well without

n'était
but for, were it not for

n'eût été
but for, had it not been for

si ce n'est (+ noun or pronoun)
if not . . ., apart from

Examples:

Il n'avait garde de contredire sa fille (Mérimée)
He took care not to contradict his daughter

Je n'ai que faire de ses conseils
I can manage very well without his advice

N'était son arrogance, il serait sûr de réussir
Were it not for his arrogance, he would certainly succeed

On ne voyait rien si ce n'est le ciel (Barbier d'Aurevilly)
Nothing was to be seen apart from the sky

Three such expressions involving other verbs are *n'en déplaise à* 'with all due respect to', *n'empêche que* 'the fact remains that', and *savoir* in the conditional, meaning 'to be able' (of the constructions listed here, these last two are the only ones that are current in conversational usage), e.g.:

N'empêche qu'il a tout à fait tort
The fact remains that he is quite wrong

Je ne saurais répondre à votre question
I can't answer your question

(c) A few proverbs beginning with *il n'est* . . . 'there is not', e.g.:

Il n'est pire eau que l'eau qui dort
Still waters run deep (*lit.* There is no worse water than sleeping water)

Il n'est pire sourd que celui qui ne veut pas entendre
There is none so deaf as he who will not hear

(ii) Ne *as a literary alternative to* ne . . . pas

561 In a variety of constructions, the use of *ne* alone is still possible, particularly in the literary language. The principal constructions in question are:

(a) With the verbs *cesser* 'to cease' (but only when followed by *de* and an infinitive), *daigner* 'to deign', *oser* 'to dare', *pouvoir* 'to be able', and occasionally *bouger* 'to move', e.g.:

Il ne cesse de pleurer	He never stops crying
Je n'ose l'avouer	I dare not admit it
Je ne peux vous aider	I cannot help you
Ne bougez d'ici!	Don't move from here!

(b) With *savoir* followed by an indirect question (in which case it is better to use *ne* alone rather than *ne . . . pas*), e.g.:

Je ne sais pourquoi
I don't know why

Il ne sait quel parti prendre
He does not know what course to take

or in answer to a question:

Qu'allez-vous faire? – Je ne sais encore
What you going to do? – I don't yet know

(c) In rhetorical or exclamatory questions introduced by *qui?* 'who?', *quel?* + noun 'what?', *que?* 'what?' or *que?* 'why', e.g.:

Qui ne court après la Fortune? (La Fontaine)
Who does not chase after Fortune?

Que ne dirait-on pour sauver sa peau?
What would a man not say to save his skin?

Que ne sommes-nous arrivés plut tôt!
Why did we not get here sooner! If only we had got here sooner!

(d) After *si*, especially when the main clause is negative, e.g.:

Je ne vous lâcherai pas si vous ne l'avouez
I will not let you go unless you confess

Le voilà qui arrive, si je ne me trompe
Here he comes, if I am not mistaken

(e) After *non que, non pas que, ce n'est pas que* 'not that', e.g.:

Non qu'il ne veuille vous aider . . .
Not that he does not want to help you

Ce n'est pas qu'il ne fasse des efforts, mais qu'il oublie tout
It is not that he doesn't try, but that he forgets everything

(f) In relative clauses taking the subjunctive after a negative (expressed, or implied in a question) in the preceding clause, e.g.:

Il ne devrait être personne qui ne veuille apprendre le français
There ought to be no one who does not want to learn French

Y a-t-il personne qui ne veuille apprendre le français?
Is there any who . . .? etc. (= Surely there is no one who . . . etc.)

Il n'y a si bon cheval qui ne bronche
There is no horse so good that it never stumbles

(g) In a *que*-clause expressing consequence after *tellement* or *si* meaning 'so', e.g.:

Il n'est pas tellement (or *si*) *bête qu'il ne comprenne cela*
He is not so stupid $\left\{ \begin{array}{l} \text{as not to} \\ \text{that he does not} \end{array} \right\}$ understand that

(h) In a dependent clause meaning 'without . . .-ing'; *que . . . ne* in this sense is equivalent to *sans que*, e.g.:

Je ne le vois jamais $\left\{ \begin{array}{l} \textit{qu'il ne me prie} \\ \textit{sans qu'il me prie} \end{array} \right\}$ *de passer chez lui*
I never see him without his asking me to drop in on him

(i) As an alternative to *ne . . . pas* in conditional sentences with inversion of the subject (see **424**), e.g.:

Il se serait retiré, n'eût-il (pas) pensé qu'il se ferait remarquer
He would have withdrawn had he not thought he would attract attention

(j) For *ne* or *ne . . . pas* after *depuis que*, etc., see **567**.

(iii) Ne *inserted where English has no negative*

562 *Ne* alone occurs in a number of constructions that are not, strictly speaking, negative though, as we shall see, there is usually a negative implication of some kind or other. This *ne* is often referred to as 'redundant *ne*', 'pleonastic *ne*' or 'expletive *ne*'. In speech the *ne* is dropped more often than not and it is also often dropped in writing in an informal style.

The constructions in question can be classified as follows:

(a) after comparatives (563)

(b) after verbs and expressions of fearing (564)

(c) after certain other verbs and their equivalents (565)

(d) after the conjunctions *avant que* 'before' and *à moins que* 'unless' (566)

(e) after the conjunction *depuis que* 'since' and comparable expressions (567).

563   (a) *Ne* after comparatives

In an affirmative clause after a comparative and *que* 'than', e.g. *Il en sait plus qu'il n'avoue* 'He knows more than he admits'; the use of *ne* can be explained by the fact that the *que*-clause contains a negative implication, viz. 'He does not admit to knowing as much as he does'. Other examples:

> *Il a agi avec plus d'imprudence que je ne croyais*
> He has acted more rashly than I thought

> *Il est moins riche qu'il ne l'était*
> He is less rich than he was

Also with *autre(ment) que* 'other than, otherwise than', e.g.:

> *Il agit autrement qu'il ne parle*
> He acts differently from the way he speaks

Note, however, that, when the main clause is interrogative or negative, the *ne* is not usually used unless the negative of the first clause also covers the second clause, e.g.:

> *Avez-vous jamais été plus heureux que vous l'êtes maintenant?*
> Have you ever been happier than you are now?

Jamais homme n'était plus embarrassé que je le suis en ce moment

Never was a man more embarrassed than I am at this moment

Vous ne réussirez pas mieux que nous n'avons réussi nous-mêmes

You will not succeed any better than we have
(i.e. 'We have not succeeded and you will not succeed')

(*Ne* is sometimes used after questions, particularly when the question is rhetorical, e.g.:

Peut-on être plus bête qu'il ne l'est?
Can anyone be stupider than he is?)

564   (b) *Ne* after verbs and expressions of fearing

The use of *ne* after verbs and expressions of fearing such as *craindre que* 'to fear that', *avoir peur que* 'to be afraid that', *de crainte que, de peur que* 'for fear that', is explained by the fact that a fear that something may happen implies a hope or wish that it may not happen; for example, *J'ai peur que ce ne soit vrai* 'I am afraid it may be true', and *Il est parti de peur qu'elle ne le voie* 'He left for fear she might see him', imply respectively a hope that it might not be true and that she should not see him.

Note that after a verb of fearing that is itself negative there is no *ne* and that the problem does not, of course, arise when the verb of the *que*-clause is itself negative. We therefore have the following constructions:

Je crains qu'il ne vienne
I am afraid he will come

Je ne crains pas qu'il vienne
I am not afraid he will come

Je crains qu'il ne vienne pas
I am afraid he will not come

Je ne crains pas qu'il ne vienne pas
I am not afraid he will not come

565   (c) *Ne* after other verbs and their equivalents

After *douter* 'to doubt' when negative or interrogative, e.g.:

Je ne doute pas qu'il ne vienne
I have no doubt he will come

Doutez-vous qu'il ne vienne?
Do you doubt whether he will come?

but, after *douter* in the affirmative:

Je doute qu'il vienne   I doubt if he will come

Il n'est pas douteux que . . . takes either the subjunctive with or without *ne* or the indicative without *ne*, e.g.:

Il n'est pas douteux qu'il (ne) vienne ⎫   There is no doubt
Il n'est pas douteux qu'il viendra ⎭   that he will come

Other negative expressions of doubt are usually followed by the indicative without *ne*, e.g.:

Il n'y a pas de doute qu'il viendra ⎫   There is no doubt
Sans doute qu'il viendra ⎭   that he will come

Nier 'to deny' when affirmative follows the same rule as *douter*; but, when negative, it can have any of the constructions illustrated below:

Je nie qu'il l'ait fait   I deny that he did it

Je ne nie pas qu'il ne l'ait fait
Je ne nie pas qu'il l'ait fait   I do not deny that he did it
Je ne nie pas qu'il l'a fait

After *nier* in the interrogative, the verb of the *que*-clause is usually in the subjunctive, with or without *ne*, e.g.:

Niez-vous qu'il (ne) l'ait fait?
Do you deny that he did it?

Note that, if the person is unchanged, the infinitive can be used, e.g.:

Il ne nie pas l'avoir fait
He does not deny doing it (that he did it)

Empêcher que 'to prevent' and *éviter que* 'to avoid' are usually but not invariably followed by *ne* whether they are used affirmatively or negatively, e.g.:

Rien n'empêche qu'on (ne) fasse la paix
Nothing prevents peace from being made

J'évite qu'il (ne) m'en parle
I avoid having him speak to me about it

But note that *empêcher* is very frequently followed by an infinitive, e.g. *Il m'empêche de partir* 'He prevents me from leaving'.

Ne is optional after *peu s'en faut que* or *il s'en faut que* (for which no even approximately literal translation is possible), e.g.:

Peu s'en fallut qu'il (ne) tombât dans la mer
He very nearly fell into the sea

Il s'en faut de beaucoup que cette somme soit suffisante
This sum is far from being enough

A few moments' thought ought to be enough to identify the negative implication in the above examples – for example, 'to prevent something from happening' is 'to ensure that it does not happen'.

566   (d) *Ne* after *avant que* 'before' and *à moins que* 'unless'

The use of *ne* after *avant que* 'before' and *à moins que* 'unless' is optional, but it is in general preferred in modern literary usage (much more so than in Classical French), e.g.:

Je le verrai avant qu'il (ne) parte
I shall see him before he leaves

Avant qu'ils n'eussent atteint la galerie . . . (J. Green)
Before they had reached the gallery . . .

Il va y renoncer à moins que vous (ne) l'aidiez
He is going to give up unless you help him

The negative implication of such examples as these is clear – 'he has not yet left', 'they had not reached the gallery', 'if you do not help him'.

Note that the use of *ne* after *sans que* 'without' that one sometimes comes across is best avoided, e.g.:

Il est parti sans que ses parents le sachent
He left without his parents knowing about it

567   (e) *Depuis que* and comparable expressions

The two interlocking problems that arise with the use of *depuis que*, viz. that of the choice of tense and that of the choice between *ne* and *ne . . . pas*, can best be explained if we first take an example. 'Ten years have passed since I saw him' (a sentence in which, in

English, there is no negative) may be translated either by:

Dix ans se sont écoulés depuis que je ne l'ai vu

(i.e. with the perfect tense and *ne*), or by:

Dix ans se sont écoulés depuis que je ne le vois pas (or *plus*)

(i.e. with the present tense and either *ne . . . pas* or *ne . . . plus*). The sense of the second of these forms becomes plain if one takes *depuis que* as an equivalent of 'during which', i.e. 'Ten years have passed during which I do not (*or* I no longer) see him'.

Furthermore, the first type has influenced the second and so one often comes across the construction:

Dix ans se sont écoulés depuis que je ne l'ai pas vu

Alternative constructions to *depuis que* are provided by *il y a, voici, voilà* + expression of a period of time (e.g. *dix ans* 'ten years', *longtemps* 'a long time') + *que*, e.g.:

$$\left.\begin{array}{l} \textit{Il y a} \\ \textit{Voici} \\ \textit{Voilà} \end{array}\right\} \quad \textit{dix ans que je ne le vois pas (or plus)}$$

It is ten years since I saw him

or, alternatively:

$$\left.\begin{array}{l} \textit{Il y a} \\ \textit{Voici} \\ \textit{Voilà} \end{array}\right\} \quad \textit{dix ans que je ne l'ai vu}$$

Another alternative construction is provided by *cela (ça) fait*, e.g. *Ça fait dix ans que je ne l'ai pas vu*. But note that since *cela (ça) fait* is a somewhat informal construction and the use of *ne* alone is a literary construction, the two should not be combined, i.e. with *cela fait* or *ça fait* always use *ne . . . pas*.

Similarly with reference to the past:

$$\left.\textit{Dix ans s'étaient écoulés depuis}\atop \textit{que}\right. \quad \left\{\begin{array}{l} \textit{je ne l'avais (pas) vu} \\ \textit{je ne le voyais pas (or plus)} \end{array}\right.$$

Ten years had elapsed since I saw (*or* had seen) him

$$\left.\begin{array}{l} \textit{Il y avait} \\ \textit{Voilà} \end{array}\right\} \quad \textit{dix ans que} \quad \left\{\begin{array}{l} \textit{je ne l'avais (pas) vu} \\ \textit{je ne le voyais pas (or plus)} \end{array}\right.$$

It was ten years since I had seen him

Note that the use of *pas* or *plus* is optional with the compound tenses (i.e. the perfect and the pluperfect) but compulsory with the simple tenses (the present and the imperfect). Generally speaking, *plus* is more widely used than *pas* with the simple tenses.

De, du, etc., *un(e)* and the direct object of negative verbs

568   *De* is normally substituted for the partitive or the indefinite article with the direct object of a verb in the negative (for exceptions, see **569** and **570**), e.g.:

Nous avons une maison
We have a house

Nous n'avons pas de maison
We haven't a house

Ils vendent du fromage
They sell cheese

Ils ne vendent pas de fromage
They don't sell cheese

Nous avons eu de la difficulté
We have had some difficulty

Nous n'avons jamais eu de difficulté
We have never had any difficulty

Note that, in the construction *il y a* 'there is, there are' followed by a noun (e.g. *Il y a des pommes* 'There are (some) apples'), the noun is the direct object of the verb *a* (from *avoir*) and so the rule applies (e.g. *Il n'y a pas de pommes* 'There aren't any apples').

Note too that *ne . . . que* 'only' is not negative in sense and so does not follow the rule, e.g. *Il n'y a que des pommes* 'There are only apples'.

569   The use of the indefinite article, *un, une*, is not impossible after a negative, but there is a difference in meaning between this construction and the usual construction with *pas de* discussed in **568**. Whereas *pas de* expresses the negation in an unemphatic way ('not a'), *pas un* is somewhat emphatic ('not one, not a single'), e.g.:

Il n'y a pas de communiste qui soit capitaliste
There is no communist who is a capitalist

Il n'y a pas un communiste qui soit capitaliste
There is not a single communist who is a capitalist

Je ne vois pas de cheval
I can't see a horse

Je ne vois pas un cheval
I can't see a single horse

(This last sentence might be spoken to express one's disappointment, for example, at not seeing any horses in circumstances where one had been expecting to see some.) Some circumstances virtually exclude the construction with *pas un*: for example, one might very well say of a woman *Elle n'a pas de mari* 'She hasn't got a husband', but it is difficult to imagine any kind of normal context in which one could say, as a complete sentence, *Elle n'a pas un mari.*

Similarly in negative questions. Whereas *N'avez-vous pas de crayon?* merely means 'Haven't you got a pencil?', to ask *N'avez-vous pas un crayon?* has something of the same implication as 'You haven't (by any chance) a pencil, have you?' (i.e., if so, may I borrow it?).

570   The construction discussed in **568** must be clearly distinguished from others that are superficially similar (or even, in English – but not in French – identical), but have a very different meaning.

One of these is the construction in which the negation applies, according to the sense, not to the verb but to the direct object. For example, 'I didn't buy a typewriter' may carry the implication that, or be followed by a specific statement that, 'I bought something else (e.g. a video-recorder)'. So, in French we have *Je n'ai pas acheté une machine à écrire* (*mais un magnétoscope*). The meaning in effect is 'I bought not a typewriter but a video-recorder', i.e. the negation, according to the sense, applies not to the verb 'bought' but to the direct object 'typewriter'.

Another similar construction is that in which the negation applies, according to the sense, neither to the verb nor to the direct object but to some other element in the sentence. For example, an utterance such as 'One doesn't keep a dog in order to eat it' has the implication 'If one keeps a dog, it is not in order to eat it'. So, in French one has *On n'a pas un chien pour le manger.*

B *The negative conjunction* ni *'neither, nor'*

571 *Ni* is the equivalent both of 'neither' and of 'nor'. There are important differences between the two languages in the use of these conjunctions:

(i) When they apply to finite verbs (see **341**), 'neither' is *ne* and 'nor' is *ni ne* (and note that both negative elements are essential here – *ni* alone will not do), e.g.:

Je ne peux ni ne veux y consentir
I neither can nor will agree to it

Il ne m'écrit ni ne vient me voir
He neither writes to me nor comes to see me

(ii) When they apply to elements other than a finite verb, each of the elements in question (which may be, for example, the subject, the direct or indirect object, past participles, infinitives, adjectives, adverbs, prepositional phrases, etc.) is preceded by *ni* while the finite verb is preceded by *ne*, e.g.:

Ni lui ni moi ne serons prêts à temps
Neither he nor I will be ready in time

Il ne comprend ni l'anglais ni le français
He understands neither English nor French

Je ne le donne ni à Pierre ni à Jean
I am giving it neither to Peter nor to John

Je ne les ai ni vus ni entendus
I have neither seen nor heard them

Il ne veut ni m'écrire ni me téléphoner
He will neither write to me nor telephone me

Je ne suis ni riche ni avare
I am neither rich nor miserly

Il ne vient ni aujourd'hui ni demain
He is coming neither today nor tomorrow

Nous n'allons ni à Paris ni à Strasbourg
We are going neither to Paris nor to Strasburg

(iii) the construction (*ne*) . . . *ni* . . . *ni* is also the equivalent of 'not . . . or . . . (either)', 'Not . . . either . . . or', etc.; for example, the second, third, fourth and last examples in ii above could also be translated 'He doesn't understand (either) English or French', 'I am not giving it either to Peter or to John', 'I haven't seen them or heard them', 'We are not going to Paris or to Strasburg either', and similar alternative translations could be provided for the other examples except the first (in which 'neither . . . nor' relate to the subject of the verb).

(iv) French uses *ni* where English uses 'and' or 'or' after a negative or after *sans* or *sans que* 'without', e.g.:

sans père ni mère
without father or mother, with neither father nor mother

Il faut le faire sans qu'il voie ni (qu'il) entende rien
It must be done without his seeing or hearing anything

La vieille aristocratie française n'a rien appris ni rien oublié
The old French aristocracy has learnt nothing and forgotten nothing

(v) Note the use of *ni* to introduce a kind of afterthought after a negative construction with *ne . . . pas*, e.g.:

Il ne faut pas s'asseoir ni même si remuer avant que la reine n'ait donné le signe
No one must sit down or even move till the queen gives the signal

Il ne comprend pas le français, ni l'anglais d'ailleurs
He doesn't understand French, or indeed English

When the newly introduced element is the equivalent of the subject, English has the construction 'neither (*or* nor)' + some such verb as 'is, has does, shall, will, can, must' + the subject; French has the construction *ni* (optional – see below) + subject (disjunctive form if it is a personal pronoun) + *non plus*, e.g.:

Il n'y va pas, (ni) son frère non plus
He is not going (and) neither is his brother

Je ne regarde jamais la télé, (ni) ma femme non plus
I never watch TV, (and) neither (*or* nor) does my wife

(Ni) moi non plus
Neither am I (have I, can I, do I, etc.)

Elle ne travaillait jamais. – (Ni) lui non plus
She never worked. – Neither did he

In speech, the form without *ni* is the more usual, the form with *ni* being rather more emphatic.

C *Negation of an element other than a verb*

572 'No' or 'not' as the equivalent of a negative sentence.

The English 'no' in answer to a question, or by way of being a comment, an objection, a warning, etc., is translated by *non* or, more emphatically, by *mais non!*, e.g.:

Vous partez demain? – Non, monsieur
Are you leaving tomorrow? – No, sir

Non! non! non! Ce n'est pas comme ça qu'il faut le faire!
No! no! That's not the way to do it!

Vous partez demain, n'est-ce pas? – Mais non! Je reste encore trois jours
You're leaving tomorrow, aren't you? – No! I'm staying another three days

573 As an exclamatory negative (usually with a sense of protest against the suggestion made), *que non* is sometimes used, e.g.:

A votre avis, votre mari est-il coupable? Oui, ou non? – Que non! Oh, que non!

In your opinion, is your husband guilty? Yes, or no? – No! Oh, no!

574 After verbs of saying or thinking and a few others such as *espérer* 'to hope', and after certain adverbs of affirmation or doubt (see **627–628**) such as *heureusement* 'fortunately' and *peut-être* 'perhaps', 'not' or 'no' can take the place of an object clause; e.g. 'I hope not' as an answer to 'Is he coming?' is the equivalent of 'I hope he is not coming' (it is not therefore the equivalent of 'I do not hope'). The French equivalent of this, and also of 'not . . . so' in such sentences as 'I don't think so', is *que non*, e.g.:

Il part déjà? – J'espère que non / Je crois que non
Is he leaving already? – I hope not / I don't think so

Tu viens à la piscine? – J'ai déjà dit que non
Are you coming to the swimming pool? – I've already said
no (*or* . . . said I'm not)

Vous feriez mieux de ne pas lui écrire. – Peut-être que non.
You had better not write to him. – Perhaps not.

(For a similar use of *que oui* and *que si*, see **628**,ii.)

Non, non pas, pas 'not'

575   When 'not' negates some element other than the verb, there
are three possible forms, viz. *non, non pas,* or *pas.* These are
interchangeable in some circumstances but not, unfortunately, in
all circumstances. We have to distinguish between a number of
different constructions. The following summary is based on the
admirably clear explanation given by R.-L. Wagner and J.
Pinchon in their *Grammaire du français classique et moderne,*
Paris, Hachette, 1962, pp. 401–2.

All depends on whether (i) two items are presented as being
in opposition to one another, or (ii) two elements are presented
as being alternatives, or (iii) only one item is expressed (and, of
course, in the negative). Further distinctions are necessary in (i)
according to whether it is the first or the second element that is
negatived, and in (ii) according to whether or not the second
element is or is not expressed. These distinctions should become
clear from the examples that follow.

576   (i) Two elements are presented as being in opposition (i.e.
we have one or other of the constructions 'not X but Y' or 'X
not Y'):

(a) The first element is negatived – 'not' is *non* or *non pas*, e.g.:

Il a l'air non fatigué mais malade
Il a l'air non pas fatigué mais malade
He looks not tired but ill

Elle arrive non mardi mais jeudi
Elle arrive non pas mardi mais jeudi
She is arriving not on Tuesday but on Thursday

*Henri sera mon cavalier, non (pas) qu'il soit beau, mais parce
qu'il danse à ravir*
Henry shall be my partner, not that he is handsome, but
because he dances divinely

(b) The second element is negatived – 'not' is *non, non pas*, or
pas:

Il a l'air fatigué, non malade
Il a l'air fatigué, non pas malade
Il a l'air fatigué, pas malade
He looks tired, not ill

Elle arrive mardi, non jeudi
Elle arrive mardi, non pas jeudi
Elle arrive mardi, pas jeudi
She is arriving on Tuesday, not on Thursday

Il l'a fait par mégarde, non (non pas, pas) avec intention
He did it by mistake, not on purpose

577 (ii) Two elements are presented as being alternatives (i.e.
we have one or other of the constructions 'X or not X' or 'X or
not'):

(a) The second element is expressed – 'not' is usually *pas*, e.g.:

Fatigué ou pas fatigué, il part demain
Tired or not tired, he is leaving tomorrow

Qu'il parle bien ou pas bien, peu importe
Whether he speaks well or not well, it doesn't much matter

(b) The second element is not expressed – 'not' is *non* or *pas*,
e.g.:

Fatigué ou non, il part demain
Fatigué ou pas, il part demain
Tired or not, he is leaving tomorrow

Qu'il parle bien ou non, peu importe
Qu'il parle bien ou pas, peu importe
Whether he speaks well or not, it doesn't much matter

Les uns l'aiment, les autres non
Les uns l'aiment, les autres pas
Some like it, others not

578 (iii) Only one (negative) item is expressed – not is *non* or *pas*, e.g.:

> *Il habite non loin de Paris*
> *Il habite pas loin de Paris*
> He lives not far from Paris

> *Il était furieux et non content de ce qu'il avait vu*
> *Il était furieux et pas content de ce qu'il avait vu*
> He was angry and not pleased with what he had seen

579 We therefore have the following pattern:

(i)	a	*non*	*non pas*	—
	b	*non*	*non pas*	*pas*
(ii)	a	—	—	*pas*
	b	*non*	—	*pas*
(iii)		*non*	—	*pas*

Note in particular:

(a) that *non pas* is used **only** to express opposition;

(b) that *pas* may be used in all constructions **except** to negative the first of two elements in opposition.

Note also that, where there is a choice between *non* and *pas*, the former is characteristic of a more formal, the latter of a more familiar style.

580 *Non* is used before a past participle not compounded with *être* or *avoir*, e.g.:

une leçon non sue	a lesson not known
vin non compris	wine not included
les pays non-alignés	the non-aligned countries

before a present participle used purely as a noun or qualifying adjective, e.g.:

un non-combattant	a non-combatant

and to form compounds (many of them technical) with various nouns and adjectives, e.g.:

> *non-conducteur*
> non-conductor

le point de non-retour
the point of no return

non-réussite
failure

non valable
invalid (excuse, etc.), not valid (ticket, etc.)

une manifestation non-violente
a non-violent demonstration

Interrogative sentences (questions)

Introduction

581 Questions are either:

(i) Direct – e.g. 'Are you coming?', 'What is he doing?', 'Why did the cat eat the goldfish?'

or (ii) Indirect – e.g. '(He asked) if I was coming', '(I wonder) what he is doing', '(Nobody knows) why the cat ate the goldfish'.

Direct questions fall into one or other of two categories:

(i) Total interrogation – i.e. 'yes–no' questions, e.g. 'Is she happy?', 'Have you any change?', 'Did the cat eat the goldfish?';

(ii) Partial interrogation – i.e. questions introduced by an interrogative expression, e.g. 'Who?', 'What?', 'When?', 'Where?', 'How?', 'Why?', 'How many?', 'Which book?', 'For what reason?'

We shall discuss interrogative sentences under the following headings:

A: Direct questions: total interrogation
B: Direct questions: partial interrogation
C: Indirect questions

582 In direct questions, in either total or partial interrogation, English makes much use of the verb 'do', which has no function other than to turn a statement into a question, e.g.:

I saw him	Did I see him?
My brother smokes too much	Does my brother smoke too much?

She bought a book	What did she buy?
They eat too much	Why do they eat too much?

Note that, in French, the verb *faire* 'to do' is never used in this way.

A *Direct questions – total interrogation*

583   The basic interrogative form of a 'yes–no' question when the subject is a personal pronoun or one or other of the pronouns *on* or (with *être* only) *ce* is obtained by inverting the subject, i.e. placing it after the verb, e.g.:

je suis	*suis-je?*	*vous venez*	*venez-vous?*
elle chante	*chante-t-elle?*	*ils peuvent*	*peuvent-ils?*
on dit	*dit-on?*	*c'est vrai*	*est-ce vrai?*

For the interrogative conjugation of a typical verb, see **387**.

For the use of *-t-* when a verb form ending in a vowel is followed by *il, elle* or *on*, see **388**.

Note that, in the present tense, the inversion of *je* is not possible with most verbs (see **389**).

Further examples:

Puis-je vous aider?
May I help you?

A-t-il terminé son travail?
Has he finished his work?

Viendra-t-elle nous voir?
Will she come and see us?

Aviez-vous beaucoup de voisins?
Did you have many neighbours?

584   A noun subject cannot be inverted in total interrogation. The equivalent construction is obtained by leaving the noun subject at the beginning and inverting the appropriate personal pronoun, e.g.:

Le chat a-t-il mangé le poisson rouge?
Has the cat eaten the goldfish?

Marie habitait-elle à Paris?
Did Mary live in Paris?

Les Français boivent-ils trop de vin?
Do the French drink too much wine?

Vos sœurs seront-elles contentes?
Will your sisters be pleased?

585   An alternative and widely used way of asking questions is
to preface the affirmative form with *Est-ce que . . .?* (literally 'Is
it that . . .?' – but it must not be translated thus), e.g.:

Est-ce qu'elle viendra nous voir?
Will she come and see us?

Est-ce que Marie habitait à Paris?
Did Mary live in Paris?

This is an effective way of coping with those contexts in which *je*
cannot be inverted, e.g.:

Est-ce que je parle trop?
Do I talk too much?

Est-ce que je pars tout de suite?
Do I leave immediately?

Note that *est-ce que* is often used for the sake of emphasis,
expressing indignation, surprise or doubt, e.g.:

Est-ce que je vais me confier à de telles gens?
Do you think I am going to entrust myself to such people?

586   The excessive use of *est-ce que* should be avoided. In writing, this can be done by using inversion (see **583–584**). In speech,
questions are very frequently formed by means of intonation
alone, keeping the same word-order as in statements, e.g.:

Je parle trop?	Am I talking too much?
Tu pars déjà?	Are you leaving already?
Mon père est sorti?	Has my father gone out?

587   The only French equivalent for English tag-questions, i.e.
brief questions such as 'Don't I?', 'Isn't she?', 'Haven't you?',
'Won't they?', tacked on to an affirmative sentence, is *n'est-ce
pas?*, e.g.:

Elle est très heureuse, n'est-ce pas?
She's very happy, isn't she?

Vous êtes allé à Paris, n'est-ce pas?
You've been to Paris, haven't you?

Ils voyageaient beaucoup, n'est-ce pas?
They used to travel a lot, didn't they?

Vous me prêterez votre voiture, n'est-ce pas?
You'll lend me your car, won't you?

N'est-ce pas? can also be used after a negative, as the equivalent of 'Is she?', 'Did they?', etc., e.g.:

Tu ne pars pas maintenant, n'est-ce pas?
You're not leaving now, are you?

Il n'a jamais dit ça, n'est-ce pas?
He never said that, did he?

B Direct questions – partial interrogation

588 For questions involving the interrogative pronouns *qui?* 'who?', *qu'est-ce qui?*, *qu'est-ce que?*, *que?*, *quoi?* 'what', *lequel?* 'which?', see **280–290**.

For questions introduced by *combien?* 'how much?', 'how many?', see **326**.

589 In questions introduced by one of the interrogative adverbs *où?* 'where?' (or *d'où?*, *jusqu'où?*, *par où?*), *quand?* 'when?', *comment?* 'how?', *pourquoi?* 'why?', or an interrogative phrase including *quel?* 'which?', the subject, if a personal pronoun, *on* or (with the verb *être* only) *ce*, is inverted, as in total interrogation, e.g.:

Où avez-vous garé la voiture?
Where have you parked the car?

Quand viendra-t-elle nous voir?
When will she come to see us?

Pourquoi dit-on cela?
Why do they say that?

Comment le savaient-ils?
How did they know?

Pour quelle compagnie travaille-t-il?
Which company does he work for?

Où est-ce?
Where is it?

As in total interrogation, *est-ce que?* may be used, in which case the order Subject–Verb remains, e.g. (as alternatives to the above):

Où est-ce que vous avez garé la voiture?
Quand est-ce qu'elle viendra nous voir?
Pour quelle compagnie est-ce qu'il travaille? etc.

590 When the subject of a question introduced by *où?*, *quand?*, *comment?*, *pourquoi?*, a preposition + *qui?* or *quoi?*, or an expression including *quel?*, is a noun (or a pronoun other than a personal pronoun, *on* or *ce*), it may (contrary to what is the case in total interrogation, see **584**) be inverted, subject however to certain restrictions (see **591–592**), e.g.:

Où travaillait votre père?
Where did your father work?

Quand arrivent les enfants?
When are the children coming?

D'où est venue cette idée?
Where has that idea come from?

Avec qui voyage votre frère?
Who is your brother travelling with?

A quelle heure est la conférence?
What time is the lecture?

An alternative is to invert the appropriate subject pronoun, in which case the noun subject may go either before or after the interrogative word, e.g.:

Votre père où travaillait-il?
Où votre père travaillait-il?

Again, in speech in particular, *est-ce que?* provides a further alternative, e.g.:

Où est-ce que votre père travaillait?
Quand est-ce que les enfants arrivent?

591   The inversion of the noun subject is not possible with *pourquoi* and tends to be avoided with other interrogative words and phrases of more than one syllable. In such cases, one or other of the constructions referred to in **590** should be used, e.g.:

Pourquoi les enfants pleuraient-ils?
Why were the children crying?

Comment est-ce que votre frère le sait?
How does your brother know?

Combien votre sœur a-t-elle perdu?
How much has your sister lost?

592   The noun subject cannot be inverted when the verb has a direct object (other than a conjunctive pronoun) or some other complement to which it is closely linked and from which it should not be separated; an alternative construction must therefore be used, e.g.:

Où est-ce que votre frère gare sa voiture?
Where does your brother park his car?

Quand les étudiants passent-ils leurs examens?
When do the students sit their exams?

Quand les enfants partaient-ils en vacances?
When were the children leaving on holiday?

593   (i) A non-literary construction that is very current in speech is to put the interrogative word not first but after the verb (and, in most cases, at the end), e.g.:

Vous allez où?	Where are you going?
Henri est arrivé quand?	When did Henry arrive?
Ton frère part quel jour?	What day is your brother leaving?
Vous en voulez combien?	How much (How many) do you want?
Il fait a ça pourquoi?	Why did he do that?
Elle écrit à qui?	Who(m) did she write to?
Il est où ton sac?	Where's your bag?
C'est quand ton examen?	When is your exam?

(On the use of both noun and pronoun subjects in the last two examples, see 602.)

(ii) A construction that occurs widely in informal spoken French, especially when the subject is a conjunctive personal pronoun (see 193–198), or *on*, *ce*, or *ça*, is that in which the interrogative word or phrase remains at the beginning (contrast i above) but the subject is not inverted, i.e. it remains before the verb (contrast 589), e.g.:

Où vous avez trouvé ça?	Where did you find that?
Pourquoi tu (ne) veux pas venir?	Why don't you want to come?
A quelle heure il est parti?	What time did he leave?
Combien ça coûte?	How much does it cost?
Quel âge il a?	How old is he?

This construction occurs in the informal speech even of educated speakers and there is no good reason why it should not be copied, in informal speech, by foreigners whose conversational French is generally fluent and correct at a normal speed. It is particularly common with *comment?* 'how?', e.g. *Comment tu t'appelles?* 'What is your name?', *Comment vous avez trouvé ce vin?* 'How did you find (i.e. What did you think of) this wine?', and is firmly established in the expression *Comment ça va?* 'How are things?'

(iii) Yet another construction but, in this case, one which is generally regarded as substandard and which should therefore be avoided by foreigners, even in informal speech, is that in which the interrogative word or phrase is followed by *que*, e.g.:

Combien que je vous dois?	How much do I owe you?
Pourquoi que tu dis ça?	Why do you say that?
Avec quoi qu'il écrit?	What is he writing with?

C Indirect questions

594 Indirect questions corresponding to total interrogation are introduced by *si* 'if, whether', and take the appropriate tense as in English; e.g. (corresponding to *Pouvez-vous m'aider?* 'Can you help me?', *Est-ce que le train arrivera à temps?* 'Will the train arrive in time?', *Est-ce qu'il viendra?* 'Will he come?'):

Il m'a demandé si je pouvais l'aider
He asked me if I could help him

Nous ne savions pas si le train arriverait à temps
We didn't know whether the train would arrive in time

Je me demande s'il viendra
I wonder if (whether) he will come

Je me demandais s'il viendrait
I wondered if (whether) he could come

Note the use of this type of *si*-clause with ellipsis of the main clause where English would use an echo-question (i.e. a repeat question by way of seeking confirmation of the tenor of the original question – cf. **595**), e.g.:

– *M'aimes-tu?* – *Si je t'aime?* (Balzac)
'Do you love me?' – 'Do I love you?' (i.e. 'Are you asking me if I love you?')

This sometimes has an exclamatory value, e.g.:

– *Voulez-vous y aller?* – *Si je le veux!*
'Do you want to go?' – 'Do I want to!' (= 'I should think I do!')

595 Indirect questions introduced by one of the interrogative expressions discussed in **588–589** have the same word-order as in affirmative clauses, e.g.:

Nous ne savions pas pourquoi il était parti
We didn't know why he had left

Il m'a demandé à quelle heure le train partait
He asked me what time the train left

Je me demande où mon frère va acheter sa nouvelle voiture
I wonder where my brother is going to buy his new car

However, inversion of the noun subject is possible provided the indirect question is not introduced by *pourquoi* and there is no direct object and no other complement closely linked to the verb, e.g.:

Dites-moi où habite votre frère
Tell me where your brother lives

Je ne comprends pas comment vivaient les hommes des cavernes
I don't understand how cavemen lived

Note the use of an indirect question with ellipsis of the main clause where English uses an echo-question (cf. **594**), e.g.:

– *Pourquoi es-tu venu? – Pourquoi je suis venu?* (Loti)
'Why have you come?' – 'Why have I come?'

– *Où êtes-vous? – Où je suis? Mais je suis chez moi*
'Where are you?' – 'Where am I? I am at home'

These correspond to something like 'You ask why I have come?' and 'You ask where I am?'

Inversion

596 In most contexts, the subject in French precedes its verb, e.g. *Il chante* 'He sings', *Mon frère habite ici* 'My brother lives here', and this can therefore be considered the normal word-order in French. In certain circumstances, however, the subject follows the verb: this is known as 'inversion'.

There are in fact three types of inversion in French:

(i) the pronoun subject follows the verb, e.g.:

Est-il arrivé? Peut-être viendra-t-il demain
Has he arrived? Perhaps he will come tomorrow

(ii) the noun subject follows the verb, e.g.:

C'est là qu'habite mon frère
That is where my brother lives

Non, monsieur, répondit le garçon
'No, sir', the boy replied

(iii) A noun subject comes first and the corresponding conjunctive pronoun is added after the verb, e.g.:

Peut-être ma mère avait-elle changé d'avis
Perhaps my mother had changed her mind

Vos enfants sont-ils en vacances?
Are your children on holiday?

Types (i) and (ii) are sometimes known as 'simple inversion' and type (iii) as 'complex inversion'.

597   For inversion:
in direct questions, see **583–584** and **589–592**

with the subjunctive, expressing wishes, see **476–477**

in hypothetical constructions, in the sense of '(even) if, supposing, etc.', see **478.**

598   (i) Inversion may occur when the subject is a noun (for exceptions, see ii, below) in indirect questions, relative clauses, and other subordinate clauses, e.g.:

Je ne comprends pas ce que dit mon professeur (or *ce que mon professeur dit*)
I don't understand what my professor says

Savez-vous de quoi se fâchait son père? (or *de quoi son père se fâchait?*)
Do you know what his father was getting angry about?

Je ne connais pas le monsieur dont parlait mon père (or *dont mon père parlait*)
I don't know the man my father was talking about

Voici le livre qu'a acheté mon frère (or *que mon frère a acheté*)
Here is the book my brother bought

Elle avait été heureuse tant qu'avait vécu son époux (or *tant que son époux avait vécu*)
She had been happy for as long as her husband had lived

(ii) Inversion of the noun subject is not, however, possible in such clauses if this would have the effect of separating the verb from some element with which it is closely linked, such as a direct object, e.g.:

Voici la librairie où mon frère achète ses livres
Here is the bookshop where my brother buys his books

or the complement of *être* or another linking verb (see **518**), e.g.:

C'est en 1959 que de Gaulle est devenu Président de la République
It was in 1959 that de Gaulle became President of the Republic

or an adverbial complement modifying the verb, e.g.:

. . . tant que son époux avait travaillé à Paris
. . . for as long as her husband had worked in Paris

(iii) Inversion is not possible in such clauses when the subject is a conjunctive personal pronoun, or *on* or *ce*, e.g.:

Je ne peux pas deviner ce qu'il veut faire ici
I cannot imagine what he wants here

Je ne connais pas les hommes dont il parlait
I do not know the men of whom he was speaking

. . . tant qu'il avait vécu
. . . for as long as he had lived

(iv) It goes without saying that inversion is impossible when *qui* or *ce qui* is itself the subject.

599 In short parenthetical expressions reporting someone's words, inversion is essential. This applies not only to verbs explicitly referring to speech, such as *dire* 'to say', *s'écrier* 'to exclaim', *demander* 'to ask', *continuer* 'to continue (speaking)', *répondre* 'to reply', but also to a few verbs such as *penser* 'to think', *se demander* 'to wonder' when they imply that the subject is inwardly addressing herself or himself, e.g.:

Je ne sais pas, répondit mon frère
'I don't know,' my brother answered

Hélas! $\left\{\begin{array}{l}\textit{dit-il,}\\\textit{cria-t-il,}\\\textit{s'écria-t-il,}\\\textit{pensa-t-il,}\\\textit{a-t-il dit,}\\\textit{disait-il,}\end{array}\right\}$ *que vais-je devenir?*

'Alas!' he said (he shouted, he exclaimed, he thought, he said), 'what will become of me?'

With other verbs that occasionally have a similar value, inversion is optional, e.g.:

$$C'est\ bizarre, \left\{ \begin{array}{l} ai\text{-}je\ réfléchi \\ j'ai\ réfléchi, \end{array} \right\} qu'il\ n'en\ ait\ rien\ dit$$

It is odd, I reflected, that he has not mentioned it

600 Certain adverbs and adverbial expressions cause inversion more or less regularly (though not invariably) when they stand first in the clause. In the case of a noun subject, we have complex inversion (see **596**, end).

Of the expressions in question, *à peine* 'scarcely' nearly always causes inversion, and *peut-être* 'perhaps' and *sans doute* 'doubtless' usually do so (except when followed by *que* – see below and **642**), e.g.:

A peine se fut-il assis que le train partit
Scarcely had he sat down when the train started

Peut-être arrivera-t-il demain
Perhaps he will arrive tomorrow

Sans doute ma sœur vous a-t-elle écrit
Doubtless my sister has written to you

but also, as an alternative, *Peut-être qu'il arrivera demain*, etc.
Toujours is always followed by inversion in the expression *toujours est-il que . . .* 'the fact remains that . . .'
Among other adverbs and adverbial expressions that frequently (and in some cases more often than not) cause inversion are:

ainsi, thus	*encore plus*, even more
aussi, and so	*en vain*, in vain
aussi bien, and yet	*rarement*, rarely
du moins, at least	*tout au plus*, at most
(et) encore, even so	*vainement*, vainly
encore moins, even less	

Inversion also sometimes occurs after various other adverbs. Examples:

Ainsi la pauvre dame a fini (or *a-t-elle fini*) *par s'échapper*
Thus the poor lady ended by escaping

En vain luttait-il (or *il luttait*)*; rien ne lui réussit*
In vain he struggled; nothing went right for him

*Vous avez demandé des nouvelles de son mari! mais on vient
de l'arrêter; du moins on le dit* (or *le dit-on*)
You inquired after her husband! he has just been arrested;
so they say at any rate

Tout au moins auriez-vous pu m'en avertir plus tôt
At least you might have warned me sooner

Note that 'at least' in its literal sense, i.e. before an expression
of quantity, is always *au moins* and that, in this case, there is no
inversion, e.g.:

Au moins trois cents personnes en moururent
At least three hundred people died of it

601   A different type of inversion is that in which the verb (which
may or may not be preceded by an adverbial expression) has
relatively little significance and serves mainly to introduce the
subject which is the really important element. In equivalent sentences in English, the verb is regularly introduced by a meaningless 'there' or 'it', e.g.:

Suivit une âpre discussion en russe (Duhamel)
There followed a sharp discussion in Russian

Restent les bijoux (Chamson)
There remain the jewels

Reste à voir ce qu'il fera
It remains to be seen what he will do

A ce moment surgit un petit homme en casquette (Benoit)
At that point there appeared a little man in a cap

Dislocation and fronting

602   (i) Spoken French (for literary French, see v below) makes
considerable use of a procedure known as 'dislocation' whereby
an element is taken out of the main structure of the clause,
repositioned before or after the rest of the clause, and recalled
or anticipated by a conjunctive pronoun, e.g.:

(a) *Paul, je le connais*
(b) *Je le connais, Paul*
    I know Paul

which, literally, mean 'Paul I know him' and 'I know him Paul' respectively: the direct object *Paul*, is taken out of the main structure of the clause and recalled (in a) or anticipated (in b) by the corresponding direct object pronoun *le*. Because of the positions the dislocated elements occupy on the printed page, type (a) is known as 'left dislocation' and type (b) as 'right dislocation'.

If the dislocated element is a personal pronoun, the disjunctive form (see **215**) is used, e.g. *Moi je le déteste* or *Je le déteste, moi* 'I hate him'.

It is impossible here to discuss all the multifarious forms taken and roles played by dislocation. These depend on a complex interplay of factors which include the level of formality or informality of the discourse, the identification of the theme or topic of the sentence (i.e. what the sentence is talking about), and emphasis. Furthermore, two or more sentences containing dislocation that are identical in print may be clearly differentiated in speech by intonation and/or emphasis.

The following notes cannot do more than draw attention to some of the more common types of dislocation.

(ii) A sentence such as *Je connais Pierre* 'I know Peter' can be dislocated in the following ways, with differences in intonation and subtle differences in role:

Moi, je connais Pierre
Je connais Pierre, moi
Pierre, je le connais
Je le connais, Pierre
Moi, Pierre, je le connais
Pierre, moi, je le connais
Je le connais, moi, Pierre
Je le connais, Pierre, moi
Moi, je le connais, Pierre
Pierre, je le connais, moi

As a further complication, note that some or all of the commas (representing pauses) in the above examples could be omitted.

The above examples involve dislocation of the subject and/or direct object. However, other elements can also be dislocated as the following examples show:

Je lui écris souvent, à Pierre
A Pierre, je lui écris souvent
I often write to Peter

J'y vais souvent, à Paris
A Paris, j'y vais souvent
I often go to Paris

J'en connais beaucoup, d'Américains
I know a lot of Americans

(iii) Right dislocation, as in *Je le connais, Pierre* 'I know Peter' and the last three examples in ii above, tends to be thematic, i.e. to clarify the information given by the conjunctive pronouns (*le = Pierre, lui = à Pierre, y = à Paris, en = Américains*) – the 'core' of the meaning, the 'new' information, is conveyed in these examples, but not necessarily in all sentences, by the verb; e.g. in *Je lui écris souvent à Pierre* and *Il y va souvent à Paris*, the new information the speaker wishes to convey in relation to the theme (Peter and Paris respectively) is that 'I write to him' and 'He goes there'.

Left dislocation can also be thematic, but sometimes with greater emphasis on the dislocated element than with right dislocation.

(iv) In left dislocation, but *not* in right dislocation, there is a further possibility which is perhaps most clearly illustrated by such examples as the following:

Pierre, je lui écris souvent
I often write to Peter

Paris, j'y vais souvent
I often go to Paris

in which the preposition *à* does not figure before *Pierre* and *Paris* even though the meaning is 'to Peter', 'to Paris' – it is sufficient that this is made clear by the conjunctive pronouns *lui* and *y* respectively. What we have here is what is known as a 'hanging topic', i.e. one that is not integrated into the grammatical structure of the sentence. The following is a further example:

Des Américains, j'en connais beaucoup
I know a lot of Americans (*lit.* Americans, I know a lot of them)

This procedure can be taken further, in that the hanging topic relates not to some element expressed as such in the rest of the sentence but to something that is merely implied, as in Baudelaire's well-known line:

Moi, mon âme est fêlée
My soul is cracked

in which *moi* 'I, me' relates to the personal pronoun that is implied in the possessive *mon* 'my'.

This construction can have an emphatic value, as in:

Mon père, il ne faut rien lui dire
My father mustn't be told anything

(v) As has been mentioned above, dislocation is especially characteristic of informal spoken French. It has, however, become the norm in literary French in the following circumstances:

(a) in certain contexts when a personal pronoun is to be stressed (see **216**,i)

(b) with complex inversion (see **596**,iii).

(vi) Fronting
'Fronting' (which is sometimes considered as yet another type of dislocation) means bringing to the beginning of the clause an element that normally follows the verb. It differs from dislocation (as defined above) in that the fronted element is not recalled by a conjunctive pronoun, e.g.:

Ces gens-là je connais
Those people I (do) know

It is much less common than dislocation and care must be taken not to use it in contexts where left dislocation, with the use of a conjunctive pronoun, is the appropriate construction. Fronting often serves to mark a contrast, e.g.:

Je n'aime pas Paul mais Pierre j'aime beaucoup
I don't like Paul but Peter I like very much

Il téléphone souvent à sa sœur mais à sa mère il écrit
He often phones his sister but to his mother he writes

Je vais de temps en temps à Paris mais à Strasbourg je vais souvent
I go to Paris occasionally but Strasburg I often go to

Adverbs, Prepositions and Conjunctions

Adverbs

Introduction

603 Adverbs can be conveniently classified as follows:

A: Adverbs of manner; these generally, but not invariably, end in *-ly* in English and in *-ment* in French (see 604–613)

B: Adverbs of time (see 614–623)

C: Adverbs of place (see 624–625)

D: Adverbs of quantity (see 'Quantifiers', 320–337)

E: Adverbs of affirmation or doubt (see 627–628)

F: Adverbs of negation (see 544–558)

G: Interrogative adverbs (see 630–631)

A   Adverbs of manner

604 Most adverbs of manner, and some others that for convenience we shall include in the following sections, are formed

from adjectives by adding *-ment* (which corresponds to English *-ly*, as in 'slow, slowly'), according to the rules set out in sections 605–607.

605 (i) With the exceptions noted in ii below and in sections 606 and 607, *-ment* is added to the *feminine* form of the adjective (the reason is that *-ment* derives from the Latin *-mente*, a form of the word *mens* 'mind' which was feminine, so one had constructions like *placida mente* 'with a placid mind', hence 'placidly'), e.g.:

clair, fem. *claire*, clear	*clairement*, clearly
complet, fem. *complète*, complete	*complètement*, completely
doux, fem. *douce*, gentle	*doucement*, gently
fou, fem. *folle*, mad	*follement*, madly
nouveau, fem. *nouvelle*,new	*nouvellement*, newly
premier, fem. *première*, first	*premièrement*, firstly
public, fem. *publique*, public	*publiquement*, publicly
sec, fem. *sèche*, dry	*sèchement*, drily
soigneux, fem. *soigneuse*, careful	*soigneusement*, carefully
tendre, fem. *tendre*, tender	*tendrement*, tenderly
utile, fem. *utile*, useful	*utilement*, usefully

(ii) Exceptions:

(a) While most adjectives having a final *-e* in both masculine and feminine form their adverbs regularly (see, for example, *tendre* and *utile* at the end of the list in i above), the following adverbs take *-é-* before the adverbial *-ment*:

aveugle, blind	*aveuglément*, blindly
commode, convenient	*commodément*, conveniently
conforme, in accordance with	*conformément*, in accordance with
énorme, enormous	*énormément*, enormously
immense, immense	*immensément*, immensely
incommode, inconvenient	*incommodément*, inconveniently
intense, intense	*intensément*, intensely
uniforme, uniform	*uniformément*, uniformly

(b) Adverbs from the following adjectives also take *-é-* before the adverbial *-ment*:

commun, fem. *commune*, common	*communément*, commonly
confus, fem. *confuse*, confused	*confusément*, confusedly
diffus, fem. *diffuse*, diffuse	*diffusément*, diffusely
exprès, fem. *expresse*, express	*expressément*, expressly
importun, fem. *importune*, importunate	*importunément*, importunately
inopportun, fem. *inopportune*, inopportune	*inopportunément*, inopportunely
obscur, fem. *obscure*, obscure	*obscurément*, obscurely
opportun, fem. *opportune*, opportune	*opportunément*, opportunely
précis, fem. *précise*, precise	*précisément*, precisely
profond, fem. *profonde*, deep	*profondément*, deeply
profus, fem. *profuse*, profuse	*profusément*, profusely

(c) The adverbs corresponding to *bon* 'good' and *mauvais* 'bad' are *bien* 'well', *mal* 'badly'.

The 'regular' adverb *bonnement* exists, but only in the expression *tout bonnement* 'just, simply, merely', e.g. *il a répondu tout bonnement que . . .* 'he merely answered that . . .', *Je lui ai dit tout bonnement la vérité* 'I just told him the truth, I told him the plain truth'.

(d) The adverb corresponding to *bref* 'brief' is *brièvement* (from an old adjective *brief*, feminine *brième*, that no longer exists)

(e) The adverb corresponding to *gentil*, fem. *gentille* 'nice' is *gentiment*.

(f) The adverb corresponding to *traître* (originally a noun), fem. *traîtresse* 'treacherous', is *traîtreusement*.

606 (i) Most adjectives ending in the vowels -*ai*, -*é*, -*i* (but not -*oi*), -*u* (but not -*eau* or -*ou*) or -*û* form their adverbs by adding -*ment* to the masculine form, e.g.:

aisé, easy	*aisément*, easily
dû, due	*dûment*, duly
poli, polite	*poliment*, politely
vrai, true	*vraiment*, truly

and the following adjectives in -*u* (for other adjectives in -*u*, see ii,b below):

absolu, absolute	*absolument*, absolutely
ambigu, ambiguous	*ambigument*, ambiguously
éperdu, frantic	*éperdument*, frantically
ingénu, ingenuous	*ingénument*, ingenuously
irrésolu, irresolute	*irrésolument*, irresolutely
résolu, resolute	*résolument*, resolutely

(ii) Exceptions:

(a) The adverb from *gai* 'gay' is written either *gaiement* (the form preferred by the Académie française) or *gaîment*.

(b) The following five adjectives in *-u* change this vowel to *-û* before adverbial *-ment* (for adverbs in *-ument*, see i above):

assidu, assiduous	*assidûment*, assiduously
continu, continuous	*continûment*, continuously
cru, crude	*crûment*, crudely
goulu, greedy	*goulûment*, greedily
incongru, unseemly	*incongrûment*, in an unseemly manner

The adverb from *nu* 'naked' is written either *nûment* (the form preferred by the Académie française) or *nuement*.

(c) Corresponding to the adjective *impuni* 'unpunished' is the highly irregular adverbial form *impunément* 'with impunity'.

607   (i) Most adjectives in *-ant* or *-ent* form their adverb in *-amment* or *-emment* respectively, e.g.:

brillant, brilliant	*brillamment*, brilliantly
constant, constant	*constamment*, constantly
fréquent, frequent	*fréquemment*, frequently
récent, recent	*récemment*, recently

(ii) However, three adjectives in *-ent* form their adverbs by adding *-ment* to the feminine form of the adjective in line with **605** above:

lent, fem. *lente*, slow	*lentement*, slowly
présent, fem. *présente*, present	*présentement*, at present
véhément, fem. *véhémente*, vehement	*véhémentement*, vehemently

608   The adverbs *journellement* 'every day', *notamment* 'notably, in particular', *nuitamment* 'by night', *précipitamment* 'hurriedly', *sciemment* 'knowingly', have no corresponding adjective. Nor has *grièvement*, which exists only in the expression *grièvement blessé* 'gravely wounded'.

609 As in English, a few adjectives can be used as adverbs qualifying certain verbs, e.g.:

Elle marcha droit devant elle
She walked straight ahead

Il travaille très dur
He works very hard

The following list gives the adjectives most commonly used as adverbs and the verbs with which they are generally used:

bas, with *jeter*, 'down'; with *chanter, parler*, 'low, in a low voice' (often *tout bas*)

bon, with *sentir*, '(smell) good, nice'; with *tenir*, '(hold) fast, (stand) firm'

cher, with *acheter, coûter, vendre*, 'dear'

clair, with *voir*, 'clearly'

court, with *s'arrêter*, '(stop) short'; with *couper*, '(cut) short'; with *demeurer, rester, se trouver*, 'be at a loss for words'

droit, with *aller, marcher*, 'straight'; also *tout droit* 'straight ahead'

dru, with *pleuvoir*, 'hard'; with *semer*, 'thickly'; with *tomber* 'thick and fast'

dur, with *travailler, jouer*, 'hard'

faux, with *chanter, jouer*, 'out of tune'; with *sonner*, 'have a false ring'

ferme, with *discuter*, 'vigorously'; with *tenir*, '(stand) fast, firm'; with *travailler*, 'hard'

fort, with *déplaire, douter*, etc., 'greatly'; with *sentir*, 'have a strong smell'; with *frapper, jouer*, 'hard'; with *crier, parler*, 'loudly'

gros, with *écrire*, 'big'; with *gagner, perdre*, 'heavily, a lot'

haut, with *lire*, 'aloud'; with *parler*, 'loudly'; with *placer*, 'high'

juste, with *tirer*, '(shoot) straight'; with *deviner, raisonner, voir*, 'correctly, accurately'

long, in *en savoir long sur quelque chose*, 'to know all about something'

lourd, with *peser*, 'heavy, heavily'

mauvais, with *sentir*, '(smell) bad'
net, with *se casser*, 'snap in two'; with *dire, parler*, etc.,
  'plainly'; with *refuser*, 'point blank'; with *trancher*, '(cut)
  short (e.g. a discussion)'; with *tuer*, 'outright'; etc.
ras, with *couper, tondre*, 'close'
sec, with *boire*, 'heavily'; with *parler, répondre*, etc., 'curtly'
serré, with *jouer*, 'cautiously'

610 (i) The above follow the verb they qualify and are
invariable, e.g. *Elle travaille dur* 'She works hard'. But note that
frais 'freshly' used adverbially before a participle, and *grand* and
large 'wide' before the one participle *ouvert* 'open', vary like
adjectives, e.g.:

des fleurs fraîches cueillies
freshly picked flowers

les yeux $\left\{ \begin{array}{l} \textit{grands} \\ \textit{larges} \end{array} \right\}$ *ouverts*
with wide open eyes

une fenêtre grande ouverte
a wide open window

(ii) In *(tout) battant neuf, (tout) flambant neuf* 'brand new', *tout*
and *neuf* normally agree but *battant* and *flambant* are usually
invariable, e.g. *des vêtements (tous) battant neufs* 'brand new
clothes', *une voiture (toute) flambant neuve* 'a brand new car' –
but occasionally the form in *-ant* agrees (and, just to complicate
things, sometimes *neuf* does not, e.g. *des bâtiments flambant neuf*
'brand new buildings').

(iii) For a general statement of the conditions in which *tout* does
or does not vary when used adverbially, see **317**,v,b.

611 French sometimes uses adverbial phrases of the type *de* or
d'une façon, de or *d'une manière* + (feminine) adjective, i.e. 'in
such-and-such a way', as the equivalent of an adverb of manner
modifying a verb, e.g. *agir discrètement* or *d'une manière discrète*
'to act discreetly', *différemment* or *de manière différente* 'differently', *inexplicablement* or *d'une façon inexplicable* 'inexplicably'.
  Another possibility is to use *avec* and a noun, e.g. *soigneusement*
or *avec soin* 'carefully', *impatiemment* or *avec impatience*
'impatiently'.

Note that these alternative constructions can be used **only** when they modify a verb or the clause in general; so, *agréablement* could not be replaced by *d'une manière agréable* in, for example, *agréablement surpris* in which it modifies a participle.

In the case of a small number of adjectives that have no corresponding adverb, some such alternative construction **must** be used, e.g. *d'une manière tremblante* 'tremblingly', *Il regardait autour de lui d'un air content* 'He looked contentedly around him', *avec concision* 'concisely'.

612 Adverbs of manner that have no corresponding adjective include:

ainsi, thus
debout, standing
exprès, deliberately, on purpose
vite, quickly

and also, taking the term 'adverb of manner' in a very wide sense:

ensemble, together   *plutôt*, rather

For *bien* 'well' and *mal* 'badly', see **161–163**.

613 *Comme* and *comment*

(i) With *être* and sometimes with other linking verbs such as *devenir* 'to become', *paraître* 'to appear', *comme* after an adjective expresses a comparison in a large number of fixed expressions such as:

Il est fort comme un bœuf
He is as strong as an ox

Elle est devenue blanche comme un linge
She turned as white as a sheet

malin comme un singe
as artful as a monkey

noir comme (du) jais
as black as soot (*lit.* jet)

blanc comme neige
as white as snow

Note that this construction is limited to such expressions and is **not** used as a general equivalent of *aussi . . . que . . .* (see **157**);

it could not, for example, be substituted for *aussi . . . que . . .*
in *il est aussi intelligent que son frère* 'he is as intelligent as his
brother'.

(ii) As a conjunction expressing a comparison between two verbs,
comme means 'as', e.g.:

> *Il écrit comme il parle*
> He writes (in the same way) as he speaks
>
> *Il se conduit comme se conduirait un enfant*
> He behaves as a child would behave

When, as is frequently the case, the verb of the second clause
would merely repeat the first, e.g. 'He behaves as a child behaves',
'I consider him as I (would) consider a brother', it may be omitted
in French as in English, e.g.:

> *Il se conduit comme un enfant*
> He behaves like a child
>
> *Je le considère comme un frère*
> I consider him as a brother

and in many expressions of the type:

> *courir comme un lièvre*
> to run like a hare
>
> *travailler comme un forçat*
> to work like a galley-slave

(iii) In the sense of 'how', *comme* must not be confused with
comment.

(a) In direct questions, 'how?' is *comment?* (see **589–590**)

(b) With an exclamatory value, 'how' is translated as *comme* or
as *que* when qualifying an adjective, e.g.:

> *Comme il est* (or *Qu'il est*) *facile de se tromper!*
> How easy it is to be mistaken!
>
> *Comme elle est* (or *Qu'elle est*) *belle!*
> How beautiful she is!

but usually as *comme* when modifying a verb or adverb, e.g.:

> *Comme elle a pleuré!*   How she wept!
> *Comme elle chante bien!*   How well she sings!

Conversational alternatives are *ce que* and, in an even more familiar style, *qu'est-ce que*, e.g.:

Ce qu'elle est belle!	*Qu'est-ce qu'elle est belle!*
Ce qu'elle a pleuré!	*Qu'est-ce qu'elle a pleuré!*
Ce qu'elle chante bien!	*Qu'est-ce qu'elle chante bien!*

(c) In indirect questions either *comme* or *comment* may be used, with, however, a significant difference in meaning. *Comment* refers strictly and objectively to the way something is done, e.g.:

Observez bien comment il travaille
Notice how he does his work

while *comme* (in line with b above) is somewhat exclamatory and conveys the idea of the extent to which something is done, e.g.:

Observez bien comme il travaille
Notice how hard he works

(d) *Comment!* is also the equivalent of exclamatory 'What!', e.g.:

Comment! Tu es toujours là!
What! You're still there!

B Adverbs of time

614 Adverbs of time include, among a number of others:

actuellement, at present
alors (see **615**), then
après, afterwards
aujourd'hui, today
auparavant, beforehand
autrefois, formerly
avant, before
bientôt (see **622**), soon
déjà, already
demain, tomorrow
depuis, since
désormais, henceforward
donc (see **615**), then

encore (see **616**), again
enfin, at last
ensuite (see **615** and **617**), then, next
hier, yesterday
jamais (see **618**), ever, never
longtemps, for a long time
lors (see **619**)
parfois, sometimes
maintenant (see **620**), now
précédemment, previously
puis (see **615**), then (next)
quelquefois, sometimes
souvent, often
tard (see **621**), late
tôt (see **622**), early
toujours, always, still

615   *Alors, puis, ensuite, donc, lors* 'then'

(i) The above five adverbs can all be translated as 'then', but in fact they mean very different things and, apart from *puis* and *ensuite*, they are not in general interchangeable.

(ii) *Alors* means 'then' in the sense of:

(a) 'at that time' (see also **620**), e.g.:

> *Nous étions à Paris en 1943. La France était alors sous l'occupation allemande*
> We were in Paris in 1943. France was then under German occupation

(b) 'so, therefore, in that case, etc.', e.g.:

> *Alors, tu viens ou non?*
> Well, are you coming or not? (Are you coming or not, then?)
>
> *Il a été très impoli. – On ne l'invite plus, alors*
> He was very rude. – We shan't invite him again, then

(iii) *Puis* and *ensuite* mean 'then' in the sense of 'next, afterwards', e.g.:

> *Je suis allé d'abord à Bruxelles et puis* (or *ensuite*) *à Paris*
> I went to Brussels first and then to Paris

With reference to space, however, *puis* (not *ensuite*) should be used, e.g.:

Vous voyez les champs de blé et puis le chemin de fer
You can see the fields of wheat and then the railway line

On *ensuite*, see also **617**.

(iv) *Donc* means 'therefore, so, then', and, with the meaning of 'therefore' (i.e. expressing the conclusion of a logical argument), it comes first in the clause, e.g.:

Je pense, donc je suis
I think, therefore I exist

When meaning 'therefore' in a rather weaker sense, i.e. 'so, then', it usually follows the verb, e.g.:

On m'a téléphoné; je sais donc ce qui est arrivé
They telephoned me; so I know what has happened

Il est donc de retour?
So he's back? (He's back then?)

Donc also frequently expresses surprise or irritation or some other emotional reaction, in which case it never comes at the beginning of the clause; there may well be no specific equivalent in the corresponding English utterance (see the second example below); e.g.:

Vous habitez donc ici!
So this is where you live!

Dépêchez-vous donc!
Do hurry up!

(v) For *lors*, see **619**.

616 *Encore* 'again, still, yet'

(i) Strictly as an adverb of time, *encore* has three senses:

(a) 'Again', e.g.:

J'espère y aller encore
I hope to go there again

Encore une fois '(once) again' is often used in this sense, e.g.:

Il m'a téléphoné encore une fois
He has phoned me again

(b) 'Still' (i.e. continuing into the present, or into some other period of past or future time indicated by the context), e.g.:

> *A minuit il était encore là*
> At midnight he was still there
>
> *Vous travaillez encore?*
> Are you still working?

In contexts where *encore* could be ambiguous ('again' or 'still'?), it is advisable to use *toujours* (which is in any case probably more common in this sense) for 'still', e.g.:

> *Vous travaillez toujours?*
> Are you still working?

(c) With a negative, '(not) yet', especially in the expression *pas encore* 'not yet' but also with other negatives such as *personne* 'no one', *rien* 'nothing', *jamais* 'never', in which case it normally follows the verb (the auxiliary in the case of compound tenses), e.g.:

> *Ne partez pas encore!*
> Don't go yet!
>
> *Personne n'a encore terminé? – Pas encore*
> Hasn't anyone finished yet? – Not yet
>
> *Rien n'était encore prêt*
> Nothing was yet ready
>
> *Je ne les ai encore jamais vus*
> I have never yet seen them

(ii) *Encore* is sometimes the equivalent of 'as well, in addition, too', e.g.:

> *Outre l'amende, il fut encore condamné à trois mois de prison*
> Besides the fine, he was sentenced to three months' imprisonment as well

(iii) Note the distinction between *encore un(e)* 'another', in the sense of 'one more, an additional one', and *un(e) autre* 'another', in the sense of 'a different one', e.g.:

> *Il demanda encore un verre de vin*
> He asked for another (= an additional) glass of wine
>
> *Il demanda un autre verre*
> He asked for another (= a different) glass

(In conversational usage, however, *un(e) autre* can have the meaning of *encore un(e)*, as in *Une autre bière?* 'Another beer?')

Likewise, 'more' meaning 'some more' can be rendered by *encore* and the partitive article (but note that 'no more' is *ne . . . plus*), e.g.:

> *Désirez-vous encore du vin? – Merci, je n'en veux plus*
> Would you like some more wine? – No thank you, I don't want any more

(iv) Note that 'even' with a comparative must be translated by *encore* (cf. English 'yet more' = 'even more'), not by *même*, e.g.:

> *Elle est encore plus intelligente que ses collègues*
> She is even more intelligent than her colleagues

> *J'aime encore mieux votre maison que la mienne*
> I like your house even better than my own

617   *Ensuite* and other expressions based on *suite*

Ensuite (see **615**) was originally two words, viz. *en suite*, and it is worth noting a number of other adverbial and prepositional expressions formed on the basis of *suite*:

à la suite	in succession, one after another
à la suite de	following, in consequence of
et ainsi de suite	and so on
dans la suite	later (on), subsequently
de suite	(1) in succession, running; (2) immediately
par la suite	later (on), subsequently
par suite	consequently, therefore
par suite de	owing to, as a result of
tout de suite	at once, immediately

Examples:

Il est mort à la suite d'un accident	He died following an accident
Il m'a téléphoné dix jours de suite	He phoned me ten days running
Je reviens de suite	I'll be right back

618   *Jamais* 'ever'

Jamais is used particularly in direct and indirect questions, after comparisons, and after *si* 'if', e.g.:

L'avez-vous jamais vu?
Have you ever seen him?

Je t'aime plus que jamais
I love you more than ever

Si jamais je le vois, je le lui dirai
If ever I see him, I'll tell him

and in a few expressions like *à jamais, à tout jamais* 'for ever'.
For *jamais* in the sense of 'never', see **550** and **558**.

619   *Lors*

Lors is not used on its own but only when preceded or followed
by a preposition. The combinations *depuis lors* and *dès lors* mean
'since then, from that time, thenceforth', *pour lors* means 'for the
time being, at the moment' (with reference to the past), while
the prepositional phrase *lors de* means 'at the time of, in the days
of', e.g.:

Lors de son mariage, il était bibliothécaire à Rouen
At the time of his marriage, he was a librarian at Rouen

Although *lors* is normally written as one word with a following
que in the conjunction *lorsque* 'when', it is separated from it by
the adverb *même* in the expression *lors même que* 'even if'.

620   *Maintenant, or* 'now'

The normal equivalent of 'now' with reference to present time is
maintenant. Where English uses 'now' with reference to past time,
alors is more usual in French though *maintenant* also occurs, e.g.:

Alors ils se rendirent enfin compte du danger
Now at last they realized the danger

Son pouls était presque insensible maintenant (Flaubert)
Her pulse was now almost imperceptible

Or, which always comes at the beginning of its clause, does not
refer to time but is the equivalent of 'now' serving to introduce
a statement (which, in many cases, represents the next stage in a
narration or an argument), e.g.:

*Tous s'écrièrent encore, disant: Non pas celui-ci, mais
Barabbas. Or Barabbas était un brigand*
They all cried out again: Not this man, but Barabbas. Now
Barabbas was a robber

621   *Tard, en retard* 'late'

Tard is 'late' as the opposite of 'early', without any suggestion of 'too late', 'later than arranged', etc., e.g.:

Je me couche toujours tard
I always go to bed late

Il compte arriver tard – peut-être pas avant minuit
He expects to arrive late – perhaps not before midnight

En retard, on the other hand, always has the idea of 'late (for an appointment, etc.)', e.g.:

Il est en retard, comme d'habitude
He is late, as usual

The noun *retard* is also used in other expressions, e.g.:

Le train a dix minutes de retard
The train is ten minutes late

622   *Tôt* 'soon, early' and compounds thereof

It should be noted that there are a number of restrictions on the use of *tôt* – the usual word for 'soon' is *bientôt* and 'early' is more often than not best translated by *de bonne heure*.

(i) *Tôt* is used in a number of fixed expressions, e.g.:

arriver (partir) tôt
to arrive (leave) early

se coucher (se lever) tôt
to go to bed (get up) early

(ii) *Tôt* may be freely qualified by quantifiers such as *assez* 'rather, quite', *aussi (si)* 'as', *plus* 'more', *trop* 'too' and words for 'very', e.g.:

Il est parti assez tôt
He left quite early

Nous arrivons très tôt – trop tôt en fait
We are arriving very early – too early in fact

Je vais commencer plus tôt que d'habitude
I am going to begin earlier than usual

au plus tôt
(1) as soon as possible; (2) at the earliest

Je n'y serai pas aussi (or *si*) *tôt que vous*
I shall not be there as early as you

(iii) The following adverbs are the result of the fusion of some
other adverb and *tôt* in one word (e.g. *tantôt* from *tant* + *tôt*):

aussitôt, immediately
bientôt, soon
plutôt, rather
sitôt, as soon
tantôt, this afternoon
tantôt . . . tantôt, sometimes . . . sometimes

e.g.:

J'irai aussitôt, bientôt, etc.
I will go at once, soon, etc.

Je vous écrirai aussitôt que je pourrai
I shall write to you as soon as I can

Il était tantôt heureux, tantôt triste
He was sometimes happy, sometimes sad

Aussitôt and *sitôt* may be used with past participles, e.g.:

Aussitôt (sitôt) dit, aussitôt (sitôt) fait
No sooner said than done

Aussitôt (sitôt) la lettre reçue, il partit
As soon as the letter was received, he left

and have also come to be used as prepositions (e.g. *aussitôt mon
arrivée* 'immediately upon my arrival').
   Note the distinction between *plus tôt (que)* 'earlier (than)' and
plutôt (que) (originally from *plus* + *tôt*) 'rather (than)', e.g.:

Il est arrivé plus tôt que prévu
He arrived earlier than expected

Je prends celui-ci plutôt que celui-là
I'll take this one rather than that one

623   *Tout à coup* and *tout d'un coup*

These both mean 'suddenly, all at once' but, in addition, *tout
d'un coup* has the meaning (which can also be expressed by *d'un
seul coup*) of 'at one go, at one (fell) swoop, etc.'.

C *Adverbs of place*

624   Adverbs of place include:

ailleurs (see **625**), elsewhere	*devant*, in front
autour, around	*ici*, here
dedans, inside	*là*, there
dehors, outside	*loin*, far
derrière, behind	*partout*, everywhere
dessous, below	*près*, near
dessus, above	*proche*, near

625   *Ailleurs* 'elsewhere' and *d'ailleurs* 'besides, moreover'

Ailleurs is 'elsewhere, somewhere else', e.g.:

Il n'habite pas ici, il habite ailleurs
He doesn't live here, he lives somewhere else

'Elsewhere' may also be expressed by *autre part*, but note that 'everywhere else' can only be *partout ailleurs*.
D'ailleurs means either

(a) 'from elsewhere, from somewhere else', e.g.:

Ils ne sont pas d'ici, ils sont venus d'ailleurs
They are not from here, they have come from somewhere else

or (b) 'besides, moreover', e.g.:

Je ne peux pas quitter Londres; d'ailleurs je n'aime pas voyager
I can't leave London; besides, I don't like travelling

D *Adverbs of quantity*

626   For adverbs of quantity, see **320–337** ('Quantifiers').

E Adverbs of affirmation or doubt

627 Adverbs of affirmation or doubt include:

apparemment, apparently
assurément, most certainly
certainement, certainly
certes, of course, admittedly
peut-être, perhaps
probablement, probably
oui (see **628**), yes
si (see **628**), yes
sûrement, certainly
volontiers, willingly
vraiment, really
vraisemblablement, in all likelihood

628 (i) French has two words for 'yes', *oui* and *si*. In most contexts *oui* is used, but *si* is used in answer to a question expressed in the negative or to contradict a negative statement, e.g.:

Ne m'avez-vous entendu? – Mais si, je vous ai entendu
Didn't you hear me? – Oh yes, I heard you

Vous n'y réussirez jamais. – Mais si!
You will never succeed. – Oh yes I shall!

Que si and *si fait* are sometimes found as emphatic alternatives for *si*.

(ii) Note the use of *que oui* and *que si* after verbs of saying or thinking, after *espérer* 'to hope', and after *peut-être* 'perhaps', e.g.:

Est-ce qu'il peut partir maintenant? – J'ai déjà dit que oui
May he leave now? – I've already said yes (said so, said he can)

Est-ce qu'il arrive aujourd'hui? – J'espère que oui (Je crois que oui)
Is he arriving today? – I hope so (I think so)

Il n'acceptera jamais de le faire. – Ah, je crois que si
He will never agree to do it. – Oh, I think he will

Peut-être que oui
Perhaps so

(Cf. the use of *que non*, **574**.)

F Adverbs of negation

629 For adverbs of negation, see **544–558**.

G Interrogative adverbs

630 The interrogative adverbs (see also **589–593** and **595**) are:

combien? (see **326**)	how much? how many?
comment?	how?
où?	where?
pourquoi?	why?
quand?	when?
que . . . ne . . . ? (see **631**)	why . . . not . . .?

631 On the basis of *où?* 'where?' is formed *d'où?* 'whence? where from?', e.g.:

D'où vient-il?
Where does he come from?

In the literary language, *que?* can have the meaning of 'why?', expressing at the same time an emotional reaction such as regret or surprise; in practice, this construction now seems to occur only in negative questions (though this restriction did not always apply in Classical French), and note that *que . . . ne . . .?* 'why . . . not?' is not accompanied by *pas*, e.g.:

Olivier et Roland, que n'êtes-vous ici? (Hugo)
Oliver and Roland, why are you not here?

Interrogation is also expressed by a variety of adverbial phrases, e.g. *de quelle manière?* 'how? in what way?', *pour quelle raison?*

'why? for what reason?', *à quel moment?* 'at what time?', *pendant combien de temps?* 'for how long?'

The comparison of adverbs

632 For the comparison of adverbs, see 'The comparison of adjectives and adverbs' (155–174).

The position of adverbs

633 The position of adverbs is to some extent a matter of taste and may vary in the interests of special emphasis or other stylistic effect. The observations that follow should therefore be taken as indications of general practice, which is often deviated from, rather than as hard-and-fast 'rules'.

Adverbs in *-ment*

634 Like their English equivalents in *-ly*, French adverbs in *-ment* may modify either (i) a verb (see **635**), or (ii) some other element within a clause (see **636**), or (iii) the clause as a whole (see **637**).

635 (i) When it modifies a verb, the adverb follows it, even if its English equivalent precedes its verb, e.g.:

Ils se battent fréquemment
They frequently fight (*or* fight frequently)

Les socialistes rejettent totalement cette proposition
The socialists totally reject this proposal

Essayez d'écrire lisiblement
Try to write legibly

In compound tenses, the adverb usually comes between the auxiliary and the past participle, but may also follow the participle, e.g.:

Ils se sont fréquemment battus
Ils se sont battus fréquemment
They fought frequently

Nous avions longuement discuté là-dessus
Nous avions discuté longuement là-dessus
We had argued about it at length

When the adverb has other words depending on it, it *must* follow the participle, e.g.:

Ils se sont battus indépendamment les uns des autres
They fought independently of one another

(On the position of adverbs with participles used adjectivally, see **636**.)

(ii) When the verb is closely linked to some following element (e.g. a direct or indirect object or a prepositional phrase), the adverb may follow this element, particularly if it is as long as or longer than the other element or if it is in any way emphasized, e.g.:

Il prononce ses mots distinctement
He pronounces his words clearly

Je vais à Paris fréquemment
I go to Paris frequently

636   When an adverb modifies an element other than a verb, it normally precedes it. Such elements include adjectives and adjectival phrases, other adverbs and adverbial phrases, and occasionally pronouns (on past participles used as adjectives, see below).

Examples:

Il nous a donné une explication complètement incompréhensible
He gave us a completely incomprehensible explanation

Comme spectacle, cette pièce est absolument sans pareille
As a spectacle this play is absolutely without equal

Elle chante exceptionnellement bien
She sings exceptionally well

Il faut partir absolument tout de suite
We must leave absolutely immediately

Ils sont pratiquement tous morts
They are practically all dead

Adverbs may either precede or (though less usually) follow past participles used as adjectives, e.g.:

Il est complètement guéri
He is completely cured

Un diner parfaitement cuit (or *cuit parfaitement*)
A perfectly cooked dinner (*or* a dinner cooked perfectly)

637   Adverbs modifying the clause as a whole have considerable flexibility of movement and the choice of position depends upon such factors as emphasis and the rhythmic balance of the clause, e.g.:

Malheureusement, je ne peux pas y aller aujourd'hui
Je ne peux malheureusement pas y aller aujourd'hui
Je ne peux pas y aller aujourd'hui, malheureusement
Unfortunately, I can't go there today

638   A small group of adverbs in *-ment* expressing certainty or probability (*apparement* 'apparently', *assurément* 'certainly', *certainement* 'certainly', *probablement* 'probably', *sûrement* 'certainly', *vraisemblablement* 'probably') together with *heureusement* 'fortunately' can serve as the equivalent of a clause (= 'it is certain, probable, fortunate (that)') and be followed by *que*, e.g.:

Assurément qu'il a tort
He is certainly wrong

Heureusement que vous le connaissez
Fortunately you know him

Probablement qu'il arrivera mardi
Probably he will arrive on Tuesday

(Note that, whereas *être heureux que* takes a subjunctive, e.g. *Je suis heureux que vous le connaissiez* 'I am happy that you know him' (see **485**), *heureusement que* takes the indicative.)

Adverbs not ending in *-ment*

639   (i) Manner

(a) *Bien* 'well', *mieux* 'better' and *mal* 'badly', like adverbs in

-ment (see **635**), follow verbs (and, in the case of compound tenses, usually follow the auxiliary) and precede other elements that they modify, e.g.:

> *Elle chante bien mais son frère chante mieux*
> She sings well but her brother sings better
>
> *Il était mal habillé*
> He was badly dressed

However, when modified by another adverb such as *si* 'so', *trop* 'too', or when followed by *que* 'as, than', they may precede or follow the past participle in compound tenses, e.g.:

> *Il a si bien chanté que tout le monde a applaudi*
> *Il a chanté si bien que tout le monde a applaudi*
> He sang so well that everyone applauded

Finally, an adverb modified by another adverb or followed by *que* 'as, than' may follow some other element closely linked to the verb such as a direct object (cf. **635**,ii), e.g.:

> *Il prononce ses mots très bien*
> He pronounces his words very well
>
> *Il a prononcé son discours si mal que personne n'a compris*
> He delivered his speech so badly that no one understood

(b) Other adverbs of manner, such as *exprès* 'deliberately, on purpose', *gratis* 'for nothing, for free', *volontiers* 'willingly', follow the verb, or some element such as a direct object or prepositional phrase closely linked to the verb (cf. **635**,ii) and, in compound tenses, do *not* come between the auxiliary and the past participle, e.g.:

> *Mon père passera volontiers vous voir*
> My father will willingly call and see you
>
> *Il l'a fait exprès*
> He did it deliberately
>
> *Nous allons assister au spectacle gratis*
> We are going to see the show for free

640 (ii) Time and place

The position of adverbs of time and place is flexible, as in English, and is governed by a wide range of stylistic factors. It is not possible to give clear-cut rules but, fortunately, in most contexts the position is the same as in English, e.g.:

Il est fatigué aujourd'hui
He is tired today

Il est toujours fatigué
He is always tired

Two important considerations to be borne in mind are:

(a) that, like other adverbs, when they qualify a verb they normally follow it, or some element closely linked to it (cf. 635,ii), and that, in compound tenses, they *follow* the past participle (cf. 639,b, and contrast 635,i), e.g.:

Il n'est pas arrivé aujourd'hui, mais il arrivera demain
He hasn't come today but he will come tomorrow

Je vous ai cherché partout
I've been looking everywhere for you

and (b) that to express contrast or for other stylistic reasons they may, as in English, come at the beginning of the clause, e.g.:

Devant, il y avait une pelouse, et derrière, un grand jardin
In front, there was a lawn, and behind, a big garden

Aujourd'hui je ne peux pas
Today I can't

Aujourd'hui il est fatigué mais demain il va travailler
Today he is tired but tomorrow he is going to work

Like adverbs in *-ment*, these adverbs of time and place usually have the same position as in English.

641   (iii) Quantity

Adverbs of quantity generally stand after the verb in simple tenses and between the auxiliary and the participle in compound tenses and the past infinitive, e.g.:

Il voyage beaucoup
He travels a lot

Il a beaucoup voyagé
He has travelled a lot

Vous avez tant souffert
You have suffered so much

Nous avons assez travaillé
We have worked (long) enough

Il croyait avoir trop bu
He thought he had drunk too much

642   (iv) Affirmation or doubt

Peut-être 'perhaps' and the adverbial phrase *sans doute* 'doubtless' can either stand after the verb or else come first and be followed by *que*, like *heureusement*, etc. (see **638**), or, in addition, they can come first and be followed by inversion of the subject pronoun (see **600**), e.g.:

Mon frère vous écrira sans doute ⎫ My brother will
Sans doute que mon frère vous écrira ⎬ doubtless write to you
Sans doute mon frère vous écrira-t-il ⎭

Il viendra peut-être mardi ⎫ Perhaps he will
Peut-être qu'il viendra mardi ⎬ come on Tuesday
Peut-être viendra-t-il mardi ⎭

643   (v) Interrogatives

In literary French, interrogative adverbs always precede the verb both in direct and in indirect questions, e.g.:

Pourquoi veut-il y aller?
Why does he want to go there?

Je me demande pourquoi il veut y aller
I wonder why he wants to go there

Quand partez-vous?
When are you leaving?

But note that in spoken French there is a widespread tendency to put the interrogative last in direct questions, e.g.:

Vous partez quand?   When are you leaving?
Vous en voulez combien?   How many do you want?

For more on this, see **593**,i.

Prepositions

Introduction

644   In this section we consider both:

(a) simple prepositions, i.e. those consisting of a single word, e.g. *avec* 'with', *sur* 'on' (see **645**), and

(b) complex prepositions, consisting in most cases of an expression ending in *à* (e.g. *grâce à* 'thanks to') or, more frequently, *de* (e.g. *à côté de* 'beside') together with a few others, e.g. *à travers* 'across' (see **647–648**).

Simple prepositions

645

    à, to, at
    après, after
    avant, before (of time)
    avec, with
    chez, at the house of
    concernant, concerning
    contre, against
    dans, in, into
    de, of, from
    depuis, since, from
    derrière, behind
    dès, from (of time)
    devant, before (of place)
    durant, during
    en, in, into
    entre, between
    envers, towards
    hormis, except
    hors, outside, except
    malgré, in spite of
    moyennant, in return for, on payment of

outre, besides
par, by, through
parmi, among
pendant, during
pour, for
sans, without
sauf, except, save
selon, according to
sous, under
suivant, according to
sur, on, upon
vers, towards

There are in addition the literary and somewhat archaic prepositions *nonobstant* 'notwithstanding' and *touchant* 'concerning'.

The forms *après, avant, depuis, derrière, devant* are also regularly used as adverbs. Other forms used as adverbs in specific contexts (a good dictionary should be consulted) are *avec, contre, outre, pour* and *selon*.

646   The following past participles are now used in certain circumstances in such a way that they must be considered as being, in effect, prepositions (see **134**):

attendu, given, considering
(y) compris, including
excepté, except
passé, after, beyond
vu, in view of, considering

Complex prepositions

647   **Complex prepositions ending in *à* or *de***

It is a moot point whether expressions such as *dans le but de* 'with the aim of', *à l'insu de* 'without the knowledge of', *à raison de* 'at the rate of' should or should not be included in a list of complex prepositions. In order not to inflate the list inordinately, we have excluded such expressions when either (a) the meaning of each of its elements seems to be still noticeable (e.g. *dans le but de*) or (b) the expression is relatively uncommon and unlikely to be much needed by the learner who can, in any case, find out its meaning from a dictionary when it is encountered in reading (e.g. *à l'insu de*). But such decisions are necessarily subjective – the list could have been much longer. The list follows the alphabetical order of the main components (so, for example, *en face de* comes before *au lieu de*).

The English equivalents given here do not always cover the whole range of meanings of the French preposition in question; for fuller information, consult a good dictionary.

(i) Forms ending in *à*

grâce à, thanks to
jusqu'à, up to, as far as, until
quant à, as for

(ii) Forms ending in *de*

auprès de, near, compared with
autour de, around
à cause de, because of
à côté de, beside
du côté de, to or from the direction of
au ⎫
en ⎬ *dedans de*, inside
au ⎫
en ⎬ *dehors de*, outside
au delà de, beyond
au-dessous de, below
au-dessus de, above
en face de, opposite
faute de, for lack of
au lieu de, instead of
au (or *le*) *long de*, along, throughout
lors de, at the time of
près ⎫
proche ⎬ *de*, near
à propos de, in connection with, apropros of
au sujet de, about
au travers de, through
en travers de, across, athwart
vis-à-vis, opposite, in relation to

648 Complex prepositions not ending in *à* or *de*

A few complex prepositions do not end in *à* or *de*. Those in common use are:

d'après, according to, in the style of
à travers, through, across
par derrière, behind, round the back of (see **669**)
par-dessous, 'under', *par-dessus* 'over' (see **671** and **684**)

Government of verbs by prepositions

649 (i) Whereas, in English, many prepositions are followed by the gerund ('on hearing', 'after deciding', 'while singing', etc.), the only French preposition that may be followed by the gerund is *en*, e.g. *en travaillant* 'by working, while working, etc.' (on the various meanings of this construction, see **445**).

(ii) The only part of the verb that can follow other prepositions is the infinitive, e.g.:

Je commence à m'inquiéter
I am beginning to get worried

Essayez de comprendre
Try to understand

Elle était près de s'évanouir
She was nearly fainting

Je l'ai fait pour vous aider
I did it to help you

Il est entré sans frapper
He came in without knocking

(iii) *par* + infinitive occurs only after verbs of beginning or finishing (and occasionally after *continuer*, but *continuer en* + gerund is more usual, e.g. *Il continua en me posant plusieurs questions* 'He continued by asking me several questions'), e.g.:

Je vais commencer par vous montrer le jardin
I am going to begin by showing you the garden

Il a fini par me remercier
He ended by thanking me

and likewise after *débuter* 'to begin', *achever, conclure, terminer* 'to end'.

(iv) 'Before' with an infinitive is *avant de* and never *avant* alone, e.g. *avant de partir* 'before leaving'.

(v) *Après* always takes the perfect infinitive, i.e. *avoir* and the past participle or, in the case of those verbs that form their perfect tense with *être* (see **347**), *être* and the past participle (which agrees with the implied subject), e.g. *après avoir chanté* 'after singing, after having sung', *Après être tombée, elle a voulu se reposer* 'After falling, she wanted to rest'.

(vi) For the construction preposition + infinitive as the complement of a verb, see **530–538**.

(vii) For the construction preposition + infinitive as the complement of an adjective, see **688**.

Repetition of prepositions

650 à, de, en
The prepositions *à, de* and *en* are almost invariably repeated before each item they govern and, in most cases, it is unacceptable not to repeat them, e.g.:

Il doit son succès à son intelligence et à sa bonne volonté
His success is due to his intelligence and good will

Il commence à grandir et à se développer
He is beginning to grow and develop

Vouz avez besoin de repos et de tranquillité
You need rest and tranquillity

Est-ce qu'il arrive de Metz ou de Troyes?
Is he coming from Metz or (from) Troyes?

J'y vais chaque année en avril et en septembre
I go there every year in April and September

Je vais en France et en Suisse
I am going to France and Switzerland

Il répondit en riant et en se moquant de leurs conseils
He replied by laughing and making fun of their advice

651   Other prepositions

Prepositions other than *à, de* and *en* need not be repeated except when two or more complements express opposite or alternative concepts, e.g.:

Dans la prospérité et dans l'adversité il montra la grandeur de son âme
In prosperity and adversity he showed his greatness of soul

Réponds-moi seulement par oui ou par non (Bourget)
Just answer me yes or no

When the two complements express much the same idea, the preposition is usually not repeated, e.g.:

Il est amolli par le luxe et l'oisiveté
He is enervated by luxury and idleness

In other cases, repetition is optional.

The meaning and use of individual prepositions

652   There is only an approximate equivalence between the meanings and uses of prepositions in different languages. In figurative and idiomatic expressions in particular, one language will use a preposition that does not correspond to its literal equivalent in another language. This is frequently so with French and English. Some of the main correspondences and differences between the two languages are given in the following sections, but an exhaustive treatment is impossible – and does not, indeed, exist anywhere else either though, to a considerable extent, uncertainties can be resolved by consulting a good large dictionary.

653   *à*, primary meanings 'to, at'
(i) The preposition *à* denotes possession when used with the verb *être*, e.g.:

A qui est ce livre? Il est à Charles, mais l'autre est à moi
Whose is this book? It is Charles's, but the other one is mine

or with disjunctive personal pronouns, particularly for purposes of emphasis, e.g.:

Il a des idées à lui
He has ideas of his own

mes amis à moi et ses amis à elle
my friends and *her* friends

(ii) Note the use of *à* + infinitive as the equivalent of an English present participle expressing a way of spending time, e.g.:

Il était perché sur le toit à regarder attentivement l'horizon
He was perched on the roof carefully scanning the horizon

Il passe son temps à lire des romans
He spends his time reading novels

(iii) The expression *à la* (which has also passed into English) is a reduction of *à la mode* (with adjectives) or of *à la mode de* (with nouns), e.g. *à l'américaine* 'in the American way', *des petits pois à la française* 'peas French-style', *des poésies à la Victor Hugo* 'poems in the style of Victor Hugo'.

(iv) French uses *à* where English uses 'with' to indicate characteristic features, permanent or temporary, e.g.:

une personne à l'esprit vif	a quick-witted person
un garçon aux cheveux longs	a boy with long hair
le monsieur au parapluie	the man with the umbrella

(v) For the use of the dative *à* with verbs denoting 'to take something from someone', see **524**.

(vi) The following is a selection of idioms using *à* where the English equivalents have one or other of a range of other prepositions:

(1) by	*à force de*	by dint of
	peu à peu	little by little
	deux à deux	two by two, i.e. two at a time
	fait à la main	made by hand, handmade
	vendre au poids	to sell by weight
	vendre aux enchères	to sell by auction
	à l'heure	by the hour
	à la lumière d'une bougie	by candle light

(For *à* meaning 'by' see also **433**,ii.)

(2) for	*à jamais*	for ever
	mot à mot	word for word

(3) in	*à la campagne*	in the country
	au bois	in the wood
	au lit	in bed
	à l'ombre	in the shade
	au milieu de	in the middle of
	à mon avis	in my opinion
	à la hâte	in haste
	à temps	in time
	avec un bâton à la main	with a stick in his hand
	au désespoir	in despair
(4) on	*à bord*	on board
	à pied	on foot
	à cheval	on horseback
	à droite, à gauche	on the right, left hand side
	à son départ	on his departure
	il se mit à genoux	he knelt down (*lit.* placed himself on his knees)
	à condition que	on condition that
	au contraire	on the contrary
	à l'heure	on time
(5) with	*à grandes enjambées*	with long strides
	avoir affaire à quelqu'un	to have to deal with someone
	abattre un arbre à coups de cognée	to fell a tree with (blows of) an axe
	à grand-peine	with great difficulty
	à regret	with regret
(6) within	*à portée de fusil*, etc.	within range (of rifle, etc.)
	à portée de la main	within reach
	à portée de voix	within hail
	à portée de vue	within sight

654   *à, en, de* as linking prepositions

The prepositions *à*, *en* and *de* can all be used to link two nouns, the second of which qualifies the first. They are, however, not interchangeable:

(i) *à* expresses

(a) purpose, use, function (= 'for'), e.g.:

une tasse à café	a coffee-cup (i.e. cup for coffee)
un moulin à café	a coffee-mill (i.e. for grinding coffee)
un ver à soie	a silkworm (i.e. for producing silk)
un tuyau à gaz	a gas pipe (i.e. for conducting gas)

(b) characteristics (including the method by which something is fuelled, driven, etc.), e.g.:

une chemise à rayures bleues	a shirt with blue stripes
un moulin à eau	a water-mill
une cuisinière à gaz	a gas cooker

(ii) *en* refers to the material of which something is made, or to shape, e.g.:

une montre en or	a gold watch
une maison en pierre	a stone(-built) house
un escalier en colimaçon	a spiral staircase
un assemblage en queue d'aronde	a dovetail joint

(note also *un compte en banque* 'a bank account').

(iii) *de* expresses a multiplicity of relationships, many of them also expressed by 'of' in English, e.g.:

une tasse de café	a cup of coffee
un marchand de légumes	a greengrocer (*lit.* seller of vegetables)
une robe de soie	a silk dress (i.e. made of silk)
une jauge d'essence	a petrol gauge
un professeur d'histoire	a history teacher
une mine de charbon	a coal mine
une carte de crédit	a credit card

à, dans, en

655   Great care is needed in translating 'at, to, in, into' when used of place. The three usual equivalents are *à, dans* and *en*, each of which can be used both of motion towards (= 'to, into') or of position at a place (= 'at, in') – but **they are not interchangeable**, e.g.:

Il est à la maison
He is in the house

Il vient à la maison
He is coming to the house

Il se trouvait dans la chambre
He was in the room

Il entra dans la chambre
He went into the room

Il est en prison
He is in prison

On l'a envoyé en prison
He has been sent to prison

For further details, see **656–659**.
For the use of these prepositions with reference to time, see
709 and **710**.

656 (i) 'To', 'at' and 'in' with names of towns are all translated
by *à*, e.g.:

Je vais à Paris	I am going to Paris
Je demeure à Paris	I live in Paris
Il est étudiant à Dijon	He is a student at Dijon

If the name of the town includes an article, as in *Le Havre* and
les Andelys, the usual contractions apply (see **25**), i.e. *au Havre,
aux Andelys*, but, in the feminine singular, *à la Haye* 'at or to
The Hague'. See also **659**,ii, for the use of *dans* with names of
towns.

(ii) With place-names other than names of towns, the situation is
much more complicated. Here too there is no difference between
'in' (i.e. situation) and 'to' (i.e. motion towards) but, in terms of
the actual preposition used, the choice depends on a number of
factors including gender (see **52**,b), whether the name begins with
a consonant or a vowel, whether the name is singular or plural,
and, to some extent, the type of geographical entity referred to.
There are four main possibilities (but see also iv below): (1) *en*
alone (i.e. with no article); (2) *à* alone; (3) *à* + definite article;
(4) *dans* + definite article. The following rules cover the great
majority of cases:

(1) *en* alone is used:

(a) with feminine singular names of continents, countries (but see
b), provinces, American states, large islands that are not also
countries, and (to use a necessarily vague term) regions, e.g.:

en Afrique	in, to Africa
en France	in, to France
en Picardie	in, to Picardy

en Californie	in, to California
en Toscane	in, to Tuscany
en Sardaigne	in, to Sardinia
en Sibérie	in, to Siberia

(b) with masculine singular names of countries etc. beginning with a vowel, e.g.:

en Iran	in, to Iran
en Anjou	in, to Anjou
en Ontario	in, to Ontario

(c) with names (of either gender) of French departments of the type *X-et-Y*, e.g. *en Lot-et-Garonne* (masc.), *en Meurthe-et-Moselle* (fem.), *en Indre-et-Loire* (fem.)

(2) *à* alone is used with the names of certain islands that are also countries, e.g. *à Chypre* (fem.) 'in, to Cyprus', *à Cuba* (fem.) 'in, to Cuba', *à Malte* (fem.) 'in, to Malta', *à Madagascar* (masc.) 'in, to Madagascar'; also *à Terre-Neuve* (fem.) 'in, to Newfoundland', *à Guernesey* 'in, to Guernsey', *à Jersey* 'in, to Jersey'

(3) *à* + definite article is used:

(a) with masculine singular names of countries beginning with a consonant, e.g. *au Danemark* 'in, to Denmark', *au pays de Galles* 'in, to Wales', *au Pérou* 'in, to Peru'

(b) with feminine names of some small islands (especially non-European islands), e.g. *à la Martinique* 'in, to Martinique', *à la Réunion* 'in, to Réunion'

(c) with plural names of countries and groups of islands (but see also iv below), e.g. *aux États-Unis* (masc.) 'in, to the United States', *aux Pays-Bas* 'in, to the Netherlands', *aux Philippines* (fem.) 'in, to the Philippines', *aux Açores* (fem.) 'in, to the Azores'; on the use of *dans* with other plural geographical names, see 4,c below)

(4) *dans* + definite article is used, meaning both 'in' and 'to':

(a) with names (of either gender or number) of French departments, except those of the *X-et-Y* type (see 1,c above), e.g. *dans le Gard, dans le Maine, dans la Nièvre, dans les Vosges.*

(b) with masculine singular names beginning with a consonant of French provinces, Swiss cantons, British counties, American states, and various other territorial units, e.g. *dans le Poitou, dans le Valais, dans le Yorkshire, dans le Texas* (but *en* also occurs with masculine names of French provinces, e.g. *en Poitou*)

(c) With plural geographical names (of either gender) other than those of countries or groups of islands (see 3,c above), e.g. *dans les Flandres* 'in, to Flanders', *dans les Balkans* 'in, to the Balkans', *dans les Grisons* 'in, to the Grisons'.

(iii) Note that *à la* (or *à l'*) is used with feminine names of countries, etc., and *à l'* with masculine names beginning with a vowel when the preposition means neither 'to' in the sense of 'motion towards' nor 'in', e.g.:

Je préfère la Suisse à la Belgique
I prefer Switzerland to Belgium

La CE va accorder une aide financière à la Pologne
The EC is going to grant financial aid to Poland

En matière de cuisine, la France est supérieure à l'Angleterre
As far as cooking goes, France is superior to England

Il pense toujours à la Grèce
He is always thinking of Greece

quant à l'Afghanistan
as for Afghanistan

This construction is *not* used with such verbs as *écrire, téléphoner* and *envoyer*, e.g.:

Il écrit (or *téléphone*) *souvent en France*
He often writes to (*or* phones) France

Je viens d'envoyer le manuscrit en Allemagne
I have sent the manuscript to Germany

In a few uncommon contexts it is also possible to have *en la*, e.g.:

Il a confiance en la France
He has confidence in France

(iv) With names of islands when the word *île* or *îles* is included, *sur* is used to mean not only 'on' but also 'in' or 'to', e.g. *sur l'île de Ré* 'on, in, to the île de Ré', *sur les îles d'Hyères* 'on, in, to the îles d'Hyères'.

657 Distinction between *dans* and *en*

(i) *En* is not used with the definite article except in certain fixed expressions such as the following:

en l'absence de
in the absence of

en l'air
in the air (lit. and figurative)

en l'an 1980
in the year 1980

en l'espace de
within the space of (a period of time)

en l'honneur de
in honour of

en la matière
on the subject, in the matter (e.g. *je suis ignorant en la matière*)

en la personne de
in the person of

en la présence de
in the presence of

Note that all the above expressions involve the use of *en l'* or *en la*; the use of *en* with *le* or *les* is very rare and should be avoided as it is usually unacceptable.

(ii) *Dans*, on the other hand, must always be followed by an article – definite, indefinite or partitive – or by another determiner (see 23), except with names of towns or people (see 659,ii), e.g. *dans le tiroir* 'in the drawer', *dans votre sac* 'in your handbag', *Dans quel roman avez-vous trouvé cette citation?* 'In what novel did you find that quotation?', *dans trois villes différentes* 'in three different towns'.

The result of this is that *dans* is in many cases more specific than *en*, e.g.:

Il est en prison
He is in jail (place unspecified)

Il est dans la prison de Poitiers
He is in Poitiers jail (a definite place)

658   Idiomatic uses of *en*
Note the following idiomatic uses of *en*:

(a) as the equivalent of English 'as':

Il le traita en enfant
He treated him as a child

déguisé en agent de police
disguised as a policeman

Je l'ai reçu en cadeau
I got it as a present

(b) where English uses 'on', e.g.:

en garde	on guard
en pente	on a slope
en vacances	on holiday
en moyenne	on (an) average

(c) with reference to the material of which something is made (see also **654**,ii), colour, or shape, e.g.:

une maison bâtie en brique(s)	a house built of brick
être en noir, en blanc, etc.	to be dressed in black, in white, etc.
un mur peint en blanc	a white-painted wall
en croix	in the shape of a cross

(but note *habillé en blanc, en noir,* or *de blanc, de noir,* etc. 'dressed in white, in black, etc.').

(d) with reference to dress, e.g.:

des policiers en tenue	uniformed police
en civil	in civilian clothing, plain-clothed
en bras de chemise	in one's shirt sleeves

(e) with verbs of 'changing into' and 'dividing into', e.g.:

Le cinéma va être transformé en supermarché
The cinema is going to be turned into a supermarket

La grenouille s'est changée en prince
The frog changed into a prince

changer des dollars en francs
to change dollars into francs

Il coupa le gâteau en tranches
He cut the cake into slices

(f) with reference to months, seasons, years, e.g.:

en juin (or *au mois de juin*)
in June

en été, en automne, en hiver
in summer, in autumn, in winter

| *en 1934* | in 1934 |
| *en quelle année?* | in what year? |

but *au printemps* 'in spring'.

(g) before *plein* when English has 'in' (or occasionally 'on'), e.g.:

Il le frappa en pleine poitrine	He hit him right in the chest
en plein hiver	in the middle of winter
en plein jour	in broad daylight
en pleine mer	on the high seas

(h) with a wide range of adverbial expressions of which the following are only a selection:

en arrière	behind, backwards
en avant	in front, forwards
en bas	below, downstairs
en face	opposite
passer quelque chose en fraude	to smuggle something through
en guerre	at war
en haut	above, upstairs
en plus	in addition
en tout	altogether
en tout cas	anyway, at any rate
en vain	in vain

(i) in the construction *de . . . en . . .* in such expressions as:

d'année en année	from year to year
de mal en pis	from bad to worse
de porte en porte	from door to door, from house to house

and with comparatives of the type 'more and more' or 'less and less' + adjective or adverb, e.g.:

de plus en plus difficile	more and more difficult
de moins en moins souvent	less and less often
de mieux en mieux	better and better

659 Distinction between *à* and *dans*

(i) When 'in' is more or less the equivalent of 'at' or in other contexts in which the idea of being 'inside' is only weakly present, its French equivalent is often *à* not *dans*, e.g.:

Est-ce que votre père est à la maison?
Is your father in the house? (i.e. as distinct from being somewhere else)

Je n'ai jamais étudié l'anglais à l'école
I never studied English in (*or* at) school

Il a toujours une cigarette à la bouche
He's always got a cigarette in his mouth

Il tenait un couteau à la main
He was holding a knife in his hand

Il a été blessé à l'épaule
He has been wounded in the shoulder

as contrasted with:

Il est quelque part dans la maison
He is somewhere in the house

Il est dans l'école en ce moment
He is in(side) the school at the moment

Cette viande fond dans la bouche
This meat melts in your mouth

Il tenait une pièce de dix francs dans la main
He was holding a ten-franc piece in his hand

Il a toujours une balle dans l'épaule
He still has a bullet in his shoulder

(ii) 'In' or 'at' with the name of a town, regarded as a place where something is situated or where some event takes place, is normally *à*, e.g. *Il travaille à Londres* 'He works in London', *Je l'ai vu à Paris* 'I saw him in Paris'. *Dans* may, however, be used to express the idea of 'within, (right) inside', e.g. *L'ennemi est déjà dans Paris* 'The enemy is already inside Paris', or to stress the idea of the town as an area (within which one can move about, for example) rather than as a point on a map, e.g. *J'aime me promener dans Paris* 'I like going for walks in Paris, walking about Paris'. *Dans* is also used if the name of a town is qualified by an adjective or adjectival expression, e.g.:

A l'exposition on se plonge dans le vieux Paris
At the exhibition we plunge into old Paris
Dans le Paris d'aujourd'hui on ne sait guère s'orienter
In present-day Paris one can hardly find one's bearings

With the name of a person, *dans* means 'in the works of', e.g.
Vous le trouverez dans Molière 'You will find it in Molière'.

(iii) Note the use of *dans* where English uses 'out of' in such contexts as:

On a bu dans ce verre
Someone has been drinking out of this glass
un article découpé dans le journal
an article cut out of the paper
Prenez un mouchoir dans le tiroir
Take a handkerchief out of the drawer

– i.e. French indicates where the object was before it was moved while English expresses the direction in which it is moved (cf. *sur* 'on' where English uses 'from, off', **685**).

(iv) *dans* + *les* and a numeral means 'about, approximately' with reference to prices, quantity, time and age, e.g.:

Cela va vous coûter dans les deux cents francs
That will cost you about two hundred francs
Je compte mettre dans les trois ou quatre mois pour l'achever
I expect to take about three or four months to finish it
Il faudra acheter dans les dix mètres de corde
We shall have to buy about ten metres of rope
Elle doit avoir dans les quarante ans
She must be about forty

(v) *dans* is widely used in figurative senses, e.g. *dans les affaires* 'in business', *dans ces conditions* 'in these conditions', *dans la misère* 'in poverty', *dans ce but* 'with this aim in view', *dans les limites de la légalité* 'within the law'.

(vi) For the distinction between *dans une heure* and *en une heure* 'in an hour', etc., see **709**.

660 *après*, primary meaning 'after'

(i) In such contexts as the following, *après* can be rendered in English by 'next to':

Après le ski, j'aime mieux la natation
Next to skiing, I like swimming best

(ii) In a spatial sense, *après* 'past, beyond, the other side of', e.g.:

Son bureau est juste après l'église
His office is just beyond (past, the other side of) the church

For *après* with a past infinitive (e.g. *après avoir mangé* 'after eating'), see **649**,v.

661 *à travers, au travers de, en travers de*

In spite of what some grammars say, there is little or no distinction in meaning between *à travers* and *au travers de* meaning 'through'; *à travers* (which, note, is never followed by *de*) is the more usual, e.g. *à travers un verre, les nuages, la foule*, 'through a glass, the clouds, the crowd', *Il avait reçu un coup d'épée au travers du bras* (or *à travers le bras*) 'He had received a sword-thrust through the arm'. *A travers* occasionally means 'across', e.g. *à travers champs* 'across country', but note carefully the following points in connection with the translation of 'across':

(a) 'across' meaning 'placed across, lying across' is *en travers de*, e.g. *Il y a un arbre en travers de la route* 'There is a tree (lying) across the road' (but *un pont sur le ruisseau* 'a bridge across the stream')

(b) when 'across' means 'on the other side of', none of the forms based on *travers* will do, e.g. 'I saw him across the square' is best rendered by *Je l'ai vu de l'autre côté de la place*

(c) where English uses a verb of motion (e.g. 'to swim, to run') and 'across', French normally uses *traverser* 'to cross' and an adverbial expression expressing the type of motion involved, e.g.:

traverser la Manche à la nage
to swim across the Channel

Il traversa la place en courant
He ran across the square

but 'to walk across' is often just *traverser*, e.g. *traverser le pont* 'to walk across the bridge'.

662 *auprès de*

Auprès de is a complex preposition based on *près* 'near' and still occasionally has its original meaning, especially when its complement is a person, *auprès de quelqu'un* 'near someone', but more usually it expresses closeness in less literal senses, in which case it is translated by various prepositions in English, e.g.:

> *Il était ambassadeur auprès du Saint-Siège*
> He was ambassador to the Holy See

> *Il était bien auprès du ministre*
> He was in good standing with the minister

> *faire des démarches auprès de quelqu'un*
> to take a matter up with someone

663   *avant, devant*, primary meaning 'before, in front of'

(i) *avant* refers to time, e.g.:

> *Il va partir avant la fin du mois*
> He will be leaving before the end of the month

> *Je suis arrivé avant mon frère*
> I arrived before my brother

and is also used to express preference, e.g.:

> *Je choisirais cela avant tout*
> I should choose that before (in preference to) anything else

Note also the complex preposition *en avant de* which, contrary to the simple preposition *avant*, is used with reference to place in the sense of 'ahead of', e.g.:

> *marcher en avant du défilé*
> to walk ahead of the procession

(ii) *devant* refers to place, position, e.g.:

> *Vous verrez la statue devant la gare*
> You will see the statue in front of the station

> *Il fut amené devant le juge*
> He was brought before the judge

and is also used in a number of figurative senses, e.g.:

> *Tous sont égaux devant la loi*
> All are equal before (in the eyes of) the law

> *Je ne reculerai pas devant mes responsabilités*
> I shall not back away from my responsibilities

(further examples may be found in any good dictionary).

Note also the complex preposition *au-devant de* which occurs with verbs of motion used either literally or figuratively in such contexts as the following:

> *Il courut au-devant de son père*
> He ran to meet his father
>
> *Il va toujours au-devant du danger*
> He always goes to meet danger
>
> *aller au-devant des désirs de quelqu'un*
> to anticipate someone's wishes

664   *avec*, primary meaning 'with'

Used in most of the senses of English 'with', but see throughout this section the use of other prepositions where English uses 'with'.

665   *chez*, primary meaning 'at the house (or shop) of'

> *Il est chez lui*
> He is at his house, at home
>
> *Il sort de chez lui*
> He is coming out of his house
>
> *Je l'ai vu chez Jean*
> I saw him at John's
>
> *chez le boulanger*
> at the baker's

Also used in sense of

with	*C'est une habitude chez moi*	It's a habit with me (or 'of mine')
among	*Ça se fait chez les Anglais*	This is done among the English
in (the works of)	*l'emploi du subjonctif chez Racine*	the use of the subjunctive in Racine

and note too *chez nous* 'in our country', etc.

666   *contre*, primary meaning 'against'

Also used in sense of

with	*se fâcher contre quelqu'un*	to get angry with someone
from	*Il s'abrita contre le vent*	He took shelter from the wind

for	*la haine qu'elle éprouvait contre son gendre*	her hatred for her son-in-law
	échanger x contre y	to exchange x for y
to	*six voix contre cinq*	six votes to five

667 *de*, primary meanings 'of, from'

(i) One important construction involving the use of *de*, and one that must be carefully noted since it does not correspond at all to English usage, is the compulsory insertion of *de* when such indefinite pronouns as *quelqu'un* 'someone', *personne* 'nobody', *quelque chose* 'something', *rien* 'nothing', *aucun, pas un* 'not one', are followed by an adjective or past participle, e.g.:

Quelqu'un d'important demande à vous parler
Somebody important is asking to speak to you

Je ne connais personne de plus charmant
I don't know anyone more charming

Il y a quelque chose de louche dans cette affaire
There's something suspicious about this business

Rien de grave!
Nothing serious!

Je n'ai jamais rien vu de pareil
I've never seen anything like it

Parmi tous ces hommes il n'y en avait aucun (or *pas un*) *de capable*
Among all these men there wasn't one who was efficient

Note in particular *personne d'autre, rien d'autre, quoi d'autre?* 'nobody else, nothing else, what else?'

(ii) The same rule applies after such expressions as *ce qu'il y a* 'what (= that which)', *quoi?* 'what?', *qu'est-ce qu'il y a?* 'what?', *il n'y a . . . que . . .* 'there is nothing . . . but', e.g.:

Ce qu'il y a d'intéressant c'est que . . .
What's interesting is that . . .

Quoi de neuf?
What news?

Qu'est-ce qu'il y a ⎫
Quoi ⎭ *de plus beau que . . .?*
What is more beautiful than . . .?

Il n'y a d'important que la vérité
There is nothing important but truth

Note that in both of these types the adjective remains invariable (contrast iii below).

(iii) The same construction can also occur (a) after a noun introduced by an indefinite article, in which case the preposition serves to detach the adjective from the noun in much the same way as a relative clause, e.g.:

si vous avez une journée libre
if you have a free day

but

si vous avez une journée de libre
if you have a day (which is) free

and (b), with a similar value, after a numeral or some other expression of quantity such as *plusieurs* 'several', *la moitié* 'half', *encore un* 'another one', *beaucoup* 'a lot', *combien?* 'how many?', e.g.:

Sur ces quatre verres, il y en a trois de sales
Of these four glasses, there are three dirty

Il y a déjà la moitié de mes crayons de perdus
There are already half my pencils lost

Encore une journée de perdue!
Another day wasted!

Il y aura beaucoup de soldats de tués
There will be a lot of soldiers killed

Note that in type (iii) the adjective or participle agrees in gender and number with the noun or pronoun to which it refers (contrast i and ii above).

Another idiomatic use of *de* is found in French (where English also often has 'of') between two nouns, the first of which qualifies the second, e.g.:

un vrai fripon d'enfant
a regular rascal of a boy

un pauvre diable de mendiant
a poor devil of a beggar

un imbécile de douanier
a fool of a customs officer

une chienne de vie
a rotten life

un amour de petit chien
a cute little dog

Note:

(a) that, in this construction, *diable* is often treated as feminine with a following feminine noun, e.g. *une diable d'affaire* 'a wretched business', *une diable d'idée* 'a weird idea'

(b) the use of *un* or *une drôle de* meaning 'strange, odd', e.g. *un drôle de type* 'a strange fellow', *une drôle d'idée* 'an odd idea'; note too *la drôle de guerre* 'the phoney war' (i.e. the first few months of World War II when nothing much seemed to be happening).

Notice that all the above constructions express some kind of value judgement (in most – but not all – cases unfavourable).

(iv) The following is a selection of the many idioms using *de* where the English equivalents have one or other of a wide range of other prepositions:

(1) for	*le respect de la vérité*	respect for truth
	de longue date	for a long time (past)
(2) with	*de tout mon cœur*	with all my heart
	rouge de colère (see also **526**, **687**)	purple with rage
(3) in	*d'un ton sec*	in a dry voice
	(cf. *le ton dont il parlait*, the tone in which he spoke)	
	de cette façon	in this way
	augmenter (baisser) de prix (see also **171**)	to go up (or down) in price
	jamais de la vie	never in my life

Also with words denoting physical or mental qualities or defects, e.g.:

sain de corps et d'esprit	sound in body and mind
aveugle de chaque œil et boiteux d'un pied	blind in both eyes and lame in one foot

(4) by	*de naissance*	by birth
	de vue	by sight
	de nature	by nature
	de nom	by name

Also of time:

		Il est parti de nuit (see also under *par* and 171)	He left by night
(5) on	*de tous côtés*		on all sides
	de garde		on duty

For discussion elsewhere in this volume of other uses of *de* the index should be consulted.

668 *depuis*, primary meaning 'since'

In French, *depuis* is used to indicate not only 'time since when', e.g.:

Il est absent depuis mardi
He has been away since Tuesday

but also 'period since the beginning of which', where English uses 'for', e.g.:

Il est absent depuis un an
He has been absent for a year

(For the tense, see **413,iv**. For *depuis lors* see **619**.)

Depuis is also used in the sense of 'from' of time or place, e.g.:

depuis le matin jusqu'au soir
from morning till evening

La France s'étend depuis les Alpes jusqu'à l'Océan
France stretches from the Alps to the Ocean

669 *derrière, en derrière de, par arrière*, primary meaning 'behind'

Derrière is used only in a literal sense, e.g.:

Il se cacha derrière la porte
He hid behind the door

'Behind' in a figurative sense ('behindhand with') is *en arrière de* (which may also be used in a literal sense), e.g.:

Il est en arrière des autres élèves
He is behind the other pupils (i.e. in his school work)

Par derrière implies movement, e.g.:

Il est passé par derrière la maison
He went round the back of the house

670 *dès*, primary meaning 'from the time of, right from'
Examples:

dès sa première enfance	from his earliest infancy
dès le début	right from the beginning

Dès is also used with expressions of place when these denote a point in time, e.g.:

Dès Orange le train augmente de vitesse
From (the moment of leaving) Orange the train's speed increases

(For *dès lors* see **619**.)

671 *dessus, au-dessus de, par-dessus*, primary meanings 'above, over'
Dessus, which survives as an adverb, is no longer in normal use as a preposition, its place having been taken in most contexts by *au-dessus de*, whether the meaning is literal or figurative, e.g.:

Son portrait pend au-dessus de la cheminée
His portrait hangs over the mantelpiece

Il est au-dessus de moi (dans la hiérarchie)
He is above me (in the hierarchy)

les enfants âgés au-dessus de dix ans
children aged over ten

être au-dessus de la flatterie
to be above flattery

au-dessus de la moyenne
above average

The English equivalent is sometimes 'beyond', e.g.:

être au-dessus de tout éloge
to be beyond praise

Cette tâche est au-dessus de ses capacités
This task is beyond his capabilities

Par-dessus is used when there is an implication of motion from one side of something to the other and in a variety of idiomatic expressions, e.g.:

Il sauta par-dessus la haie
He jumped over the hedge

Il a jeté la balle par-dessus le mur
He has thrown the ball over the wall

lire par-dessus l'épaule de quelqu'un
to read over someone's shoulder

Il porte un manteau lourd par-dessus son pull
He wears a heavy coat over his pullover

par-dessus le marché
into the bargain

672 du côté de

Du côté de means 'in the area of', 'in the direction of' and 'from the direction of', e.g.:

Il habite du côté de la place de la République
He lives somewhere near the Place de la République

La voiture filait à toute vitesse du côté de Vendôme
The car was speeding in the direction of Vendôme

Le vent vient du côté de la mer
The wind is coming from (the direction of) the sea

(This complex preposition represents a specialized use of the adverbial expression *du côté* + adjective 'on, to the . . . side', as in *de l'autre côté de la rue* 'on, to the other side of the street', *du côté sud de la place* 'on the south side of the square'.)

673 entre, parmi

The primary meaning of *entre* is 'between' and that of *parmi* is 'among', e.g.:

Son bureau est situé entre la mairie et la gare
His office is between the town hall and the station

Essayez d'arriver entre midi et quatorze heures
Try and arrive between twelve and two

Parmi les invités il y avait plusieurs Américains
Among the guests there were several Americans

Il se cachait parmi les buissons
He was hiding among the bushes

While *parmi* is not used as the equivalent of 'between', *entre* is sometimes used instead of *parmi* (as 'between' is instead of 'among'), especially with verbs denoting selection or distinction, e.g.:

> *Il nous faut choisir entre plusieurs possibilités*
> We have to choose between (among) several possibilities

> *Moi je ne fais pas de distinction entre mes enfants*
> I make no distinction between (among) my children

> *Le ciel vous prépare une place entre les immortels*
> Heaven is preparing a place for you among the immortals

674   *d'entre*

In addition to meaning 'from between', *d'entre* is used instead of *de* to link a numeral or an indefinite or interrogative pronoun to a following personal pronoun, e.g.:

> *deux d'entre nous*
> two of us

> *certains d'entre vous*
> some of you

> *plusieurs d'entre eux*
> several of them

> *la plupart d'entre nous*
> the majority of us

> *Personne d'entre vous ne sait rien*
> None of you know(s) anything

> *Lequel d'entre eux a dit ça?*
> Which of them said that?

However, *de* + a disjunctive pronoun is possible as an alternative to *d'entre* after *chacun* 'each', *l'un* 'one', *pas un* 'not one', *aucun* 'not one', *qui?* 'who?', and occasionally *la plupart* 'most', e.g.:

> *chacun d'eux* (or *d'entre eux*)
> each of them

> *l'un de nous* (or *d'entre nous*)
> one of us

> *qui de vous?* (or *d'entre vous?*)
> who among you?

Note that *de* (not *d'entre*) must be used when the pronoun is qualified, e.g. *Personne de nous trois n'est coupable* 'None of us three is guilty'.

675 *envers* (see also **687**,c), *vers*, primary meanings 'towards, to'

Envers denotes conduct or attitude towards people. *Vers* refers to physical motion towards; with expressions of time it means 'about'.

Examples:

> *sa générosité envers sa famille*
> his generosity to (towards) his family

> *Il courut vers moi*
> He ran towards me

> *Il leva les yeux vers le ciel*
> He raised his eyes to (towards) heaven

> *vers trois heures*
> about three o'clock

676 *hormis, sauf, excepté*, primary meaning 'except'
Hormis is archaic; *sauf* and *excepté* are used just like English 'except':

> *Tout le monde est arrivé, sauf ma sœur*
> Everybody has come except my sister

> *Ils sont tous partis, excepté les trois Allemands*
> They have all left, except the three Germans

Note, however, that *excepté*, which was originally a past participle, occasionally follows the noun to which it refers, and then it agrees with it in gender and number, e.g. *Elles sont toutes mariées, la fille aînée exceptée* 'They are all married, the eldest daughter excepted (apart from the eldest daughter)' (see also **134**).

677 *hors, hors de, en dehors de, fors*, primary meanings 'out of, outside'
In this literal sense *hors* is chiefly confined to fixed phrases, e.g.:

> *hors commerce*
> not on general sale

> *hors jeu*
> offside

hors ligne
incomparable, outstanding

mettre hors la loi
to outlaw

It is also, though rarely, used in the sense of 'except'.

Hors de and *en dehors de* are both used literally of place, e.g.:

Ils se trouvèrent hors de la ville, or *en dehors de la ville*
They found themselves out of the town, *or* outside the town

Hors de can also be used metaphorically, e.g.:

Il est hors de danger
He is out of danger

hors d'haleine
out of breath

hors de combat
disabled, out of action

Fors is an old form of *hors*, meaning 'except', and has now gone almost totally out of use except in the saying *Tout est perdu fors l'honneur* 'All is lost save honour'.

678 *malgré*, primary meanings 'in spite of, notwithstanding', e.g.:

Malgré sa colère il ne dit rien
In spite of his fury he said nothing

malgré tout
in spite of everything

malgré moi
in spite of myself, against my better judgement

679 *outre, en outre de*

Outre, whose primary meaning is 'beyond', is little used with that meaning as a preposition (it is also an adverb) except in such compounds as:

outre-Manche, across the Channel (i.e. in Britain)
outre-mer, overseas
outre-Atlantique, across the Atlantic

outre-Rhin, beyond the Rhine
outre-tombe, beyond the grave

and in a small number of fixed expressions, in particular *outre mesure* 'excessively' (*lit.* 'beyond measure').

It also has the secondary meaning 'in addition to, besides', e.g.:

outre cela
in addition to that

outre le fait que
besides the fact that

Outre ses névralgies, elle souffrait de maux de cœur fréquents (Boylesve)
In addition to her neuralgia, she suffered from frequent heart disorders

En outre de has the same meaning as *en plus de*, i.e. 'in addition to', e.g. *en outre de son épouse légitime* (Montherlant) 'in addition to his lawful wife'.

680 *par*, primary meanings 'by, through'

(a) 'by'

Par is the equivalent of 'by' expressing the agent or instrument of a passive verb, e.g.:

Le radium fut découvert par Pierre et Marie Curie
Radium was discovered by Pierre and Marie Curie

Il fut tué par les soldats (or *par une balle*)
He was killed by the soldiers (*or* by a bullet)

La ville sera entourée par les insurgés
The town will be surrounded by the rebels

Note, however, that when the agent's role is a fairly inactive one, as is often the case with verbs of the emotions and sometimes with verbs such as *entourer*, *environner* 'to surround', *accabler* 'to overwhelm', *inonder* 'to flood', when they express a state rather than an action, *de* is frequently used rather than *par*, e.g.:

Mazarin était fort détesté des Parisiens (A. France)
Mazarin was greatly hated by the Parisians

Il est aimé de tout le monde
He is loved by everybody

une ville entourée de remparts
a town surrounded by ramparts

Elle est toujours entourée d'admirateurs
She is always surrounded by admirers

Je suis inondé de travail
I am swamped by work

Par also corresponds to 'by' in a variety of other contexts, e.g.:

deux par deux	two by two
par avion	by air, by airmail
par centaines	by the hundred
par cœur	by heart
par hasard	by chance
par la poste	by post
par tous les moyens	by every possible means
(saisir quelqu'un) par le bras	(to grab someone) by the arm
(payer) par chèque	(to pay) by cheque
(voyager) par le train	(to travel) by train

(b) 'through', e.g.:

passer par la Belgique	to pass through Belgium
par le trou de la serrure	through the keyhole

(c) In other expressions, *par* corresponds to one or other of a wide range of English prepositions (for further examples, consult a good dictionary), e.g.:

par avance	in advance
par contre	on the other hand
par écrit	in writing
par exemple	for example
par habitude	out of habit
par moments	at times
par pitié	out of pity
par temps de pluie	in rainy weather
(être couché) par terre	(to be lying) on the ground
(tomber) par terre	(to fall) to the ground

(d) Note also such idiomatic constructions and expressions as:

deux fois par jour	twice a day

cent francs par personne	a hundred francs a head (per person)
par ailleurs	otherwise, in other respects, moreover
par conséquent	consequently
par ici	this way, hereabouts

681 *pour*, primary meaning 'for'

The use of *pour* often corresponds to that of 'for', e.g.:

Je l'ai acheté pour mon frère
I bought it for my brother

Il part pour Paris
He is leaving for Paris

Je pars pour trois semaines
I am leaving for three weeks

With reference to time, however, it is used only when there is an idea of intent, as in the last example. For 'for' expressing duration, see **708** and **711,iii**.
Pour is also used in percentages, e.g. *dix pour cent* 'ten per cent'.
For 'for' with expressions of price, see **712**.

682 *sans*, primary meaning 'without'

Examples:

Ils sont partis sans moi	They left without me
sans difficulté	without difficulty
sans répondre	without answering
Cela va sans dire	That goes without saying

Other English equivalents are 'but for' or a negative element such as 'un-' or '-less(ly)', e.g.:

Sans vous, j'aurais pu être tué	But for you I could have been killed
C'est sans espoir	It's hopeless
une robe sans manches	a sleeveless dress
sans cesse	ceaselessly
sans y avoir été invité	uninvited, without being asked

un repas à 200F sans le vin	a meal at 200F not including wine

683 *selon*, primary meaning 'according to'
Examples:

Selon lui nous partons demain	According to him we leave tomorrow
l'évangile selon saint Luc	the Gospel according to St Luke
à chacun selon ses besoins	to each according to his needs
agir selon les règles	to act according to the rules

684 *sous, au-dessous de, par-dessous*, primary meanings 'under(neath), beneath, below'
These prepositions are not, generally speaking, interchangeable. The distinction is basically as follows:

(a) *sous* means 'under (literally or figuratively)', e.g.:

sous la table	under the table
être sous l'influence de quelqu'un	to be under someone's influence

Note also such expressions as the following in which prepositions other than 'under' are used in English:

sous mes yeux	before my (very) eyes
sous presse	in the press
sous tous les rapports	in every respect
passer sous silence	to pass over in silence
sous forme de cachets	in tablet form
sous la forme d'une sorcière	in the shape (guise) of a witch
sous peine de mort	on pain of death
sous serment	on oath
sous (le) prétexte que	on the pretext that

(b) *au-dessous de* means 'beneath, below, lower than (literally or figuratively)', e.g.:

au-dessous du genou	below the knee
Le thermomètre est au-dessous de zéro	The thermometer is below zero

Cette tâche est au-dessous de   That task is beneath him
  lui

or 'under' in such contexts as *les enfants au-dessous de dix ans*
'children under ten'.

(c) *par-dessous* usually implies motion, e.g.:

ramper par-dessous la haie   to crawl under the hedge

685 *sur*, primary meanings 'on, on to, over'

(a) 'on, on to'

Examples:

Tes livres sont sur la table
Your books are on the table

Il monta sur la table
He got up on to the table

sur votre gauche
on your left

Je n'ai pas mon passeport sur moi
I haven't got my passport on me (with me)

(b) 'over'

Examples:

La ville s'étend sur vingt kilomètres
The town extends over twenty kilometres

On va construire un pont sur la rivière
They are going to build a bridge over the river

Je n'ai aucune influence sur lui
I have no influence over him

sur une période de dix jours
over a period of ten days

(c) Two frequent uses of *sur* are as the equivalent of 'by' in
measurements and of 'out of' with reference to a fraction, e.g.:

Cette pièce mesure cinq mètres sur dix
This room measures five metres by ten

treize sur vingt
thirteen out of twenty

deux mariages sur trois
two out of every three marriages

(d) *sur* frequently corresponds to some other preposition in English, e.g.:

un livre sur Paris	a book about Paris
tirer sur quelqu'un	to shoot at someone
sur invitation	by invitation
La clef est sur la porte	The key is in the door
parler sur un ton dédaigneux	to speak in a scornful tone
prendre un livre sur la table	to take a book (from) off the table

Prepositions used with adjectives or past participles

686 Prepositions frequently link an adjective or past participle to a following noun (or pronoun). There are, however, considerable discrepancies both within the same language (e.g. English 'full *of*' but 'covered *in* or *with*') and between languages (e.g. English 'greedy, hungry, avid *for*' but French 'avide *de*' – see **687**). (Note that with a following verb a different preposition may be required, e.g. English 'ready *for* action' but 'ready *to* go'; on this, see **688**.)

687 (a) In this section we list some of the commoner adjectives and past participles and the prepositions used to link them to a following noun or pronoun; for *de* meaning 'by' with certain past participles, see b below; for *envers* 'to(wards)', see c below; for other adjectives and participles, a good dictionary should be consulted:

agile de	nimble with
avide de	greedy, hungry, avid for
bon à	good for (see below)
bon pour	good to, for (see below)
certain de	certain, sure of
confus de	embarrassed at, by
content de	pleased with, at
couvert de	covered in, with
différent de	different from, to

expert en	expert in, at
fort à or *en* (see below)	good at
fou de	mad with
furieux contre	angry with, at
heureux de	happy at, with, about
inquiet de	worried about, at
ivre de	drunk, intoxicated with
lourd de	heavy with
mécontent de	discontented with
orné de	decorated with
plein de	full of
prêt à or *pour*	ready for
propre à	suitable for
ravi de	delighted with, at, about
reconnaissant de	grateful for
responsable de	responsible for
satisfait de	satisfied with
semblable à	similar to
soigneux de	careful with, about
sûr de	sure of
trempé de	soaked in
voisin de	adjacent to, bordering on

Examples:

Il est très agile de ses doigts
He is very nimble with his fingers (nimble-fingered)

avide de pouvoir
hungry, greedy for power

Cette machine n'est bonne à rien
This machine is good for nothing (no good for anything)

C'est bon pour la santé
It's good for your health

Il a toujours été très bon pour moi
He has always been very good to me

Il est fort au tennis, aux échecs
He is good at tennis, at chess (*à* with reference to games, etc.)

Il est fort en anglais
He is good at English (*en* with reference to academic subjects)

fou de colère
mad with rage

une atmosphère lourde de menaces
an atmosphere heavy with threats

Je vous suis très reconnaissant de votre aide
I am very grateful for your help

Qui est responsable de cette décision?
Who is responsible for this decision?

trempé de sueur
soaked in sweat

(b) Note the use of *de* as the equivalent of 'with' or 'by' with a number of past participles used as adjectives (cf. **526**), e.g.:

une femme admirée et adorée de tout le monde
a woman admired and loved by everyone

des nuages chargés de neige
clouds laden with snow

une maison entourée d'arbres
a house surrounded by trees

une voiture suivie d'un bus
a car followed by a bus

and likewise *aimé de* 'loved by', *enchanté de* 'enchanted by', *encombré de* 'laden, encumbered with', *précédé de* 'preceded by', and many others.

(c) With adjectives or past participles indicating attitude or conduct towards people, 'to, towards' is rendered by *envers* if the emphasis is on the person's attitude (see also **675**), e.g.:

Il a toujours été doux (dur) envers ses enfants
He has always been gentle (harsh) towards his children

Je suis bien disposé envers les Américains
I am well disposed towards Americans

though *pour* may be used if the focus is on the person's actual behaviour, e.g.:

Il a toujours été très gentil pour sa mère
He has always been very kind to his mother

Other adjectives falling into this category include *aimable* 'kind, amiable', *cruel* 'cruel', *généreux* 'generous', *indulgent* 'indulgent', *injuste* 'unjust, unfair', *juste* 'just, fair', *rigoureux* 'harsh, strict', *sévère* 'harsh, severe'. Others that normally take only *envers* include *bon* 'good' (see also a above), *grossier* 'rude', *impoli* 'impolite, rude', *insolent* 'insolent, impertinent', *poli* 'polite', *respectueux* 'respectful'.

688   An adjective or past participle is linked to a following infinitive either by *à* or by *de*:

(i) Adjectives taking *à* include *apte* 'fit, suitable', *bon* 'good', *habile* 'clever, skilful', *hardi* 'bold', *prêt* 'ready', and *propre* 'fit, suitable', e.g.:

> *Cela n'est pas bon à manger*
> That is not good to eat
>
> *Il est très habile à donner une impression de sincérité*
> He is very clever at giving an impression of sincerity
>
> *Je suis prêt à partir*
> I am ready to leave
>
> *une personne propre à occuper une position de responsabilité*
> a fit person to occupy a position of responsibility

(ii) Adjectives and participles taking *de* include *certain* 'certain, sure', *confus* 'embarrassed', *content* 'glad, pleased', *libre* 'free', *ravi* 'delighted', *reconnaissant* 'grateful', *soucieux* 'anxious', *sûr* 'sure', *surpris* 'surprised', *triste* 'sad', e.g.:

> *Je suis content de vous voir*
> I am glad to see you
>
> *Vous êtes libre d'essayer*
> You are free to try
>
> *Je vous suis reconnaissant d'être venu*
> I am grateful to you for coming

Conjunctions

Introduction

689   Conjunctions, as the term suggests, serve as linking or 'conjoining' elements. They fall into two categories, (i) coordinating conjunctions and (ii) subordinating conjunctions – though the

distinction is not as absolute as some grammars suggest, and *car* 'for' (see **690**,iii) seems to occupy an intermediate position on the border between the two categories.

690   Coordinating conjunctions

(i) Coordinating conjunctions like *et* 'and' join together two elements of similar status, which may be either two (or more) clauses (e.g. *Il est parti hier* et *il revient demain* 'He left yesterday *and* he is coming back tomorrow') or constituent elements of a clause such as verbs (*Il mangeait* et *buvait trop* 'He ate *and* drank too much'), nouns (*les chats* et *les chiens* 'the cats *and* the dogs'), adjectives and/or adjectival expressions (*noir* et *blanc* 'black *and* white'), adverbs and/or adverbial expressions (*Elle m'écrit souvent* et *dans les moindres détails* 'She writes to me often *and* in great detail'), etc.

(ii) The universally recognized French coordinating conjunctions are:

(a) *et* 'and', *ou* 'or', *ni* 'nor', which, when repeated, are also the equivalents of 'both . . . and', 'either . . . or', 'neither . . . nor', respectively, e.g.:

Je les ai vus et à Paris et à Londres
I saw them both in Paris and in London

Il est ou malade ou fatigué
He is either tired or ill

Il ne comprend ni l'anglais ni le français
He understands neither English nor French

Note, however, that French has at its disposal a number of alternative constructions to the repetition of *et*, e.g.:

Il craignait en même temps qu'il désirait de parler
He both feared and wished to speak

C'était un enfant à la fois sage et espiègle
He was a child both well-behaved and mischievous

(On the syntax of *ni*, see **571**.)

(b) *mais* 'but' which, like its English equivalent, introduces either a clause, e.g.:

Mais je vous l'ai déjà dit
But I've already told you

Il est malade mais il veut venir quand même
He's ill but he still wants to come

or the second of two other elements of similar status, e.g.:

Ce livre est difficile mais très intéressant
This book is difficult but very interesting

Je l'ai connu non à Londres mais à Paris
I met him not in London but in Paris

(iii) *Car* 'for' is usually classified as a coordinating conjunction, though its usage is much more restricted than that of *et, ou, ni* and *mais* since, normally (but see note b below), it can serve only to introduce a clause, e.g.:

Il était très fatigué, car il travaillait depuis l'aube
He was very tired, for he had been working since dawn

Note:

(a) that *car*, like 'for', introduces the second of two clauses (as in the example above) and cannot introduce the first clause, whereas subordinating conjunctions can, e.g. *Puisqu'il travaillait depuis l'aube, il était très fatigué* 'Since he had been working since dawn, he was very tired' – *car* or 'for' cannot be substituted for *puisque* or 'since' in such circumstances: this is the main justification for considering *car* and 'for' as coordinating rather than subordinating conjunctions;

(b) that, by analogy with the use of *parce que* 'because' in such contexts as *Le puritanisme est faux (parce que contraire à la nature humaine)* (Maurois) 'Puritanism is false (because [it is] contrary to human nature)', *car* is occasionally found introducing an adjective, but this should not be imitated.

(iv) *Or* 'now' is sometimes considered to be a coordinating conjunction but in this grammar is treated as an adverb (see **620**).

691   Subordinating conjunctions
The subordinating conjunctions are:

  (i) *comme* 'as' (see **613**)
      si 'if' (see **414**,iii; **415**; **418–422**)
      quand 'when' (see **315**,iv; **414**,iii; **422**)
      que 'that' (see **692**; **699–704**) and 'as, than' (see **157**; **166**)

and (ii) a considerable number of compounds of *que*, a few of which are written as one word (*lorsque* 'when', *puisque* 'since', *quoique* 'although') though most are written as two or more words (e.g. *bien que* 'although', *jusqu'à ce que* 'until') (see 694–698).

692   In this grammar, *comme, si, quand* and *que* are considered as 'simple conjunctions' while compounds of *que* (including those that are written as one word, see 691,ii) are termed 'compound conjunctions'. (Note that some grammars consider *lorsque* etc. as simple conjunctions, while some French grammars use the term *locutions conjonctives* for conjunctions consisting of more than one word.)

Compound conjunctions not requiring the subjunctive

693   The following conjunctions take the indicative or the conditional, not the subjunctive. In the case of those listed in 694, *que* is comparative and means 'as'. In the case of those listed in 695, *que* is not comparative and so is not translated as 'as' (except in the one case of *dès que* which, though not itself based on comparative *que*, corresponds to an English expression based on comparative 'as', viz. 'as soon as').

For the use of the future tense after temporal conjunctions such as *aussitôt que, tant que, après que, lorsque, pendant que*, etc., see 414,iii.

In some contexts, other English equivalents than those given here may be appropriate; for the full range of meanings of each French conjunction a good dictionary should be consulted.

694

> *ainsi que*, (just) as
> *(au fur et) à mesure que*, (in proportion) as
> *aussi . . . que*, as . . . as
> *aussitôt que*, as soon as
> *autant que*, as much as, as far as (but see 490)
> *de même que*, just as
> *selon que*, according to whether
> *si . . . que*, as . . . as (after negatives only – see 157)
> *sitôt que*, as soon as

suivant que, according to whether
tant que, as long as, while (see **696**)

695

alors que, whereas
après que, after
attendu que, seeing that, since
depuis que, since (the time when)
dès que, as soon as
étant donné que, since, given that
excepté que, except that
lorsque, when
outre que, besides the fact that
parce que, because
pendant que, while (see **696**)
puisque, since
sinon que, except that
tandis que, while, whereas (see **696**)
vu que, seeing that, since

696 *péndant que, tant que, tandis que*
Pendant que 'while' and *tant que* '(for) as long as' are both temporal conjunctions, but whereas *pendant que* merely indicates an action during the course of which something else happens, *tant que* refers to an action throughout the whole time of which something else happens, e.g.:

Pendant que j'étais en Espagne j'ai visité l'Escurial
While I was in Spain I went to see the Escorial

Tant que j'étais chez eux, il a fait affreusement chaud
While (i.e. all the time) I was with them it was terribly hot

Tandis que 'while' originally had the same value as *pendant que* and sometimes still does in literary usage, but its normal value nowadays is that of 'whereas', i.e. it implies a contrast, e.g.:

Son père a peiné jusqu'à la mort, tandis que lui n'a jamais rien fait
His father laboured to the end of his life, while he has never done anything

Compound conjunctions requiring the subjunctive

697   The following conjunctions take the subjunctive:

afin que (see **489**), in order that
en attendant que (see **488**), until
avant que (see **488** and **566**), before
bien que (see **487**), although
de crainte que . . . ne (see **491**, **564**), for fear, lest
encore que (see **487**), although
jusqu'à ce que (see **488**), until
(bien) loin que (see **491**), far from . . . -ing
malgré que (see **698**), despite the fact that, although
à moins que (see **490**), unless
non que, non pas que (see **491**), not that
de peur que . . . ne (see **491**, **564**), for fear, lest
pour peu que (see **490**), if only
pour que (see **489**), so that, in order that
pourvu que (see **490**), provided that
quoique (see **487**), although
sans que (see **491**), *que . . . ne* (see **561,h**), without . . .
   -ing
soit que . . . soit que (see **480,iii,c**), whether . . . or
à supposer que, supposé que (see **490**), supposing that

698   *malgré que*

Although frowned on by some grammarians, *malgré que* is widely used in speech, and increasingly in literary usage too, with the meaning 'although', e.g. *malgré qu'il ait obtenu tous les prix de sa classe* (Mauriac) 'although he won all the prizes in his class'.

Que as a subordinating conjunction

699   In subject or object clauses

Except in indirect questions introduced by *si* (see **594**), if the subject or object of a verb is itself a clause then that clause is introduced by *que*, e.g.:

(i) The *que*-clause is the subject:

Qu'il soit mécontent est certain
That he is displeased is certain

This also applies when the grammatical subject is a 'dummy' subject, *il*, and the logical subject, represented by the *que*-clause, follows:

Il est évident qu'il a tort
It is obvious that he is wrong (= 'That he is wrong is obvious')

(ii) The *que*-clause is the object:

Il dit qu'il y a eu un accident
He says there has been an accident

Je crains que ce ne soit trop tard
I fear it may be too late

Je veux qu'il s'en aille
I want him to go away

(See also **480**,ii.)

700   In alternative conditional clauses

In alternative conditional clauses introduced in English by 'whether . . . or', each clause is introduced in French by *que*, e.g.:

Qu'il pleuve ou qu'il fasse beau, je vais sortir
Whether it's raining or whether it's fine, I shall go out

Qu'il soit d'accord ou non, moi je reste ici
Whether he agrees or not, I am staying here

(See also **480**,iii,d.)

701   *Que* in conditional constructions

Note the following construction (on which see also **422**) in which the French main clause is the equivalent of an English subordinate clause introduced by 'even if' and the French subordinate clause introduced by *que* and having its verb in the conditional tense is the equivalent of the English main clause:

Et je vous promettrais mille fois le contraire,
Que je ne serais pas en pouvoir de le faire (Molière)

And even if I were to promise you the contrary a thousand times, I should not be able to do it

702   *Que* as the equivalent of other conjunctions

When two or more subordinate clauses in English are introduced by the same conjunction, the conjunction is frequently not repeated, e.g. 'Because it was raining and he had to go out [= and because he had to go out']. In French, on the other hand, each subordinate clause must be introduced by a conjunction unless (a) they have the same subject and it is not repeated and (b) the verbs are in the same tense, e.g. *lorsqu'il est entré et a vu son frère* 'when he came in and saw his brother', *puisqu'il était fatigué et ne savait pas où chercher un hôtel* 'since he was tired and didn't know where to look for a hotel'. The second clause is normally introduced not by a repetition of the same conjunction but by *que*. This applies both to simple and to compound conjunctions, e.g.:

(i) Simple conjunctions

> *Comme c'était le dimanche matin et qu'on ne se lèverait que pour la grand'messe . . .* (Proust)
> As it was Sunday morning and we should only be getting up in time for high mass

> *Quand la leçon fut finie, et que les autres élèves se furent dispersés, Louis s'approcha* (Romains)
> When the lesson was over and the other pupils had gone, Louis came up

> *Si je vais en Égypte et que j'y sois tué . . .* (Stendhal)
> If I go to Egypt and (if) I am killed there . . .

Note that, whereas *si* is followed by the indicative, *que* standing in for *si* is usually followed in literary French by the subjunctive (see the last example). The indicative is possible, however, and is usual in conversational French, e.g.:

> *Si c'est vrai et que Vous êtes venu pour servir . . .* (Claudel)
> If it is true and if You have come to serve . . .

> *Si quelque chose vous retient et que vous avez le temps, envoyez-moi un petit mot*
> If something delays you and (if) you have time, drop me a line

Note, too, that when *si* is the equivalent of 'whether' in indirect questions it cannot be replaced by *que*, e.g.:

> *Il m'a demandé si j'allais à Londres et si j'avais mon billet*
> He asked me if I was going to London and if I had my ticket

(ii) Compound conjunctions

> *Puisqu'il pleuvait et qu'il était fatigué, il alla se coucher*
> Since it was raining and he was tired, he went to bed

> *Lorsqu'il est entré et qu'il m'a souri, je me suis rendu compte que tout allait bien*
> When he came in and smiled at me, I realized that all was well

> *Il va vous écrire afin que (pour que) tout soit clair et que vous compreniez ce qu'il veut faire*
> He is going to write to you so that everything shall be clear and so that you shall understand what he wants to do

> *Bien qu'il soit arrivé très tôt et que sa fille l'ait reconnu, ils ne se sont rien dit*
> Although he arrived very early and his daughter recognized him, they did not say anything to each other

> *Il faut tout préparer avant que ton frère arrive et que ta mère le voie*
> We must get everything ready before your brother arrives and your mother sees him

Note that *que* standing in for a compound conjunction takes the same mood (indicative or subjunctive) as the conjunction in question (see examples above).

703 Note that, in certain circumstances, *que* may have the value of one or other of a number of compound conjunctions even when no repetition is involved. In particular:

(i) After an imperative (and occasionally elsewhere), it can express purpose (i.e. it serves as the equivalent of *pour que* or *afin que*), e.g.:

> *Mettez-vous là que je vous voie mieux*
> Stand there so that I can see you better

(ii) It occasionally expresses consequence, e.g.:

Il tousse qu'il en secoue toute la maison (Flaubert)
He coughs [so loudly] that he makes the whole house shake

(iii) Particularly after questions (and occasionally elsewhere), it has a vaguely causal value (in which case it is more or less the equivalent of *puisque*), e.g.:

Est-ce que vous avez des amis de ce côté-là, que vous connais-sez si bien Balbec? (Proust)
Do you have friends thereabouts, since you know Balbec so well?

(iv) After a negative clause it can serve as the equivalent of *sans que* 'without' (see 491) (in which case the verb in the clause it introduces takes *ne*), e.g.:

Il ne se passait pas de semaine qu'il ne fût terrassé par une migraine atroce
Not a week passed without his being laid low by a fearful migraine

(v) In certain circumstances, particularly (but not exclusively) after *déjà* 'already' or after a negative, it has a temporal value, often expressing total or partial simultaneity between two events, e.g.:

J'étais déjà dans la rue qu'il cherchait toujours ses clefs
I was already in the street while he was still looking for his keys

Elle n'était pas là depuis cinq minutes, qu'il sortit (Zola)
She hadn't been there for five minutes when he came out

(vi) The use of *que* as the equivalent of 'when' is particularly common after *à peine* 'scarcely', e.g.:

Elle était à peine sortie de la chambre que la porte s'ouvrit (Bourget)
She had scarcely left the bedroom when the door opened

A peine Kyo avait-il fait cent pas qu'il rencontra Katow (Malraux)
Kyo had hardly gone a hundred steps when he met Katow

704   For *que* in comparisons, see **166**; after *tout*, **310**,i; after *quelque*, etc., **308–310**, **315**.

Appendix

The expression of age, time, price, dimensions, speed, fuel consumption

Age

705 In asking about or expressing age in French, the verb *avoir* 'to have' is used, together with an appropriate noun such as *âge* 'age', *an(s)* 'year(s)', *mois* 'month(s)', which cannot be omitted, e.g.:

Quel âge avez-vous?
How old are you?

J'ai dix-huit ans
I am eighteen

Je ne sais pas quel âge elle a
I don't know how old she is

Le bébé a deux ans et trois mois
The baby is two and a quarter

un garçon de vingt ans (or *âgé de vingt ans*)
a boy of twenty

Time

706   The time of day

(i) In asking about or expressing the time of day, the word *heure(s)* 'hour(s)' is used (except with *midi* 'noon, midday' and *minuit* 'midnight'), and cannot be omitted, e.g.:

Quelle heure est-il?
What time is it?

A quelle heure arrivez-vous? (note that *à* cannot be omitted)
(At) what time are you arriving?

Il est midi (minuit)
It is twelve o'clock (twelve noon, midnight)

Il est (presque) trois heures
It is (almost) three o'clock

Il est cinq heures passées
It is after five (o'clock)

Il est sept heures précises
It is exactly seven (o'clock)

When necessary, 'a.m.' can be rendered by *du matin* 'in the morning' and 'p.m.' by *de l'après-midi* 'in the afternoon' or *du soir* 'in the evening', e.g. *à huit heures du matin* 'at eight a.m.'.

(ii) 'Half past' is *et demi* with *midi* and *minuit* but *et demie* when the word *heure* is involved, e.g.:

Il est midi et demi
It is half past twelve

Il arrive à deux heures et demie
He arrives at half past two

'Quarter past' and 'quarter to' are usually *et quart* and *moins le quart* (though *un quart* and *moins un quart* also occur), e.g.:

A minuit et quart j'ai été réveillé par l'orage
At a quarter past midnight I was woken up by the thunderstorm

Attendons jusqu'à trois heures moins le quart
Let's wait until a quarter to three

Otherwise, 'so many minutes past the hour' is expressed by the appropriate figure, and 'so many minutes to the hour' by *moins* and the appropriate figure, usually without the word *minutes* in either case, e.g.:

Il est trois heures dix-sept
It is seventeen minutes past three

Je pars à quatre heures moins vingt
I am leaving at twenty to four

(iii) Time is frequently expressed according to the 24-hour clock, not only for administrative purposes (timetables, appointments, radio and TV programmes, etc.), but in ordinary conversational usage too. This is very easy. All hours are expressed, as in the other system (see i and ii above), by *heures*, including twelve noon (*douze heures*) and twelve midnight (*vingt-quatre heures* or *zéro heure*). Minutes are expressed as minutes past the hour (never as so many minutes 'to' the hour), e.g.:

02h.15 (deux heures quinze) two fifteen (a.m.)
18h.35 (dix-huit heures trente- six thirty-five (p.m.)
cinq)

707 Days of the week, months, seasons, years

(i) Capital initials are not used for the names of the days of the week and the months, e.g. *lundi* 'Monday', *janvier* 'January'.

(ii) Apart from *le premier* 'first', dates are expressed by using the cardinal (i.e. not the ordinal) numerals (for these terms, see 178), and no preposition is used corresponding to the English use of 'of', e.g.:

le premier mars the first of March
le quatorze juillet the fourteenth of July

Note that 'What is the date today?' is *Nous sommes* (or *C'est*) *le combien aujourd'hui?*

(iii) Where English uses 'on' with days of the week or month, French has no preposition. Note too the difference between *lundi*, etc. (no article) 'on Monday' (i.e. one particular Monday, last Monday or next Monday) and *le lundi* (singular, definite article) 'on Mondays' (i.e. regularly), but *le* (+ day) + date.

Examples:

Je l'ai vu samedi
I saw him on Saturday

J'écrirai lundi
I will write on Monday

J'y vais toujours le samedi
I always go there on Saturdays

Il est parti le quinze août
He left on the fifteenth of August

Il doit arriver le vendredi premier septembre
He is due to arrive on Friday, September 1st

(iv) With reference to months or years, 'in' is *en*, e.g. *en décembre* 'in December', *en quelle année?* 'in which year?', *en 1980* 'in 1980', though with reference to months *au mois de* is also used, e.g. *au mois de mars* 'in March'.

(v) Note that 'in summer, in autumn, in winter' are *en été, en automne, en hiver*, but that 'in spring' is *au printemps*.

(vi) 'BC' and 'AD' are, respectively, *av. J.-C.* (= *avant Jésus-Christ*) and *ap. J.-C.* (= *après Jésus-Christ*), e.g. *au IVe siècle av. J.-C.* 'in the 4th century BC', *en 336 ap. J.-C.* 'in 336 AD'.

708   Duration of time

(i) *Pour* 'for' is usually not the correct equivalent of English 'for' with relation to time. It is, however, used with reference to a period of time that is later than the time of the action expressed by the verb, in which case it also includes an idea of purpose, e.g.:

Je croyais qu'il n'était venu que pour trois jours
I thought he had only come for three days

Je vais à Paris pour une semaine
I am going to Paris for a week

Note that in such contexts 'for' does not express the time that the action (of coming or going respectively) lasts.

(ii) 'For' meaning 'time during which' is usually to be translated by *pendant* 'during', e.g.:

L'an dernier j'ai été malade pendant trois mois
Last year I was ill for three months

(iii) Note the use of *depuis* 'since' instead of *pendant* with reference to a period of time that still continues at the time of the action expressed by the verb, e.g.:

> *J'insiste là-dessus depuis dix ans*
> I have been insisting on it for ten years (and still am)

709 *En* and *dans* with reference to a period of time

'In' with reference to a period of time is sometimes *en* and sometimes *dans*, but with a very clear distinction of meaning between the two:

(i) *en* refers to duration, to the length of time required to do something, e.g.:

> *On peut traverser la Manche en quarante minutes*
> One can cross the Channel in forty minutes

> *Je le ferai en deux heures*
> I shall do it in two hours (i.e. it will take me two hours to do it)

(ii) *dans* refers to the period of time that will elapse before the action takes place, e.g.:

> *Nous partons pour Paris dans un quart d'heure*
> We are leaving for Paris in a quarter of an hour

> *Je le ferai dans deux heures*
> I shall do it [not now but] in two hours' time

710 'From' with reference to time

The time from which something starts may be expressed in various ways, including *de* 'from', *dès* 'as from', *depuis* 'since' (see **668**), *à partir de* 'as from, starting from', and *après* 'after', e.g.:

de neuf heures à midi	from nine to twelve
dès maintenant	as from now
dès le début	from the outset
à partir de dix heures	from ten o'clock onwards
après neuf heures	after nine (o'clock)
de temps en temps, or *de temps à autre*	from time to time

711 Miscellaneous points

(i) *Ici* and *là* (literally 'here' and 'there' respectively) are used of time in a few expressions such as *jusqu'ici* 'up to now, so far' and *d'ici là* 'between now and then'.

(ii) *Souvent* 'often' cannot be used in any French equivalent of 'how often?' which is usually *combien de fois?* (literally 'how many times?'), e.g.:

> *Combien de fois êtes-vous allé à Paris?*
> How often have you been to Paris?

but, with reference to something that occurs on a more or less regular basis, *tous les combien?* (cf. *tous les trois jours* 'every three days') is used, e.g.:

> *Tous les combien y a-t-il des trains qui vont d'ici à Chartres?*
> How often do trains run from here to Chartres?

(iii) The translation of 'how long?' depends on whether it means 'how much time?', e.g.:

> *Combien de temps vous faudra-t-il pour faire cela?*
> How long will it take you to do that?

or 'for how long?', e.g.:

> *Pour combien de temps est-il parti?*
> How long has he gone for?

or 'for [in the sense of "during"] how long?', e.g.:

> *Pendant combien de temps allez-vous travailler?*
> How long are you going to be working for?

or 'since when?' (cf. 413,iv), e.g.:

> *Depuis combien de temps* (or *Depuis quand* 'since when?')
> *y habitez-vous?*
> How long have you been living there?

(iv) 'Whenever' meaning 'every, each time that' must be translated by something meaning just that, e.g.:

> *Chaque fois* (or *Toutes les fois*) *qu'il venait, il était le bien-venu*
> Each time (Whenever) he came he was welcome

For 'whenever' meaning 'no matter when', see 315,iv.

(v) For 'last' and 'next' with reference to moments or periods of time, see 142.

(vi) Note the use of the preposition *par* in the construction *plusieurs fois par jour* 'several times a day', *deux fois par mois* 'twice a month', *dix fois par an* 'ten times a year', etc.

Price

712   (i) No preposition corresponding to English 'for' is normally used to indicate the price for which something is bought or sold, e.g.:

Il a acheté (vendu) ce tableau 150 000 francs
He bought (sold) this picture for 150,000 francs

(though *pour 150 000 francs* is also possible).

Ces pommes se vendent 8F. le kilo
These apples sell (*or* are sold) at 8 francs a kilo

Note too that *payer* means not just 'to pay' but also 'to pay for', so no preposition is used in such contexts as:

J'ai payé ces billets 200 francs
I paid 200 francs for these tickets

Je les ai déjà payés
I have already paid for them

(ii) In the absence of a verb, the price at which something is sold (i.e. 'at' meaning 'costing') is indicated by *à*, e.g.:

du vin à cinquante francs la bouteille
wine at fifty francs a bottle

du tissu à cent francs le mètre
material costing a hundred francs a metre

trois timbres à cinq francs
three five-franc stamps

(iii) With *coûter* 'to cost' and *valoir* 'to be worth, to cost', the construction is the same as in English, e.g.:

Ce tissu coûte (vaut) 50 francs le mètre
This material costs 50 francs a metre

(iv) For the use of the definite article where English uses the indefinite article (*dix francs le kilo* = 'ten francs a kilo'), see **29,** i,a.

Dimensions

713   (i) Dimensions may be expressed in a number of ways:
(a) adjective + *de* + measurement, e.g.:

> *une tour haute de quarante mètres*
> a tower forty metres high
>
> *un lac profond de vingt mètres*
> a lake twenty metres deep

and likewise with *épais* 'thick', *large* 'wide', *long* 'long'

(b) *de* + measurement + *de* + adjective, e.g.:

> *une tour de quarante mètres de haut*
> a tower forty metres high
>
> *un champ de cent mètres de long*
> a field a hundred metres long

and likewise with *large* but *not* with *épais* or *profond*

(c) *être* + adjective + *de* + measurement, e.g.:

> *La tour est haute de quarante mètres*
> The tower is forty metres high
>
> *Le lac est profond de vingt mètres*
> The lake is twenty metres deep

and likewise with *épais, large* and *long*

(d) *avoir* + noun + *de* + measurement, e.g.:

> *La tour a une hauteur de quarante mètres*
> The tower is forty metres high ('has a height of forty metres')
>
> *Le lac a une profondeur de vingt mètres*
> The lake is twenty metres deep

and likewise with *une épaisseur* 'thickness', *une largeur* 'breadth', *une longueur* 'length'

(e) *avoir* + measurement + *de* + noun, e.g.:

La tour a quarante mètres de hauteur
The tower is forty metres high

Le lac a vingt mètres de profondeur
The lake is twenty metres deep

and likewise with *épaisseur, largeur, longueur*

(f) *avoir* + measurement + *de* + adjective, e.g.:

La tour a quarante mètres de haut
The tower is forty metres high

Le champ a cent mètres de long
The field is a hundred metres long

and likewise with *large*, but note that this construction is *not* possible with *épais* and *profond*.

(ii) To ask 'how high?', etc., the appropriate noun must be used, e.g.:

Quelle est la hauteur de la tour? (*lit.* 'What is the height of the tower?')
or *Quelle hauteur a la tour?* (*lit.* 'What height has the tower?')
How high is the tower?

and likewise with *épaisseur, largeur, longueur* and *profondeur*.

(iii) Note that 'by' in expressing two or more dimensions is expressed by *sur* (see **685**,c), e.g.:

six mètres sur dix
six metres by ten

cinq mètres sur cinq
five metres square (i.e. 'five metres by five' – but *cinq mètres carrés* 'five square metres')

Speed

714   Speed is expressed as follows:

Cette voiture fait du cent (à l'heure)
This car does a hundred kilometres an hour

Fuel consumption

715   Fuel consumption is expressed not, as in English, according to the distance covered for a certain quantity of fuel (a gallon), but according to the amount of fuel consumed in covering a given distance (a hundred kilometres), e.g.:

> *Sa consommation d'essence est de onze litres au cent (kilomètres)*
> *Elle (= cette voiture) consomme onze litres au cent*
> It (= this car) does 26 miles to the gallon (*lit.* 'It uses eleven litres to the hundred kilometres')

Index

predicative use of adjs 127
prédire 377, 378
préférable 482, 485
préférer 353, 485, 529
premier 182, 183
  mood after 494
premier-, plural of nouns in 111
prendre 377, 524
préparer 531
prepositional phrases
  after *celui*, etc. 245
  forming adverbial expressions 38
  with or without art. 38, 46
prepositions 644–688
  after adjs and past parts 686–688
  before infin. 649
  complex 644, 647–648
  derived from past participles 134
  government of verbs by 649
  questions with prep. + *qui?, quoi?,*
    quel? 590
  repetition 650–651
  simple 644–646
  used as adverbs 645
  used as nouns, plur. 117
  various Eng. prepositions transl. as
    à or *de* 526, 527
  verbs requiring a preposition in
    Eng. but direct obj. in Fr.
    523
  with or without art. 38, 46
  with pres. part. (only *en*) 445, 649
prescrire 376, 536
present indicative
  after *si* 419
  expressing the fut. 414
  historic present 404
  where Eng. uses perfect 413
present participle 439–446
  absolute use 443
  after (*s'en*) *aller* 441
  differing from verbal adj. 446
  in Eng. but past part. in Fr. 379,
    444
  invariable when used as part. 441
  rendered by past part. of verbs
    denoting position 379, 444
  rendered by rel. clause 442
  used as adj. 148, 440, 444
  used as gerund (*en . . . -ant*) 445
present subjunctive 496–506
  endings 345
  in independent clauses 497
  instead of imperf. subjunct. 502,
    504

stem 346
présider 525
presque 332
  elision 12
(se) presser 535, 537
prétendre 367
prétendu, position of 148
preterite
  after *si* 'if' 418
  endings 345
  in Eng. but pluperf. in Fr. 411,
    413
  in Eng., French equivalents of 400
  spoken language 410
  written language 407, 408
prévaloir 377, 378
prévenir 377, 450
prévoir 377, 378
price, expression of 712
prier 535
probability expressed by future or
  future perfect 414
probable 483
probablement 627, 638
  precedes *pas* 544
prochain 28, 142
produire 374
profond 713
progressive action (tense) 399, 444
projeter 534
promettre 376, 521, 534, 536
promouvoir 377
pronouns (*see* demonstrative,
  indefinite, interrogative,
  personal, possessive, reflexive,
  relative pronouns)
proposer 536
proscrire 376
protéger 353
'provided that' 490
provinces, names of, gender 52
provoquer 531
puis 615
puisque, elision 12
punctuation 5
  in decimal numerals 192
punir 535

quand
  interrogative 589, 590
  meaning 'even if' 422
  meaning 'whenever' 315
  tenses after 414
  + future 414
  + past anterior 411